This work focuses on the economic challenges the American economy has met during the post-World War II era and on the new challenges – represented notably by the competing economies of Japan, Germany, and the entire European Union – which confront it as the 21st century approaches. The book shows how the transformations brought about by international competition fit into the long-term processes of economic growth and change with respect to structural mutations, technological development, the role of government, and the evolution of government-business relations.

Professor Spulber presents a detailed critique of the thesis alleging that the American economy has experienced some kind of decline. He demonstrates not only that such a decline has not taken place but also that the economy will continue to strengthen if growth and change are primarily left to emerge from the impulses and incentives of the private economy.

Cambridge studies in economic policies and institutions

The American economy

Cambridge Studies in Economic Policies and Institutions

Editor
Professor Mark Perlman, University of Pittsburgh

Economic ideas are most obviously revealed through economic policies, which in turn create and are implemented by economic institutions. It is vital, therefore, that students of economics understand the nature of policy formation, policy aims, and policy results. By examining policies and institutions in a detailed yet accessible manner, this series aims to provide students and interested laypeople with the tools to interpret recent economic events and the nature of institutional development, and thus to grasp the influence of economic ideas on the real economy.

Other books in the series
Herbert Giersch, Karl-Heinz Paqué, and Holger Schmieding *The fading miracle: four decades of market economy in Germany*
Shigeto Tsuru *Japan's capitalism: creative defeat and beyond*

The American economy

The struggle for supremacy in the 21st century

Nicolas Spulber

CAMBRIDGE
UNIVERSITY PRESS

PUBLISHED BY THE PRESS SYNDICATE OF THE UNIVERSITY OF CAMBRIDGE
The Pitt Building, Trumpington Street, Cambridge CB2 1RP

CAMBRIDGE UNIVERSITY PRESS
The Edinburgh Building, Cambridge CB2 2RU, United Kingdom
40 West 20th Street, New York, NY 10011-4211, USA
10 Stamford Road, Oakleigh, Melbourne 3166, Australia

First published 1995
Reprinted 1997
First paperback edition 1997

Printed in the United States of America

Library of Congress Cataloging-in-Publication Data is available.

A catalog record for this book is available from the British Library.

ISBN 0-521-48013-2 hardback
ISBN 0-521-59583-5 paperback

For Sue, Dan, Rachelle, Aaron, and Ben

Contents

Figures

Tables

Preface

This book focuses on the economic challenges which the American economy has had to meet during the post-World War II era, and on the new challenges – represented by the competing economies of Japan, Germany, and of the entire European Union – which confront it in the perspective of the 21st century. The book shows how the transformations brought about by *challenge and response* fit into the long-run processes of economic growth and change with respect to structural mutations, technological development, the role of the government, and the evolution of government-business relations. The book presents a detailed critique of the thesis according to which the American economy had reached its developmental "summit" in the late 1960s/early 1970s, since when supposedly it has been drawn increasingly into a process of decline. This downward slide, which is said to parallel the alleged decline of the United Kingdom in the 19th century, could, according to the partisans of this thesis, be averted only by a crucial shift of U.S. policies toward more investment, a holistic approach to industrial-technological change, and the selective targeting for "absolute advantage" in foreign trade of certain high-tech industries and products. The book demonstrates not only that such a decline has not taken place, but also that the American economy will continue to move forward energetically, enterprisingly, and successfully if growth and change are left to emerge from the impulses and incentives of the private economy.

Before the U.S.'s encounter with the supposedly increasing menace of the triple juggernaut of Japan, Germany, and the European Union competing with it in the contest for industrial-technological supremacy in the 21st century, one should not forget that the United States had already successfully met other great challenges. From 1917 until 1991, the world's main economic, political, and military developments had been deeply impacted, directly or indirectly, by the epochal changes which had taken place in the former empire of the Russian Tsars. Throughout its life span of over 70 years, the anti-Western and anti-capitalist Soviet system exercised a totalitarian dictatorship over the peoples of the Romanov's great domain covering one sixth of the surface of the globe. In addition, after World War II it commanded a vast allegiance from and an immense influence over the rest of the world, thanks to the illusions it had generated about the nature and the purpose of its rule, as well as about its supposed capacity to harness the "vagaries" of the market and to plan growth and change in an orderly fashion. Soon after World War II Soviet military power reached its apogee. But the Soviet economy, saddled with a growing military burden, was increasingly falling behind that of the rapidly developing United States and its Western allies. Yet the Soviet Union's mastering of nuclear technologies and the beginning of its space exploration placed that country in a nightmarish balance of terror with the world's leader, the United States. This paradoxical "bipolar" era lasted until the collapse of the Soviet Union in 1991.

Throughout these perilous post-World War II years, the United States met Soviet military challenges head on while steadfastly providing an effective shield behind which the entire Western world could continue to grow and develop. Finally, by 1991, the Soviet economy collapsed, the Soviet empire disintegrated along multiple fault lines, and the Soviet military threat receded. For a still unspecified time, the deepening of vast and unrelenting economic, social, and ethnic crises in the former USSR, the long and agonizing efforts to restructure its society on a new basis, and, last but not least, the end of the so-called cold war, removed this challenge from the horizon and opened up a new historical epoch.

Even while the Soviet military threat was still an important presence, the United States started to face another kind of challenge, represented by the rising and rapidly growing competitive economies of Japan (along with certain minor Asian countries), of Germany, and of the expanding European Union. Under the impact of these conflicting factors, how exactly did the United States maintain its world economic leadership, undergo the appropriate economic transformations, and confront both the Soviet military challenge and the rising economic challenge posed by reindustrialized Japan and Germany? What directions did it chart as the old balance of power started to break down and as the other kinds of challenges began to grow? Finally, how has the United States decided to approach the complex contest for industrial supremacy in the 21st century?

Certainly, immediately after World War II, triumphant America enjoyed an unchallenged economic hegemony which remained uncontested until the mid 1960s. From then on, the U.S. supremacy started to be eroded by a number of vexing and at times apparently unrelated problems both at home and abroad. At home, the great U.S. postwar economic expansion began to falter in the late 1960s, toward the end of the Vietnam War, as the American economy stumbled through combinations of stagnation and inflation punctuated by intermittent but painful recessions. By the early 1970s, the American economy was beginning to experience serious stress under the unfolding of vast yet subtle and apparently unrelated mutations in regard to production processes, interrelations between manufacturing and services, business organizational patterns, and the volume and structure of foreign trade. Abroad, large-scale transformations shook the economic environment at an unrelenting pace. While the United States was still providing the West's military shield, the American economic leadership seemed to be overshadowed by the advances of its new competitors. Their high rates of savings and investment, massive adoption and adaptation of certain U.S. technologies, and faster economic growth rates nurtured a growing challenge to the U.S. performance.

What exactly happened then to the worldwide economic position of America, to its powerful and complex manufacturing, to its skills, to its traditional inventiveness and daring innovation? Was the U.S. falling behind certain critical technological changes which were taking place at dizzying speed in the rest of world, particularly with regard to management strategies and organization, commercial research and development, and foreign trade? Had it been riveted, so to speak, to its ever-advancing military technologies, while its ex-enemies and competitors had been transforming, updating, and upgrading their civilian-oriented industries? Had a final industrial realignment among the great powers already occurred – a realignment which was irremediably affecting the contest for industrial and technological supremacy in the 21st century? Was the U.S. government forced to attempt post-haste, as it were, the reshaping of the American economy's structure – its patterns of manufacturing, technology, output, and employment – through global administrative intervention based on an all-out industrial-technological strategy?

In discussing these issues and their wide-ranging implications, this book falls into four parts. In Part I, I focus on the processes of U.S. economic growth and change while the nation countered the Soviet military challenge from the end of World War II to the threshold of the 1990s. In Part II, I examine the form and content of the competitive challenge presented by the revitalized ex-enemy countries, Japan and Germany, and by the European Union; sketch the basic features of so-called organized capitalism; and argue against the criticisms of our "individualistic" reliance on market-determined outcomes. In Part III, I place our present situation in historical perspective, focusing on the structural transformation of the American economy from the threshold of the 1870s to the threshold of the 1990s. I pay particular attention to long-run changes in income, employment, and public expenditures, consider in detail the shifts in manufacturing and in services, and conclude with a comparison of U.S. performance with that of the other industrially developed countries. Finally, in Part IV, I discuss the main *directions* of U.S. policies as the struggle for technological leadership in the 21st century grows in scope and intensity. I examine in detail the tenor of the industrial-technological proposals advanced by the Clinton-Gore administration, which are bound to have a deep impact on a number of fundamental issues, including the framework of future government-business relations. As we shall see, these proposals indeed concern United States policies with regard to the crucial question of the allocation of the national product between consumption and investment; the relationship between government and business, particularly as it affects the growth and development of U.S. manufacturing and technology; and the approaches to competition and cooperation in what has become known as the "global market." The suggested changes involve, more specifically, a shift in emphasis from the demand to the supply side (a perspective now commonly shared by centrist Democrats and Republicans); a transition from a policy of ad hoc intervention in the market to a fully integrated industrial policy; and the search for new strategies in foreign trade, encompassing not only export targeting for high-tech industries but also various barriers (other than tariffs) to foreign penetration, and the creation and expansion of a regional trade bloc (NAFTA).

It is interesting to note that notwithstanding the historically preponderant strength of the powerful U.S. industrial machine, whenever a great challenge rises on the horizon – be it Soviet nuclear and outer-space defiance in the 1950s, or the intense Japanese industrial and economic competitive confrontation from the 1980s on – quite a number of our decisionmakers, policy analysts, and guiders of public opinion seem ready to assume that the United States is losing its leadership, is falling behind, and is incapable of rapidly adjusting to change. Eventually, a subtle mobilization of energies does take place in U.S. policy and the economy, a gathering of forces which finally shapes, first of all under the impulses and incentives of the market, new responses which more than counterbalance the presumed scope and strength of the foreign contenders. Thus, the former Soviet Union did open up the outer-space era with the launching of Sputnik in the late 1950s, but the United States leadership, with the concourse of the nation, eventually succeeded in achieving an undisputed lead in space exploration. Japan's rapid industrial growth in the 1980s bested the United States in some respects for a while. However, ultimately, powerful growth and change in the American economy, along with the difficulties experienced by the Japanese economy in the early 1990s, finally made Japan recede in the American consciousness both as a *threat* and as a *model*. But paradoxically, the policy proposals which germinate in the periods in which America is alleged to be in decline are those which may finally shape its basic policies at a time when the presumed decline is already perceived as unfounded. In a strange fashion, then, the aging challenges and their deferred policy repercussions ultimately shape, to a large extent, the future's development.

This book is addressed to economists, historians, and policymakers, but hopefully it will also be of interest to the educated public at large. The research on which it is based was funded in part by generous grants-in-aid extended to me by Professor George Walker, Vice-President and Dean, Research and University Graduate School, Indiana University. I am also greatly indebted to my colleagues Professors Robert A. Becker, Roy Gardner, and Elyce Rotella, who read part or all of the manuscript and made invaluable suggestions. I am in debt to Professors Matei Calinescu, Tom Kniesner, and David Wildasin for advice and comments, as well as for the useful materials they kindly put at my disposal.

Finally, I am very grateful to the librarians of the Reference Department and of the Government Publications Department of the Indiana University Library for the continuous and very useful help they extended to me during the preparation of this work. My debt is also great to Ms. Suzanne Hull, of the Graphic Services Department of Indiana University, who with understanding and ability produced the graphs included in the text; to Ms. Ruth Fishel, who carefully and intelligently typed the various versions of the manuscript; and to Ms. Peg Hausman for her wise and precise editorial help. Evidently, I am responsible for all remaining errors.

Part I

A challenge met

Introductory note

Over four decades of complex American growth and change are encompassed between the early post-World War II years and the time of the final collapse of East European and Soviet communism in the late 1980s and early 1990s. During this extraordinary interval, decisive structural transformations took place in the U.S. economy, along with vast changes and a powerful expansion of the movement of resources in world markets. As the Soviet communist danger was slowly receding, a new kind of challenge to the U.S. started to loom on the horizon, the challenge of powerful and innovative economic competitors.

In order to sketch the directions of change in the 21st century, it is indispensable to take stock of the deep transformations brought about by the entire cold war 1947/48–1989/90 era, and to take a close look at the interconnections it forged at home and abroad between policies, growth, economic fluctuations, structural changes, and the capacity to compete in world markets. The time has come to assess the triumphs and the failures of that period as far as the United States economy is concerned, and to evaluate its legacies on the threshold of a new era.

In the opening chapter of Part I, I first point out that the U.S. economy continued to grow significantly over the entire postwar era under review. It developed an enormous production machine, and its multiple and increasingly complex interindustry flows reached into the trillions of dollars annually from the end of the 1970s on. Its GNP had risen to well over $5 trillion by the end of the 1980s. With respect to rates of growth, of unemployment, of inflation, and of productivity, one can conveniently distinguish two main cycles divided into four sub-periods. In Chapter 1, I map out the structural changes that the economy underwent in each of these four sub-periods vis-à-vis income, employment, and technological changes, particularly in various manufacturing branches, and also examine the role of these branches in foreign trade. After an analysis of the usual measurements of "competitiveness," I focus on the interactions between the changing structure of imports and exports and the problems concerning the current-account position of the U.S. in relation to the level of national savings and the budget deficit.

In Chapter 2, I indicate the ways in which the economic policies of successive Democratic and Republican administrations coincided and diverged in their basic approaches to business activity and growth. Afterwards, I discuss the nature and scope of the government's interventions in the market and examine in detail the government's regulatory, supervisory, allocative, and promotional measures and processes that in a variety of fashions shaped the growth and development of business. I then turn to the impact on the development of science and technology of the research and development (R&D) outlays of the federal government, industry, the states, and institutions of higher learning.

In the conclusion to Chapter 2, which also concludes Part I, I focus on various transformations that business underwent during the period, considered in terms of (1) adjustments to the spread of *technologies;* (2) strategies of *growth;* (3) responses to the *globalization of trade;* and (4) measures for cross-border *integration* of formerly separate and competing national firms. I address the other complex issues of the United States' relationships with its new economic challengers in Part II.

1   Postwar growth and change

1-1   *Phases and issues*

The postwar years can be conveniently divided into two intervals with distinctly different characteristics. During the first, from 1947 to 1973, the U.S. was successful at home in almost all economic directions, while its military and economic supremacy confronted the then powerful communist military challenge on a world scale. During the second interval, from 1974 through the end of the 1980s – a time of increasing doubt and disappointment – the U.S. economy had to grapple with mounting difficulties at home and with a rising competitive challenge in its domestic as well as its foreign markets. These setbacks became a matter of growing concern and generated all kinds of efforts to chart new paths for the country.

For a close examination of the evolving economic policies, the indicated basic spans of time can each be appropriately subdivided into two phases. During the *first* postwar phase, from 1947/48 through 1960, the U.S. economy evolved under the combined influence of countercyclical policies at home and policies of "containment" of communism abroad. During the *second* phase, from 1961 through 1973, the American economy developed powerfully in the early 1960s under the impulse of growth-oriented policies at home, but toward the end of that decade its successes started to be marred both by the consequences of its effort to contain communism territorially in Vietnam and by the beginnings of competitive assertiveness on the international markets by the ex-enemy countries, rehabilitated under the policy of containment.

The second basic span also falls into two clear-cut phases. During the *first*, a relatively short one from 1974 to 1982, the country faced a critical combination of stagnation and inflation at home, which compared unfavorably with the faster economic growth and increasingly wider participation in the foreign markets of its new and powerful competitors, Japan and Germany. During the *second* phase, from 1983 through 1989/90, the U.S. economy registered a noteworthy recovery with regard to both output and inflation; but, along with these successes, new problems arose concerning painful readjustments in manufacturing output and employment, widening budgetary and current-accounts

Table 1-1. *U.S. growth, employment, and inflation during main economic phases, 1947–1990*

	1947	1960	1973	1982	1990
GNP in billions of 1982 dollars	1066.7	1665.3	2744.1	3166.0	4155.8
Index 1982 = 100	33.7	52.6	86.7	100.0	131.3
Annual Growth Rate	3.5	3.9	1.6	2.8	
Employment: Civilian Labor Force (millions)	57.0	65.7	85.0	99.5	117.9
Index 1982 = 100	57.2	66.0	85.4	100.0	118.5
Annual Growth Rate	1.1	1.9	1.7	2.1	
Av. Unemploy. Rate	4.5	4.8	7.1	6.7	
CPI (1982-84 = 100)	22.3	29.6	44.4	96.5	130.7
Annual Growth Rate	2.2	3.3	9.0	3.8	

Source: Computed from Economic Report of the President Transmitted to the Congress February 1991, Washington, D.C., GPO, 1991, pp. 69, 288, 322, 351.

deficits, and massive increases in the national debt. Thus, particularly from the early 1970s on, the U.S. path ceased to be a straightforward and smoothly ascending one, as it had been during the first postwar period. The United States had to cope now with recessions, unemployment, stagnation, inflation, and the needs of uneasy, costly, and complex adjustments to both increasing military expenditures and rising foreign competition at home and abroad.

The key elements defining the *economic profile* of each of these four phases are presented in Table 1-1.[1] Let us now consider these elements in some detail. From 1947 through the 1960s, the U.S. economy had to cope with the requirements posed by the transition from war to peace and, internationally, with the assertive expansion of Soviet communism. Notwithstanding their philosophical differences, under Democratic and under Republican administrations the focus was kept on full employment and on the moderation of cyclical swings.

Externally, the emphasis was on the building of a credible defense against Soviet international assertiveness. This led, *inter alia,* to the launching of the Marshall Plan, a daring operation aimed at rehabilitating the devastated capitalist economy of Germany, along with other rehabilitation measures in Asia to benefit another former enemy, Japan. As can be seen from Table 1-1, during this phase the average yearly rate of growth in real GNP was on the order of 3.5 percent, a rate significantly above that of the pre-World War II years (1900–38) of 2.3 percent. The average yearly rate of unemployment was 4.5 percent (with the lowest rate registered in the early 1950s and the highest in the late 1950s). The average annual rate of increase in the Consumer Price Index (CPI) remained generally quite low, except for the late 1940s and again for the early 1950s. The policy of active containment of communism brought about not only the indicated rehabilitation of the former enemies – with lasting and multiple economic consequences for decades to come – but also rising U.S. defense expenditures, as well as diplomatic confrontations and ultimately direct military conflict (the Korean War).

In the second phase, 1961–73, governmental policy passed from one of moderation of cyclical swings to one of growth acceleration. This change was due in part to illusions about what the government could effectively do in regard to macroeconomic 'fine tuning' and sustained economic growth, and in part came about as a reflex to the increasing growth rates of Japan, of the other industrialized countries, and of the allegedly rapid growth of the Soviet Union and of its satellites. The Kennedy and Johnson administrations, and then the Nixon administration, stressed the necessity of increasing the growth rate in order to cope – as Nixon himself put it–"in the deadly competition . . . not only with the men in the Kremlin, but [also] the men in Peking." Under the Democratic administrations the economy meandered at first through a peaceful stretch of increasing growth rates, with reasonable monetary stability and slowly falling unemployment rates. But soon afterwards the country got embroiled in the unsettling misfortune of the Vietnam War. Inflationary pressures started to mount, and, along with them, unemployment rates. From 1961 to 1973 the average yearly rate of growth of GNP rose to 3.9 percent, the highest average rate of the entire postwar period under review. The pace of growth of GNP was supported by increases in the net stock of business's fixed capital at the impressive annual rate of 3.9 percent and of net capital per worker at 2.4 percent. Paralleling these trends, productivity grew at the average yearly rate of 3.3 percent between 1948 and 1966, though the rate fell to 2.1 percent between 1966 and 1973. Moreover, the wide availability of U.S. technological innovations, through assistance programs and through the growth of affiliates, opened up for the United States avenues for both international cooperation *and* competition with its new challengers. But at the same time, inflation increased its pace to 3.3 percent per year, while unemployment stood at around 4.8 percent per annum. U.S. increases in GNP and capital growth were overshadowed in part by the faster growth of the other main industrialized countries, in particular of Japan, and by the latter's felicitous application of advanced technological discoveries to the production of goods of mass consumption (advances applied in the U.S. mainly to weaponry and other military goods). As noted by the *Economic Report of the President* (henceforth *ERP*) of January 1989, between 1950 and 1973 capital per man-hour grew over one and a half times as fast as in the U.S. in the next six largest industrialized nations, while their investment and productivity grew twice as fast.[2]

During the third phase under review, the U.S. economy was grievously affected by stagnation and inflation. The legacies of the Vietnam War and the fruits of post-Keynesian misconceptions concerning the government's ability to fine-tune economic processes turned out to be equally bitter. From 1974 through 1982 the economy experienced no fewer than three recessions, two of which were severe. The first recession, which at the time was the longest and deepest since the great depression of the 1930s, started in November 1973 and dragged on for 16 months, until March 1975. A big hike in the price of oil caused by an Arab embargo accelerated the inflation inherited from the preceding phase and precipitated a fall in stock market prices. The second recession unfolded for six months in early 1980, under the Carter administration, against the background of a further increase in inflation stimulated by a new Arab oil price hike. Finally, the third recession, this time engineered by the then new Reagan administration in order to bring down the alarming inflation rate, also dragged on for 16 months – from July 1981 to November 1982. During this entire phase, the average yearly rate of growth of the GNP fell to a low of 1.6 percent, while the average unemployment rate hovered around 7 percent and the average inflation rate reached 9.0 percent per year. (See Table 1-1.) Between the first quarter of 1976 and 1980 the U.S. experienced its highest postwar inflation rates, and the value of the dollar plummeted. As one might have expected in such troubled times, the average yearly rate at which nonfarm businesses acquired new plant and equipment fell from the level of 3.9 percent (reached during 1947 to 1973) to 2.0 percent (between 1973 and 1982). Productivity fell even more sharply. The trends toward price escalation, mounting budget deficits, and expanding money supply for a while seemed unstoppable. The federal budget deficit as a percentage of GNP increased steadily to 6.3 percent per annum, its highest level since World War II. As the value of the dollar fell, the value of U.S. exports increased at a higher rate per year than that of imports – a situation exactly opposite to that which had prevailed in the 1960s. But this success was overshadowed by global current-account deficits: by the end of the 1970s, trade balances in both merchandise (excluding the military) and services were in the red. In addition, while the U.S. was experiencing the combination of miseries that came to be known as *stagflation,* the economies of Japan and Germany continued to develop at much faster rates and to register huge trade surpluses.

The fourth and last phase of the postwar epoch, ending in 1989/90, exhibited, especially from 1985 on, a noteworthy recovery marked by a quickening pace in growth of the GNP and a significant fall in the average yearly rate of inflation. As can be seen from Table 1-1, the rate of growth of the GNP increased significantly between 1982 and 1990, though at a lower rate than that prevailing before 1973. Nonfarm business acquisitions of plant and equipment expanded at a high rate, namely, at an average of 5.2 percent per year. And while the average yearly rate of unemployment decreased noticeably – still remaining at levels higher than those prevailing from 1947 to 1973 – the rate of inflation was brought down sharply, to an average yearly rate of 3.8 percent. Concomitantly, the value of the dollar started to climb, a fact which adversely affected the United States' international transactions. Until 1983, all the measures of external balance (current-account balance and net exports balances, in current and constant dollars) stayed within the ranges which had prevailed throughout the previous postwar years. However, from 1983 on, these accounts changed dramatically. The U.S. began to experience trade deficits of a magnitude not seen since the 19th century. The deficit in real net exports reached its peak (4.1 percent of real GNP) in 1986, and in current prices (at the level of $159 billion) in the last quarter of 1987. As is well known, external trade deficits imply inflows of capital. From the early postwar years up to 1980 the U.S. had built up large international holdings as a counterpart of its annual current-account surpluses. By the beginning of the 1980s, the pattern of international capital flows had reversed. From 1985 on, the United States moved from a net creditor into a net debtor position. The total value of foreign assets in the United States (direct investments and common stock and bonds) exceeded the total value of similar holdings abroad of U.S. citizens. The borrowed resources actually enabled the U.S. to expand its investment, raise its productivity, and increase its future output. But, as we shall see further on, many critics saw in this reversal of position ominous signs for the future.

Notwithstanding the important variations within and between the indicated phases, over the entire period under review, from 1947 to the beginning of the 1990s, the main growth indicators – real GNP, real disposable per capita income, real investment, employment, productivity – showed significant average annual rates of increase. Indeed, between 1947 and the end of the 1980s real GNP (at 1982 prices) increased almost four times, at an average rate of 3.3 percent per year.[3] Real disposable income per capita increased faster: it more than quadrupled during these years, at an average rate of 3.4 percent per annum. (These upward trends are shown [for 1965–1989] in Fig. 1-1.) Total nonfarm business acquisition of new plant and equipment increased at an average annual rate of 3.7 percent. Government investment in physical and

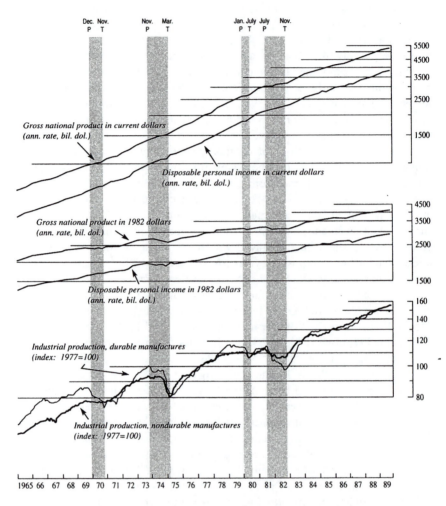

Figure 1-1. United States industrial production, 1965–1989. *P* and *T* indicate peaks and troughs of recessions. *Source:* U.S. Department of Commerce, Bureau of Economic Analysis, *Business Conditions Digest,* January 1990.

human-capital infrastructure also increased significantly until 1973 and continued to rise at a somewhat slower pace from then on. Real gross private domestic investment, which had been on the order of 16.7 percent of GNP in 1947 and of 17.4 percent in 1989, moved over the entire period at an average rate of growth of 3.4 percent per year. The employed labor force also increased at the moderate average rate of 1.7 percent per year. Finally, notwithstanding wide variations in output per hour in the business sector between the phases considered, the United States' productivity growth of 2.28 percent per year for the period as a whole remained consistent with its historic labor productivity growth rate.

Significant shifts in industrial structure occurred during the entire postwar epoch. From 1947 to the end of the 1980s, appreciable changes took place in the relative contributions made to real GNP by the economy's three major components: *agriculture; industry* – mining, construction, manufacturing, power and light, other utilities, transport, and communications; and nongovernmental *services*. Used in its broadest sense, this latter term includes distributive services (trade, wholesale and retail); finance/insurance/real estate; business, professional, and technical services; and personal services. As can be seen from Table 1-2, the share of agriculture fell from some 5 percent to less than half that amount; the share of industries contracted from 44 percent to some 40 percent by 1988. Big drops were registered in the shares of mining and construction. While not strictly comparable (because of changes in the underlying statistical methods), the share of manufacturing fluctuated narrowly at around 20 percent of total GNP, while the combined share of utilities and transportation remained close to the 9–10 percent range (except in 1960). On the side of nongovernmental services, the highest relative expansions were registered in the contributions of finance/insurance/real estate and of certain other services, in particular miscellaneous business services and health services. On the other hand, the government's contribution to the GNP decreased, from over 14 percent to about 10½ percent.

Even broader changes took place within and between the indicated major components of the economy with respect to labor force distribution. The share of civilian employment in agriculture fell from 10.3 million in 1947 to 3.1 million by the end of the 1980s. The combined share of the indicated industries during this time rose from 22.3 million to 30.8 million gainfully employed. However, within this total, significant changes in the *pattern* of labor force distribution took place, particularly from 1973 on: employment in mining and manufacturing contracted while it expanded in construction, in utilities, and in transport and communications. The share of the heterogeneous conglomerate called services (excluding government) increased dramatically from 17.7 million to 57.4 million, with vast increases particularly in trade (from 9.5 million to 25.1 million) and other services (from 6.3 million to 25.6 million). Government employment also increased, from 5.1 million to 17.3 million.

Output per person employed was markedly higher in some of the so-called goods-producing industries than in services. Productivity was especially high in mining and in manufacturing, for instance – less so in construction and agriculture. On the service side, the highest productivity was registered in

Table 1-2. U.S. real gross national product: agriculture, industry, services, and government (percentages): selected years, 1947–1988 (underlying data in 1982 dollars)

Years	GNP (billions of 1982 $)	Agric.		Industries					Services					Govern- ment	Residual*
		Agric., Forestry & Fishing	Total	Mining	Con- struction	Manu- facturing	Utilities & Transp. & Commun.	Total	Trade, Wholesale & Retail	Finance, Insurance, Real Estate	Other Services			
1947	1,066.7	5.2	44.1	6.3	7.2	21.2	9.4	36.1	14.8	9.6	11.7	14.6	--
1960	1,665.3	4.1	43.6	5.7	9.8	20.4	7.7	38.5	14.7	12.4	11.4	14.4	0.6
1973	2,744.1	2.6	42.6	4.9	6.2	22.6	8.9	41.7	15.9	13.4	12.4	12.6	0.5
1982	3,166.0	2.8	37.8	4.2	4.5	20.0	9.1	45.6	16.0	15.0	14.6	12.1	1.7
1988	4,024.4	2.3	40.4	3.2	4.4	23.1	9.7	46.9	17.2	14.5	15.2	10.4	--

*statistical discrepancy: includes "Rest of the World."
Source: Computed from Economic Report of the President . . ., 1991, p. 299.

finance/insurance/real estate. The least productive services were in trade and in government. Projections for the year 2000 do not forecast significant changes in the observed relationships among the indicated major components of the economy.

Of course, the divisions underlying our calculations are subject to many caveats. Utilities, notably electricity and gas, as well as water purification, transportation, and communications, are often included in services. Some services are closely tied to the goods-producing sectors, others are not. Government – erroneously, I believe – is usually included in services, while in fact its functions in the economy are complex, specific, and *sui generis*. Certain statistical groupings concerning manufacturing divide its production into durable and nondurable goods, a division which is based on the life span of the goods produced, but which conveys the incorrect impression that it corresponds respectively to heavy vs. light industries. (This is a division of a different kind, based on the capital and technological needs of an industry, i.e., for massive or relatively light capital investments.) Fortunately, the interrelations between each type of industry, in terms of sales and purchases, can be ascertained with the help of input-output (IO) tabulations. Even a small table of this type (say, a 10×10 matrix) can disclose the relationships which necessarily exist at a certain point in time between the value added in the economy (the GNP) and the very large-scale transactions which must take place for the purpose of production between all the economy's industries, be they "goods-producing" or "service-producing."

I shall turn to these issues in Section 1-2 below. In Section 1-3, I shall focus on the determinants of growth and on their impact during the entire period under review. In Section 1-4, I shall consider the issues related to changes in the volume and structure of our foreign trade and their interconnections with competitiveness and cooperation in international markets. The chapter's concluding section, Section 1-5, will examine the problems of current-account and budget deficits and the issues connected with the transformation of the U.S. from a creditor to a debtor nation.

1-2   A powerful processor

Behind the production of goods and services for consumption, investment, and exports lies a powerful industrial processor composed of a complex web of interindustry transactions. Let us make a preliminary sketch of this processor's constituent parts. Input-output analysis divides outputs (or sales) of industry i into sales to all other industries (intermediate demand) and into consumption plus investment plus net exports plus government spending, all of which equals final demand (or GNP). And further, it divides outlays (purchases) of industry j into purchases from all other industries (interindustry purchases) and into outlays on employee compensation, profit-type income and capital consumption allowances, and indirect business taxes (all of which constitute value added, or Gross National Income [GNI]). In an n-sector model, row i shows the sales of industry i to all other industries (interindustry flows) and to final demand (that is, to persons [Consumption], investors [Investment], foreigners [net exports], and government). On the other hand, column j shows the purchases of industry i from all other industries and its outlays on employee compensation (wages and salaries [$w + s$]), profit income and capital consumption allowances (interest, rents, and profits [herein denoted as r, v, π], and depreciation [D] plus indirect taxes [T]). Summing up along row i and column j respectively, we obtain:

$$X_i \quad = \sum_{j}^{n} X_{ij} \qquad\qquad + (C_i + I_i + E_i + G_i)$$

$$\begin{array}{l}\text{Total} \\ \text{Gross} \\ \text{Output}\end{array} = \begin{array}{l}\text{Interindustry} \\ \text{Demand}\end{array} + \begin{array}{l}\text{Final Demand} \\ \text{(Gross National Product)}\end{array}$$

$$X_j \quad = \sum_{j}^{n} X_{ij} \qquad\qquad + (w + s + r + v + \pi + D + T)$$

$$\begin{array}{l}\text{Total} \\ \text{Gross} \\ \text{Outlay}\end{array} = \begin{array}{l}\text{Intermediate} \\ \text{Purchases}\end{array} + \begin{array}{l}\text{Value Added} \\ \text{(Gross National Income)}\end{array}$$

(See Fig. 1-2.)

In the IO tables of the U.S. economy prepared by the Interindustry Economics Division of the Bureau of Economic Analysis of the U.S. Department of Commerce, productive activities are usually grouped into 85 industries as defined (at various points in time) in the Standard Industrial Classification (SIC). Imports used for production which are substitutable for domestic goods and services are treated like secondary products; those which are not substitutable are shown as purchased directly by the consuming industry or final market. In order to make the row total equal to the output of each industry, inventories are shown for each industry regardless of which industry actually owns or holds inventories. Setting aside the inventory items, the entries in a row add up to the *total* consumption (i.e., both industrial and final use) of its products or services. To show the links between producing and consuming industries or final markets, the tables do not trace *actual flows* to and from the trade industry. If trade was shown as buying and reselling, the connections would be between producing industries and trade, and the consuming industries would also make their purchases from trade. In the input-output tables, the output of trade is measured only in terms of total margins, that is, operating expenses plus profit. Finally, the valuations underlying the tables are based on producers' prices.

		PRODUCERS									FINAL MARKETS				GROSS OUTPUT
		Agriculture	Mining	Construction	Manufacturing	Transportation	Trade	Finance	Services	Other	Persons	Investors	Foreigners	Government	
PRODUCERS	Agriculture														
	Mining														
	Construction			*INTERINDUSTRY FLOWS*							*Personal consumption expenditures*	*Gross private domestic investment*	*Net exports of goods and services*	*Government purchases of goods and services*	
	Manufacturing														
	Transportation														
	Trade														
	Finance														
	Services														
	Other														
VALUE ADDED	Employees	*Employee compensation*													
	Owners of Business and Capital	*Profit-type income and capital consumption allowances*													
	Government	*Indirect business taxes*													
	GROSS OUTLAY														TOTAL

Figure 1-2. Input-output table: a schematic presentation. *Sources:* Based on tabulation of the U.S. Department of Commerce, Bureau of Economic Analysis, Interindustry Economics Division; U.S. Department of Commerce, *Survey of Current Business,* February 1974.

Table 1-3. *Global input-output flows in the American economy, 1967, 1977, 1982, and 1987 (billions of dollars at current prices)*

Rows / Columns	Intermediate Demand	Final Demand	Total Gross Output
1967 Interindustry Purchases Value Added Total Gross Outlay	725.088	795.388	1,520.476
1977 Interindustry Purchases Value Added Total Gross Outlay	1,682.667	1,991.227	3,673.894
1982 Interindustry Purchases Value Added Total Gross Outlay	2,745.558	3,166.245	5,911.804
1987 Interindustry Purchases Value Added Total Gross Outlay	3,502.814	4,531.300	8,034.114

Sources: Interindustry Economics Division, "The Input-Output Structure of the American Economy: 1967," "The Input-Output Structure of the U.S. Economy: 1977," and "Annual Input-Output Accounts of the U.S. Economy," 1982, 1987, in U.S. Department of Commerce, Survey of Current Business, February 1974, May 1984, April 1988, April 1992.

The endogenous sphere – that is, the economy's *processor* (the web of interindustry transactions) – adjusts its input demands and its outputs so as to respond as efficiently and effectively as possible to the evolving demands of the final users. Its structure is determined by the network of its *couplings* and by the *operation* of its components. This operation is conditioned not only by technological elements but also by given cultural patterns of response to various stimuli, and by given ownership relations, forms of income distribution, and forms of intervention in the economy. Put differently, the activity of the processor is shaped by the incessant interplay of technical, behavioral, and institutional relationships. Within this framework, there are of course wide variations among industries in regard to pace of technological change, responses to stimuli, proportions of the output sold either to other producers or to final demand, and so on. Some industries (e.g., primary iron and steel manufacturing; producers of chemical and selected chemical products) sell most of their products to other industries; others (e.g., footwear, leather goods, household furniture) sell most of their output to final markets. Heavy interdependence among industries is a key feature of the powerful, incessantly expanding, technologically advancing American economic processor and the vast markets it serves. The intense activity of the endogenous sphere and its enormous capacity for generating incomes and products are illustrated in Table 1-3. The web of interindustry purchases, which amounted in current dollars to $725 billion in 1967, had risen to close to $2 trillion 10 years later. In the next 10 years, it more than doubled again. Meanwhile, the ratio of value added to interindustry purchases rose from around 110 in 1967 to 118 in 1977. After falling to 115 in 1982, this ratio then rose again to 129 in 1987, reflecting an increasing efficiency in the processor. At constant (1982) prices, GNP (equivalent to value added as defined) rose from $2,271.4 billion in 1967 to $2,958.6 billion 10 years later and then to $3,845.3 billion 10 years further down. By the end of the 1980s, real GNP had reached over $4.1 trillion.

1-3   The determinants of growth

Growth theory emphasizes as determinants of the pace of economic growth the rates at which productive capacity expands, private investment increases, the labor force grows and adjusts to change, productivity per man-hour grows, technology progresses, and the efficiency with which capital, resources, and labor are used rises. Public policy can accelerate growth, notably by increasing the stock of public physical capital (roads, water systems, schools, hospitals) and by improving the education, skills, and motivations of the labor force.

During the postwar years considered, the yearly expenditures on *new plant and equipment of nonfarm industries* (i.e., manufacturing plus nonmanufacturing [mining, transportation, public utilities, commercial, and others]) were on the order of 9 to 9.5 percent of GNP from the mid 1940s to the mid 1960s. This figure rose to around 10 percent to 10.5 percent during the ensuing years until the late 1970s; it then rose again, from 10.5 percent to close to 12 percent during the early 1980s. Out of these shares, about one third was spent, year in and year out, in manufacturing. At constant (1987) dollars, the *yearly* investment in equipment and structures in manufacturing was on the order of $257 billion in the 1960s, $82 billion in the 1970s, and $97 billion in the 1980s. From 1947 to 1989, the *net* stock of nonresidential private capital in manufacturing increased (in 1987 dollars) over four times – namely, from about $240 billion in 1947 to over $998 billion in 1989.[4] Concomitantly, however, important changes were registered in the public capital stock. Roughly one quarter of the total U.S. capital stock is owned by federal, state, and local governments. This capital increased at the impressive rate of 4.9 percent a year in the 1950s and 1960s, but at the rate of only 2.2 percent a year in the 1970s and of only 0.9 percent a year in the 1980s – with some adverse effects in the latter years on the state of buildings, roads, and bridges, as well as on overall productivity growth.[5]

For most of the postwar era, U.S. *domestic saving* was sufficient for financing domestic investment. Gross private domestic investment was roughly 16 percent of yearly GNP from the 1950s through the 1980s. However, in the

1980s the share of national savings fell by more than 2 percent of GNP. While private (household and business) savings continued as usual at 16.7 percent of GNP, government's dissaving of 2.6 percent reduced the share of national savings to 14.1 percent of GNP. The balance, pulling the total up to the level of close to 16 percent, was provided by inflows of foreign capital.[6]

Total *nonfarm employment* grew during the postwar years, from less than 46 million in 1947 to around 105 million by 1988. Employment in manufacturing rose from 15.1 million in 1947 to between 19 and 20 million from 1966 on. In these totals, great shifts took place between and within industries. In a highly developed economy such as the U.S., industrial firms must, under the penalty of economic death, be constantly immersed in a variety of processes of growth and transformation. At the end of the 1980s there were 370,000 American manufacturing establishments (out of which some 355,000 were small or mid-sized firms with under 500 workers). Whatever its size, each firm had to cope effectively and efficiently with the continuous pressures of domestic and foreign competition. Besides expenditures on equipment, reequipment, and structural transformations, this also requires adequate organization at all levels of management; ceaseless attention to current and impending technological alternatives; proper selection, training, and retraining of the labor force; and good marketing strategies. Unfortunately, as we shall see later on, many manufacturing firms, particularly the small and midsized ones, failed to take full advantage of the key imperatives of technological change.

The *largest gains in employment* were registered in radio and TV communication equipment, plastic products, computing equipment, electric components, machinery, aircraft equipment, semiconductor devices, and missiles. Gains were also scored in commercial printing, lithograph operations, and newspapers. On the other hand, large *losses in employment* were recorded in steel mills, vehicle and car body works, pig iron foundries, farm equipment, and construction machinery. (By the end of the 1980s, the U.S. share of the domestic market for car and truck sales accounted for 67 percent, that of Japan for 29 percent, and that of others for 4 percent.) Large losses of employment were also exhibited in cotton mills, women's dresses and footwear, and men's suits and coats.[7] I shall consider later whether so many branches and firms had to shrink and lose their market shares because of obsolescence – and failure to improve technology, engineering, product design, and quality – or marketing. Let me add that further deep changes are bound to be brought forth by the end of the cold war. The processes of demobilization are bound to affect not only Russia and the other former Soviet republics but, in different and very complex ways, the U.S. economy as well. Confronted by the Soviet military-nuclear challenge, in the 1980s the U.S. federal government spent, on the average, about 6 percent of yearly GNP on defense. Defense absorbed as much as 30 percent of the country's technical manpower and about 40 percent of its durable goods production. The country's vast and complex defense needs were met first of all by some 20 giant corporations, then by some 25,000 to 30,000 other prime contractors, and, finally, by numerous subcontractors working on defense electronic components, aircraft engines and equipment, shipbuilding and repair, ammunition, and so on. Among the giant recipients of defense contracts were (and still are) such illustrious corporations as Lockheed, Boeing, Martin Marietta, General Electric, McDonnell Douglas, Rockwell International, IBM, Westinghouse Electric, General Dynamics, Hughes Aircraft, Grumman, Sperry Rand, TRW, Raytheon, United Technologies, RCA, Honeywell, Ford Aerospace Communications, ITT, and Texas Instruments.[8]

While U.S. military requirements have certainly not dissolved with the disintegration of the USSR, the U.S. is bound to downsize its defense expenditures over a number of years (e.g., to 3.5 percent of the 1995 GNP). The U.S. will sharply reduce its armed forces and extensively restructure its weapons systems. Unfortunately, the defense-oriented companies which have ventured in the past into commercial markets have not found the transition easy. As the *ERP* for 1991 points out, defense industries cannot effortlessly transfer their engineering and production capacity to civilian uses. Such a transition requires dealing with an entirely different set of products. Producers of military aircraft, military radio and TV communication equipment, missiles, space vehicles, and ships are bound to incur large adjustment costs and employment losses.[9] Yet new prospects may develop in the 1990s – for instance, in the aerospace industry, which looks to the realization of future aerospace products and spin-off applications in key technologies involving low-cost commercial aircraft, ultrasafe cars, ultrasurvivable aircraft, new space systems, highly secure air traffic control, and a variety of information services.[10]

Throughout the postwar years under review, owing to the vast demands of the domestic markets, the different characteristics of the commodities involved, the impact of competition, and the variability of access to foreign markets, America's manufacturing industries participated in the country's exports in varying degrees. At the end of the 1980s, U.S. manufacturers' exports of food, apparel, furniture, printing, and publishing remained at or below 5 percent of their total shipments. Textile mill products, lumber, petroleum and coal products, leather and leather goods, and stone, clay, and glass products oriented from 5 to 10 percent of their shipments toward foreign markets. The tobacco, paper, fabricated metal products, transport equipment, chemicals, and instruments industries exported from 10 to 15 percent of their total shipments. Finally, primary metal industries, machinery and heavy equipment industries, and electric and electronic equipment manufacturers directed over 20 percent of their shipments toward foreign buyers.[11] The largest merchandise exports involved aircraft and spacecraft, road vehicle and tractor parts, office machine parts, computers, electronic components and parts, passenger motor vehicles, organic chemicals, and measuring instruments.

On the other hand, at the end of the 1980s, the so-called import penetration ratio – i.e., the ratio of imports to new supply (product shipments plus imports) – was for manufactured goods as a whole close to 13 percent. For nondurables, the ratio was on the order of 8 percent; for durables, close to 17 percent. Among the durables, the most notable increases in import penetration in relation to early 1970 levels were registered by the industries manufacturing primary metal products, fabricated metal products, machinery, electrical and electronic equipment, transportation equipment, and instruments and related products. Yet it is interesting to note that in terms of U.S. output, total manufacturing nearly doubled its production from the early 1970s to the end of the 1980s, as did transportation equipment production, while the output of electrical machinery and instruments almost tripled and that of nonelectrical machinery nearly quadrupled. Clearly, with the exception of the primary metal industries (which increased over their 1970 production by only one half), the import penetration was *heavier* in the industries which were expanding (rather than contracting) their output and were also successful in terms of exports. Indeed, the key characteristics of advanced industrial economies is that, both in their exports and in their imports, equipment and reequipment play critically important roles.[12]

Achievements in regard to output per hour and unit labor costs in manufacturing were not always encouraging. According to data released by the Bureau of Labor Statistics of the U.S. Department of Labor, manufacturing productivity increased at an average annual rate of 3.3 percent during 1960–73, dipped to 1.4 percent per year during 1973–79, and increased again to an annual average rate of 3.6 percent from 1979 to 1989. For the entire period 1960–89, the annual average rate of change of output per hour was on the order of 3.0 percent. This, as we shall see, compares unfavorably with the trends prevailing in the other industrial countries. In regard to unit labor costs, the rates of change were particularly detrimental in the highly inflationary years 1973–79. The average annual rates of increase in the unit labor cost were 1.8 percent for 1960–73, 8.2 percent for 1973–79, and 1.9 percent for 1979–89, bringing the average rate to 3.1 percent for 1960–89.[13]

I turn now to the specific characteristics of international competition and international cooperation in world markets, and then to the problems which in the postwar years effected the changes in the U.S. current-account position.

1-4   Competition and cooperation in global markets

In the four decades of the postwar period 1948–88, international trade expanded vigorously, as did that of the United States. (See Fig. 1-3, illustrating the period 1965–89.) Simultaneously, enormous changes took place in the shares of world trade held by most countries and, above all, by the main industrialized ones, first in the period from the mid 1940s to around the mid

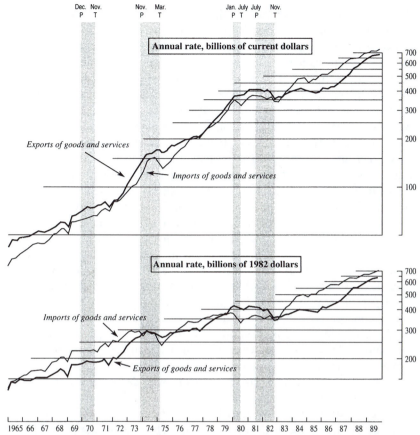

Figure 1-3. United States foreign trade, 1965–1989. *P* and *T* indicate peaks and troughs of recessions. *Source:* U.S. Department of Commerce, Bureau of Economic Analysis, *Business Conditions Digest,* January 1990.

1960s, and then from the late 1960s onward. Further, deep changes also took place during these years in the structure and direction of trade and in capital movements.

Increases in a country's share in total world exports are often considered indicative of that country's increased competitiveness, while increases in its imports are often taken to reflect the increased competitiveness of its rivals. Those who relate these increases (or decreases) to the expansion of the volume of world trade may overlook two critical factors: (1) the increase in the number of nations participating in that trade; (2) the critical relation between each country's trade and its total output of goods and services. For instance, a country's share in world exports (and imports) might have declined even though the volume of its foreign trade reached increasingly higher levels, both in absolute and in relative terms (in relation to its GNP).

Consider these relations in the case of the United States. Immediately after World War II, the U.S. share of the world's merchandise trade reached unprecedented heights. In 1948, U.S. exports amounted to close to 22 percent of world exports, compared to less than 16 percent in 1929 and to around 14 percent in 1938. In 1948, U.S. merchandise imports were on the order of 11 percent of the world's total, compared to 12 and about 9 percent in 1929 and 1938 respectively. In the early postwar years, the former enemy countries accounted for very small shares of the world's merchandise trade. In 1948, West Germany's share of world merchandise exports amounted to less than 1.5 percent; that of Japan, to less than 0.5 percent. In regard to imports, their shares were 3 and 1 percent. Twenty years later, in 1968, the U.S. share of world merchandise exports had fallen back to 14 percent, while that of West Germany had risen to close to 9 percent and that of Japan to over 5 percent. Another 20 years down the road, in 1988, the U.S. share was on the order of 11 percent – exactly matched by West Germany's share but exceeded now by Japan's, which reached over 14 percent of world merchandise exports. Import figures over the same periods tell an equally dramatic tale. In 1968, the U.S. share of the world's imports was about 5 percent. Again, 20 years later the U.S. share of world merchandise imports had increased to 16 percent, while that of West Germany had fallen to 9 percent and that of Japan had stayed at around 6 percent. Upon initial inspection of these figures, the temptation may be great to correlate different countries' losses and gains with decreases and increases in their competitiveness.

But consider the impact of other factors on these relations, as well as other ways of measuring them. Clearly, fundamental changes took place between 1948, 1968, and 1988 in world markets as the first devastated and then reconstructed and expanded West German and Japanese economies reentered world trade in full force. Though the U.S. is relatively less export-oriented than smaller industrialized countries, since it has a large and quite wealthy domestic market, it has become *more* rather than less internationalized as far as trade is concerned during the post-World War II years. This can be ascertained in a number of ways. From 1948 to 1988, the U.S.'s real GNP (in 1982 dollars) grew at an average annual rate of 3.3 percent, while U.S. exports grew at an average annual rate of 5.4 percent. Before World War II, U.S. exports at current prices accounted for 7 percent of GNP in 1929, 4–5 percent in the 1930s, and 7 percent in the early 1940s. Since then exports have increased significantly, reaching 12.8 percent of GNP in 1988.[14] During the entire postwar period, imports grew even faster than exports, i.e., at an average annual rate of 6.6 percent. Imports were on the order of 4.2 percent of our GNP in 1948; they were on the order of 15.5 percent in 1988.

To properly evaluate these changes one would have to take into account the multilateral reductions in tariffs since World War II and the impact of nontariff barriers erected as alternatives; the ways of breaching these trade barriers; the increasingly complex relationships between the flows of exports and imports; and the rationale behind the continually expanding direct foreign investments. One would have also to consider the volumes and the combined trade of the parent companies of multinationals, as well as their majority subsidiaries in other countries; the factors that determine the competitiveness of firms in their local markets and those which shape the competitiveness of their subsidiaries and affiliates abroad; the patterns of expansion of competition multilaterally involving various world areas; and the specific sources of trade deficits.

I shall return in more detail to some of these issues later on, in Chapters 5 and 7. For the moment let me simply point to the expanding role played by multinational enterprises (MNEs), particularly since the mid 1960s, in *all the industrialized countries*. In the advanced economies abroad, American MNEs have started to sell more goods through their subsidiaries than other American exporters have been able to. In certain countries, local production by these subsidiaries, as well as by minority affiliates, has granted U.S.-based MNEs far greater market access than the access secured by other U.S. exporters of manufactured goods. Conversely, foreign MNEs, including the Japanese ones, have invested in majority subsidiaries and in minority affiliates (e.g., in Isuzu, Mazda, and Mitsubishi subsidiaries and in various U.S.-owned automaker affiliates) which have also served as both final markets and intermediary channels for the products of the parent Japanese companies and for Japan's exports to the U.S. in general. Transplant production in the automotive industry, for instance, has grown into a significant portion of overall North American automotive production, accounting by the end of the 1980s for more than 50,000 jobs in assembly and parts-making operations and for about 16 percent of the U.S. production capacity of 14.8 million vehicles annually. Most of the "Japanese" goods produced locally in the U.S. have accounted for roughly three quarters of the American deficit with Japan. Moreover, in some cases it may be argued that the high proportion of U.S.-Japan trade produced by trade between Japanese companies and their foreign affiliates may also have acted as a barrier to the entry of foreign firms in Japan.[15]

The U.S. has consistently been the world's largest market for high-tech products (goods that exhibit high ratios of R&D expenditures, such as those in the aerospace, electrical machinery, electronics, scientific instruments, and pharmaceutical industries). It has continued to consume nearly half the global production of these goods. Increased imports of these and other goods (produced by foreign majority subsidiaries, or incoming from other sources) have been viewed by some as the proof of loss of U.S. leadership and of our dependence on foreigners. It is true that accessibility to our market is as decisive for foreign-based MNEs as it is for our MNEs and for our exporters with regard to foreign markets. But of course there is more to international cooperation and to its intensification than the breaching of one another's trade barriers. In certain cases, what may seem crucial is the capacity to exploit globally dispersed resources and technical abilities. In still other cases, the goal may be to achieve products of higher quality and reliability at affordable prices and to spread the risks.

High-tech cooperation may lead to all kinds of alliances – more or less stable – both within a country and over its borders. For instance, as Lawrence W. Clarkson, a senior vice-president of Boeing Commercial Airplane Group, has indicated, in aircraft manufacturing the buying of parts abroad has expanded at an increasing rate. The 767, the first Boeing production airplane with significant foreign content – 24 percent – counted 1,300 suppliers in eight countries. The Boeing 747-400 includes even more suppliers, and the 777 involves more complex agreements with a variety of Japanese firms as well (Mitsubishi, Kawasaki, and Fuji Heavy Industries). Further, the building of a second-generation supersonic plane, the so-called High-Speed Civil Transport, involves both domestic and foreign cooperative agreements, viz. of Boeing with McDonnell Douglas, as well as with the French Aerospatiale, British Aerospace, and Deutsche Aerospace along with Whitney and General Electric (the last-named being itself involved with other companies, including British and Japanese ones, in the study of a "combined-cycle engine").[16] Certain U.S. high-tech industries are bound to develop still more new international alliances, as I shall point out further on. Moreover, it should be noted that U.S. high-tech manufacturing firms already maintain a higher portion of their assets in foreign affiliates than do other U.S. manufacturers. (Again, I shall return to some of these issues in detail in Section 2-5.)

The evolving complexity of the network which connects the domestic economy and foreign markets, continuously impacted by changes in demand, output, prices, quality, design, technical innovations, and ways of breaching trade barriers, appears in vivid relief when one considers the changes in the structure of U.S. merchandise exports and imports (excluding military). In the mid 1960s, about 24 percent of U.S. merchandise exports consisted of agricultural goods, while 76 percent was accounted for by industrial supplies, capital goods, automotive products, and other goods. By the end of the 1980s, the share of agriculture had fallen to less than 12 percent, while that of all the other goods combined grew to over 88 percent, with massive increases in capital goods. On the import side, the oil story, while well known in its broad outlines, is nonetheless dramatic in its specifics. Less than 10 percent of import expenditures in the mid 1960s went toward oil and oil products. During the upward pressure on oil prices in the next decade this share grew rapidly, until it reached close to 32 percent of the value of all imports in 1980. With the fall in oil prices during the 1980s, this share fell back to around 10 percent. Over the entire period under review, big changes took place with respect to the import shares of industrial goods, capital goods, and automotive products. The shares of the last two types of goods grew enormously: from 7 and roughly 4 percent of total merchandise imports in the mid 1960s, to 24 and 18 percent, respectively, by the end of the 1980s.[17] (Actually, the automotive import percentage is much higher if one takes into account the cars the Japanese makers produce for the big American companies.) The vast expansion of these imports is usually viewed as the most critical indicator of the vigorous foreign penetration in our domestic markets since the early 1970s, and is the subject of much oratory. But on the other hand, this picture is blurred by the many complex cooperation arrangements between U.S. and foreign firms (particularly European and Japanese ones) concerning *joint production, supply of engines and parts,* and *joint financial arrangements.* These modes of cooperation have become in some cases the rule rather than the exception, as we shall see later on.

Throughout the postwar years, income and employment in the service-producing industries registered massive growth in relation to the goods-producing industries (refer back to Table 1-2). Notwithstanding these changes, the growth of services in exports, and even more so in imports, has according to the official data been moderate. In the four decades between 1948 and 1989, merchandise exports grew at an average annual rate of 5.2 percent; service exports (as officially defined), at an average annual rate of 6.2 percent. In imports, the average annual rates were 6.8 and 6.1 percent. At current prices, the share of services in relation to the share of tangible goods has increased only in exports, not in imports. During these four decades the share of services increased in total exports from 24 percent to 41 percent; in imports, that share remained roughly the same, around 28 percent.[18] These figures should be taken with certain caveats. Besides various questions which can be raised concerning the official definitions of services in foreign trade, it is certainly correct to say that the relatively smaller share of services in that trade arises from the fact that the services which absorb most of the labor force at home (mainly retail trade, certain business services, legal services, health, education, housing, and public administration) are not the same as those involved in international service trade (mainly tourism, shopping, brokerage, insurance, and various types of professional services in engineering and management). Moreover, service activities are highly regulated, and the available statistics more often than not may understate the actual magnitude of this trade.[19]

The interrelations of the pace of economic growth with rates of expansion and with the changing structures of exports and imports raise a host of problems concerning the current-account position of the United States and its complex rapports with the level of national savings and the budget deficit. Equally problematic are the implications of these interrelations for understanding the change of the U.S. from a net lender and investor abroad to a net borrower. It is to these issues that I shall now turn.

1-5   *"Twin" deficits and U.S. indebtedness*

The three closely related measures of external balance – nominal current account, net exports and imports at current prices, net exports and imports at constant prices – show, for the entire postwar period, broadly consistent patterns underlying the main directions of change which finally led in the 1980s to the reversal of the net asset balance of the United States. The current-account position (the difference between exports and imports minus net transfer payments to foreign residents), already negative in 1972 and 1974 and again from 1977 through 1979, declined precipitously from 1982 through 1990, ending that year with a $92 billion deficit. The nominal net export-import balance of goods and services, which had been positive from 1946 through 1982 (with surpluses ranging from $1.5 to $3 billion to $15 to $33 billion) also turned increasingly negative from 1983 through 1990, plunging to –$114.7 billion in 1987. Finally, the real net export-import balance (in 1982 dollars), which was negative in most of the years from 1958 to 1978 (ranging from –$2 billion to –$35 billion), also yielded increasingly onerous deficits each year from 1983 through 1990, reaching a low point of –$129.7 billion in 1986.

This current-account deficit implies that U.S. residents bought more goods and services than they produced (i.e., more than the value of the American GNP). The counterpart of this excess is a capital-account surplus – that is, a *net capital inflow* provided by foreigners to finance our extra spending. The net capital inflow is analogous to net foreign investment, and equals (with minor accounting adjustments) the difference between national savings and national investment. Put differently, the current-account deficit also implies that *domestic saving fell short of domestic investment* and that foreigners have been accumulating claims on the United States, or else reducing their liabilities thereto. Furthermore, inasmuch as the government budget deficit counts as a negative component of the national savings rate, this deficit also contributes to the deterioration of the national savings-investment balance. Hence the tendency of some writers to couple the current-account and budget imbalances under the popular label of "twin" deficits – actually according to some critics only a "twin" illusion, since no direct statistical link has been found to exist between them.

Yet many factors interacted to bring about the string of deficits in the current-account balances characteristic of the 1980s. Not only did increases in U.S. total demand (spurred by demand for imports) and decreases in foreign demand for U.S. products (dampened by an overvalued dollar) play significant roles, but so did differences in the rates of return on capital at home and abroad,

U.S. inflation, price hikes (above all for oil), changes in exchange rates, and development of the complex ways of bridging various nontariff barriers – in particular, via (1) joint ventures and direct (foreign) investments in U.S. production and (2) efforts to build market share unconstrained by so-called voluntary export restraints. Reports of the President's Council of Economic Advisers pointed out that in the 1950s and the first half of the 1960s the rates of return on capital were lower and the wage rates were higher in the United States than in the other industrial countries. As the U.S. capital stock had not been damaged by the war and as the rates of return on investments abroad were attractive, the U.S. invested heavily there, thus achieving a persistent surplus in current transactions – including merchandise trade. By the 1970s, after the other countries had eliminated the differences between their capital and labor costs and those of the United States, the demand for new capital abroad started to subside. By the mid 1980s, the United States had ceased to be a net exporter of capital, and the current-account balance ceased to be in surplus. In the 1980s, a deep shift in the tax structure and higher domestic demand relative to the growth of GNP at home, along with the growth of American spending abroad, brought about a rapid deterioration in the savings-investment balance and, along with other causes, brought about an increase in the inflow of capital. This increase was also fueled by the strengthening of the dollar, which cheapened U.S. imports and increased the price of U.S. exports.[20] Moreover, the government budget deficits, along with the external deficits – not associated *in any systematic fashion* – further negatively influenced the current account. (Such association does not exist even when both kinds of deficits are adjusted for both inflation and market value changes.)[21]

The acquisition of U.S. assets by foreigners during the second half of the 1980s, at a faster rate than the acquisition by the U.S. of similar assets abroad, resulted in the transformation of the U.S. from a *net lender* into a *net debtor* nation – even though many of the foreign holdings involved equity claims rather than debt. (See Table 1-4.) On the basis of estimates at current cost, the reversal in the U.S. position took place in 1986 (in 1985 the U.S. still had $64.3 billion in surplus asset holdings). While throughout the 1980s U.S. holdings of assets abroad continued to grow in nominal terms, from $1.1 trillion in 1982 to $1.7 trillion in 1990, during the same period foreign holdings of assets in the U.S. (bonds of all kinds, common stock, and direct investment) rose from $736 billion to over $2.1 trillion . While in 1982 direct investments in the U.S. by foreigners amounted to about 46 percent of U.S. direct investments abroad, in 1990 the former equaled close to 78 percent of the latter. In 1990, as Table 1-4 shows, the measured U.S. net external indebtedness had reached over $412 billion; that total, it is true, was equivalent to only about 8.4 percent of that year's GNP. However, from the mid 1980s on, the trend has certainly been toward a declining U.S. asset position.

Table 1-4. *U.S. international investment position (billions of dollars): selected years, 1970–1988*

	1982	1985	1990
Net Intern. Investment Position	364.0	64.3	-412.1
U.S. Assets Abroad	1,100.6	1,173.9	1,764.1
of which U.S. Private Assets	882.5	968.2	1,508.2
of which Direct Investments	374.0	379.6	598.1
Foreign Assets in the U.S.	736.6	1,109.5	2,176.2
of which Direct Investments	173.2	227.2	465.9

Note: All data at current cost.
Source: U.S. Department of Commerce, Survey of Current Business, June 1991, p. 26.

I shall examine later on (particularly in Chapter 7) the impacts on U.S. industrial policies of the trade deficits and of the indicated changes in the U.S. assets position. Let me recall for now that by the end of the 1980s, Paul A. Samuelson, the Nobel laureate, was painting the U.S. situation, and its prospects, in mixed black and gray hues. In testimony before a Senate committee in which he stated that he did not wish "to darken the bad spots nor whitewash the subtle and insidious degenerations," he affirmed that both the trade and chronic budget deficits must be "reduced toward zero." As to the use of foreign savings, they certainly did increase our capital formation, but the results of this increase, he added, were mixed. In Samuelson's view, the productivity wages which our citizens would earn in the 1990s would increase, but the fruits of these investments – dividends and interest – would go abroad.[22]

Other economists reject the idea of "subtle and insidious degenerations" and contend that the figures show simply that the U.S. was a good place to invest. Are we really in danger of going down the road of discredited debtor nations? Is it true that we are henceforth at the mercy of foreign financiers and of foreign financial markets who sit "in finger-wagging judgment over the budget and are braced to lower the boom on stocks, bonds and the dollar if the [budget] deficit is not cut substantially and soon"? Peter T. Kilborn, the author of this quotation, rightly points out that this is far from being a general opinion, either in the markets or among economists.[23] Professor Samuelson himself noted in the testimony quoted above that even though "by the year 2000 America will owe an appreciable fraction of her total wealth," the U.S. will still be only "at bare beginnings" of the process of running into debt, a situation far different from that of poor nations with debt obligations. The last report of President Reagan's Council of Economic Advisers quietly recalled that the U.S. continued to have the largest aggregate wealth in the world and that both the country and its citizens could easily maintain their contractual obligations. By the end of the 1980s, interest payments made to foreigners amounted to about 2.6 percent of government outlays and to less than 20 percent of the government's interest payments. The inflow of foreign funds for which these interest payments served as compensation, added the report, helped to keep our interest rates at close to world levels, while the foreign capital invested productively would help to increase future income. Hence, this investment might be expected to compensate for the interest payments due to the foreigners who financed it.[24] Other economists, C. Fred Bergsten for instance, note that the United States "differs" from other industrial debtor countries because it borrows primarily in its own currency, so that it can never "run out of foreign exchange."[25] This assertion is actually irrelevant: a country with valuable assets abroad, as the United States continues to be, can always sell them for foreign exchange.

Nevertheless, aren't the United States' business ventures still subject to the discretion of foreign financiers, who might withdraw their funds or cease to extend us new loans while our current account is in deficit? The short answer is that as long as there is a capital market, each participant is certainly affected by the behavior of all others. This is so whether or not we eliminate our external deficit and "reorient" the economy toward exports and private investment, as Bergsten would like us to do.[26] The different interpretations of the significance of the change in the U.S. position from a creditor to a debtor nation actually reflect different interpretations of the significance of (1) the inflow into the U.S. of foreign capital and (2) the interrelations of our budget deficits with our *levels of public and private saving and investment* (which, of course, impact also the gross public debt of the U.S. Treasury).

What are the orders of magnitude involved? According to official data, from 1949 to 1969 the U.S. budget deficit fluctuated between 0.1 percent and a maximum of 3.3 percent (in 1968) of yearly GNP. During the 1970s, the deficit oscillated between 0.6 percent of the GNP and a maximum of 4.2 percent (in 1976). In the early 1990s the maximum was scheduled to reach 6.7 percent. These large deficits are, of course, far below those registered during the war years, when a maximum of 31.6 percent of GNP was reached in 1942. The spread between receipts and expenditures in current and constant prices for selected postwar years is presented in Table 1-5.

The connections between the growth of foreign assets in the United States and the decrease in our assets abroad, between investment levels and the trade deficit, and between the level of saving and the budget deficit have been differently assessed by two main schools of thought. Perhaps the best expositor of the first has been Paul Krugman of MIT, and of the second, Robert Eisner of Northwestern University.

According to Krugman, simply put, if the U.S. sells to foreigners more U.S.

Table 1-5. *U.S. budget receipts, outlays, and surplus or deficit at current and constant prices as percentages of GNP: selected years, 1945–1989*

	Receipts	Outlays	Surplus/ Deficit (-)	Receipts	Outlays	Surplus/ Deficit (-)
1945	20.6	43.6	-22.9	24.0	49.3	-25.3
1960	16.2	16.1	-0.1	20.5	20.4	0.1
1973	14.4	15.6	-1.2	18.1	19.2	-1.1
1982	15.1	18.9	-3.8	19.5	23.6	-4.1
1989	14.2	18.2	-4.0	19.1	22.1	-3.0

Sources: Historical Tables: Budget of the United States Government, Fiscal Year 1992, Washington, D.C., Executive Office of the President, Office of Management and Budget, 1991, pp. 15, 17. Constant computed from ibid., p. 17, and Economic Report of the President . . . 1991, p. 288.

assets than it buys abroad, it must necessarily buy more goods from abroad than it sells there. The dependence of the U.S. on foreign capital to finance its investments thus has its inevitable counterpart in our trade deficit. Now, this trade deficit also reflects a decline in U.S. saving (which finances our investments both at home and abroad), a trend which in turn is partly due to the budget deficit. Put differently, in order to increase savings – and to cut the trade deficit and reverse the existing relations between the increase of foreign assets in the U.S. and the relative decrease in our assets abroad – we must cut the budget deficit. Even if one rejects the formula that the budget deficit and the trade deficit are "twins," there are no better ways for the federal government to make room for a smaller trade deficit than by balancing its budget. How about our competitiveness? Does not the loss of our markets abroad help explain our trade deficits? Krugman's answer is a resolute *no.* "Competitiveness does matter, but not for the trade deficit." If U.S. savings remained high, the loss of competitive advantage (even assuming that, up to a point, such a loss existed) would not lead to a trade deficit but to a depreciation of the dollar, which could compensate for the loss of competitive advantage by making our goods cheaper.[27] In short, Krugman's argument hinges on the idea that reducing the budget deficit is the way to increase the real and financial resources available for private investment. But is it that certain that this reduction will necessarily generate that additional investment?

Robert Eisner challenges various aspects of this thesis, as well as the inferences of C. Fred Bergsten concerning the role of our budget deficits. He posits that these deficits have been associated with increases both in consumption and in investment and that they have not been detrimental to private investment. While conceding that they did increase trade deficits, he notes that the imports due to the trade deficits also contributed to stimulating growth. To measure the true impact of the budget deficits, Eisner asserts, we need a measure of the deficits which would be uncontaminated, to start with, by the economy's cyclical fluctuations; it would also be adjusted to take inflation into account. Such a "clean" measure is, according to Eisner, the so-called *full employment budget* – that is, the estimates of budgetary receipts, outlays, and deficits computed at full employment (i.e., at a constant rate of unemployment) – adjusted in the indicated ways. Plotting the percentage changes in real GNP for 1956–84 against *lagged* price-adjusted high-employment deficits, Eisner concludes that the greater the budget deficit (as defined), the greater the next year's increase in the GNP, and the less the deficit, the greater the decline in the next year's GNP.[28] While some of Eisner's conclusions have been rejected by some as simply "hoary Keynesian arguments" (to which we shall return immediately below), his methods of adjusting the data by taking inflation into account and by excluding from the deficit the federal spending for capital investment – adjustments which made Eisner state that with them "we may have no deficit at all" – have been welcomed even by anti-Keynesians as properly putting "deficits and debt into perspective."[29]

But Krugman retorts that in the 1980s, for instance, the attempts to cut down government expenditures (except for defense) resulted in larger cuts in investments rather than in consumption. Be that as it may, Krugman adds that in the 1980s the government moved sharply toward budget deficits, thus contributing to further declines in national savings. Most important, even if one accepts Eisner's arguments that there are *no* budget deficits, one cannot fail to see that we do have trade deficits and that these cannot be cut without raising savings, which cannot be raised without cutting the budget deficit, the "only reliable tool" for this purpose.[30]

Herbert Stein, former chairman of President Nixon's Council of Economic Advisers, has noted that after World War II budgetary policy was viewed as an instrument of the federal government for maintaining *high employment and stabilization*. The prescription consisted in reliance on automatic variations in revenue and expenditure which come with business fluctuations and are unaffected by business changes except in a deep depression. The rationale was the Keynesian one: an increase in government expenditures and a decrease in revenues (in a recession), whether occurring automatically or as a result of budgetary action, would sustain total demand for goods and services and thus reverse the situation. The strategy implied acceptance of the deficits that come with a recession but discouraged deficits in "normal" times. The standard for appraising the budget position was not the *actual* deficit or surplus, but – as we

Table 1-6. *U.S. gross federal debt (billion dollars): selected fiscal years, 1945–1989*

	Total Gross Debt	Held by the Public	Gross National Product	Ratios 1 ÷ 3	Ratios 2 ÷ 3
	1	2	3	4	5
1945	260.1	235.2	212.4	122.5	110.7
1960	290.5	236.8	506.7	57.3	46.7
1973	466.3	340.9	1,281.4	36.4	26.6
1982	1,136.8	919.2	3,139.1	36.2	29.3
1989	2,867.5	2,190.3	5,131.3	55.9	42.7

Source: Economic Report of the President . . . 1991, p. 375. Columns 4 and 5 computed.

also saw in Robert Eisner's demonstration above – the *hypothetical* deficit or surplus obtaining under "stable" conditions, namely at an accepted (later called "natural") unemployment rate. After all kinds of policy failures and attempts to correct them, the Keynesian-inspired deficit rule fell into disuse. What took its place is what Stein calls "unrealistic and irrational fears" concerning a substantial increase in the ratio of debt to GNP which will cause "increases of interest rates in the future." In short, as Herbert Stein pointed out, the fall into disuse of the old Keynesian rule in effect left with decisionmakers *no* guidance as to the desirable size of the surplus or deficit.[31] In practice, the annual size of the budget deficit was left to arduously negotiated "budget agreements" poorly reconciling the different priorities of the Republicans and Democrats in Congress within the bounds of an ill-defined bipartisan commitment to balance the budget and to cut the national debt "in the very near future."

The rate of increase in the debt-to-GNP ratio certainly accelerated during the 1980s at a time of rising defense expenditures. The gross federal debt held by private investors – commercial banks, money market funds, insurance and other companies, and individuals – more than tripled at current prices from 1980 to 1989 (rising from $709 billion to $2,190 billion). Further, as can be seen from Table 1-6, the ratios to GNP of the total gross public debt as well as of the debt held by private investors, after significantly decreasing from the war levels to the 1970s, rose at a very rapid pace from the early 1980s through the rest of the decade. Still, only a small part of this total was held by foreigners. Our gross liabilities to foreigners (i.e., not netted by their liabilities toward us) amounted in 1989 to $714. (We shall turn in more detail to these years in Chapter 6.) As the 1980s passed into history, the American public and decisionmakers were increasingly pulled between what Herbert Stein called

Table 1-7. *Major industrial countries: net public debt of the general government* in percentage of GNP/GDP, 1980, 1982, and 1989*

Countries	1980	1982	1989
United States	19.0	21.7	30.7
Canada	12.9	16.5	37.8
Japan	17.3	23.2	14.1
Germany (West)	14.3	17.4	22.1
France	14.3	17.8	24.8
Italy	53.6	63.4	95.6
United Kingdom	43.5	42.1	33.2
Average (seven countries)**	21.5	25.5	30.6

* Definitions of central government and the public sector vary across countries. Net debt equals gross liabilities less gross financial assets. Since assets include social security assets, which are sizable in many countries, there may be substantial differences between the levels of gross and net debt in individual countries. For example, gross debt of the general government in Japan was roughly equivalent to 71 percent of GNP in 1989.
**On the base 1987 GNP/GDP weights and exchange rates.
Sources: World Economic Outlook: A Survey by the Staff of the International Monetary Fund, Washington, D.C., International Monetary Fund, October 1990, p. 89; OECD, Economic Outlook, No. 48, December 1990, p. 113.

the "unrealistic and irrational fears" that the rising ratios of debt to GNP would make our interest obligations unbearable and mortgage our future, and assurances that what we were really bequeathing to the future were not budget deficits that add to the "public's own burden and that of future generations" but rather "our physical and human capital" financed by these "deficits."

I believe that to a large extent the fears nurtured by the rising ratios of debt to GNP are exaggerated. It is certainly true that a significant part of the population has since the early 1980s viewed the debt as a key cause of our economic problems – the dragon which must be slain if we are to get back to the good times. Yet let me point out that our ratios of net debt to GNP are still well within manageable limits, as our own war experience and the postwar experience of *all* major industrial countries clearly show. For instance, according to data furnished by the International Monetary Fund, the net debt (i.e., gross liabilities less gross financial assets) of the government sector increased in the 1980s much faster than GNP in *all* major industrial countries except Japan and the United Kingdom. As can be seen from Table 1-7, by the end of the 1980s the net public debt of our government corresponded roughly to the average ratio of debt to GNP of all the industrial countries.

It is certainly erroneous to *mechanically* project into the future certain trends which developed during the postwar years up to the end of the 1980s. Throughout that epoch the United States focused on countering the enormous Soviet challenge, a task which obliged it to adjust its economic activities in many different ways. The collapse of communism on the threshold of the 1990s removes an enormous danger and brings in its wake vast changes around the globe, changes which are bound to deeply modify not only our world military commitments, our supporting military infrastructure, and our defense budgets, but also our views concerning national priorities and the allocation of a GNP in the $6 trillion range in the 1990s and beyond.

2 Government-business relationship

2-1 Divergent and convergent policies

The analysis of even a speculative proposal of an American "industrial policy" or of an American "foreign trade strategy" – both of which are supposed to counter the new competitive challenge facing America (and on which I shall focus in detail in Part II) – requires a preliminary examination of the nature and scope of the federal government's traditional pattern of intervention in the economy, of the economic instruments available for this purpose, and of the ways in which these instruments have been put to use. After the broad review of America's economic development in the postwar years presented in the preceding chapter, we now turn to the mapping of the relationship which prevailed during that period between business and the federal government.

These interrelations did, in some respects, differ under Democratic and Republican administrations. I shall start the discussion by first examining the ways in which the traditional Democratic and Republican conceptions actually diverge respecting the roles of the federal government and of private business in the shaping of the country's economic activity. I shall consider afterwards the specific issue of the instruments available, their gamut and their scope – from various forms of supervisory procedures to promotional methods. I shall also indicate the influence on science and technology of R&D outlays by the federal government, industry, the states, and the colleges and universities. In the conclusion, I shall focus on the transformations business has undergone from the points of view of forms of organization, growth strategies, and adjustments to the rapid spread of technologies and to the speeded-up processes of their worldwide commercialization.

Consider first the nature and extent of the conceptual differences between Democrats and Republicans concerning the economic roles and functions of the federal government and of private business. What specific approaches do they condition in regard to the economy's *modus operandi*? To what extent are the measures which these approaches yield adequate for the goal(s) pursued? To start with, one should note that these differences proceed from the acceptance (or the rejection) of the *primacy* of the federal government's or of private business' activity in affecting the problems of consumption and investment, employment, stability, and economic growth. The recognition of one or the other primacy implies different views of the possible impacts of taxation and of the volume, structure, adequacy, and timing of government expenditures.

In a cogent essay entitled "Some Current Cleavages Among Economists," written way back in 1947, the economist J. M. Clark pointed up a basic division among economists – and by implication among policymakers – shaped particularly by the experiences of the 1930s. This division involves differing conceptions of the nature and scope of public and of private spending and of the adequacy of each to ensure economic stability and growth.[1] According to Clark, when attempting to define *adequate* spending in the national economy, some economists think mainly of "private consumer spending, plus public spending of whatever sort, for consumption or investment, and neglect private investment and the necessary incentives thereto." They assume that the major determinant of private investment is the volume of consumers' expenditures. It is the latter, in this way of thinking, which pushes private business to make capital outlays and to expand capacity to adequately handle effective demand. Possible low rates of return can be countered by low rates of interest. Finally, a redistribution of income via wage increases, at the expense of profits, ultimately increases employment by favoring consumption as well as economic growth.

On the opposite side, adds Clark, are economists who reverse the logic of consumption and hold that "the way to high consumption is high employment and the way to high employment is investment." What matters for them are the incentives for stimulating *private investment.* They regard public spending as "largely unproductive or inherently wasteful." They focus instead "on those incomes which furnish the reward of private investment and the incentives to it." They are against schemes of income redistribution, profits limitation, and any tax system "which loads the dice against risk-taking investment of equity capital." Finally, they dismiss the idea that low interest rates have a determining effect on investment, especially in the case of pioneering endeavors and high-risk ventures in conditions of rapid economic progress, when accelerated obsolescence is the rule.

Close to half a century after Clark's essay, in 1991, an observant *New York Times* reporter, David E. Rosenbaum, noted that the main Democratic and Republican confrontations – as in the early 1930s and the 1940s – still swirled around the question of the taxing of capital gains. The main tenet of the Democrats' tax policy in the early 1990s, remarked Rosenbaum, was that the wealthy should be taxed as needed to finance government programs, while the Republicans continued to believe that if rich people's taxes were reduced they would invest more money. That, in the Republican view, would cause the economy to grow, leading to more jobs and prosperity for all Americans.[2] Let us see now how and to what extent Democratic and Republican presidential policies and measures conformed to and deviated from these old tenets in the variously changing conditions which confronted them through the post-World War II period up to the turn of the 1990s. We start with the Democratic presidencies.

Intensely preoccupied with the avoidance of "mass unemployment and ruinous depression," the Democratic administration of the early postwar years, that of President Truman, asserted that its responsibility, as enshrined in the Employment Act of 1946 – called by some labor's Magna Carta – was to aim for "maximum production and the purchasing power that makes for high consumption."[3] For this purpose, the administration indicated that it would try to strike a very special balance between business, consumers, and the federal government, a balance requiring that business' income and investment "should be large enough to make full use of our technology, our inventions"; that consumers' income and spending "should be sufficient to clear the market of goods and provide for still more business enterprise"; and that the government's expenditures "should be large enough to provide those services which our resources permit."[4] At the crucial juncture of 1949, when war-inflated purchasing power had waned and when both unemployment and inflationary pressures were rising, the indicated balance was to shift in favor of consumption via a complex set of measures involving voluntary price-wage adjustments, increased minimum wage, farm price supports, and government help for the unemployed and the millions whose incomes were lagging behind inflation. In addition, increases in corporate taxes were to "offset decreases in government revenues."[5] This special balance was, however, thrown out of gear by the rapidly rising defense requirements of the early 1950s. Indeed, in the words of the *ERP* of January 1952, the outlays for national security almost doubled in 1951, while concomitantly a series of direct and indirect controls had to be put in place in order to limit "prices, wages, credit, and the expansion of incomes."[6] As we shall see, this was not to be either the only or the last situation in which policies had to conflict with the professed economic philosophy. In another order of ideas, it is interesting to point to a disclosure of Truman's last *ERP,* of January 1953. The report indicated that for several years the administration's economic advisers had worked on projecting maximum levels of employment, production, and purchasing power, both for a year and for several years ahead, and had estimated the magnitudes of the income flows to consumers and investors needed to achieve these levels. But the projections had only an "educational" purpose, i.e., they were strictly academic.[7] However, during the next Democratic administration, as we shall see, such estimations became the very substance of practical policies.

The next Democratic administration, that of President John F. Kennedy (who in 1961 followed the Republican President Eisenhower), shifted the focus of its economic policy from moderation of the business cycle toward realization of the full employment *potential* of the economy. The shift was proclaimed imperative because of the "disturbing" economic situation at home and the lagging of the U.S. growth rate behind that of all the other industrialized countries. After a little more than a week in office, in his State of the Union address of January 30, 1961, the president drew a somber balance sheet of the country's situation. He asserted that he was taking charge of the country after "seven months of recession, three and a half years of slack, seven years of diminished economic growth, and nine years of falling farm income."[8] And in his immediately following "Special Message to the Congress: Program for Economic Recovery and Growth" of February 2, 1961, he added that the country could not afford to "dissipate its opportunities for economic growth" and that it had to expand its productive capacity at a rate that would demonstrate the "vigor and vitality" of its economy.[9] The economic proposals addressed to the Congress on the basis of these messages were, however, not very striking. The president asked notably for improved unemployment compensation, more food for the families of the unemployed, redevelopment of areas of chronic labor surplus, stimuli for housing and construction, a higher minimum wage, and tax increases for "sound plant investment." It was in the *ERP* of January 1962 that Kennedy and his Council of Economic Advisers (CEA) took the decisive step of clearly *defining* both their economic goals and the means for reaching them. The goal – the meeting of the "standing challenge" posed by the Employment Act of 1946 of maximum production, employment, and purchasing power – was specified to involve a temporary unemployment target of 4 percent and a long-term yearly economic growth target of 4½ percent, along with a stabilization policy implying minimization of deviations "from a rising, not from an unchanging average." The main measures proposed for reaching the goals were, notably, tax credits for gross investment in depreciable machinery and equipment, a stand-by authorization for the president to initiate accelerated capital improvements with public funds, and a procedure for quickly making a temporary across-the-board reduction in the individual income tax.[10] Subsequently, in his State of the Union address of January 14, 1963, and in his final *ERP*, also delivered that month, the president took innovative steps toward both tax cuts and tax reform. The need for early action, stated the report, lay not in the prospect of a recession, i.e., in a "cyclical emergency compelling immediate action," but rather in an undue "slowing down of our long-term growth." After asserting that our obsolete tax system exerted "a drag on private purchasing power," as well as on profits and employment – a tax system designed in earlier years to check inflation and now checking growth instead – the president proposed (both in the message and in the report) the following drastic targets: reduction of the individual tax rates from their 20–91 percent levels to 14–65 percent; and reduction, in stages, of the corporate tax rate from

52 to 47 percent. He and the CEA predicted that the proposed tax reductions would directly increase the disposable income and purchasing power of consumers and of business, whose spending would set in motion a process of cumulative economic expansion. Interestingly, the report dismissed as unfounded the suggestions of those who claimed that the proposed tax reductions were either too small in relation to paychecks or that they would be "frittered away," since what mattered was that all purchases would finally lead to production, which generates income and provides employment.[11]

After the assassination of President Kennedy, the idea of the great tax cut, along with ideas about the need to "overcome poverty" (first affirmed by President Roosevelt) and to "extend the equality of opportunity," included in the *ERP* of January 1962,[12] were vigorously reasserted by President Lyndon B. Johnson in his first "Annual Message to the Congress on the State of the Union," of January 8, 1964. In this message, the president invited the current session of Congress to be known as the session which "enacted the most far-reaching tax cut of our time"; "declared all-out war on human poverty and unemployment"; "recognized the health needs of all our older citizens"; and "helped to build more homes, more schools, more libraries, and more hospitals than any single session of Congress in the history of our Republic."[13] Kennedy's tax-cut program of 1963, embodied in the Revenue Act of 1964 and representing President Johnson's first major legislative victory – the largest stimulative fiscal action ever undertaken until then – became effective in July 1965. The "unfinished task of prosperous Americans" was declared to be the "building of a Great Society" involving the achievement of full employment without inflation, increased economic efficiency, and extension of the benefits of prosperity to the disadvantaged. All this was to be carried out according to the Democrats' traditional scenario, thanks to strong growth in the confidence of consumers, who "will respond to rising earnings, higher social security benefits, and a cut in excise taxes by lifting their purchases, thereby providing a market for a full two-thirds of our expected over-all gain in production."[14] The "war on poverty" was supposed to "strike at the roots" of misery with programs of community action, education, training, and work experience.

By January 1966, Lyndon Johnson could note in his *ERP* that only seven countries of the world could claim total yearly output as large as the *increase* in U.S. output in 1965; that the U.S.'s stock of private plant and equipment had *increased* in 1965 alone as much as in the four years 1957 through 1960; and that in spite of the tax cuts, the increase in Federal cash receipts between fiscal 1961 and 1967 would exceed the entire cash receipts of the federal government in any fiscal year prior to 1951. As the president spoke, however, the Vietnam War had already started to cast an increasingly dark shadow over the country as 200,000 of our citizens and billions of our resources were engaged in battle and as defense needs were becoming an increasingly important economic factor.[15]

As the Vietnam War dragged on, an economic slowdown set in in 1966 and continued through the first half of 1967. By the end of 1967, the fall in federal tax receipts, rising inflation, the mounting deficit, and the dollar's decline abroad forced the president to start a politically difficult reversal, namely a request to Congress for a "temporary" 10 percent surcharge on corporate and individual income taxes, along with the continuation at their current levels of various excise taxes which had been scheduled to drop in April 1968. In his last budget proposal and in his valedictory *ERP* for 1969, the president finally requested that the adopted 10 percent income tax surcharge be extended further, until June 30, 1970. By the end of 1968, the president's Council of Economic Advisers, guided by the brilliant Arthur M. Okun, had, sadly, to warn that though the country had experienced eight years of economic expansion, the attainment of its "full employment potential" had proven much more elusive than it had seemed in January 1961 at the beginning of two self-confident Democratic administrations. The January 1969 report of the CEA did reaffirm that the task of federal fiscal and monetary policy was to affect demand to the extent that an appropriate balance would be maintained with the "potential," but this potential itself was not an absolute technical ceiling on output. It was rather something less stringent, less determinant, namely something allowing "for some margin of idle resources." The *choice* of a specific margin would revive the rather old dilemma of the proper balancing of the goal of high unemployment with that of stability – obviously an arduous choice, since, as Okun wistfully reminded us, it is always difficult to balance the costs of inflation against those of an absolute loss of output and employment, which are "quantitatively and qualitatively" different.[16] The great Kennedy-Johnson policy shift from moderating the cycle to raising the economy to its "full employment potential" thus ended on a melancholy note, whose echo was to resound even more poignantly under the Democratic administration of the 1970s, that of President Carter.

As this Democratic administration came into office, at the beginning of 1977, it was faced with the severe consequences of the deep recession of 1974–75 (to which I shall return below). Unemployment still affected close to 7 million workers – roughly 7 percent of the labor force – while the yearly inflation rate was also inching toward the level of 7 percent. The administration began with a *stimulus program* (partly enacted in 1977) which consisted notably of a rebate on the 1976 tax, combined with a permanent increase in the personal tax deduction; a choice for business firms between an investment tax credit and a new higher credit against employer-paid social security taxes; and an increase in the authorization for emergency public works, plus an increase of federal grants to the states and localities. To press for growth, the *ERP* of 1978 proposed a further tax reduction meant "to strengthen consumer purchasing power and expand consumer markets." The proposal was for an across-the-board reduction in personal income taxes, along with significant improvement in the progressivity of the tax system. The overall corporate business tax was to be reduced also – initially, from 48 to 45 percent; by 1980, to 40 percent. Concomitantly, an energy program would provide for the expansion of an oil reserve buffer against upward price movements. While Congress was wrangling about the Humphrey-Hawkins Full Employment and Balance Growth Act and its five-year projections of what seemed fancifully low unemployment and inflation rates, the CEA was also projecting more modest yet still rather unrealistic growth rates for the real potential GNP of between 3.3 and 3.8 percent for 1978–81 (with a benchmark unemployment rate of 4.8 percent.)[17]

As it turned out, by mid 1978 the administration was compelled to completely reverse itself. It abandoned the traditional policy of "strengthening consumer purchasing power" and focused instead on the mounting inflation. Fiscal and monetary restraint was declared to have become imperative, while unemployment fluctuated at around 6 percent of the labor force, and inflation was climbing rapidly above 9 percent. As indicated by the *ERP* of 1979, the key objective became the *slowing down of economic growth* while avoiding a recession by delaying the tax cuts and slowing down wage and price increases on a "voluntary" basis (using explicit numerical ceilings set by the administration). At the same time, the CEA again lowered its sights for the future. While the Humphrey-Hawkins Act had finalized rather incredible targets for 1983, the CEA carefully reevaluated its own previous estimates about the economy's past performance and "reinterpreted" its former optimistic assumptions about the future accordingly.[18] Finally, the CEA stated in its own report accompanying the *ERP* for 1980 that the Humphrey-Hawkins targets of a 3 percent unemployment rate and a 4 percent inflation rate, both set for 1983, had to be "deferred" to 1985 and 1988 respectively. Coping with the productivity decline and counteracting inside and outside inflationary pressures could not be carried out "by relying solely on aggregate demand policies," i.e., fiscal and monetary restraint and voluntary pay and price controls. To improve the economy's performance – by then, registering a 7 percent unemployment rate and a 13.3 percent inflation rate – a series of long-term measures was required, involving *inter alia* regulatory reform (previously suggested by a Republican administration), a long-term energy policy, grain reserve policies, and trade policies. Acting fully in the logic of the time, the Democratic administration was now proclaiming that *restraining aggregate demand* was to remain the country's highest priority *for an extended period,* and that, if inflation was to be reduced over the long run, the growth of nominal national income had to decline.[19] In its final report (1981) the Carter administration seemed literally ready to throw in the towel. It was now looking wherever possible for ways of bringing down "a stubborn inflation without choking of economic growth" and was stressing the need to channel a much larger share of our national output to *investment* in order to "reverse a decade-long decline in productivity growth." In considering the past 15 years (i.e., fiscal 1965 to 1980), it affirmed that "excessive demand in the economy," fed by an overly large federal budget deficit or excess growth in the money supply, was the *major factor* in "one of the three inflationary episodes [of the period] and played a subsidiary role in the other two." The first of these "excessive demands" was said to have occurred in the late 1960s, "when the Vietnam war and the Great Society programs were financed for a number of years without a tax increase," while the other two had taken place in the 1970s, at the time of the massive oil price increases.[20] Thus the traditional Democratic assertion of the primacy of consumption had finally to be abandoned by the Carter administration – a change which would eventually exercise a profound impact on the "center" of the party, as we shall see later on.

Let us now turn to the Republican administrations. Were their policies and their measures continuously consistent with their basic premises – specifically, the primacy of business initiative and investment as the royal road to high employment, adequate purchasing power, and an expanding economy?

The first postwar administration, that of President Eisenhower, clearly delineated its economic philosophy in its earliest presidential reports. In the first *ERP*, that of January 1954, the new administration indicated that the federal government would continue to pursue the broad objectives of the preceding Democratic administration concerning the stimulation of output and employment and the avoidance of contraction or inflation, but would do it without "constant stirring or meddling" in the economy. People did not wish or expect their government to "give them jobs and thereby gain control over their individual lives," added the report. In order to have expanding *private* employment, employers' prospects of reward had to be sufficient to impel them to assume risks. In this connection the federal government would remove price controls, redraw the line separating public and private activities, privatize certain unprofitable federal enterprises, grant investors more deductions (notably for research and development), liberalize depreciation allowances, encourage investment abroad, and, in general, "improve the climate" for risk assumption.[21] The same ideas were to be stressed again, without much variation, in the second *ERP* of January 1955. However, as time went on and the recession that had begun in 1957 dragged on, the *ERP* of 1959 suddenly revealed a much more active ideal of federal government than the earlier presidential reports might have led one to envision. Reviewing federal activities at a time of "contractive influences," the report noted that the government had acted "vigorously" to ensure an ample supply of credit, had pressed for the enactment of legislation temporarily extending unemployment benefits, had taken steps to accelerate federal construction projects under way, and had speeded up projects supported by federal financial assistance.[22] At the same time, to counter the then increasing Soviet threat, a vast military procurement program was put into place. The president's "Annual Budget Message to the Congress – Fiscal Year 1959" stressed that the weapons and equipment to be bought in 1959 were to be totally different from those purchased four years earlier. Hardly "a single production model aircraft on the Air Force's proposed list for 1959" had been in its program in 1955; this was also true for all types of missiles.[23] And the "Annual Message to the Congress on the State of the Union," of January 9, 1959, pointed out that national security programs accounted "for nearly sixty percent of the entire Federal budget for this coming fiscal year."[24] Eisenhower's valedictory *ERP* of January 1961 ended, however, on a disappointing note. After a successful recovery in 1959, which had continued during the first half of 1960, the economy was again showing signs of contraction in the form of increasing unemployment and decreasing business expenditures on plant and machinery. Faced with a new recession, the administration concluded wistfully that the moderation of economic fluctuations indeed remained "a major challenge" to government and industry – one whose diagnosis and prescription had the experts divided both on the appropriate countermeasures and on their eventual repercussions as well.[25]

The next Republican administration, that of President Nixon, emphasized in a series of documents starting from the beginning of its term in January of 1969 that *inflation* was then the main enemy – an enemy which had been "allowed" to run unchecked into its fourth year. These documents repeatedly contended that the previous Democratic administrations had tried through "jawboning" to put the blame for inflation on business, while in fact the primary culprit in the disturbance was the government itself. It was now incumbent on the government to turn away from budgets propelling this "form of economic aggression" against the population and move toward budgets with strong surpluses that would curb inflation.[26] Deriding "the overflowing rhetoric of the sixties" and its emphasis on the word "war" in measures taken against poverty, misery, disease, and hunger, the president listed among his "urgent priorities" the replacement of the welfare system – which "penalizes work, breaks up homes, robs recipients of dignity" – with programs of income support, job training, and work incentives. After stressing the continuing difficulties of transiting toward a peace economy (a process begun in 1969, when 400,000 military and civilian personnel were released by the armed forces), the president asserted that notwithstanding the increased pressures of inflation and unemployment, he would "not take the Nation down the road of wage and price controls, however politically expedient that may seem.. . . Wage and price controls only postpone a day of reckoning."[27]

Two and a half years later, however, the government's efforts at "rooting out" inflation were faring badly. Toward the middle of 1971 the president signaled that the time had come for a *New Economic Policy*. On August 15, 1971, he imposed a 90-day freeze on wage and price increases, a freeze which was to continue with a lot of confusion, variations, changing rules, and different "phases" until April 30, 1974. The following January, the president and his economic advisers explained this extraordinary reversal for a Republican administration as follows: "The American economy was beset by a conflict among four objectives: faster growth, higher employment, greater price stability and a more balanced external position.. . . . The price and wage control system has provided more room for expanding growth and employment even while inflation and inflationary pressures are reduced."[28] The controls, coupled with a devaluation of the dollar, constituted an extraordinary experiment, given that the economy was not dominated by war and its immediate aftermath over 1972 and 1973. Yet after about two years of it, the president had to admit that progress had been made in regard to output, employment, and the expansion of net exports, but not in regard to *inflation*, the main object of the New Economic Policy. Conjunction of a number of factors – lagging food production and then sharply rising food prices and consumer prices, as well as energy prices (boosted then by the Arab boycott) – raised the yearly inflation rate to almost 9 percent, "outstripping the earlier period of control as well as the rate of earlier periods without controls" and dashing the hopes and the expectations of the Nixon presidency.[29]

The full mandate of the Nixon administration was completed under the presidency of Gerald R. Ford in the painful aftermath of the Watergate scandal. The first *ERP*, of February 1975, stressed that the country was then facing *three* problems: the immediate problem of recession and unemployment, the continuing problem of inflation, and the newer problem of reducing America's vulnerability to oil embargoes. To cope with the recession, this Republican administration decided on an immediate tax cut "to restore purchasing power, rebuild the confidence of consumers, and increase investment incentives for business." But it had to resort to some Democratic prescriptions as well. In particular, asserting that the expansion of "purchasing power" was "essential," it had to accept a sharp rise in unemployment benefits, even though such a rise would clearly increase the federal deficit and thwart the achievement of price stability.[30] After adoption of the indicated one-time tax cut in March 1975, the administration continued to advocate permanent reductions in personal and corporate taxes, stressing (allegedly in opposition to Congress) that stimuli should be provided to the economy via tax reductions rather than via increases in government spending. In addition, under the chairmanship of Alan Greenspan, the Council of Economic Advisers (CEA) drew attention to two significant issues which were to be amply and heatedly debated in the future. One concerned various auguries of an apparent "permanent downward shift in the level of productivity." The other involved the expanding role of the government in the economy and the imperative need for regulatory reform, which the administration was at this time able to initiate in regard to airlines, railroads, trucking and related areas, and the refining and marketing of natural gas and gasoline.[31]

The next Republican administration, that of President Reagan, which followed the one-term intermission of the Carter administration, asserted that its first and foremost objective was "to improve the performance of the economy by *reducing the role of the Federal government* in all its many dimensions." The new administration rejected "paternalism" as a basis for policy. The scaling down of the government was to involve above all a broad-based tax cut, along with reductions in spending and in the size of the federal and in the scope of regulations. Except for providing certain temporary forms of insurance for income loss (e.g., welfare payments and unemployment compensation), taxes were no longer to be used to "redistribute existing incomes," but rather to encourage people to save and invest. According to the administration, the new tax policy would involve far more than a simple reduction in tax burdens: it would mean *a change in the basic character of taxation,* a change meant to energize the economy via the shifting of the burden of taxation "away from capital income." The Economic Recovery Tax Act of 1981, embodiment of the administration's new tax "experiment," scheduled reductions of marginal tax rates on given levels of nominal income while indexing personal exemptions and, in addition, *lowering the top tax rate on income from capital* from 70 to 50 percent. The compass of government regulatory intervention was likewise scheduled to shrink, being henceforth predicated on cost-benefit analysis with a view to eliminating regulations whose costs would exceed their benefits. Finally, the government set out to pursue a resolutely noninflationary monetary policy, whose credibility would be maximized (thus reducing the transition costs of eliminating inflation) by announcing beforehand, and conforming to, a *rate of growth of the money supply* consistent with a desired path of price level performance.[32]

Reviewing the performance of the administration during its first term in office, the *ERP* of February 1985 focused first of all on its major achievements concerning taxes, inflation, unemployment, and growth. It hailed as "one of the most important accomplishments" the reduction of individual income taxes and of the "effective tax rates on the income from new investments." It pointed out that the inflation rate, as measured by the GNP deflator, had declined dramatically, from 9.0 percent in 1981 to 3.5 percent in 1984. It noted that civilian unemployment had also fallen during the same period, from 9.5 percent of the civilian labor force during the height of the recession of August-December 1982 to 7.4 percent in 1984. It then stressed that after the recession, the recovery had been very rapid, with the rate of growth of GNP peaking at 6.0 percent per annum. Significant changes had been effected in the *structure* of government spending, though the total of federal outlays, contrary to the administration's stated key goal, had increased rather than decreased, reaching 23 percent of GNP in 1984 (as against 22.7 percent in 1982). The basic structural change involved defense vs. nondefense outlays. Defense purchases (including federal investment outlays) increased, while transfer payments, grants-in-aid, and nondefense purchases declined.

The administration registered its biggest disappointments in regard to the budget deficit, the foreign trade deficit, the total gross federal debt, and the United States' international investment position. A fortuitous conjunction of decreasing tax rates and decreasing federal receipts, along with the strengthening dollar (supported by anti-inflationary high interest rates), boosted the budget and foreign-trade deficits and sharply reduced the nation's net international investment surplus (i.e., the value of U.S. assets abroad minus the value of foreign assets in the U.S.).[33] In addition, high interest rates accelerated the decline of economic capital among savings and loan institutions (S&Ls), as well as among a number of banks.

During President Reagan's second term in office, the trends which emerged during the first term were further accentuated. By the end of 1988 the economy had officially registered six years of continuous expansion: from the end of 1982 to the end of 1988, real output had grown on the average at the rate of 4.2 percent per year; the inflation rate had averaged 3.6 percent per year; the rate of unemployment had fallen to 5.3 percent. Business productivity had grown at the rate of 1.7 percent per year – more than double the rate in the stagflation period 1973–81.

Total productivity growth, however, did not match the increases reached during the period preceding the stagflation, namely 1948–73. Further, the discrepancy between federal receipts and expenditures remained substantial, with the 1988 deficit amounting to 3.2 percent of the GNP. In the same year the gross federal debt held by the public climbed to 42.9 percent of the GNP, compared to 26.3 percent in 1981 and 35.2 percent in 1984. Moreover, the negative current accounts of the 1980s year by year increased the net claims foreigners held on the United States. In 1985 the United States turned from a creditor into a debtor nation. During the second term, the difference between the value of U.S. assets abroad and that of foreign assets in the United States grew nearly five times, reaching, as already noted, over half a trillion dollars.[34]

The Reagan presidency, notwithstanding substantive achievements, ended with disappointing results in matters it had considered decisive. The expected incentive effect of the tax cut evoked barely a response in regard to personal saving, investment, and productivity growth. The tax cuts were not "self-financing": they did not increase the propensity to save and did not result in reduced government spending, but rather in an increasing deficit (which helped bring about the increases in GNP growth rates). The federal government did not shrink in many of its dimensions – including the overall size of federal employment and of the federal budget.

At the beginning of the new Republican administration – that of George Bush – the economy continued its expansion, but at a far slower pace. By the end of the 1980s, real GNP was growing at the rate of only 1.8 percent per year; in 1990 this rate dropped to 0.3 percent. Toward the end of 1990, the economy entered into its longest recession since World War II: in the fourth quarter of that year all the economic indicators pointed downward, while uncertainty increased rapidly, particularly after Iraq invaded Kuwait and so destabilized the world's oil prices. The growth slowdown during 1989, and still more in the early 1990s, was concentrated in residential investment, commercial and residential real estate, and consumer spending on durable goods. In addition, export growth slowed down. All this severely hit manufacturing production and employment. America's businesses, households, and government continued to save at a lower rate than in other industrial countries. During the 1980s, the national savings rate actually *dropped substantially below its average over the previous three decades,* and foreign capital inflow rose to about one sixth of the U.S. investment.[35] It would thus appear (as many economists had predicted) that the vaunted tax cut on income from capital, together with tax reform, meant to prevent income redistribution and to encourage savings, actually failed to affect positively the U.S. savings patterns and may have had a negative effect on growth, except for growth stimulated by the inflow of foreign capital.

In sum, under the pressure of circumstances, both the Democrats and the Republicans may have espoused policies and measures that were in conflict with their traditional orientations (e.g., Nixon's adoption of wage and price controls, Ford's emphasis on "purchasing power," and Carter's recognition of the need to restrain aggregate demand and to focus instead on investment). As a rule they tried – but did not always succeed in doing it – to ground their main policies on their old strategies: for the Democrats, the expansion of consumer purchasing power; and for the Republicans, the stimulation of private investment. This does not mean, however, that their approaches converged only during stubborn recessions and periods of high inflation. Even in other situations, their basic approaches have tended to be adjusted. For instance, as defense began the process of downsizing following the collapse of the USSR in 1991, broad agreements started to develop among policymakers in favor of providing both certain infrastructural investments and various forms of support to private business. Attention has shifted in particular toward the expansion of social overhead capital (i.e., transportation, natural resource development, conservation, urban renewal); the upgrading of human capital via some form of national health insurance; vocational education and training; and the expansion of information and of communications technologies. I shall briefly examine some of these issues below, returning to them in more detail in Part IV.

Let me recall first that Democratic and Republican agreement has prevailed, as a rule, with regard to direct support for housing and for small business development. The parties have also agreed on reducing risks for private investment, both at home and in the case of some foreign operations. This risk reduction has been achieved via insurance, via subsidies, and, in exceptional cases – which may, unfortunately, endanger certain other sectors – via bailouts (for certain big banks and most S&Ls). Finally, some agreement has developed with regard to certain tax cuts. On the other hand, interparty divergences remain formidable regarding the broader roles of government and the significance of the *tax system,* particularly taxes on income from capital and the marginal rates of taxation of upper incomes. Often-unbridgeable disagreements also remain on the size and structure of welfare spending, defense cuts, the budget deficit, the size and the structure of spending, various fiscal and monetary measures, and the scope and financing of regulatory activities.

Given the flexibility of the policy framework in which such agreements and disagreements are played out under alternating Democratic and Republican administrations, how extensive and consistent are the *actual* interventions of our government in market relations and the operation of private business? To what extent do these interventions differ from one administration to the next? What is the range of the instruments the government uses, and how do they interact? Do these interactions respond to concerted unidirectional influences, or to variously motivated and conflicting pressures? I shall turn to these issues in Section 2-2. I shall examine the potential changes in the direction of government interventions in Chapter 7.

2-2   The traditional compass of economic intervention

The government determines and enforces the *legal matrix* within which the market operates. This involves the definition of the nature and uses of property rights, the extent and the limits of enforceable contracts, the rules governing firms and associations (including trade unions), and the scope of the regulations which shape the economic environment and which structure the decision-making processes of the market's participants. The legal framework evolves slowly or rapidly under the impulse of such events as significant price changes; severe quantity restrictions from foreign or domestic causes; pressing needs – and changing perceptions of need – among the population or among various groups within it; vast socioeconomic and technological transformations affecting the economy as a whole.

Within the legal framework, the government discharges *macroeconomic* and *microeconomic* functions. To achieve certain central national objectives such as high output and employment, price stability, and a balance in foreign trade, the federal government develops various policies – fiscal, monetary, wage-price, and foreign economic. For implementation, the first entails governmental expenditures and taxation; the second, changes in money supply (effected by the Federal Reserve System); the third, wage-price guidelines or controls; and the fourth, export and import adjustments and exchange rates management.

Possible microeconomic actions comprise a vast array of interventions in markets in order to eliminate trade restrictions, enhance efficiency, stimulate competition, promote equity, and protect workers and consumers. Interventions in the play of supply and demand attempt to cope notably with certain *market failures* and also to modify, in a socially desirable way, some of the market's outcomes concerning, in particular, *distribution of income.* Thus, laws and administrative regulations aim to prevent, modify, or eliminate monopolistic trade restrictions interfering with competition; the insufficient provision of public goods and the increasing costs of public and personal services; misallocations of resources (e.g. between the present and the future); unacceptable distributions of income; and harmful economic spillovers. A vast number of instruments in a wide variety of combinations are called into play in order to carry out these objectives.

In order to better grasp the compass of government's distinct but often overlapping interventions in the market, and also in order to better ascertain the range and interplay of the instruments used by the government, I shall classify these activities under the following headings: (a) *regulatory processes* oriented primarily, though not exclusively, toward restructuring or eliminating interference with effective competition and efficient allocation; (b) *supervisory processes* affecting specific phases of a business' operation; (c) *allocation processes* concerning the attribution of certain rights and privileges and the rationing of certain scarce resources; (d) *promotional processes* aiming at assisting the growth and development of business; and, finally, (e) activities involving the government as a large *buyer* in various markets, as well as a *producer* and an owner of certain business enterprises.

(a) Consider in turn the laws and regulatory mechanisms concerning antitrust, the measures against labor discrimination and for equal opportunity, and, in the same vein, the question of asymmetric information preventing rational consumer choices in the marketplace. As we shall see further on (in Chapter 6), the antitrust policies framed from the end of the 19th century onwards have been directed first of all against monopolization, price discrimination, some types of mergers, and certain unfair business practices. Originally, the policies reflected public concern with industrial concentration and the political power of trusts. Eventually, antitrust administrative rules have provided foundations for wider extensions and applications – to pricing types, output, product variety, innovation, share in sales of small businesses, and the link between market structure and the economic efficiency of the market equilibrium.[36] Traditionally, antitrust has not affected a class of businesses involving the "public interest," e.g., the public utilities industries such as electricity, telecommunications, and pipelines. These businesses have been functioning as *controlled monopolies* with special attention to their operating costs, capital expenditures, rate of return – and have been obligated to charge fair, nondiscriminatory rates and to render satisfactory service. In exchange, they have been allowed a "fair return" on their investment. This situation is in process of change. A famous antitrust decision of 1982 led finally to the breakup of the Bell System in 1984. AT&T was assigned the long-distance and manufacturing functions of the Bell System, and local exchange services were divided among seven regional Bell companies. This breakup has in fact increased the government's involvement in the market. Other changes are impending with respect to electricity. In the 1980s, through a combination of federal laws and the utility industry's reluctance to build new plants because of their cost, a whole new industry of independent power producers has sprung up. The independents are pressing to sell power to any and all industrial consumers, but the transmission system is still controlled by the regulated utilities.[37]

The idea that when equal opportunity is enhanced, competition is the determining element of one's real "economic worth" has gained increasing currency since the 1960s. A massive legal and administrative apparatus has been developed, aiming at protecting labor against most forms of discrimination in regard to employment and rewards – discrimination concerning race, national origin, religion, sex, age, or any criterion other than professional qualification. The goal of equal opportunity is evidently linked to income distribution, and the pursuit of equality of opportunity has been reinforced by the principle of *affirmative action,* i.e., of commands to employers to correct discriminatory imbalances, especially in regard to women's and nonwhites' hiring, firing, and promotion. Notwithstanding numerous gains in these matters, the movement toward equal distribution of income remains uneven and limited.[38]

Another element interfering with the efficient allocation of resources is the presence of *incomplete and asymmetric information* among buyers and sellers, consumers and firms – a presence, open or insidious, which prevents rational choices in the marketplace. Laws and regulations against such unfair practices as adulteration or mislabeling of foods, drugs, and cosmetics; false advertising; deceptive warranties; and risky health products, along with various standard-setting processes aimed at helping buyers make better informed purchasing decisions, have consistently tried to cope with this kind of market failure. A major overhaul of food labeling standards is in process with regard to the deceptive use of such labels as "fresh" (from concentrates), "light," "fat-free," "low cholesterol," and the like. The process encompasses 80,000 types of foods and 300,000 labels. In the words of the commissioner of the Food and Drug Administration, Dr. David A. Kessler, "The misleading stuff is going off the label. There will be confidence that when you see claims on the label the words will have meaning."[39]

(b) Let us now examine government's *supervisory processes* concerning various *phases* of a business operation, including rights of entry into service, nature of the product to be sold, methods of production, financing, and working conditions. The supervisory measures concerning all these issues have been developed in response to distinct and quite diverse public needs or concerns, e.g., screening the unfit or the unqualified out of certain professions; guaranteeing efficient production of important public services; and coping with spillover problems. While each supervisory measure has been focused on a specific, *partial* aspect of business management, in the long run they have sometimes coalesced into a quite comprehensive supervisory system, one never aimed at in the diverse underlying laws and regulations. In principle, a completely unregulated company could reach free managerial decisions in such crucial areas as "the determination of the nature of the product to be offered, the market in which to sell it, the volume to be offered for sale, the price at which to sell it, the method and practices of production and sale, the methods of financing capital investment, and the utilization of material and human resources in production and sale."[40] But for most businesses, this is certainly not the prevailing situation.

To start with, in certain cases licensing is needed – i.e., a governmental agency's permit, certificate, approval, registration, charter, membership, statutory exemption, or other form of permission – before a business may begin to operate. Moreover, such permission may be revoked, suspended, or otherwise subject to compulsory or restrictive action once a business does enter into operation.[41] Before setting up in business, physicians, dentists, beauty experts, private investigators, and taxicab operators must obtain permits. So also must persons who wish to open a bank or brokerage company, operate an airline, manufacture certain drugs or other restricted materials, or maintain facilities that treat, store, or dispose of hazardous waste. The same goes for bus companies, railroads, electric light and power companies, and radio and television stations.[42]

In regard to "the nature of the product to be offered," many changes have already taken place, especially concerning foods, drugs, and cosmetics, as I pointed out. The process of establishing and enforcing truth in labeling will necessarily affect both the content of processed foods and their prices.[43] Many other kinds of prices are regulated. In numerous states, utility commissions regulate not only electricity, telecommunications, and natural gas, but also water, sewage, transportation, banks, securities, insurance, and in some cases warehouses. Regulation of the prices charged by these utilities occurs in the context of public rate hearings in which the regulated firms, their customers, and other interested parties attempt to influence the decision. Finally, various taxes, such as sales taxes and corporate taxes, play a decisive role in the determination of many industries' policies.

As for "the method and practices of production and sale" of a whole range of industries and of products, vast changes have been brought about, in particular by the complex legislation on protection of the environment, i.e. on the patterns of utilization of the soil and subsoil and of the precious public goods air and water. Deep public concern with the adverse health effects of industrial air and water pollution, of solid waste accumulation in incredible proportions, of the ubiquity of chemicals of all kinds, of the use of agricultural pesticides, and of the damaging consequences of noise and radiation have led to the adoption of an enormously ramified corpus of environmental laws and regulations and the setting and enforcement of a gamut of standards under the monitoring and supervisory aegis of the Environmental Protection Agency. From the early 1970s on, yearly outlays on capital and operating costs in order to conform to legislated pollution controls have reached into the billions of dollars, in manufacturing and nonmanufacturing alike. The most serious impact of this legislation has been on coal mining, steel works, paper manufacturing, water works, and automobile production. Of course, business has regarded the cost of pollution abatement as a part of their total costs which must be passed on to the consumer. But the actual extent to which this has taken place has depended, of course, on the elasticities of demand and supply and on the degree of competition in the given market.[44]

In many cases, business firms' current expenditures on capital equipment exceed their current income, so when they plan to expand they must resort to the financial markets. (They usually will borrow if the market rate of interest is less than the rate of return on the planned capital investment.) They must then seek out the appropriate lenders, taking account of the financial alternatives and the maze of regulatory measures which affect the financial markets and the financial institutions within it: securities brokers and dealers for *direct finance,* and the commercial banks, S&Ls, mutual savings banks, life insurance companies, pension funds, and credit unions for *indirect finance.* Affecting these "professionals in finance" is the system of federal financial regulations, involving portfolio restrictions, capital adequacy requirements, and other measures directed at monitoring the activities and the solvency of these institutions. In the case of a commercial bank, for instance, besides determining who can open a bank, the regulations specify what products it can sell and at what prices; how it can expand, and what it can do with its funds. Before a charter is issued to it, a bank must show that it has an adequate degree of capitalization. As it engages in business, it must avoid directly holding certain types of assets, such as common stock or real estate. Moreover, it must have its portfolio examined periodically to ensure that it possesses adequate liquidity. Finally, any and all firms must, in at least one of their accounting books, follow the business accounting procedures set out by the Internal Revenue Service, and conform in their public reporting to the detailed requirements of the Securities and Exchange Commission.[45]

Last but not least, the scope of managerial decisions is limited in regard to the utilization of "human resources" in production and sale. Though workplace health and safety regulations, for instance, date back to 1867, the Occupational Safety and Health Act (OSHA) of 1970 now constitutes the major statute establishing the regulatory health standards to be met by employers. Two interesting things about this 1970 legislation are that it defines and enforces these regulatory standards without regard to incentive-based instruments, and that it opens channels for achieving both improvements not obtainable through collective bargaining and various wage concessions (e.g., for not reporting violations to OSHA).[46]

(c) Government's *allocation processes* involve the authority to allocate the use of certain natural resources (e.g., of navigable waters, of timber on public lands, of hydropower sites), as well as the power to grant, revoke, or withhold licenses for the use of channels and frequencies in the radio and television broadcasting spectrum. Permits for the transporters of ideas are analogous in essence to those needed for railways, steamships, or airline routes. Frequencies for AM, FM, UHF, and VHF are, of course, a scarce resource. The fact that as a rule an administrative rather than a market process like auctions has been favored to allocate them raises a host of fascinating problems concerning the standards to be applied in selecting the "winners," in renewing their permits when the latter expire, and in implementing and enforcing the standards set. Indeed, a plethora of standards are called into play in the process of allocating frequencies, notably involving *legal* qualifications (citizenship and compliance with ownership rules), *financial* qualifications (sources of capital, amounts, and estimated costs and revenues), proposed *program* service (structure and mode of operation), and *engineering* qualifications (frequency, power, area served, etc.). The effect of many standards, however – as Justice Stephen Breyer has pointed out – "is virtually the same as having none at all. There is no clear indication as to which standards are more important, how they are to be individually applied, or how varying degrees of conformity are to be balanced."[47] Such issues would increase to the *n*th degree if the process of "picking winners" were to be extended to a host of industries (if not to manufacturing as a whole), as some proponents of industrial policies advocate. (We shall return to these issues in detail in Part II.)

(d) To support and promote business, the government uses a vast gamut of instruments, including credit safeguards, investor protections, loans, subsidies, tax incentives, export supports, import restrictions, and the transfer to private entrepreneurs of businesses initiated by the government.

The federal government's credit programs may involve *direct loans* by federal departments and agencies (e.g., federally financed bank loans and agricultural loans), loans granted and issued by federal departments and agencies, and loans by federally sponsored and privately owned agencies. Specialized governmental enterprises perform specialized credit functions directed in particular toward housing, education, and agriculture. Thus certain operations in the housing financial market are served by the Federal National Mortgage Association (Fannie Mae), the Federal Home Loan Mortgage Bank (Freddie Mac), and the Federal Home Loan Banks. In education, nearly all student loans are financed by the Student Loan Market Association (Sallie Mae). The main recipient of the largest and most complex economic aid program remains, however, American agriculture. For over half a century farming has been the object of wide-ranging support and benevolent supervision by the federal government in regard to price setting, soil conservation payments, acreage allotments via direct payments, crop insurance, marketing quotas, credits, and export subsidies. Two types of federal farm credit have been established. The largest of these is the government-sponsored Farm Credit System (FCS and its affiliated banks) for long-term farm mortgage loans and for intermediate and short-term production loans, and the Farmers' Home Administration (FHA) for emergency loans. In periods of distress (i.e., depression prices) farmers have tended to combine the government's "price support" loans with another farm program, namely government's direct subsidies for keeping land out of production, or with simple price supports to enhance total income. Paradoxically, this policy, rather than being criticized, has been welcome, since it is estimated that it is less costly to restrain the nation's productive capacity than to pay (also with federal funds) for an abundance so great that surpluses clog up the warehouses. Critics assert that while agriculture has benefitted from the great variety of programs for government price-support credit and relief for investment and growth (particularly since the 1970s and 1980s), the cost to taxpayers remains high, and the subsidy to foreign buyers continues to be very generous. In 1990, 73 percent of all farm debt had some form of federal support. Taxes, in particular the treatment of capital gains and investment credit, have had a deep impact on farm structure. As pointed out by the outstanding agriculture expert Harold G. Halcrow, these taxes and credits have favored large farms, wealthy investors, and corporations. Thus, because of investment credits in both farmland and improvements, high-income farmers have benefitted more than low-income ones; because of a unique provision concerning the reporting of income from breeding stock as capital gain, large-scale farms and ranches have been strongly favored.[48]

In contrast to its dominant credit role in housing, education, and agriculture, the government plays a relatively small role in the provision of credit to business. Federal credit is focused on export financing and on small business. In 1990 it amounted to only 2 percent of business liabilities. The specialized financial institutions are the Export-Import Bank (Eximbank), the Overseas Private Investment Corporation (OPIC), and the Small Business Administration (SBA). Eximbank provides direct loans, loan guarantees, and export credit insurance for foreign borrowers to purchase U.S. exports. In 1989 its support financed roughly 5 percent of capital goods exports. OPIC extends medium-and long-term financing for international investment. SBA supplies loans and loan guarantees to small business and victims of natural disasters.[49] But in exceptional cases, federal government loans or insurance funds have bailed out certain firms or even an entire industry in distress. The most notorious bailout occurred in 1979. It involved the rescue of Chrysler, with a mixed $4 billion government loan and loan-guarantee package approved by Congress, in order to avoid massive job losses and a decline in both federal and state taxes. An even more complex rescue operation concerns the entire S&L industry. Started in 1989, the operation has involved the forced liquidation, under direct government control, of a number of insolvent S&Ls; the merger of some weak S&Ls with healthier firms; the establishment of a new Savings Association Fund (SAF); and the creation of a new institution, the Resolution Trust Corporation (RTC), charged with solving as much as possible the fundamental problems of this industry. The Financial Institutions Reform, Recovery, and Enforcement Act (FIRREA) of 1989, besides creating the SAF and the RTC, stressed the necessity of restructuring the whole system of financial regulation and support created in the 1930s. From the disaster of the S&Ls, attention has shifted to the banking industry. Most banks are healthy, although some, including several large ones, are weak. On the other hand, the reserves of the Federal Deposit Insurance Corporation (FDIC) are severely depleted, and the resources of the Bank Insurance Fund (BIF) may not be sufficient for an emergency without a systematic capitalization effort.[50]

Of course, the most complex weapon in a government's hands is the tax system. Taxes have a crucial impact on everything which affects business: consumption, savings, investments, economic growth, structural change. Yet taxes, of course, are not only shaped by economic considerations. Effective tax rates quite often present puzzling anomalies. The rates vary widely among different nonagricultural industries in regard to *assets* (machinery, buildings, inventories), *sources of finance* (debt, new share issues, retained earnings), and *ownership* (households, tax-exempt institutions, insurance). In principle, these disparities could be overcome by a comprehensive tax system integrating the corporate and personal tax systems, recognizing depreciation and replacement costs, and avoiding special grants or incentives and wealth taxes – while fully indexing and fully taxing accrued real capital gains. Such a switch would not, however, be easy, and possibly also not desirable. Many factors hamper the taxing of *real income*. To start with, there are difficulties to identifying and measuring income, particularly in a time of inflation. Further, inconsistencies may result from the presence of diverging political objectives, or may be brought about in response to changing macro conditions. Our corporate tax system has certainly been used for *stabilization* as well as for *incentive* purposes. The tax rate, the investment credit rate, and the rate of depreciation, for instance, have all been used to provide incentives for investment – in particular, for low-cost housing. Moreover, research into correlations between the tax on income from capital and the rate of economic growth yields very surprising results. According to a study by a number of authors in *The Taxation of Income from Capital,* comparisons for 1960–80 of this tax's levels and the respective income growth of a few countries (West Germany, the United States, Sweden, and the United Kingdom) show paradoxically that West Germany, which had the highest tax on income from capital, also had the highest growth rate; the United States was second in both categories; and Sweden, third. The United Kingdom had the lowest overall effective tax on income from capital *and* the lowest growth rate.[51] The impact of this or that tax measure on business is, in practice, blurred. It cannot be fully elucidated even when examined industry by industry and, in some respects, case by case.

In regard to foreign trade, the interactions of government and business seem, at first blush, clear, at least in their broad outlines. Since the 1970s and the 1980s, the liberal economic order created in the aftermath of World War II has significantly eroded. Changes in the world output and trade of various manufactured goods; the forceful orientation toward foreign markets of Japan, Germany, and some former less developed countries; and the increasing U.S. trade deficit have all brought about repeated protectionist reactions in the U.S. These have involved not only expanding subsidies for the usual agricultural commodities and for various industrial goods (e.g., aerospace) as well, but also measures restricting imports of various items, such as steel products and automobiles.[52] We shall return to some of these issues in detail in Parts II and III.

The support given to business cannot be fully appreciated without taking into account the development of the stock of public physical capital and of the public services, fully or partially publicly supported, as the case may be, on which vital business activities depend. These include not only the maintenance of roads and waterways, the establishment of weights and measures, the collection and distribution of statistical data, and various special programs such as food inspection and grading, but also the crucial funding of R&D (including agricultural) and the creation of appropriate channels for their diffusion and, in some cases, for the commercialization of their results (an issue to which I shall turn in detail in Section 2-3).

(e) Finally, the government exercises complex and multidirectional influences on business as a whole, both as the massive *buyer* of a unique mix of military and civilian goods and as the *owner* of various types of business enterprises.

Through its vast procurement outlays, the government (federal, state, and local) wields powerful influence, exercising a buyer's monopoly power in a variety of markets. In roughly *one third* of its total purchases – those earmarked for defense and space programs, amounting, in the late 1980s, to around $65 billion per annum – the federal government, by its selection of contractors, controls entry into and exit from the market, determines the growth patterns of the firms participating, and imposes its way of doing business.[53] Furthermore, the military imposes on privately operated defense-oriented industries its specific choices concerning innovation and technological change. (I shall return to these issues in Section 2-3.) In the other two thirds of its purchases, relations between the government buyers and the sellers are as a rule not as close: bidding occurs here among "responsible" civilian-oriented firms, and *price* is the main element, though not necessarily always the decisive one, in contracting.

Until the mid 1980s, both the military buyer and the corresponding seller operated in a peculiar negotiation framework. The negotiation was based on "allowable costs," and the final selection of the weapons producer was determined, first of all, by past performance and technical capability. Formal advertising was the only form of competition required in the process. No marketing or distribution facilities entered into account. (The government took charge of distribution.) Purchases could target assistance to individual firms better than special regulations or tax incentives could. Strong ties developed among the government and its major contractors, to the point where the government could feel obligated to back a contractor in difficulty while lacking effective control over the contractor's management.[54] In the mid 1980s, this euphorically close cooperation was shattered by allegations of price abuses: overpriced spare parts, mischarged fees for certain services, and billing for various unallowable costs. As a result, as the vice-president for procurement and finance of the Aerospace Industries Association put it, "administrative discretion suffered and congressional micromangement of the procurement process grew."[55] By the end of the 1980s, the debates which followed the scandals still had not settled the final criteria for assessing implementation in ongoing production in federal contracts; the share to be borne by the contractor for certain environmental clean-up costs; the license rights of the government in regard to deliverable technological data (funded either by the government or by the industry); certain fixed-price contracts or "capped" (not to exceed a certain price) production options; or the system for taxing long-term contracts (based on the reporting of income for any given tax period of a portion of the total profit expected from the contract). All these issues are bound to continue to draw the public's attention as the defense budget declines and procurement still remains both the largest single discretionary part of the federal budget and the most visible evidence of federal expenditures.[56]

Federal enterprises, sometimes called "government proprietary enterprises," are financed wholly or in part by the fee or price charged for the goods or services they provide. Excluding the Government Sponsored Enterprises (GSEs) involved in finance and insurance, which I examined in the preceding subsection, federal public enterprises are engaged notably in the fields of energy, electricity and gas, transportation, and communications. In energy, the U.S. Synthetic Fuels Corporation constitutes a special case. It has no production role. It only finances private projects. In electricity, the main public enterprise is the giant Tennessee Valley Authority (TVA) founded in the early 1930s to accelerate the growth and development of a vast and underdeveloped southern region. In transportation, the major government enterprise is the Consolidated Rail Corporation (Conrail). It was set up in the late 1960s in response to the danger of complete cessation of rail service in the Northeast after the bankruptcy of seven northeastern railroad companies. The second important governmental train corporation, Amtrak, was created in 1970 to salvage intercity rail passenger services, also in the Northeast. (There is also the Alaska Railroad, a minor government enterprise.) In waterways and harbors, the notable corporations are the St. Lawrence Seaway Development Corporation and the Port Authority of New York and New Jersey. In the broad meaning of "communications," the main U.S. enterprises are the Corporation for Public Broadcasting, the U.S. Postal Service, and the Government Printing Office (the biggest publishing concern in the world). Including the GSEs, these comprise at least 50 major federal enterprises, employing about a million people and generating annual revenues of some $25 billion. Their share in gross fixed capital formation is on the order of 4.4 percent.[57]

2-3   Federal and industry influences on science and technology

Throughout the period under review, the federal government has exerted a decisive influence on the generation of fundamental developments in science and technology via the provision of federal funds devoted to R&D. Divided by budget function, these funds have primarily concerned national defense, health, space research and technology, general science, energy, natural resources and the environment, transportation, and agriculture. Through the 1980s, these functions accounted for 96 to 98 percent of total federal R&D funding.

Obligations for R&D are set up largely for federal agencies with mission-oriented functional divisions, e.g., agencies of the departments of Defense, Health and Human Services, Energy, Commerce, and Transportation, along with the Aeronautics and Space Administration (NASA), the National Science Foundation (NSF), and the Environmental Protection Agency (EPA). In other words, instead of a *single* R&D system there has evolved a *pluralistic R&D support system* maintained by cabinet-level agencies responsible for the direct support of long-range research objectives. At the top of the federal hierarchy in the 1980s was the Office of Science and Technology Policy (OSTP), which coordinated basic policy objectives of the administration in regard to science and technology. Policies evolved in a number of ways during the years considered. This can be seen from the changes which have taken place in the patterns of federal expenditures on various functions, as well as from the changing emphasis in regard to certain programs. The "finalized" patterns of funding depend on the manner in which executive and congressional priorities are combined and translated into budgetary appropriations. The executive's policies have tended to emphasize basic research, the identification of broad areas with particular promise for the future, and especially – though not exclusively – the development of defense and space-oriented technologies. Congress has been preoccupied, particularly since the end of the 1970s, with the transfer of federally funded technologies to industry, and with the development of technologies critical for industrial competitiveness.

Total national spending on R&D – by the federal government, by industry, by universities and colleges, and by nonprofit organizations – has grown from 1.4 percent of GNP in 1953 to 2.2 to 2.7 percent of GNP from the 1960s on. In real terms (at 1982 prices), these outlays have increased from less than $20 billion in 1953 to over $113 billion in 1990. Of the 1990 figure, roughly 46 percent was accounted for by the federal government, 49 percent by industry, and the rest by all others. The structure of the federal outlays – comprehending defense-related, space-related, and civilian-related projects – has changed in relation to their main object, namely defense-related projects. In 1953, the defense-related share stood at 89 percent of total R&D federal outlays; this percentage fell to 80 in 1960, then to about 57 in 1973 and to 53 in 1979. With the Reagan-Bush defense buildup, the share of these outlays increased in the 1980s, reaching around 61 percent in 1990. Conversely, while space-related federal outlays increased massively in the 1960s – particularly in the mid 1960s, when they absorbed 21 percent of the total – they have drifted downward since then, to a low of about 4 to 5 percent of federal R&D expenditures. Finally, civilian-related federal R&D outlays have oscillated around 9 to 15 percent of the total since the 1950s.[58]

The critical areas in which vast new technological changes are in process and in which the sharpest international competition is taking place include microelectronics, the study of matter and new materials, and biotechnology. *Microelectronics* involves notably the computational sciences, information technologies, aerospace systems, and industrial process control and automation. In turn, the computational sciences cover hardware and software for high-performance computing. Information technologies most visibly involve the development of a vast electronic high-speed, high-volume broadband nationwide network of interconnected public and private networks (to which I shall return in detail in Chapter 8), as well as high-definition systems and artificial intelligence. Aerospace systems embrace *inter alia* atmospheric satellites, new space systems, the national aerospace plane, and advanced sensor systems.

Industrial process control and automation include computer-controlled design, engineering, manufacturing, and handling systems, involving in particular computer-controlled machine tools, flexible machine centers, robots, automated transport, storage and retrieval systems, and, finally, fully integrated plants. *The study of matter,* an important part of the nation's science and technology enterprise, depends to a large extent on investments in nuclear physics, high-energy physics, and basic energy programs, requiring the development of full-sized prototype magnets and then of large magnets on an industrial scale. Technologies for new *materials* evolving advanced composites and metallic structures – carbon/carbon, polymer-matrix, metal-matrix, ceramic-matrix, and hybrid materials – are needed in particular to reduce the structural weights of spacecraft, increasing their range, payload, speed, and maneuverability. Also in this group may be included the integration of photonics (the technology based on light) with microelectronics and the development of optical materials, in particular fiber optics, for the "gigabit" national network for data and image transmission. (I shall return to this crucial issue in Section 8-3.) Finally, in regard to *biotechnology,* great scientific and technological changes are afoot, concerning food manufacturing, genetic engineering, plant and animal breeding, waste treatment, recycling and waste processing, chemical synthesis, health care, and drug discovery techniques. The various manufacturing branches directly affected by current and impending changes can be assembled not only around these *core* fields, but also around complex technology *webs* connecting them with other manufacturing branches, with other industries and sectors, and finally with the economy as a whole.[59]

Federal influences in science and technology through the 1980s involved mainly interactions among defense-oriented federal R&D expenditures, along with support for the transfer of some of the results to civilian use. These activities were carried out through certain government agencies such as the Defense Advanced Projects Agency (DARPA, originally known as ARPA), the National Aeronautics and Space Administration (NASA), the National Science Foundation (NSF), and the National Institute of Standards and Technology. Further, the government extended support of *generic* applied research through the formation of R&D consortia (involving government, industries, and university laboratories), as well as through more informal methods of government-industry collaboration.

DARPA, the Pentagon's main instrument for the support and development of major defense-oriented technical innovations, was founded in 1958, soon after the Soviet Union launched Sputnik. This "technology mission agency" played a leadership role in engineering, in electronics, and in the materials sciences.[60] By far the "biggest venture-capital fund in the world," as its ex-director Craig Fields called it, DARPA pushed the performance frontier outward in information technology, far beyond commercially available computer hardware and software, into high-performance computing, parallel processing using supercomputers, and artificial intelligence (with concentration on systems that can plan, schedule, and automatically improve their performance). In communications, in 1969 DARPA launched *the first computer network,* ARPANet, which began as a U.S. government experiment in "packet switching" involving the efficient assembly and disassembly of computer data over networks. It then supported university-based research programs, as well as those of the Software Engineering Institute, in software development, use, and reuse. Jointly with NASA and the NSF, DARPA funded the National Research and Education Network (NREN), meant to serve scientists and engineers at major research universities, supercomputer centers, and federal laboratories. NREN started as a continuation and expansion of federal support for such networks as the National Science Foundation's NSFNet, the Department of Energy's Energy Sciences Network (ESNet), and Nasa's Science Internet (NSI). Together these have constituted the core of the expanding INTERNET, which by the early 1990s connected some 20,000 networks. These federal networks, with regional networks, campus networks, and the foreign networks of Internet, now provide access to data bases and supercomputers for users in all parts of the United States and around the world. (I shall return to these issues in more detail in Chapter 8.) Federal support was also extended through DARPA to Sematech – a government-industry consortium – focused on the realization of a new generation of semiconductors and of other microelectronics tools and processes. As is well known, the semiconductor industry plays a strategic role not only in computers and telecommunications in general, but also, very specifically, in aerospace, automotives, and all industries with high electronic content. DARPA also invested in the materials sciences. It has been engaged in the pursuit of advances in structural materials, ceramic composites, intermetallic alloys, and other structural materials. It furthered work on high-density and high-power batteries virtually impervious to damage. It also contributed to the progress of research on optical materials for optical computing, and of optics based on holography. Honeywell has been commercializing the DARPA-developed optic high-speed computer.

Like DARPA, NASA was established in 1958. Its missions were to conduct space and aeronautics research and to develop the advanced technology and capabilities needed for orbital operations, manned exploration of Earth's space environment and the realization of a permanently manned space station in Earth orbit.[61] NASA's explorations have been labor-intensive, with large spending directly for jobs. But the most effective economic effects of its spending have been the long-term productivity advances from technological developments for space and aeronautical programs. NASA has eight vast space and engineering centers managing its complex aerospace research, its space programs, its assembly hardware and sub-systems, the training of astronauts, the testing and monitoring of launch services, and its specially designed Technical Utilization Program for the transfer of NASA-developed technology to the nonaerospace sectors of the U.S. economy. In 1990, with commitments from NASA and the Department of Defense, a team of aerospace contractors – General Dynamics, Rockwell International, McDonnell Douglas, and Pratt & Whitney – gained permission to work as a consortium for the development of the national aerospace plane (officially known as X30). This experimental space plane – whose conception has been heavily criticized, as we shall see – is meant to be able to take off and land on conventional runways and to fly into orbit at 25 times the speed of sound. To reach these goals, the researchers will have to overcome a host of technological barriers, particularly in regard to advanced composite materials (which make up a family of lightweight aerospace structural materials). The realization of such a craft would effectively lead to an era of low-cost access to space. In other areas, the sustained human exploration of the solar system is certainly bound to open new vistas in artificial intelligence, robotics, medical technology, and life-sustaining environments.

Until the 1990s, government-supported civilian-oriented research with generic applications advanced slowly and mostly under Congress' prodding.[62] The National Institute of Standards and Technology, or NIST (formerly the National Bureau of Standards, in existence since 1901), founded under the Department of Commerce's Technology Administration, developed a relatively low-key role in the commercialization of certain technologies by American companies. Yet NIST did become directly involved in the technological infrastructure that underlies certain advances in automation, electronics, materials, biotechnology, and quality improvement of products and processes. The funds allocated to NIST amounted to only one third of 1 percent of the federal R&D budget – about one fifth of the allocations for DARPA. Cooperation with companies and technology transfer were standard operating procedures at NIST from its inception. This cooperation, based mainly on three regional manufacturing centers (established by nonprofit institutions and aiding smaller firms), has been scheduled to expand in a number of directions including "shared centers." Such centers, both privately and state funded, would be organized to use advanced manufacturing techniques. Other steps in technology transfer have been organized by Offices of Research and Technological Applications (ORTA), whose members are appointed by federal laboratory directors. Their support organization is the Laboratory Consortium (FLC), charged with guiding firms into the federal lab system, identifying possible areas of collaboration in manufacturing technology, and funding projects to demonstrate technology commercialization. (I shall return to these developments in Chapter 7.)

Besides the direct activities of the above-mentioned government agencies in regard to applied research, a number of other mechanisms have been put in place for the support of technological development and diffusion. I mentioned above that the federal government has allowed the formation of *strategic alliances* among private industries, such as the one for the development of the national aerospace plane. On the basis of the 1984 National Cooperative Research Act (NCRA), the federal government has authorized certain companies to form various *research alliances* – consortia, joint ventures, partnerships – without incurring antitrust action. By the beginning of the 1990s there were over 250 such consortia registered with the Justice Department. The direct federal participation in Sematech has already been referred to. The attention of the federal government has also been oriented toward the formation of other critical consortia, such as the Concurrent Supercomputing Consortium, a grouping of various government agencies (Defense, Energy, NSF, NASA) and academic and industrial institutions which have jointly acquired the "Intel Touchstone Delta System," and the Advanced Battery Consortium, uniting the major U.S. auto companies, battery manufacturers, and electric utilities.

But in general, the defense-oriented thrust of federal R&D outlays, (typical until the end of the 1980s), along with other federal involvement in collaborative ventures with industry, has often been criticized, at times quite unjustly. "If the same resources had been devoted to electronics, mass transit systems and alternative technologies," stated one critic, U.S. industry "might be more competitive." The same critic then added that the "superior performance" of Japan in sectors like steel, autos, and consumer electronics, "in which the U.S. had a prior advantage, may be due to the absence of military-related production" in that country.[63] In about the same vein, other critics contended that the earlier U.S. military spending did expand the country's defense capacity, but that afterward military technology emphasized mostly "exotic technologies" with few apparent commercial spinoffs.[64] Much of this kind of criticism tends to downgrade the crucial technological advances of American science, even when primarily defense-oriented, and also overlooks the notable successes achieved by the manufacturing industries' own heavy investments in R&D.

Consider the industries' own pattern of R&D outlays. As I noted, the share of industry in real R&D expenditures (1982 prices) of the country as a whole amounted to about 49 percent in 1990. At current prices, the industry's expenditures increased from slightly over $2 billion in 1953 to some $68 billion in 1988. The number of scientists and engineers employed in industry (including part-time employees, computed in terms of their full-time equivalents) increased from 164,000 in 1953 to some 717,000 in 1988 (compared to 38,000 and 66,000 respectively in federal service). Consider further the high concentration of industry's R&D funds in the group of industries which constitute the core of manufacturing. Out of a total of 20 SIC-code industrial groups, 6 industry groups (SIC codes 33 to 38) continue to play a critical role with regard to equipment and reequipment, structural changes, productivity performance, and competitiveness. These groups are (1) *primary metal industries* (iron and steel, nonferrous metals); (2) *fabricated metal products* (especially structural metal products, metal forging, and metal stamping); (3) *industrial machinery and equipment* (including computer and office equipment and other machinery, except electrical); (4) *the new and expanding electronic and electrical equipment* (including radio and TV, communication equipment, electronic components, other electrical equipment); (5) *transportation equipment* (motor vehicles, aircraft, ships, railroads); and (6) *instruments and related products* (scientific and mechanical measuring instruments, as well as optical, surgical, photographic, and other instruments). In 1988, these 6 groups accounted for over 44 percent of those gainfully employed in manufacture and for close to 47 percent of the value added.[65] Now, out of a total of $66.4 billion of company funds spent for R&D by industry (excluding company-financed R&D contracted to outside organizations), over 66 percent was directed toward these 6 groups of industries. The largest R&D outlays were spent on industrial machinery and equipment, electronic and electrical equipment, and transportation equipment. The combined federal-industry R&D outlays were also concentrated in these groups, and particularly so in regard to the allegedly neglected transportation system.[66] It is also interesting to note that certain so-called high-tech industries – namely, those producing office and computing machines, copiers and related equipment, and electronic communications and components (i.e., groups 3 and 4 above), in which both federal and industry R&D outlays were massive – have accounted for most of the growth in total industrial production since the 1970s. According to Donald L. Losman and Shu-Jan Liang, "in terms of market aggregates, the growth rate of business equipment production has exceeded that of consumer goods. This fast growth in the 1980s has been due to the generally strong demand for computing equipment," in which rapid innovations have reduced costs and expanded usage.[67]

Incessant discussion is in process in the United States on the uses of advanced technologies, on the modernization of small and medium-sized firms, on the commercialization of defense-oriented innovations, and so on. According to a 1991 review of 94 technologies carried out by the Council on competitiveness – a nonprofit organization of leaders in business, education, and labor – at the end of the 1980s, the United States was either the leader or was highly competitive in about two thirds of the technologies considered. The nation's "highly competitive" technologies were grouped into five fields: materials and associated processing; engineering and production; electronic components; information; and power train and propulsion. The United States was viewed as a leader in, notably, computer-aided engineering, certain electronic components, a vast number of information-related techniques, and high-level software languages. The U.S. was viewed as "weak" or "likely to fall behind in the next five years" in regard to certain materials, integrated circuits, robotics, and various electronic components.[68]

The Council's list is only one of a number of lists in this genre. It is not altogether clear on what specific criteria all these technologies are chosen, classified, and granted or denied the title of leadership. In any case, one may point out that it is erroneous to assume that the U.S. must be necessarily and immutably the leader in all technological fields. It is the immediate payoff of each technology that matters. It is not sure which of these technologies will eventually play a decisive role: this may depend not only on them but also possibly on the appearance of yet another technology offering a breakthrough in some related field. New technologies do not occur at regular intervals. There is no unique way in which technologies may be applied: a technology in which the U.S. is "weak" may, in combination with another technology, yield new and unexpected results. There is neither a single identifiable path nor a clearly defined pattern of technological progress in any and all fields.

2-4   R&D in the states and the universities and colleges

When one looks at R&D from the point of view of the *sources* of expenditures for it, and from that of actual *performance,* the resulting patterns, of course, differ significantly. As I have already noted concerning the sources of outlays in 1990, as much as 46 percent came from federal funds and 49 percent from industry, with over 3 percent from universities and colleges and 1 percent from other nonprofit institutions. However, the federal government accounted for only 11 percent of actual R&D effort, while industry was responsible for 72 percent, universities and colleges (plus the federally funded R&D centers administered by universities and colleges) for 14 percent, and other nonprofit institutions for 3 percent.[69] Clearly various bonds have developed between the relevant federal agencies and industry on the one hand, and the universities and colleges on the other: federal support has obviously been significant for industry's R&D performance, and crucial to that of the universities and colleges.

A closer look at both the *sources* of expenditures on R&D and the pattern of *allocations* of these funds within universities and colleges yields some interesting results. As can be seen from Table 2-1, in 1988 over 60 percent of the R&D funds came from the federal government and over 8 percent from state and local sources. As much as 24 percent came from institutions and other sources. Industry contributed only 6.7 percent of the total: clearly the R&D interconnections between industry and the universities and colleges are still in process of development. (The 1988 pattern still closely resembles the 1981 pattern.) About two thirds of the funds used were directed toward basic research, one third toward applied research. Similarly, close to 85 percent went toward the

Table 2-1. *R&D expenditures at universities and colleges, 1981 and 1988 (millions of dollars and percentages)*

Funds and Allocations	1981	Percent	1988	Percent
Total	6,829	100.0	13,422	100.0
Sources of Funds:				
Federal	4,560	66.8	8,165	60.8
State and Local	546	8.0	1,123	8.4
Industry	294	4.3	892	6.7
Institutions	995	14.6	2,314	17.2
All Other Sources	434	6.3	928	6.3
Character of work:				
Basic Research	4,577	67.0	8,870	66.1
Applied Research	2,251	33.0	4,552	33.9
Fields:				
Engineering Total	967	14.2	2,084	15.5
All Sciences Total	5,861	85.8	11,338	84.5
Physical Sciences	765	11.2	1,531	11.4
Environmental Sciences	549	8.0	891	6.6
Mathematical Sciences	87	1.3	199	1.5
Computer Sciences	132	1.9	410	3.1
Life Sciences	3,689	54.0	7,236	53.9
Other Sciences	639	9.4	1,071	8.0

Source: Computed from National Science Foundation, National Patterns of R&D Resources: 1990, p. 73.

sciences and only 15 percent toward engineering. Within the sciences, the highest concentration was on life sciences (particularly agricultural and medical sciences) and on the physical sciences. State and regional distributions of R&D were highly concentrated. Of all R&D dollars spent in 1987 – $128 billion – one half was spent in just six states: California, New York, Michigan, Massachusetts, New Jersey, and Pennsylvania. These states, along with Texas, Illinois, Ohio, and Maryland, accounted for about two thirds of the national R&D effort. By region, some 80 percent of total R&D was accounted for by states in the Northeast (8.9 percent), the Middle Atlantic (16.2 percent), the East North Central (17.2 percent), the South Atlantic (13.5 percent), and the Western Pacific (23.3 percent).[70]

The continuous decline of a number of traditional manufacturing areas, along with the increasing importance of high-tech industries, has enhanced the interest of state administrations in the development of science policies and agencies, in the funding of business and academic research, in the creation of "business incubators" and research parks, in the encouragement of investment from domestic or foreign sources, in the expansion of a state's trade, and in the marketing of its products at home and abroad. By the end of the 1980s, the major effort of state science and technology was embodied in the application of over 200 state programs to high-technology development.[71]

In the encouragement of innovations, certain state programs have been patterned on the federal program promoting advances in small business, namely the Small Business Innovation Research (SBIR) program established by Congress in 1982. (In 1987, some 1,287 small companies were awarded about $350 million to do work for 11 federal agencies.)[72] It is primarily on the small companies that the states must focus their interest: the big companies can fend for themselves. In the 1980s, some 358,000 *small and medium-sized manufacturing firms* (those with fewer than 500 employees) – i.e., 98.8 percent of all U.S. manufacturing enterprises – accounted for 35 percent of the manufacturing workforce and for 21 percent of the value added. Their technological lag was highly disturbing. A key element of the capacity to compete on both cost and quality is modernization of the technology used to make a wide variety of products. A crucial indicator of such modernization is the use of automated machinery. For example, an investigation sponsored by the National Science Foundation was carried out in the late 1980s on the adoption of programmable machinery in metal-cutting operations in machinery-manufacturing industries. The investigation focused on a selected sample of 1,368 establishments in 21 different manufacturing industries. The sampling frame included the smallest plants (with fewer than 20 employees), as well as the largest (with more than 250 employees). According to this investigation, computer-controlled machines were still not widely in use at the time in U.S. metalworking establishments. Less than 11 percent of the total stock of machine tools in use in the industries studied was computer-controlled. Some 53 percent of the plants had not installed even one computer-controlled machine. Even among the actively innovating plants, only about one in six machines was computerized. What little investment in new production equipment was undertaken was concentrated in a small number of the large plants. The typical nonadopter of computerized automation is a small, single-plant firm. An enormous number of small businesses continue to exist in a technological and investment backwater. For the single-plant enterprise with direct sales to larger customer firms, the most important channel for technology transfer is *a close working relationship* with these customers.[73]

More than 40 states have programs to "promote technology," but most of their effort and funding is directed toward research and development in universities and colleges and for aid to start up high-technology ventures. Little is provided for helping existing firms to adopt best-practice technology. According to a survey of state programs done for the NIST at the end of the 1980s, only 13 programs in nine states had technology extension programs whose main purpose was direct consultation with manufacturers on the use of technology. Such technology – patterned on the agricultural extension services – involved the creation of an office staffed with a few engineers ready to offer technical advice to firms and to consult with their managers about implementation.[74] The Department of Commerce has moved to cooperate with the states in this respect: the Boehlert-Rockefeller Extension Program provides technical assistance for state technology outreach and for federal technology to help solve state technological problems.[75]

The states have also paid attention to the needs of small businesses for access to capital markets. They have adjusted state regulations to encourage banks to lend to small firms or to provide funds for specific targets, and in some cases have created public development funds. Further, the states have pursued their traditional mission in furthering the growth of human capital and, in some states, in developing workers' skills and in retraining displaced workers. Finally, the states have started to focus their attention on export programs designed to help small and medium-sized firms to market their products overseas, and have also created insurance programs and loan funds for exporters.[76]

2-5   Concluding comments

In the first two decades after World War II – the years of undisputed U.S. economic dominance – the big enterprises which had accumulated strength and had developed their organizational capabilities before and during the war continued to be the industrial leaders. Employment in U.S. manufacture, which had risen between 1939 and 1947 from 10.3 million to 14.3 million, continued to grow over the next two decades, eventually reaching 18.5 million. Between 1947 and 1967 impressive increases were registered in key manufacturing groups. Employment in the primary metals group (including iron and steel) rose by 11 percent; in fabricated metal products, by 38 percent; in machinery (except electrical), by 21 percent; in electrical machinery and in the newly developing electronics industry, by 134 percent; in transport equipment, by 55 percent; in scientific instruments, by 70 percent. The leading American industries opened new paths to overseas expansion, defended and expanded free trade and competition throughout the world, and swept away tariffs and other barriers that had divided Western markets.[77]

By the mid 1960s, Italian, German, and then Japanese firms started to become effective challengers in the domain of mass-produced goods, first of all automobiles – not only outside the United States but in the American market as well. This globally expanding competition started to grow at the critical historical juncture when the newly developing electronic and computer revolutions were bringing new industries into existence while forcing massive and often painful transformations in others – in their structures in their production and distribution processes, and in their patterns of employment. From 1967 to 1987, the two decades which followed the years of uncontested economic hegemony of the United States, employment in the key manufacturing groups mentioned above changed radically. Primary metals and machinery – both electrical and nonelectrical – shrank in terms of employment by 45, 2, and 17 percent, respectively. On the other hand, all fabricated metals, transport equipment, and instrumentation groups expanded their employment by 6, 9, and 150 percent. In terms of shares in the total value added by manufacture, the changes were somewhat different. For instance, between 1973–75 and 1983–85 the shares of nonelectrical machinery, transport equipment, and instruments rose respectively from 8.5 to 11.1 percent, 11.4 to 12.4 percent, and 3.1 to 4.0 percent. The shares of the other three groups shrank severely, with the biggest drop for primary metals, whose share fell from 9.3 to 6.7 percent. Within the primary metals class, the share for iron and steel works fell steeply, from 5.2 to 2.5 percent.[78]

As the advent and then the spread of electricity had done before the turn of the century, the coming of electronics intensified the demand for capital investment in certain manufacturing branches and firms and forcefully pushed them onto a higher technological plateau. Moreover, as technology spread abroad and fueled the increase in global competition, a number of firms started to move into related industries, resorting to *diversification* as a strategy of growth. This happened not only in the United States, but also in the other industrialized countries. By the end of the 1960s, the growth of conglomerates, i.e., of firms growing by acquisition in unrelated industries, had become a *preferred* route of growth for the large American industrial enterprise. But in the early 1970s the negative consequences of diversification became increasingly evident. Many American firms had little or no competitive advantage in the markets they had entered. A new wave of *divestitures* followed the wave of mergers and acquisitions which had previously swept through corporate America. Finally, buying and selling of corporations became a business in its own right.[79] At the same time, like the American machinery industry of a half a century earlier, the new American computer companies led the move into foreign markets. IBM became the leading producer of mainframe computers in Europe. And, by the mid 1980s, Apple and IBM accounted for the largest share of the world's production of personal computers.

But the rapid diffusion of technological advances to many other countries dramatically changed the world's manufacturing environment, and often created, along with new and vast opportunities, numerous difficulties for American firms. The intensity of international competition in various domains, the pressures of closing down obsolete units and the need to construct totally new facilities, the demand for heavy investment and the dangers of rapid obsolescence, and the mandate to reshape corporate growth strategies and carefully weigh the choice between domestic expansion needs and transnational opportunities have become particularly keen in one industry after another. As markets for goods and services have become increasingly "global," many countries – from Europe and the Pacific rim – have become considerably more competitive in such fields as electronics, chemicals, aircraft, and automobiles, as well as in many other lines of production and distribution. Yet, while globalization has raised a host of similar problems, it has *not* necessarily called forth exactly the same solutions to these problems and the same pace in their implementation. Consider, for instance, the case of three crucial industries – *semiconductors, aerospace,* and *automobiles* – technologically interrelated in many respects, but distinct in their orientations and functions.

The electronic components industries – semiconductors, connectors, and printed circuits – are the makers of the primary building blocks of electronics. They supply a wide range of end users, including the computer, telecommunication, aerospace, and automotive industries. They support a domestic electronics sector that employs some 2.6 million workers – more than double the number employed by the U.S. steel and auto industries combined – and account for about $300 billion a year in business. Within this group, the semiconductor industry is the *foundation* of the entire industry. The level of technological advance possible in an electronic product directly depends on the technology available in leading-edge semiconductors. Because of this, all industrialized countries and virtually all the newly industrializing nations have semiconductor development programs. Japan, Korea, Singapore, Hong Kong, Taiwan, and mainland China are now highly competitive in this field.

The U.S. lead in semiconductors, incontestable in the 1960s and 1970s, has weakened in a number of respects. A 1989 report of the Office of Science and Technology Policy of the Executive Office of the President asserted that the industry's world market was eroding and that its domestic fragmentation into relatively small firms prevented it from achieving economies of scale and of meeting head-on the large vertically integrated Japanese firms. Furthermore, the continuing downward price pressure in consumer electronics products was increasing the competition among the suppliers of components, compelling them not only to constantly improve their products but also to incessantly track technological changes in the consumer markets and to anticipate needed changes in their own design, packaging, and high-performance system interconnections. The U.S. semiconductor industry, still in the lead in a number of areas (e.g., ion implantation and mixed signal testing), has faced strong Japanese competition in other areas (particularly in logic and memory testing equipment). The Japanese have in turn suffered stiff competition from South Korean companies. In the United States, the government-industry consortium Sematech, created in 1987, was supposed to boost U.S. capabilities in semiconductor manufacturing technology, produce a new chip with ultrathin circuitry, and improve interindustry technical relationships. Sematech has yielded mixed results. It has helped improve existing American-made equipment and interindustry rapports, but has not produced any great leaps forward in semiconductor manufacturing technology. Sematech in particular failed in its efforts to develop photolithography equipment, a technology needed in the making of future generations of computer chips. In a crucial shift in what had become a bitter rivalry to dominate the computer memory-chip market IBM bypassed Sematech and joined with two foreign electronic giants, Toshiba of Japan and Siemens of Germany, to develop a memory chip scheduled to become the mainstay of computers used in the next century.[80] (However, soon afterwards IBM started to face crucial problems, to which I shall turn in Section 4-3.) IBM's decision was followed by the framing of other important international alliances, e.g., between the United States' Advanced Micro Devices and Japan's Fugitsu. With regard to photolithography, an agreement concluded, in exchange for financial assistance, between the Silicon Valley Group and its Japanese competitor Canon, Inc., made the U.S. companies dependent on Japanese suppliers for the equipment used in this critical process.

Consider now the adaptation to the internationalization of competition carried out in another key worldwide industry, the automotive industry. This is the world's largest manufacturing industry, consisting of 25 corporations making and selling cars; it accounted in the 1980s for annual business of $500 billion (at 1987 prices). The connected industrial-commercial web of firms involved in the supply of materials and services, auto fuels, and the aftermarket (such as sales of used vehicles) is six to seven times larger. The industry is a major producer and consumer of new technology. Half of the world's robot population works for it.[81] The U.S. automotive industry has changed profoundly since the end of the 1970s. It has started to restructure its product lines, modernize its factories, streamline production, reduce costs, and increase productivity in order to cope with the increased competition of a number of foreign firms, particularly those participating in the American market through the establishment of local majority subsidiaries and minority affiliates. Competition in this industry has also led to all kinds of cross-border arrangements concerning investment, joint ventures, and exports and imports. The extent to which the U.S. auto companies have become intertwined with their competitors in the U.S. and worldwide may be illustrated by a few examples involving cooperative ventures by the Big Three (General Motors [GM], Ford, and Chrysler). For instance, Chevrolets of various types are now produced in California (in a joint GM-Toyota venture), Canada (in a joint GM-Suzuki venture), Mexico, and Japan, and GM uses its Chevrolet network to market the Geo nameplate throughout the U.S. A joint Ford-Mazda venture builds Ford-"badged" variations of one car in Illinois and Michigan, which are sold respectively in the U.S. and Japan. (A badge-engineered vehicle is engineered to be sold under the nameplate of either participating company.) A Chrysler-Mitsubishi joint venture builds cars in Illinois which are sold in the U.S. by both companies. Japanese solo and joint ventures account now for *all* foreign-owned high-volume production in the United States. It is true that at the end of the 1980s, Big Three factories accounted for 78 percent of domestic production. But analysis of imports is obscured by the shift in the local market between U.S. and foreign-owned firms.

The Big Three must continue not only to implement major cost-cutting programs and to further upgrade their manufacturing facilities and products, but must also develop new types of automotives if they wish to remain the dominant producers in the U.S. market.[82] To this end, new relationships are developing between the main auto companies and the U.S. government, as we shall see in Chapter 7. Let me note for now that until 1980, investment in the U.S. auto industry was *more than double* that of Japan – while in 1988, auto industry investment was almost equal in the two countries ($10.60 and $10.17 billion respectively).[83]

Interestingly, the presence of Japanese carmakers in the U.S. has spurred imitation of some of their production and management methods, such as simultaneous group designing of car models (instead of sequential transfer of blueprints from design to production); "just-in-time" inventory control; long-term contractual relationships with suppliers of components; rapid shift of component sourcing overseas; reliance on quality control circles on the assembly line; and cultivation of worker loyalty and/or a sense of partnership.[84] In other cases, U.S.-Japanese associations have opened up U.S. firms to Japanese technological innovations. Mitsubishi's Nagoya plant, for instance, has been reconditioned to place many different models on the same production line, an idea which the General Motors seems ready to follow. At the Nagoya plant, robots reconfigure themselves automatically to put the steering wheel on the left side of one car and on the right side of the next, as needed for the Japanese or the American market.[85]

So far the Big Three have not made strenuous efforts to develop models which will appeal especially to the Japanese. Most American cars are still too big and too expensive to be attractive for most Japanese. What each of the Big Three did aim at in the past was to acquire *equity* in the Japanese auto companies as part of their global manufacturing and market programs. Now the Big

Three do hold important equity in several large and small vehicle manufacturers in Japan as well as in other countries (viz. Isuzu, Suzuki, Mazda in Japan; Lotus and Jaguar in the U.K.; Saab in Sweden; Kia Motors in South Korea; Beijing Jeep in China). The Big Three's wholly owned foreign subsidiaries, along with their numerous cross-border joint ventures, diminish the possibility that their unit exports from the U.S. will increase greatly – though the U.S. companies pursue an aggressive policy to gain foreign markets (including the Japanese, but only in high-value luxury and sports models). On the other hand, one should note that there is no direct foreign investment by any foreign vehicle maker in GM, Ford, or Chrysler – and that the first two still command the first and second positions worldwide in overall auto production.

Different approaches prevail in another key industrial group, with different characteristics and different problems, and in which the U.S. is still, and by far, in the lead: the *aerospace complex*. In its widest sense, this complex includes industries producing aircraft, aircraft engines and parts, and propulsion units and parts for guided missiles and space vehicles, as well as the aircraft equipment, missile equipment, and space-vehicle equipment industries. The aerospace sector faces particularly difficult problems, since at least half of its revenues used to be derived from defense. Cuts in defense have reduced, and are scheduled to further limit, the demand for military aircraft, missiles, and related equipment. In addition, space exploration and commercialization face uncertain prospects of large government funding. Finally, in the second half of the 1980s growth in the civil aviation sector began tapering off. In 1970 the U.S. led the global aerospace market (excluding the then Soviet Union and its satellites), with a share of almost 80 percent. In 1990 this share had shrunk to less than 60 percent. The most vigorous competition has come from the European aerospace industry, which grew almost twice as fast as the U.S. industry during the period 1978–89. The creation and development of the Airbus industrial consortium (France, Germany, Spain, and the United Kingdom) has provided Europe with a powerful manufacturing complex that is competitive worldwide. Little competition exists today from the military-oriented aerospace industry of the former Soviet Union. The Japanese, however, are expected to become competitive in the future, particularly in the domains of aircraft parts, propulsion systems, and space vehicles. While at the end of the 1980s the U.S. aerospace industry still employed 800,000 people (of whom half were production workers), top managers of the leading companies have increasingly stressed the need to transform the commercial aircraft business into a new kind of corporation, in which the majority of ownership and control will remain in the United States but *most parts and sub-assemblies* of the future jetliners will be produced outside the United States. In addition, investors in Asia/Pacific and other parts of the world will be called upon to make up a large share of the investment needed. It is doubtful that the U.S. government will remain indifferent to such developments. But in considering the problems of all defense-oriented industries, the crux of the matter for the politicians will be to balance the risks of too deep employment cuts – which would impair the nation's future military production capabilities – with the danger of misallocating scarce funds, which would sacrifice other pressing national needs.

At the core of the aerospace complex, the *aircraft engine industry* is still dominated worldwide by three companies: GE Aircraft Engines and Pratt & Whitney in the U.S., and Rolls-Royce in the United Kingdom. Each of these companies can produce a full line of state-of-the-art engines. Below these three, several U.S. and foreign companies are capable of designing and developing gas turbine engines or major parts thereof. Various alliances have been established between the prime manufacturers and the second-tier companies, but the U.S. prime manufacturers have been able to avert the erosion of their technological leadership, thanks to specific U.S. policies preventing them from allowing others access to the technologies. This, however, has encouraged other alliances – possibly one linking Rolls-Royce with Airbus, for instance. It is important to note that this industry has a long production cycle. Beginning from a well-established base, development of the initial version of an engine takes from 4 to 5 years; once development has begun, an engine program may span 30 years before the last engine is taken out of service.[86]

As our three examples show, profitable adjustment to the expanding globalization of competition may take different forms – depending on a given industry's characteristic patterns of demand for its output, positions it has already acquired both at home and abroad in various markets, price and quality of the product(s) it offers, type of technology it uses or is ready to acquire, and quality of its workforce and management. Clearly, as the internationalization of markets intensifies, the chief executive officer (CEO) of each company will have to decide *continually* what balance he or she should strike between (1) the maintenance, modernization, and expansion of plants and the consolidation of the network of domestic suppliers and (2) the development of joint ventures both at home and abroad in association with foreign competitors. These are indeed dynamic problems: one cannot determine once and for all which particular level of domestic capability must be maintained for which particular industry, though obviously beyond a certain limit it becomes increasingly more difficult – if not impossible – to rebuild a sharply shrinking industrial base and its network of local suppliers.

It is extremely doubtful that the U.S. government can stay aloof with respect to such critical managerial decisions, especially in cases affecting the growth and development of a group of industries, or ones impacting the country's defense, levels of employment, balance of payments, or competitiveness. Because of the potential conjunction of such crises, certain policymakers and economists assert that the government must turn all its attention to the "straightening out" of the economy, discard its old method of ad hoc responses to the particular needs of this or that industry, and adopt a fully integrated *industrial-technological* strategy of development. To properly evaluate the tenor and the implications of such approaches, it is necessary to examine first the nature and scope of the competitive challenge the U.S. now faces and then to ascertain whether without such a policy, the U.S. indeed risks precipitating its "decline" while its reinvigorated former enemies gain speed and overtake it.

I shall turn to some of these issues in Part II and again, from a different angle, in Part IV.

Part II

The new challenge and its implications

Introductory note

Alignments in the contest for industrial supremacy in the 21st century started, in various respects, before the collapse of the Soviet empire. Until the 1960s, few expected the United States to encounter any difficulty in consolidating the economic leadership it had acquired through and since World War II. The danger of any significant Soviet industrial breakthrough, except in some limited military technologies, seemed increasingly remote. The economies of then-divided Germany and of Japan seemed to be locked in reconstruction and in "catching up" for years ahead. Only the Common Market – the core of the future European Union – held some promise of developing into a significant economic challenger, though U.S. firms had already secured important inside positions for themselves in that still evolving aggregate.

Then all this started to change with seeming suddenness. Japan appeared to surge forward at incredible speed. Through the 1970s its rising indices of industrial production seemed to propel it above the industrial levels of the United Kingdom, the European Community, the United States (see Fig. II-1). Industrial production indices were generously displayed and often erroneously commented upon in the media. Few, except those familiar with such indices, seemed to realize that the indicators illustrated changes from *different starting points* and that they exemplified *speeds* and not interrelations between underlying industrial structures, capacities, and outputs. Few checked other evidence or compared successive index series, as I do herein. When one uses the index basis 1967 = 100, Japan "surpasses" the United States in, say, 1967; on the basis 1977 = 100, Japan crosses the line in 1979; and on the basis 1987 = 100, it "overcomes" the United States in 1989, while all the while its industrial output has not been even about half that of the United States.

As the Soviet Union faltered and then collapsed, Japan and subsequently also West Germany increasingly became the symbols of so-called young economies, in which "organized capitalism" could achieve miracles which old capitalism could no longer deliver. The inventory of Japan's successes was stressed frequently. Its rapid pace of economic growth, its systematic allocation of vast resources to gross fixed capital formation, its obvious progress in high-tech consumer-oriented production, and its impressive penetration of the

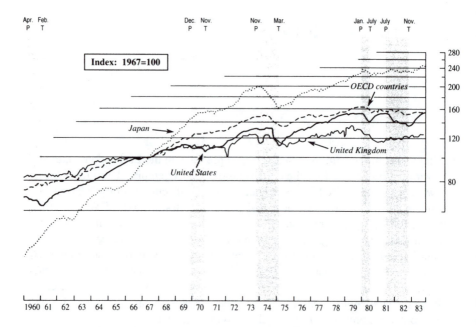

Figure II-1. Industrial production: international comparisons, 1960–1983. *P* and *T* indicate peaks and troughs of recessions. *Source:* U.S. Department of Commerce, Bureau of Economic Analysis, *Business Conditions Digest,* December 1983.

global markets all received their due. West Germany's economic recovery, the growth of its powerful chemical and machinery industries, the consolidation of its new mark, and its regaining of traditional positions in the global market were also dutifully acknowledged. After the fall of the Soviet Union and the expressed desire of its dissociated republics, including Russia itself, to join the European Union, it was the projected enlarged "House of Europe" – with Germany at its core – that was touted as the foremost candidate for the industrial domination of the 21st century. In contrast, the United States was increasingly depicted as an aging, stumbling giant, losing its preeminence and its leading abilities. From the mid 1970s on, a vast literature asserted with much conviction that the United States was "deindustrializing," losing the battle of high tech, and unduly shifting its labor force toward services while complacently accommodating itself to falling productivity, low rates of saving, low rates of capital formation, failure in export markets, incessant trade deficits, and growing international indebtedness. Few seemed to recall that some of the same telltale signs of "maturity" and of "decline" had already been diagnosed in the 1930s, when the United States was facing the same "young" challengers, namely, Hitler's Germany and Hirohito's Japan.

Yet, certainly, the contest for industrial supremacy in the 21st century is still wide open in various respects. Indeed, it still remains to be seen *to what extent* Japan and Germany, along with the European Union, actually challenge the United States' industrial leadership, technological development, and ability to compete in trade. In what ways does the "organized capitalism" of Japan and Germany operate de facto, and what are its strengths and weaknesses? On what data, and on what considerations, are the contentions based of those who assert that the United States has reached an ill-defined "maturity" that hampers its dynamism? On what premises are founded the arguments that America is deindustrializing and that it is losing in the competition for world markets? Does America need to mold its capitalism on the economic models of its rivals? These are the issues that I focus on in Part II.

Chapter 3 sketches the key features of the Japanese and German "organized" management of their private economies, compares their economic structures to those of the United States, and outlines the paths of their development. It also examines the contradictory forces which are shaping the structure and behavior of the European Union, as well as its prospects. Chapter 4 presents and assesses the theses concerning the alleged "decline" of the United States, outlines the proposals for industrial policy advanced since the mid 1970s, analyzes critically and in detail the tenor of these proposals, and points to some of their drawbacks. The concluding section of the chapter – and of Part II – discusses the implications of the notions of decline and of the allegedly faster progress possible with the help of industrial-technological policies.

3   The challenge

3-1   MITI and Japan's economy

How does the modern market-directed economy of the United States differ from the "organized capitalism" of its main competitors, Japan and Germany? In the U.S., economic management has involved – particularly since the 1930s – acceptance of the government's responsibility to avoid or shorten *recessions,* to avert *unemployment,* and to counteract *inflation.* The government's basic and at times elusive goal has been to dampen economic perturbations and to subdue the volatility of the environment, which otherwise would hamper the proper functioning of private business. The instruments used for the purpose have been the basic tools of aggregate supply and aggregate demand, occasioning in each particular case various combinations of fiscal, monetary, and, exceptionally, institutional reform. Though the prevalence of market mechanisms was recognized, this in no way superseded complex market regulations (constraints), nor governmental actions responding to specific business situations of concern for the business community, labor, and the economy as a whole, as I pointed out in Chapter 2. In the formulation of economic policies as well as in the application of ad hoc specifically tailored measures (e.g., bailouts, subsidies, R&D expenditures, grants, tariff protection) to given businesses, branches of industry, and even sectors of the economy, a wide variety of conflicting interests have had to be weighed by the president, the Congress, the administrative agencies, the state legislatures, and the courts. But the indicated ad hoc measures did not involve systematically picking "winners" or "losers": ultimately, *the market was left to make these choices.* And the ad hoc measures neither were part of a previously established economic plan nor were they integrated afterwards into some kind of unified industrial policy blueprint affecting the operations of the entire economy.

In all capitalist economies, government interventions – or *state* intervention, as it is usually called outside the United States – has been, historically speaking, complex, versatile, and not necessarily consistent at any point in time. Both the scope and the types of instruments used have depended on many factors: the institutional matrix of the given country as it emerged from its precapitalist surroundings, its evolution and transformations through time, and the changing economic philosophies and economic policies adopted by its successive governments in response to pressing social, political, economic, or military problems. Besides the routine provision of certain public services and the enforcement of certain regulatory market measures, the state has tended to intervene along the following main lines: direct involvement in the development of industries connected with the establishment and growth of defense-related or defense-supporting industries; direct or indirect state participation in the provision of key social overhead services – e.g., transportation, power, public utilities – unmet by the private sector; and incentives for domestic or foreign entrepreneurs to develop selected "indispensable" industries, both heavy and light – incentives involving tax exemptions, grants, credits, protective tariffs, and special state procurement arrangements. Such measures were aimed, more often than not, at smashing some real or assumed bottleneck hampering the activity of private industry and/or the security and development of the country as a whole. Usually, however, state involvement has tended to increase in scope and complexity as minimal requirements for private development were met and growing, coalescing pressure groups of industrialists, bankers, landowners, and workers began to act in order to obtain measures in their favor.

While in the United States the developmental role of the state tended to decrease after the Civil War, in Japan and in Germany, as well as in other countries like France, the economic role of the state tended to expand, particularly toward the end of the 19th century. These states broadened their support for various industries, amplified their ownership in a number of sectors and branches, and spread the network of their controls over a variety of economic activities. Consider first, in some detail, the specific case of Japan.

When that country emerged from its feudal surroundings at the end of the Shogunate and the beginning of the so-called Meiji Restoration (1868), it started to reshape both its traditional economic framework and its economic policies on the patterns of German nationalism and Prussian absolutism united in the first German Reich (1871) – Bismarck's Germany, then the most powerful and successful developing country in continental Europe. In numerous respects these patterns have persisted in Japan ever since. The Japanese state remains the focal point of the society. It continues to exercise an overt or covert tutelary authority over almost all important economic activities and over every sector of the society. Even the highest leaders of the private sectors – individually and collectively – tend to accept occupying a kind of meek, subservient rung in the scheme of things. They are often enmeshed in long-drawn-out negotiations with the upper echelons of the bureaucracy, and tend to rely as much as they deem convenient on the tutelary state as controller of resources, referee, adjudicator, and mediator. This specific "statist" mentality and its supporting institutional setup ("étatisme," as the French would call it), as well as the aspiration of the state bureaucracy to a guiding role in the economy (what the French aptly call "dirigisme"), have been typical of Japan since the Meiji Restoration.

After World War II, the American occupation (1945–52) carried out the purging of some major bureaucrats and military leaders and the partial disbanding of the *zaibatsu*, the interlocking industrial-banking organization of the top enterprises dominated by family holdings. As the occupation ended, though, the central bureaucracy rapidly regained its guiding economic role. The interconnections and the interplay between the bureaucracy and business started again on a vast scale. However, when the economy was in the process of reconstruction and adjustment, the bureaucratic center could easily enforce its own priorities. Subsequently, when the private sectors regained strength and assertiveness, the center adroitly chose the paths of compromise and adjustment. The state's guiding role has been discharged by the Ministry of International Trade and Industry (MITI). In the early post-occupation years, MITI focused its attention on the imperatives of reconstruction and on the needs of the infrastructure. In the 1960s, in tune with the world's preoccupation with accelerated growth, MITI fueled the economy's superfast growth with its preferential treatment of heavy industry and chemicals – a growth supported by the country's high savings rate and by the channeling of appropriate resources toward the expansion of selected production capacities. In the 1970s, the scope of MITI's guiding policies expanded in a number of directions. It first helped stabilize variously depressed industries, namely steel manufacturing; aluminum smelting; polyester, glass, and wool production; and shipbuilding, and extended all kinds of financial assistance to these and other industries for the reduction of their capacities (some of which it had previously helped to grow), as well as for the relocation, retraining, and retirement of their workers. It also promoted various consolidations and mergers, notably in chemicals, petroleum, metals, and the machinery industry, and attempted to bring about a bigger concentration in the automobile industry (though the private firms deftly avoided its directives). Finally, it asserted its interest in the growth of "knowledge-intensive industries," i.e., those involving electronics and information. In the 1980s, MITI's attention shifted to the framing of a comprehensive energy-security policy and the expansion of broad-based technologies oriented toward both domestic needs and foreign markets.

During the first postwar decades, Japan vastly benefitted from the free import of technologies from the United States. As this flow started to tighten somewhat, Japan was increasingly forced to search for new paths and to attempt to be more innovative, probing at the frontiers of both process design and new product choice.[1] Since the 1980s, MITI has channeled some of its R&D expenditures into such technologies as systems for unmanned space experiments, superconductors (materials and devices for electric power generation), solar energy, fuel-cell power generation, chemicals, super-hypersonic transport propulsion, and nonlinear photonic materials. Not all these choices have been either *unique* – many of them correspond to choices also made in the United States – or necessarily *optimal*. With or without MITI's prodding, Japanese industry has registered successes, made many false starts, and recorded failures in a number of fields. MITI's more recent failures have involved its so-called Fifth Generation Project (an effort to make quantum leaps in artificial intelligence) and fiascos in superspeed computers, jet engines, and high definition TV (HDTV), to mention but a few.[2] In short, it would be misleading for any country to look at MITI's choices – embodied in the succession of Japanese Five Year Plans from 1955 on and in the strategic priorities enshrined in decennial documents called "visions" – as reliable guides to Japan's actual industrial development.[3]

Indeed, as I pointed out above, industry responded in a variety of ways to MITI's incentives, jawboning, or cajoling. In the 1950s MITI's influence was all-encompassing and decisive. In the 1960s, many new industries bypassed MITI's focus and struck out on their own. In the 1970s and 1980s, many of these industries, now stronger and more independent, expanded further on their own, both domestically and internationally. *Pari passu,* industrial policy and central guidance (dirigisme) tended to become less important to government's overall economic policy.[4] Through all these phases, banking, trading, and industry coalesced in new patterns of cartel organization. What has emerged in Japanese business is the so-called *keiretsu* ("linkage") system of business organization along horizontal and vertical lines. The horizontal keiretsu consist of *clusters* of interdependent companies, including manufacturing companies, banks, service companies, and trading firms. The vertical keiretsu include selected component suppliers, distributors, and marketing companies, organized by leading *manufacturing* companies. Preeminent keiretsu such as Mitsui, Mitsubishi, Sumitomo, Fuyo, Saniva, and Daichi tend to have one or more member companies in almost all major industries, a fact that spurs the rivalry among them in each industrial field. In the crucial electronics industry, for instance, the Mitsui group contains Toshiba, a major force in the industry; the Mitsubishi group controls Mitsubishi Electric; the Sumitomo group includes three key electronics enterprises, namely Matsushita (i.e., Matsushita Kotobuki Electronics and Matsushita Seico), Nippon Electronic Company (the leading telecommunication equipment producer) and Sanyo Electric. Another keiretsu, the Furukawa group, also controls three important electronic enterprises: Fuji Electric; Fujitsu, the leader in computers; and Fanuc, the national champion in robotics.[5]

As Hugh Patrick points out, industry's relations with MITI and with its financial intermediaries changed radically in various respects in the 1980s. In an economy now "awash in surplus saving, most in financial assets," the traditional emphasis of industrial policy on picking "winners" lost its importance. A new problem emerged: "how to encourage businessmen, indeed anyone, to invest and spend rather than how to ration credit to them."[6] In regard to R&D expenditures, even a cursory examination shows that in relative terms these expenditures were higher in the case of Japan than in every other industrialized country. As a percentage of GNP, Japan outpaced even the United States; but, in *absolute* terms, total U.S. R&D expenditures exceeded those of its four industrial competitors *combined*, namely Japan, West Germany, France, and the United Kingdom. Paradoxically, it was *not* in Japan but in the United States that the relative share of the government in total R&D spending was the larger one. In 1989, for instance, the principal Japanese R&D source of funds was industry itself: Japanese industry contributed 72 percent of the total, compared to 19 percent contributed by the government and 9 percent by higher education and other sources. In the United States in the same year, the share of industry was 51 percent; of government, 45 percent; and of higher education and other sources, 4 percent. Note that in the then prevailing conditions of the cold war, the U.S. spent a significantly lower proportion of its GNP on non-defense R&D than Japan and West Germany did.[7]

Were the Japanese achievements – particularly those of the 1960s and 1970s in GNP and manufacturing growth, the structural transformation of the economy, the emphasis on high tech and international competition – the result of a unique combination of factors in which the government played the decisive role? Two opposite schools of thought confront each other on this issue. One of the main spokesmen of the first school, Chalmers Johnson, asserts in a very influential study that Japan resembles all *late*-industrializing states in having some special characteristics. While the first industrializing states are said to be *regulatory* states (bent on the regulation of market processes), the late industrializers are said to be *developmental* states. Incidentally, Johnson does not specify who these first industrializers are: besides England, one may assume that the term applies to the United States, France, and Germany. (A difficulty with this thesis is that the governments of *all* these countries were also developmental for long stretches of time.) Further, according to Johnson, the first industrializers are supposed to have operated in a "market-rationality" framework, while the late industrializers acted in a "plan-rationality" context. As a "plan-rational" state, post-World War II Japan allegedly focused on the structure of its domestic industry, particularly on one which would enhance the nation's international competitiveness. In contrast, the "market-rational" states concentrated on antitrust matters and showed no concern with "what industries ought to exist and what industries are no longer needed." Johnson then establishes a "model" of the Japanese developmental state, whose four basic features are (1) an "elite" bureaucracy staffed by the best managerial talent available, "which identifies the industries to be developed, and which channels toward them the best means for this purpose"; (2) a political system in which the legislative and judicial branches fend off the special-interest groups which, if catered to, would distort the priorities of the state; (3) a competitive economic environment, in which competition prevails "to as high a degree as is compatible with the state's priorities"; (4) a powerful economic organism (MITI) that combines planning, energy, domestic production, international trade, and a share of finance, and that controls the execution of the "industrial policy."[8]

The opposite school denies the validity of the development model, "or of an otherwise defined model specific to the Japanese economic system, or of the central and efficacious role of industrial policy" in the modern development of that country. The partisans of this school assert that the main source of Japan's economic growth has been a vigorous private sector that engaged imaginatively and diligently in productive investment. One proponent of the school, Philip Trezise, has argued that while Japan did indeed have an industrial policy, it was "not particularly coherent, focused or effective." Other supporters of this school rightly argued that one would expect a successfully anticipatory industrial policy to have created an industrial structure in which "winners" were overrepresented and "loser" industries underrepresented. However, this has not been the case: Japan's industrial structure is quite similar to that of the other industrial nations when adjustments are made for size. MITI's targeting of specific industries has had mixed results in practice, with high costs to consumers, savers, and taxpayers.[9] Michael E. Porter dismisses also "the story that usually assigns a starring role to government," and to Japanese management practice as well, in the country's economic success. He then asserts that "the domestic market, not foreign markets, led industry development in the vast majority of Japanese industries" and that often the essential stimuli for improvement, innovation, and the upgrading of industries were the paucity of natural resources, the proliferation of domestic rivals heavily oriented toward market share, and, finally, the explosion of this aggressive rivalry of Japanese firms in the global market. The early government intervention was constructive in such industries as steel and shipbuilding; it was disastrous when it aimed at limiting competition, and indeed led to inefficiency in a wide range of fields.[10] More broadly, Porter rejects the "outdated and static view" of international competition that posits that "low capital and labor costs, a cheap currency, and economies of scale" are the levers of competitive success. He affirms instead that competitive advantage, notably in the skill-intensive industries which are crucial in any advanced economy, results not from static efficiencies but from the processes of rapid industrial upgrading, which occur not in a comfortable domestic environment but in one in which local rivals pressure one another to advance.[11]

Table 3-1. *United States and Japan: employment patterns (percentages): selected years, 1947–1989*

	Goods-Producing Total	Goods-Producing Industries				Rest of the Economy Total
		Agric.	Mining	Construc.	Manuf.	
U.S. 1947	45.7	13.8	1.6	3.6	26.7	54.3
1957	42.0	9.3	1.3	4.5	26.9	58.0
1967	36.8	5.2	0.8	4.6	26.2	63.2
1977	31.9	3.5	0.9	5.3	22.2	68.1
1989	26.1	2.7	0.6	5.7	17.1	73.9
Japan 1979	47.2	13.6	0.2	9.9	23.5	52.8
1989	42.0	9.5	0.2	8.8	23.5	58.0

Sources: Computed from (for the U.S.) National Income and Product Accounts of the United States 1929-1976, Washington, D.C., U.S. Department of Commerce, Bureau of Economic Analysis, 1981, pp. 249-252; Economic Report of the President . . . 1991, p. 322; (for Japan) OECD, National Accounts 1977-1989, Paris, OECD, 1990.

The historical extremes of dirigisme are a fully controlled economy, at one end, and a loosely guided or prodded economy, at the other. The best example of the first is the "Kriegswirtschaft," the war economy forged by the Germans during World War I. It is the Kriegswirtschaft model which prefigured the Soviet centralized all-round planning. The other extreme of modern dirigisme is embodied in the system of so-called indicative planning long in vogue in France. The system relies on centralized suggestions of future developments which industries may or may not accept as guides to action. In many respects, MITI's plans and "visions" have oscillated between these two extremes. In the early post-occupation years MITI did guide the economy firmly toward its selected priorities; in the later years, when the industrial and banking keiretsu mustered increasing strength, central prodding slowly but surely lost its overall guiding effectiveness.

In order to choose among competing explanations of the Japanese phenomenon, some questions must be answered. How did the Japanese economy perform during the period under review? Was this development akin to or different from the one undergone by the American economy? Did manufacturing maintain a predominant share in total output? As can be seen from Table 3-1, Japanese employment patterns in 1979 and 1989 actually closely resembled those of the United States in 1947 and 1957 in terms of the relative shares of *goods*-producing industries versus those of the rest of the economy, i.e., *service* producers plus utilities and transport, as well as in terms of the relative shares of agriculture and manufacturing. While one cannot mechanically project a future Japanese development strictly parallel to that of the United States, one may note that the 1989 Japanese employment pattern could not be frozen in time any more than was the pattern of 1979, and that very likely a further *expansion* of the services closely tied to production (notably the financial intermediation services and certain professional and technical services) is in store, along with relative decreases in the economic shares of total goods-producing enterprises (agriculture and manufacturing).

The evolution of employment in Japanese manufacturing over the period 1960 to 1989 is presented in Table 3-2. As the table shows, factory employment (i.e., excluding handicrafts) peaked in 1970 at 11.6 million and then fell through the 1980s to between 10.6 and 10.9 million. In the industries surveyed – which constitute the backbone of advanced countries – the most severe losses were in iron and steel, even considered in relation to 1960. In relation to the latter year, large employment expansions did take place in all the other industrial branches; but in relation to 1970, expansions took place only in transportation equipment and electrical machinery and equipment. Total Japanese employment in manufacture was on the order of slightly over 48 percent of U.S. employment in 1960, 60 percent in 1970, and 56 percent by the end of the 1980s. In electrical machinery (including electronics), in transportation equipment, and in precision instruments – the branches most directly related to high technology production and supplies – Japanese employment relative to that of the U.S. reached 118 percent, 50 percent, and 24 percent respectively by the end of the 1980s.[12]

With regard to *productivity,* the Japanese performance has been outstanding in steel, metalworking, autos, and consumer electronics. In manufacturing as a whole, the average annual rate of change in output per hour for 1960–86 was 7.6 percent, compared to 3.0 percent for the U.S. Note, however, that the crucial divergence in the performance of the two countries took place in 1960–73: the average yearly rate of growth in output per hour was then 10.3 percent for Japan, against 3.3 percent for the U.S. The discrepancy narrowed down from 1979 to 1989, when the average yearly rate of growth for Japan was 5.5 percent, against 3.6 percent for the U.S.[13]

Awed by the Japanese successes in productivity, in manufacturing outputs, and in automotive and electronics exports, many people have tried to explain them, as Robert H. Hayes and Steven C. Wheelwright put it, "in terms of gleaming modern factories peopled by skillful robots – both human and otherwise – all under the dictatorship of 'Japan Inc.'"[14] Actually, most Japanese factories are *not* modern structures filled with high-tech equipment, and the government does not watch over their activities. Firsthand observations of

Table 3-2. *Japan: employment in manufacturing:* total and selected industries, 1960–1989*

Years	Total Establish- ments (in 1000)	Employment (in 1000)						
		Total Manu- facturing	Iron and Steel	Fabricated Metal Products	General Machinery	Electrical Machinery and Equipment	Trans- portation Equipment	Precision Instru- ments
1960	487	8,169	420	474	762	668	539	147
1970	652	11,680	552	844	1,178	1,341	881	241
1980	734	10,932	433	825	1,081	1,358	904	276
1989	421	10,962	336	818	1,147	1,918	908	241

*The Japanese official data exclude the manufacturing establishments owned by central and local governments.
Sources: *Japan Statistical Yearbook*, Tokyo, Statistics Bureau Management Coordinating Agency, 1975, pp. 175–177; 1991, pp. 216–221.

even the most advanced Japanese factories indicate that they are not superior technologically to U.S. plants in corresponding industries. The main differences are between the *operational approaches* in the two countries in regard to handling the equipment, care of the machinery, and cleanliness and orderliness in the plant. The Japanese take great care of the equipment and of its surroundings; they avoid production overloading, pay close attention to the reduction of work-in-process inventories, and elaborately monitor the production flow. Productivity and quality are viewed as interconnected: building quality into the job is viewed as mandatory. The objective of management is "crisis-free, error-free operation," an objective which seems to require careful screening of the workforce before hiring and tight discipline within the plant. Contrary to overused clichés, "lifetime employment" is not practiced in the *majority* of Japanese companies; only the elite companies do it extensively. Much of Japanese investment is devoted to *upgrading* existing equipment, while in the U.S. the emphasis is on equipment *replacement* and on building new capacity for new businesses.[15]

In examining the sources of Japan's competitive strength in automobiles, electric-electronic goods, and other high-value-added products, T. Ozawa draws attention to the effective use in these industries of a distinctive system of subcontracting. Ozawa notes that in any industrialized country the system of subcontracting exists, but it is *mono-layered* and the transactions involved are based on strict contractual relationships. In contrast, the Japanese system is *multi-layered,* with a few major assemblers at the top served by primary subcontractors, who rely in turn on other subcontractors, who are served further down the line by other sub-processors, and so on down to the very bottom, where one finds "literally tens of thousands of the cottage-type, family-owned and -operated small production units." The relationship between buyers and suppliers is often personal, based on years of mutual trust rather than on market-mediated ties. Examining the situation in the automobile industry, Ozawa points out that at the top of the pyramid are 11 core companies, followed by 168 primary sub-assemblers, by 4,700 second-stage sub-assemblers, and by a third and lowest stage of sub-processors numbering 31,600 establishments. Cost reductions come from a meticulously segmented division of labor that capitalizes on "multifarious wage structure and diverse factor intensities."[16]

As I showed in Table 3-2, the official Japanese statistics indicate that factory employment in 1989 was on the order of 10.9 million. OECD data included in *National Accounts 1977–1989* give a figure of 15.1 million for manufacturing employment for the same year, presumably including the workforce of family-owned and -operated small handicraft-type shops, many of which must also have been service-oriented. Be that as it may, the structure of manufacturing establishments itself displays a far lower degree of concentration than in the

United States. The *Japan Statistical Yearbook* shows that in 1989 the 10.9 million factory employees worked in 421,000 establishments, of which 75 percent employed fewer than 20 persons; 21 percent employed between 20 and 100 persons, and only 4 percent employed more than 100 persons. The same year 19.4 million persons worked in the 348,000 American manufacturing establishments. Of these establishments, 66 percent employed fewer than 20 persons, 24 percent counted between 20 and 100 persons, and 10 percent employed more than 100 people. In Japan, at the top of the pyramid, 662 manufacturing establishments had a workforce of more than 1,000 employees. As in all developed countries, these establishments were concentrated in electrical machinery and equipment and in transportation equipment, as well as in iron and steel. In contrast to this high peak, large portions of the Japanese economy "not only fail to measure up to the standards of the best world competitors but fall far behind them."[17]

At the end of the 1980s, Japan produced the equivalent of 70 percent of U.S. manufacturing output – 81 percent of U.S. high-tech manufacturing output and 65 percent of other manufacturing. In both countries, high-tech manufacturing represented about one third of manufacturing production.[18] These data show that Japan's achievements, while certainly very impressive, hardly constitute global economic hegemony. Yet, as I pointed out in the introduction to Part II, attention is not paid to *these* figures, which show the continuing dominant U.S. position in manufacturing production, but to the "crossover" graphs of production indices, which convey the impression that U.S. output is trailing that of Japan.

In the global market, Japan secured the highest share for certain of its high-tech manufactures. This has been the case particularly for radio and TV equipment and for all kinds of office computing machinery. In addition, Japan also acquired significant shares in the areas of drugs and medicines, chemicals, engines and turbines, and precision instruments. However, the U.S. remains powerful in all these areas, and is still dominant in aircraft, the computer industry, and scientific instruments. At the end of the 1980s, the total of Japan's merchandise exports was equivalent to over three quarters of the corresponding U.S. exports, while its imports accounted for less than half of the corresponding U.S. imports (yielding Japan a surplus of $65 billion in 1989).[19] The U.S. and the European Union will necessarily continue to be Japan's main trading partners. However, Japan has also developed informal partnerships with the Asean countries (members of the Association of Southeast Asian nations), namely Brunei, Singapore, Thailand, Malaysia, Indonesia, and the Philippines, and has also expanded its ties with certain countries of the Pacific rim, namely, China, Canada, Mexico, Australia, and Chile. It is interesting to recall in this regard that since the 1980s, some small newly industrialized countries of the Pacific rim area, the so-called Small Tigers (South Korea,

Taiwan, Hong Kong, and Singapore), have pressed forward on industrialization based on exports, and have also achieved high rates of growth equaling or exceeding Japan's. During the 1980s, the real rate of growth of the global economy was 3.0 percent per year; that of the Small Tigers, 8.0 percent. The four continue to excel in terms of real income, growth rates, low inflation, low unemployment, and vigorous participation in global trade.[20]

Analysis of Japan's GDP by end use, factor payments, and industrial origin illuminates some of the underlying factors of its rapid growth. According to OECD data, between 1960 and 1989 the share of consumption in Japan's GDP as calculated by end use (at current prices) fluctuated around 58 percent, except in the 1970s, when it fell to around 52 percent. In contrast, in the United States' GDP, the yearly share of consumption was on the order of 64–67 percent. In Japan's GDP, calculated by factor payments, the compensation of employees paid by resident producers rose from 40 percent in the 1960s to around 58 percent in the 1980s. The corresponding shares in the U.S. GDP were on the order of 58 percent in the 1960s and 61 percent in the 1980s. In the GDP calculated by industrial origin, the trends are broadly similar to those indicated for the employment patterns in Table 3-1, with differences due to variations in productivity. Thus, during the period under review, the contribution of Japanese agriculture to GDP fell from slightly over 11 percent in the early 1960s to less than 3 percent in 1989; that of manufacturing also dropped, from 34 percent in the early 1960s to less than 30 percent in 1989; finally, that of goods-producing industries contracted during the same period, from 56 percent to 44 percent. These trends parallel those which can be observed in the case of the U.S., where the contractions were of course sharper: the total share of goods-producing industries fell during the period under review from close to 40 percent to around 28 percent.[21] As these data suggest, as Japan reaches higher levels of income, the claims of both consumption and of employee compensation are bound to rise to levels closer to those of the U.S., with potentially similar repercussions on gross fixed capital formation. MITI's "vision" for the 1990s calls for new goals, including a "mellow society" and a potential re-orientation of the industrial structure from producers to consumers – though some Western experts still look with suspicion on the idea of MITI as an eventual dispenser of mellowness.[22]

Concomitantly, as we shall see further on in more detail, the need to operate at the frontiers of contemporary technology is bound to encourage the proliferation of strategic international alliances, joint venture mergers, acquisitions of foreign firms, overseas investments, and license deals, particularly with the United States. On the other hand, Japan itself will continue a major effort to develop complex Japanese counterparts to Silicon Valley – so-called Technopolises forging expanded relations between the government, business, and the universities in all parts of the country, more or less on the U.S. model.[23]

3-2   *The state, the banks, and the German economy*

Consider now the case of the second great economic challenger of the next century, united Germany. Toward the close of the 20th century, Germany reemerged economically as the most successful country of Europe, with the most developed and most efficient factories, the best technically trained labor force, the most powerful export-oriented capacity, and the strongest currency, henceforth the benchmark of European exchange rates. Since July 1990, West Germany has "taken over" East Germany, whose decaying economy, obsolete technology, and glaring inefficiencies of capital and labor have since been drawn into vast processes of transformation and restructuring. This absorption, which will require an investment at least equivalent to West Germany's net national product of 1990, has opened important opportunities for Western entrepreneurship, and in addition has most likely helped Germany to become a crucial factor in the Western trading and economic relations with the ex-Soviet empire and its former East European satellites.

How did Germany regain such a critical position in the space of only a few decades after a disastrous war which had led to the creation of two impoverished and hostile Germanies – a Federal Republic of Germany under Allied occupation and a German Democratic Republic under Communist dictatorship? In the discussion which follows I shall focus mainly on West Germany, the heart and soul of the unified country. Through unification, it is West Germany's kind of market relations, together with its patterns of production and employment, that is penetrating East Germany. However, one cannot simply add the economic statistics of West and East Germany in order to acquire a view of the unified country – first, because of the unreliability of East Germany's statistics, fraudulently manipulated by the communist regime, and second, because of the still unsettled state of that area's production and employment structures. According to German estimates, more than 60 percent of the East German working population of about 8 million will have to take up completely new jobs in the 1990s. The former East German industries, organized along autarkic, highly vertically integrated lines (the so-called *kombinate*), must be restructured in order to become profitable, competitive businesses. It is estimated that up to 40 percent of all East German companies may not survive this kind of restructuring, as vertical integration prevented both economies of scale and competitive innovation. The entire system must undergo profound mutations: it cannot be rapidly overhauled.[24]

Economic recovery and then fast growth took place in postwar West Germany as a result of the interaction of two crucial series of events. The first involved the forging of ramified connections with Western Europe – new ties rooted in the U.S.-launched Marshall Plan. The second concerned the search for and then the adoption of adroit ways of handling the country's prewar and wartime economic heritage in order to reshape its new economic framework. Let us consider these issues in turn.

The Marshall Plan, officially entitled the European Recovery Program, was both a large-scale American relief effort and a shrewd political move whose aim was to get Europe back on its feet and to forge, at the same time, a counterweight to rising Soviet power. The plan began to take effect a year before the Federal Republic officially came into existence with the acquisition of its "Basic Law" (*Grundgesetz*). The German recovery started in the spring of 1948. The Marshall Plan was launched in April of that year; the currency reform that replaced the Reichsmark (R-Mark) with the Deutschemark (D-Mark, or DM) was carried out in June; and the liberation of the economy from a vast number of oppressive administrative controls started soon afterwards. West Germany obtained much-needed foodstuffs, raw materials, and equipment as American aid. It did not have to repay the loans immediately and fully. The counterpart funds (received from the sale of these goods in Germany) were booked in a special account at the disposal of the German government in cooperation with the Plan's administration. These funds were used over many years for financing various German industries at low interest rates and for guiding a significant share of private investment.

In his famous commencement address at Harvard (on June 5, 1947), General George C. Marshall had stated that the United States was ready to put up the necessary money for European reconstruction, but that in turn "the Europeans would have to commit themselves to a new system of cooperation" in order to achieve a joint recovery through "multilateral undertakings." The first major postwar West European organization, the Organization for European Economic Cooperation (OEEC), was established with 16 founding member states in April 1948: the Federal Republic was received as a member, although it still lacked sovereign status at the time. The large and heterogeneous OEEC did not go far beyond the broad intergovernmental tasks of managing and encouraging joint economic policies. Eventually some of its functions, notably those concerning coordination of its members' policies, were taken over (in 1961) by a new organization, the Organization for Economic Cooperation and Development (OECD). In the meantime, much closer integration started to be implemented by six European states on the basis of the concurrence of objectives and interests of the United States, on the one hand, and of France and Germany on the other. In 1951 the six signed the Treaty of Paris forming the European Coal and Steel Community (ECSC), which came into operation in 1952; in 1957 the six signed the famous Treaty of Rome, which established the European Economic Community (EEC) – the so-called Common Market – and the European Atomic Energy Community (Euratom). After a series of successes in lowering trade barriers and in establishing common sectoral policies, the Common Market ran into a series of difficulties and quandaries of critical import, to which I shall return in detail in the next section.

While establishing these critical connections with its former Western enemies, the Federal Republic was groping for ways of handling its motley economic heritage and for building a new democratic post-Nazi society. A raging controversy with strong echoes of the 1920s and 1930s sprang up among the policymakers and the economists about the kind of market economy the country needed and should implement. The drive for free competition and free trade – labeled "neo-liberalism" – was supported by a large segment of public opinion, but only with the proviso that such freedom would be accompanied by a very active government. This so-called neo-liberalism had its conceptual roots in the prewar doctrine of "competitive order" or "ordo-liberalism" (meaning liberalism in an orderly structure) propounded by Walter Eucken of the University of Freiburg, and in a germane theory called "social market economy" formulated by Alfred Müller-Armack of the University of Münster. The latter theory posited the need for "organic compromises" between the government, the market, and interest groups. The neo-liberals in power since the beginnings of the postwar era were challenged by the social democrats, who were in favor of planning but who eventually settled for the more flexible guiding formula "competition as far as possible, planning as far as necessary." This formula finally gained the support of the holders of power, who were presiding over the removal of market controls and the liberalization of the movement of capital, labor, and goods and services. In practice, all these currents of thought combined with other historical legacies to lead to the shaping of a regime with a strong federal chancellor at its head – a "chancellor democracy" protected against the "whims" of parliament – and a paternalistic-dirigiste approach to government intervention in the economy.[25] (The discussion about German economic doctrine came alive again during 1990 as the prospects of German unification loomed on the horizon: in reply to the East Germans, who indicated that they preferred to look for a "third way" between capitalism and socialism, a West German writer, Willy Kraus, argued that the Federal Republic's "social market economy" already combined capitalism with the goals of socialism, with competition as their crucial link. The then state secretary in the Economics Ministry, Otto Schlecht, added the official imprimatur of the federal government to the "third way" thesis – which shows how adjustable the underlying doctrines really are.)[26]

The paternalistic-dirigiste approach consistently manifested itself in large budgets and in massive and increasing government subsidies. Federal, state, and local budgets, which had been on the order of 35 percent of GNP in the 1960s, grew to close to 50 percent in the mid 1970s and to over 50 percent in the 1980s. The federal government and various states have supported a number of industries and services, such as coal, steel, air and space, shipbuilding, and agriculture (starting, in the latter case, with payments to the Common Market's "common agricultural policy"). The level of subsidies has risen almost uninterruptedly, though it is generally recognized that they are extensive and costly. The traditional coal and steel complex is dependent on subsidies to such an extent that it could not exist without them. Though truly moribund firms are allowed to die, the government gives various forms of subsidies to some of the country's largest and most profitable concerns, such as Daimler-Benz, Bayer, Volkswagen, and BMW. Some subsidies – particularly those concerning European agriculture – have become a disruptive factor in German-American trade. Ominously, the overall volume of subsidies will have to rise yet further, as the government must unavoidably attempt to cushion a number of difficult transitions in the former East Germany.[27]

The Federal Republic inherited from previous German regimes a large state-owned sector, including railroads, most local transportation, the main utilities, the telegraph, the telephone and radio, the savings banks, and quite a number of industrial enterprises. From the 1950s on, the various German governments have taken a number of steps in the direction of privatization. They partially denationalized the large mining and smelting company Prussag, the well-known Volkswagen, and the enormous state-owned united electric and mining company Veba. But the pattern of public ownership has continued much the same in most sectors of the economy. Even with unification, the denationalization of the massive state-owned sector of the former Democratic Republic, entrusted to the management of the Treuhandanstalt agency, seems to be guided by the idea of achieving a preliminary restructuring and reorganization rather than by a drive toward precipitous dismantling and privatization (as the Germans put it, *Sanierung* rather than *Privatisirung*).[28]

Large firms are once more dominant in the German economy's key sectors – e.g., oil and gas, automobiles, shipbuilding, chemicals, electrical engineering, rubber, and asbestos – and ultimately it is such firms which are called upon to play the decisive roles in the final reshaping of the Eastern economy. In spite of the antitrust legislation of 1957 and 1965, the system remains as has traditionally been the case: lenient in regard to mergers and dominant firms. Indeed, according to Michael E. Porter, mergers and alliances among leading companies were proliferating at a high rate in the late 1980s, and almost none of these have been prohibited on antitrust grounds. However, this does not mean that domestic rivalry among the big firms does not occur: it remains, in fact, widespread among the firms commanding important shares in the global market.[29]

Behind most German firms stand the German banks. The "competitive order" has complacently adjusted itself to a historical characteristic of the German economy, namely the central position of the banks with a concomitant interlocking of banking and business. Germans put their savings into a bank rather than into stocks and bonds; the country, in fact, lacks a major international market for these commodities. Nothing in Germany rivals New York, Tokyo, and the London market. Fewer than 650 of some 2,500 German stock corporations are listed on the eight German exchanges. London trades roughly one third of German shares. German companies raise less capital from the market than their European competitors. As W. R. Smyser rightly puts it, "from the powerful Bundesbank [central federal bank] whose policies have given Germany a world currency, through the 'big three' [Deutsche Bank, Dresdner Bank, Commerz Bank] and the other banks that influence and perhaps determine the policies of the major corporations, to the corner *Sparkassen* [savings institutions] where Germans place their savings every week or month, the banks are at *the core* of the German system and of German style."[30]

The German banks function as *universal* banks; that is, they are able to furnish a full range of services in banking, savings and investment, and foreign exchange. The "big three" have been omnipresent throughout the Federal Republic's tenure and have rapidly expanded into East Germany. These are not the only big banks: certain regional banks may be even larger in their respective areas. However, these three reach into every aspect of the economy and are interlocked with all kinds of companies – manufacturing firms, utilities, insurance, trading corporations. They interlock through various channels: they hold many company shares, play an important role on company boards, and exercise controlling voting power not only on the basis of their own shares but of those of their clients as well (by proxy). According to official data from the mid 1980s, the three major banks could vote significant percentages (30–60 percent) of such major corporations as Siemens, Daimler-Benz, Bayer, BASF, Höchst, and Thyssen. Together, the voting shares held in the same companies by *all three* banks ranged from 60 to 98 percent. Thanks to the seats the banks hold on the boards of the most important corporations, they can pool information on the basis of which they steer investment throughout the country. Germany is thus endowed with a kind of unofficial "collective economic policy" which is framed not through some MITI-like public instrument but through "coordination" by private (and some public) banks. The available evidence suggests that German business is in general comfortable with this arrangement and with its perpetuation, notwithstanding some criticisms of bank power.[31]

Consider now the ways in which the German economy changed during the period under review and whether its development paralleled or diverged from that of the United States. As can be seen from Table 3-3, the Federal Republic's patterns of employment in 1980 and 1989 parallel those of the United States some 12 to 13 years earlier, and reflect the same evolutionary tendencies. In 1980, shares of agriculture, mining, and manufacturing in total German employment were rather similar to the shares held by these sectors in the United

Table 3-3. *United States and Germany (West): employment patterns
(percentages): selected years, 1967–1989*

		Goods-Producing Total	Goods-Producing Industries				Rest of the Economy Total
			Agri-culture	Mining	Construc-tion	Manu-facturing	
U.S.	1967	36.8	5.2	0.8	4.6	26.2	63.2
	1977	31.9	3.5	0.9	5.3	22.2	68.1
Germany	1980	41.4	5.2	0.9	7.9	27.4	58.6
	1989	35.9	3.6	0.7	6.6	25.0	64.1

Sources: Computed from (for the U.S.): see Table 3-1; (for Germany) OECD, National Accounts 1977-1989, and, for manufacturing, OECD, Industrial Statistics 1989, Paris, OECD, 1989, pp. 19, 22.

States in 1967; and again, 1989 German shares in the indicated sectors paralleled those of the United States in 1977. As in the case of Japan and of the United States, the shares of *all* goods-producing industries tended to decrease from one decade to the next.

As can be seen from Table 3-4, after the reconstruction years German employment in manufacturing fell sharply through the 1970s, and then continued to decrease, though at a slower pace, through the 1980s. As in all developed countries, employment in iron and steel was the most affected. The machinery industry (the traditional stronghold of German engineering), as well as the electrical equipment industry, maintained or expanded the high position secured by 1970. Consistent with historical tradition, the efficacy of the German industrial system depends on the strong technical training of the workforce. The backbone of the latter are the skilled blue-collar workers, the *Facharbeiter* who have completed an apprenticeship and received certification of their skills. Apprenticeship is required for more than 450 different job classifications. In addition, the first-line factory supervisors are skilled workers with experience, some of whom have passed the "master"-level examination in the trade they oversee. Finally, factory managers are people who have received graduate training in the technical professions and are fully knowledgeable about the technical operations of the plants they manage. These managers are not moved from place to place, as is the case in many American firms. For their skilled and highly disciplined workforce, customer orientation means delivery on schedule of finely engineered products, followed by excellent after-sale service. On the downside, this rigid system tends, perhaps, to dampen entrepreneurial activities, especially those associated with the establishment of spinoffs, i.e., new firms with managers leaving the confines of the older enterprises.[32]

Table 3-4. *Germany (West): employment in manufacturing: total and selected industries, 1960–1989*

Years	Total Establish-ments (in 1000)	Total Manu-facturing	Iron and Steel	Fabricated Metal Products	Machinery	Electrical Equipment	Trans-portation Equipment	Precision Instru-ments
				Employment (in 1000)				
1960	52	7,159	560	722	935	0,728	501	148
1970	44	8,536	784	548	1,176	1,131	742	169
1980	38	7,428	522	676	1,094	925	858	166
1989	43	6,910	261	783	1,119	1,011	927	145

Sources: First two rows: Statistisches Jahrbuch für die Bundesrepublik Deutschlands 1962, pp. 222-223; 1975, p. 226; last two rows: OECD, Industrial Structure Statistics 1989/90, Paris, OECD, 1992, pp. 19, 22.

Notwithstanding the German workforce's productivity and its high-quality output, growth has been disappointing since the 1970s. The rates of growth in total factor productivity (TFP), labor productivity, and capital productivity in the business sector decreased appreciably after 1973, compared to the 1960s levels. The average annual percentage rise in TFP in the business sector, which had been 2.6 from 1960 to 1973, fell to 1.7 from 1973 to 1979 and to 0.8 from 1979 to 1988. Note that the U.S. performance in TFP rates was also unsatisfactory, reaching even lower levels. The annual rate of change in labor productivity in German manufacturing exceeded the U.S. performance in 1960–73 and in 1973–79, but fell below the U.S. in 1979–87, which brought an average annual percentage rise of 3.7 for the U.S. but of only 1.6 for Germany. In addition, in Germany as in the United States, increasing technological transformations brought about high rates of unemployment.[33]

At the close of the 1980s, West Germany's global manufacturing output came to 37 percent of that of the U.S. and 53 percent of that of Japan. Its high-tech manufacturing was proportionally smaller – roughly one quarter of the corresponding U.S. output, and about one third of that of Japan. There can be little doubt that in time united Germany will knit together the Eastern and Western portions of the country into a vast manufacturing economy. Consistent with its historical development, Germany has already regained strong positions in the global market, and will regain dominant positions in many industrial fields. Its main strengths are in chemicals, industrial and electrical machinery, and transportation equipment; in addition, it has proven competitive across a wide range of other products. At least one third of all the jobs depend directly on exports, and many more depend on them indirectly. Indeed, at the end of the 1980s West Germany was exporting about 30 percent of its total production – a very high percentage for a country its size (the corresponding figures were 7 percent for the U.S. and 11 percent for Japan). Export shares of Germany's production ranged from 30 to 40 percent for electronics, precision instruments, and optics, and from 40 to 50 percent and over for chemicals, machine tools, and automobiles. In the global market, West Germany secured high shares for its economy in industrial chemicals, engines and turbines, aircraft, radio and TV equipment, and scientific instruments, as well as in various other industries.[34] Germany remains the world's leading exporting nation partly because of *domestic austerity*. Even a cursory analysis of the structure of its GDP – by end use and factor payments – points in this direction. Like Japan, West Germany exhibits a low share of consumer expenditures and low levels of employee compensation. OECD data on West Germany's GDP, at current prices, show that the share of private consumption was on the order of 56.7 percent of GDP in 1960 and of 54.8 percent in 1989. The compensation of employees was on the order of 47.3 percent in 1960, rising to 54.0 percent in 1989. Both series are significantly lower than in the U.S.

Since World War II the Federal Republic's main trading partners have been the Western industrialized nations. In 1990 the countries of the European Union alone absorbed close to 52 percent of its exports, and supplied as much as 53 percent of its imports. But German trade did not go only to the West. Both the Federal Republic and the GDR were important trading partners for Eastern Europe. The Federal Republic was the main Western trading partner of the Soviet Union and of Eastern Europe's Council of Mutual Economic Assistance (CMEA): by the end of the 1950s, 30 percent of the OECD's exports to European CMEA states were supplied by Germany. For its part, East Germany directed one half of its trade to the Soviet Union and one quarter to Eastern Europe. United Germany has thus become not only the main trading partner of the Western European countries but also a crucial gateway to the East. We turn to these issues in the next section.

3-3   Relations within Europe

The European Union – formerly the European Economic Community (EEC) – is poised to encompass not only the whole of Western Europe but also some East European countries as well. How is this expansion likely to affect inter-European relations? How is it likely to impact international competition? What bearing will it have on German growth and competitiveness and the country's international role? How will it influence the United States' and Japan's economic policies toward Europe?

Recall that the EEC was created in 1958 by its six founding members – Belgium, France, Germany, Italy, Luxembourg, and the Netherlands – in order to achieve certain *economic, political,* and *security* objectives. The economic objectives were to further growth and European integration via a customs union and a common agricultural policy. By 1968, the two pillars of the EEC – the customs union (i.e., the Common Market) and the Community's agricultural policy (CAP) – were in place. After a period of relative stagnation characterized by some as "Euro-sclerosis," the EEC actually started to expand from the early 1970s on, first adding Denmark, Ireland, and the United Kingdom (in 1973), then Greece (in 1981), and then Spain and Portugal (in 1986). In 1990, West Germany simply absorbed an Eastern European country, East Germany. By 1993, the EEC had been rebaptized the European Union (EU), and in 1994 it endorsed for membership also Austria, Finland, Iceland, Norway, and Sweden, in order to create a vastly expanded, loosely integrated European Economic Space (EES). The new EU evidently stands ready to expand also into Eastern Europe – extending memberships notably to the Czech Republic and Slovakia, Hungary, and Poland – thus engendering a free trade area far broader than the one France has consistently tended to prefer.[35] As has sometimes been pointed out, the U.S.-Canadian free trade agreement

(FTA), signed in 1988 and followed in 1993 by its expansion to Mexico – and thus, by the creation of a regional bloc called the North American Free Trade Agreement (NAFTA) – paralleled in some respects the European Common Market's expansion to less developed countries (viz. Greece, Spain, and Portugal). The further expansion of the increasingly large European Union into Eastern Europe, bridging the East-West divide, may also be paralleled by the eventual inclusion in NAFTA of other Latin American countries. (I shall return to some of these issues in Section 7.3.)

How does the vast European Union, with so many independent and sovereign member states – and, eventually, with more – efficiently conduct its joint business? The EU is neither an emerging state nor an international regime: rather it is a *network* pooling national sovereignties in various directions on the basis of sets of intergovernmental bargains. There is a center of authority, but its focus is on easing intergovernmental negotiations and agreements. Policy is fragmented by sectors, and within each sector informal coordination takes place among national bureaucracies. Different national ministries have different, even conflicting, interests in regard to the items on the common agenda. And, in turn, ministries are not reluctant to use either the EU bureaucracy or other national bureaucracies to further their own interests. The system functions only within the limits set by various nationally devised constraints. Though tariffs have been reduced or eliminated within the Common Market, commercial procedures which distort free competition interact in a variety of ways. The obstacles include customs procedures, technical regulations, differences in standards, internal subsidies, bidding restrictions, and a host of other impediments blocking the free movement of factors of production and of goods. The EU treaty contains provisions allowing the EU institutions to curb restrictive procedures, but these institutions in fact lack the real power to do it. It seems impossible to reach agreement on a common tax system. National financial systems are impossible to coordinate, and totally free movement of people within the EU may likewise prove elusive.[36]

From its inception, the European Common Market enjoyed, besides the blessing of the United States, a concordance between French and German interests. France saw in such an organization a means of limiting the costs of its weakness in certain sectors vis-à-vis Germany, of harnessing the latter's potential competition, and of ensuring its own overall economic growth. Germany saw in European integration a means of asserting its new international importance, of accelerating its industrial recovery and development, and of expanding its exports. Franco-German relations based on mutually beneficent bargains have continued to be at the *core* of the Common Market. Various important factors have helped to increase or diminish the tensions implicit in the negotiations underlying such bargains, but no factor has been more important than the potentially continuous growth of Germany's *industrial base,* particularly after German unification and its increasing penetration of the vast East European hinterland. (At the end of the 1980s, West Germany's manufacturing output was equivalent to 164 percent of French and 161 percent of British manufacturing output. In high-tech manufacturing, West Germany produced more than twice as much as France and about 10 percent more than the United Kingdom. Its exports were also close to double those of France, and over 220 percent of British exports.)

It is not astonishing that the French economist Jacques Lesourne remarked in the 1980s that the European industrial scene is characterized by strong solidarities as well as by intense internal tensions. Among the solidarity factors, Lesourne included notably the importance of intra-European exports in manufactures, accounting for 50 percent of total manufactured exports; what this means is that for each EU member, the rate of growth of the rest of the Union was obviously a critical determinant of its own growth. The internal tensions seem to arise from the evolution of trade balances in manufactures (favorable for West Germany and unfavorable for the United Kingdom), from insufficient cooperation between European firms and governments with respect to industry; and from the different approaches of the European governments to the management of their economies. In any case, Lesourne noted that "because of its strength, German industry structures industrial relations within Europe."[37]

With new openings to the East, united Germany may see its exports increase above the combined levels of West Germany and East Germany before unification. German businessmen have been assiduously visiting Russia and the new nations of Russia's former empire in order to establish trade contacts and to inspect investment sites. During the 1980s, West Germany's direct investments abroad exceeded direct foreign investments in the Federal Republic, thus helping to balance its trade surpluses. About half of these investments were directed toward other EU countries, but a growing share of investments started to move toward Eastern Europe. It is interesting to note that in the second half of the 1980s, just before the collapse of the communist regimes, West Germany hosted the greatest number of East-West joint ventures (68 companies) out of a worldwide total of 416 such joint ventures. This was due *inter alia* to geographic factors, trading traditions, and specific economic and commercial interests.[38] The many obstacles and objections that may be raised toward a whole set of economic moves toward the East seem to weigh less heavily on the minds of German officials, exporters, and investors than on the minds of some other Europeans.

The new interests may entail problems for older trading partners. In particular, German unification, along with the opportunities provided by the collapse of communism, may eventually make Germany a less committed partner in the EU. Germany may manifest dissatisfaction with the current onerous arrangements concerning its contribution to the EU budget for the common agricultural policy, and may also resist any further extension of existing EU commercial rules and procedures. For their part, the French have been disturbed both by the unilateral moves made by the Federal Republic during the unification process – which the Germans considered not to be within the Community's jurisdiction – and by the drift of German interests toward Eastern Europe rather than toward the southern European members of the EU. However, while the French may be reluctant to accept an enlargement of the Union that would include East European countries – an enlargement which would compromise the French goal of a tightly integrated Europe counterbalancing the United States – the latter, along with Germany and the United Kingdom, seems to favor precisely that – i.e., a broader Europe, which by its very complexity and diversity would prevent moves toward the tight, narrow Eurofederalism that these three would clearly like to avoid.[39]

Japan's direct investment in EU manufacturing is rather small, but it is growing at a rapid pace. At the end of the 1980s Japanese investment in the area was equal to one tenth of that of U.S. multinationals in the EC (representing over one half of all U.S. direct foreign investment abroad). If one defines the economic involvement of country X and country Y as including both the exports of X to Y plus the output of manufactured goods produced by X's foreign-affiliated companies in Y, then the total involvement of Japan in the EU amounted to only 17 percent of that of the U.S. The data suggest that there is great potential for more Japanese production in Europe – a prospect which not all Europeans view with equanimity. Some even say that Japan is no longer *ante portas* but is in fact *in porta*.

Be that as it may, a number of factors are *accelerating* not only Japanese but also U.S. investments in the EU:[40] these concern the possibility of new technical and financial barriers and national quotas to avoid intra-EU diversion of trade when the controls on intra-Union borders are lifted, as well as the anticipation of growing markets in Eastern Europe. The European economic network continues to be pulled in a variety of directions by its constituent national sovereignties and by outside (or internalized) pressures. The idea of a coherent, united House of Europe remains remote, notwithstanding the tendencies toward fuller integration.

3-4   *The workforce and its "S&E" core*

The microelectronic revolution has been in progress for well over half a century. Its significance was at first overshadowed by the large-scale expansion of nuclear energy. But its importance and enduring consequences have become increasingly evident. Microelectronic technologies developed at a moderate pace until the late 1940s. Since then, a number of major breakthroughs have given it nonstop impetus. Two critical changes occurred in the late 1940s. One was the construction of programmable electronic computers, the other the invention of the transistor. Subsequent developments in semiconductor electronics led to the present-day silicon chip. About 1960, solid-state devices were incorporated into computers, sharply increasing the latter's capabilities. The crucial idea of combining more than one transistor on the same piece of semiconductor material inaugurated the era of *integrated circuits,* whose ability to perform useful functions grew exponentially with each passing year. The miniaturization of transistors allowed the creation of sophisticated electronic circuits with millions of transistors on a single silicon chip, in particular the *microprocessor,* the general-purpose logic element programmable to perform an almost unlimited number of functions, and *memory chips,* boasting vast and increasingly expanding capabilities. These innovations have expanded the application of both computer and noncomputer electronics to communications and information, to military weaponry and strategy, and to the system of production of goods and services, and have reshaped our way of life in numerous respects.

How did these developments impact the demand for and the supply of labor in regard to job patterns, schooling levels, and earnings – in, for instance, the United States? How does the U.S. compare with its challengers in regard to production of the core of technological change by its scientists and engineers? Do the occupational patterns of scientists and engineers differ in the countries we have been considering?

From the 1950s on, crucial changes took place in the structure of the American workforce, some due to innovations and technological changes, others attributable to shifts in demand patterns, in productivity, in resource reallocations, in comparative advantage, and in global markets. The respective shares of *white-collar* and of *blue-collar* workers changed appreciably. Thus, white-collar workers (managerial and administrative personnel, professionals and technicians, sales personnel, and administrative support staff, including clerical) rose from 37 percent of the 59.6-million-strong employed workforce of the 1950s, to 43 percent of the total of 66.6 million employed in the early 1960s, to 47 percent of the 79.8 million employed in the early 1970s, and then to close to 57 percent of the 117.3 million employed at the end of the 1980s. The share of service occupations (protective services, health services, and personal services) also increased, while the share of blue-collar workers (craft and repair workers, machine operators, handlers, helpers, and laborers), as well as that of farm occupations, decreased. The blue-collar share fell from some 39 percent of the total workforce in the 1950s to 27 percent at the end of the 1980s.

Within the white-collar groups, the critical share of professionals and technicians among the employed rose the fastest. The numbers of these "nonacademic scientists and engineers" (S&E) – i.e., excluding those employed in educational institutions and government – rose as follows. *Scientists* (narrowly defined to include only chemists, geologists, biologists, and life scientists, as well as mathematical and computer researchers and analysts) and *engineers* (namely, aerospace engineers, electrical and electronic engineers, chemical engineers, civil engineers, and industrial and mechanical engineers) increased from close to 1.7 million in 1970 to close to 3.1 million at the end of the 1980s. Including the scientific and engineering technicians in these same categories, the S&E total rose from 2.5 million in 1970 to over 4.2 million at the end of the 1980s.[41]

During the decades considered, the years of schooling of the workforce also tended to register significant increases. According to official labor statistics, a notable decrease was registered during the 1970s and 1980s within the American *civilian labor force* (of individuals 25 to 64 years of age) in the share of the workers with less than high school education, accompanied by a corresponding increase in the workforce with one to four years or more of college. Yet, at the center, the share of those with only high school diplomas remained stationary. Thus in 1970, out of a civilian labor force of 61.7 million, 36 percent had less than a high school education, 38 percent had a high school diploma, and 26 percent had some college study or full college training. By 1989, out of a civilian labor force of 97.3 million, the percentage of the less educated had dropped to 14 percent and that of the higher educated had increased to 46 percent, while those with only a high school diploma continued to account for 39 percent of the total.[42] From the 1970s through the 1980s, the market apparently penalized the fraction of the workforce with less than 12 years of schooling (i.e., up to a high school senior) and increased the rewards of those with one to three years of college or more. According to Marvin H. Kosters, the earnings of the lowest fraction declined by some 13 percentage points. At the same time, the earnings of those with 13 to 16 years of schooling or more (i.e., of those with one to three years of college or more) increased by 7 percentage points, while the rewards of those with only the high school diploma remained roughly the same.[43] Incidentally, poverty rates are also related to the years of school completed by a householder. In 1990 the poverty rate was 21.8 percent for householders who had not completed high school, 9.3 percent for those who had graduated from high school, and 3.8 percent for householders who had completed one or more years of college.[44]

Clearly one cannot assume that throughout the economy *technological change* alone had led to redefinitions of jobs and revised earnings levels among occupational groups with different schooling. First, the effects of technological development have not been necessarily uniform throughout all sectors of the economy nor within any one sector, nor even within the special group of so-called high-tech industries. Secondly, the effects of technological change cannot be separated from other economic or demographic factors. In regard to the former, one may note for instance that the slowdown in productivity which took place through the 1970s and part of the 1980s undoubtedly affected average real hourly earnings in all private nonagricultural industries. This average rose year in and year out through the 1960s, climbing from some $6.80 (in 1982 dollars) to close to $8. After continuing to rise in the early 1970s (going up to $8.50), average hourly earnings started to decline, dropping through the 1980s from about $7.80 to $7.50 by 1990.[45] On the other hand, it should also be noted that these fluctuations did not affect the underlying basic disparities in average earnings which have traditionally prevailed among industries. Thus, through the decades considered, the average hourly earnings of production workers, going in descending order for workers in construction, mining, transportation, manufacturing, and wholesale, continued to remain *above* average hourly earnings in the economy as a whole, while they fell *below* the average for retail sales people and for other service employees. In manufacturing itself, the traditional intrasectoral disparities were not affected. By the end of the 1980s, as at the beginning of the 1970s, the average hourly earnings of production workers on manufacturing payrolls ranged in descending order as follows. The earnings of workers in petroleum and coal production, chemicals, tobacco products, motor vehicles and other transportation equipment, industrial machinery and equipment, primary metals, fabricated metal products, and printing and publishing remained above average. Workers' earnings hovered at around the average in electronic and other electrical equipment and in instruments and related products. Finally, earnings were below the average in food and kindred products, lumber and wood products, furniture and fixtures, and other miscellaneous manufactures (including notably textiles and apparel).[46] Even within the group loosely defined as high-tech industries, wide gaps continued to exist among average earnings in, say, industrial chemicals and drugs and pharmaceutical products, engines and turbines and special industrial machinery, office and computer equipment and other equipment, communication equipment, and aircraft engines. Each, of course, had grown at a different pace (in the United States as in Japan and Germany), each had a different occupational structure, and each faced a different set of demands.

A significant number of analysts still argue that jobs have been clearly shifting from the middle-paying jobs in the economy as a whole (particularly in manufacturing) to both lower- and higher-paying jobs, grinding down on the middle class. This bipolarization would be due in part to the growth of high-tech industries, and in part to the disappearance of smokestack industries, the pressures of competition, and the shift from manufacturing to service-producing industries. Other writers point out that *most* if not all production workers in the so-called high-tech industries have hourly earnings above average; i.e., these industries do not contribute to bipolarization.[47] At bottom, the conflicting arguments on the impact of high tech on jobs, earnings, and educational levels hark back to a deep-seated and never-ending debate on industrialization to which I shall return in detail in Parts III and IV of this work. For the moment, let me note that one school of thought argues that, as in all the industrialization processes of the past, the technological processes rooted in the electronics revolution necessarily simplify and routinize certain work tasks, thus eliminating entire classes of skilled and semi-skilled workers and generating low-paying jobs.[48] Others assert that the new technological processes give birth to new industries, create new jobs, and in many respects open new directions, so that one cannot look at the past and predict the future any more than one can drive a car forward by looking in the rear-view mirror.[49]

The critical forces in technological development are, as I pointed out, the scientists and the engineers (S&E). How does the U.S. achievement in this regard compare with those of its challengers, Japan and Germany? What is the pace of S&E growth in the United States and abroad? Toward the end of the 1980s, over one million Americans annually acquired their first university degree, as compared to some 383,000 in Japan and close to 75,000 in Germany.[50] Also in that year, the United States awarded over 33,000 doctoral degrees in all fields, compared to 9,000 in Japan and 17,000 in West Germany. The S&E *core* of the doctoral degrees, potentially crucial with regard to technological change, comprised over 14,600 doctoral recipients in the United States, 3,000 in Japan, and 6,000 in West Germany. While it is true that a certain portion of the U.S. degrees were awarded to foreign nationals, the United States imported over 1,000 natural scientists and over 8,000 engineers yearly through immigration during the same period.

Toward the middle of the 1980s the U.S. counted in its workforce 3.9 million nonacademic S&Es – broadly defined to include psychologists and social scientists as well as natural scientists and mathematical and computer analysts – employed in business and industry, educational institutions, and government. This total compared to 1.5 million in Japan and to some 620,000 in West Germany. However, it should be noted that the numbers of S&Es (broadly defined) per 10,000 employees in the labor force were closely similar in the three countries. Moreover, from the mid 1960s through the 1980s, great strides were made in the increase of S&Es engaged in R&D, particularly in the U.S. and Japan. From 1965 to 1987, the numbers increased in the U.S. by some 60 percent (from 76,400 to 121,600) and in Japan by 27 percent (from 47,800 to 60,800). In the other industrialized countries, notably West Germany, France, Italy, and the United Kingdom, these numbers fluctuated in each from between 20,000 and 25,000 to between 25,000 and 28,000.

The economic and technological factors which have been impacting the labor force's occupational patterns, educational levels, and earnings disparities in a variety of ways have not hindered the systematic nurturing of the S&E core of technological change in all the countries considered, nor have they diminished the United States' leadership. The U.S. continues to produce through its system of higher education, and to absorb through immigration, the S&E cohorts needed to keep up its high-quality research output, its rate of technological innovation, and its competitive growth.

3-5   Speed, size, proportions

The confluence of two distinct yet critically decisive series of events – the agony and then the implosion of the ex-Soviet Union on the one hand, and the apparently unflagging economic dynamism of Japan and Germany (up to the 1990s) on the other – have shifted the focus of the old controversy on *economic efficiency* from capitalism vs. communism to the assessment and comparison of various models of "organized" capitalism, especially as regards their capacity to effectively carry out vast technological transformations.

Let me recall briefly the key features of the economic challenge facing the primarily market-directed U.S. economy. Postwar Japan's tightly interwoven state and private economy has yielded high rates of GDP growth, high rates of growth in fixed capital formation, high productivity, and strong global trade leadership – all of which have proven difficult to match. Concomitantly, the rise of unified Germany astride both Western and East Central Europe has added to the challenge: its peculiarly interlocked banking and industrial system, its increasingly determining role not only in the European Union but throughout the entire former Soviet domain, and the decisive role of its currency as well as of its unmatched industrial machinery are bound to play critical roles in the contest for industrial supremacy in the 21st century and in the shaping of the ways in which nations and economies produce, invest, trade, and compete.

Between 1960 and 1987 the annual average growth rates of GDP were on the order of 3.3 percent for the United States, compared to the very high rates of 6.5 percent for Japan and of 13.1 for Germany. The GDP share allocated to gross fixed capital formation (GFCF), above all in Japan and then in West Germany, was consistently and significantly higher than that allocated thereto by the United States between 1960 and 1989. During these years, U.S. GFCF as a percentage of GDP fluctuated at between 16 and 17 (except in 1965, when it reached 18.7). In the case of Japan, this percentage rose from some 20 in 1960 to 25 in 1965, and maintained itself afterwards at between 29 and 32. In the case of Germany, the figure rose to 26 percent in 1965 and then declined to slightly over 20 percent by the end of the 1980s. Further, Japan's and Germany's yearly rates of investment in the business sector significantly exceeded those of the U.S. in this period (in the 1980s they reached 9.6, 7.4, and 6.2 percent respectively). Finally, with respect to both total factor productivity (TFP) in the business sector and labor productivity in the business sector, the rates attained by the challengers of the U.S. were also appreciably higher.[51] While the shape of the broad *trends* for the entire period 1960–89 was for all the countries considered closely *similar* – namely, showing a deep inflection in the mid 1970s, and descending in the 1980s in relation to the 1960s – the levels attained by each country were, of course, significantly different all along.

Yet all these changes and differences must necessarily be evaluated in relation to the *size* of the economies involved. Size, *in conjunction* with *total and per capita income*, determines the investment potential, the dimensions of the labor force, the scope of manufacturing, the breadth of the domestic market, and the potential for trade and global competition. It may be useful to examine Table 3-5, which groups various size indicators as of the end of the 1980s. To start with, Japan's population barely equaled half that of the United States, while unified Germany's population – an immense force in Central Europe – equaled about one third that of the United States. While the U.S. manufacturing labor force (based on firms' surveys) just equaled that of Japan and Germany combined, clearly each of the latter countries had made appreciable strides in regard to manufacturing productivity and output, as we shall see in detail in Chapter 4. Further, they had secured important positions in the global market. As I have already pointed out, both Germany and Japan reasserted their original important spheres of influence – the first in chemicals, fabricated iron and steel products, metal manufacturing, and machinery; the second also in machinery in general as well as in regard to new lines of penetration in high-tech manufacturing, namely communication equipment and office computing machinery, along with exports in cars, trucks, buses, and motorcycles.

Given the initial levels of development in the countries considered, the most immediate relations between speed of economic growth and underlying size are reflected in the changing proportions over time of their respective total and per capita GDPs. As can be seen from Table 3-6, toward the end of the 1980s, whichever way the GDP comparisons are made – in constant price data converted into dollars at the prevailing exchange rates, or in purchasing power parities – Japan's GDP was still roughly one third that of the United States, and West Germany's roughly one half that of Japan. While the usual economic development indicator, per capita GDP, shows that West Germany and Japan are not very far from the U.S. level in terms of total GDP, in terms of potential investment (from domestic sources), range of alternatives, size of the market, and so on, the distances between the three economies remain huge and unbridgeable.

This, however, does not mean that the United States can, or does, look complacently upon the challenge represented by the rapidly growing and highly competitive Japanese and German economies, both in the global market and even in its own domestic market. Yet does the postwar meteoric rise of Japan and Germany, contrasted to the slower pace of growth of the United

Table 3-5. *U.S., Japan, and Germany (West): selected size indicators, 1988–1990*

Countries	Population (1990)		Employment (1989)		Empl. in Manuf. (1989)		Exports (1988)		Imports (1988)	
	Millions	Percent of U.S.	Millions	Percent of U.S.	Millions	Percent of U.S.	Billion $	Percent of U.S.	Billion $	Percent of U.S.
United States	251.5	100	113.4	100	17.7	100	321.8	100	459.6	100
Japan	123.5	49	64.3	56	10.9	61	264.9	82	187.3	41
Germany*	79.5	32	27.6	24	6.9	39	323.2	100	250.4	54

*1990 data, unified Germany; other data, West Germany only.
Sources: Population: OECD, Main Economic Indicators, Paris, OECD, February 1992, p. 180; employment: OECD, Industrial Structure Statistics 1989/90, pp. 44, 72, 142; exports and imports: Statistical Yearbook, New York, United Nations, 1990, pp. 621–625.

Table 3-6. *U.S., Japan, and Germany (West): gross domestic product: total and per capita as percentage of U.S., 1970, 1980, and 1988*

	GDP*			Per	capita	GDP*
Countries	1970	1980	1988	1970	1980	1988
United States	100	100	100	100	100	100
Japan	26	32	34	52	62	68
W. Germany	17	17	15	58	63	61
United States	100	100	100	100	100	100
Japan	28	34	36	67	67	72
W. Germany	20	20	18	69	75	73

*Upper part of the table: Comparisons based on constant (1985) price data converted to U.S. dollars using 1985 exchange rates. Lower part of the table: Comparisons based on purchasing power parity (PPP), showing how many units of currency are needed in one country to buy the same amount of goods and services one unit of currency will buy in the other country.
Sources: Statistical Abstract of the United States 1991, pp. 842, 843; OECD, National Accounts 1960-1988, Paris, OECD, 1990; OECD, National Accounts 1977-1989, Paris, OECD, 1991.

States, imply that the latter has reached some obscurely defined "maturity" and that it is headed for stagnation and decline? Does it imply that the United States must hastily adjust the operations of its economy to mimic the Japanese and German managed-capitalist models in order to "save" itself? Are such adjustments actually cost-effective or even feasible, let alone "compelling"? Still, how can the United States meet the challenge – in terms of rates of growth, productivity, capital formation, and competition in the global markets? These are the questions to which I shall turn in the next chapter.

4   The implications

4-1   *The decline diagnosis*

In sharp contrast to the overconfident 1960s, anxious perceptions started to grip the United States from the mid 1970s on. Many factors contributed to the country's changing mood: first, the deep and, it was supposed, unusual shifts in employment away from manufacturing and toward services; second, the concurrence of unemployment and inflation; third, the new and unfamiliar relations between saving, investment, and the inflow of foreign capital; fourth, the increasing competition in world markets; and fifth, management's apparent failure to adjust efficiently to the complex needs generated by all these transformations. In the 1970s the country was experiencing its seventh postwar recession – called by some the "second coming," with reference to the 1930s – a recession which was indeed deeper than the six which had preceded it. The crisis hobbling the economy – the slowdown in growth of the GNP, the low rates of capital formation and productivity, the high rates of unemployment and of inflation, the sharpening competition in international markets – all seemed to indicate, at least to some economic and political analysts, that America was losing its vitality and dynamism along with its leadership in the world economy. Concerns with the economy's performance stimulated intense debate on the causes of the country's "decline"; on the conduct and scope of the government's policies, particularly toward manufacture and trade; on whether the traditional tools of fiscal and monetary policy were sufficient to address the economy's problems or whether the entire matrix of government-business relations had better be completely overhauled. Approaches to the latter issues involved a series of proposals under a variety of titles ranging from "economic revitalization" to "economic renewal" and "reindustrialization," stressing the need for a "holistic" or "coherent" industrial policy. I shall first sketch the outline of this theory and then examine critically its flawed assumptions and conclusions.

The decline thesis, as it took shape in the early to mid 1970s, and as it was further elaborated throughout the 1980s, was predicated on the assertion that the country was engaged in a complex process of deindustrialization – a process allegedly evidenced by the "aging" and decay of our "basic" industries; the contraction of manufacturing employment; the slow emergence of new technologically advanced industries capable of absorbing the slack in employment; the sluggish pace of innovation and of development of new products; the increasing transfer of production facilities abroad; the falling rates of capital formation; the loss of former key positions in foreign markets; and the increased penetration of foreign goods and capital into our markets and domestic industries. America's decline trajectory was said to be, in fact, similar to that followed by Great Britain from the end of the last century onward.

Consider these contentions in turn. Assertions about the impact of the alleged *aging* of American industry are not new. Similar allegations had been made in the 1930s, long before their reemergence in the late 1970s. However, the answers to the questions involved were different in the two periods. These questions, according to R. D. Norton, are: Why do industries tend to show, in the process of economic change, a retardation in output and employment growth? And why does aging erode industrial competitiveness in world markets? According to the theories in fashion in the 1930s – as formulated then most notably by Alvin Hansen – in the earlier development of American technology there was a continual tendency toward capital deepening, that is toward an increase in the ratio of investment to output. Expansion of the stock of capital per capita was especially favored by the appearance of new industries of major importance (viz. turnpikes and canals, then in turn the railroads, the electrical industry, and the automobile). However, as technology matured, investment began to fall behind output. Stagnation set in because of the dearth of great new industries, the shrinkage of investment opportunities, and the increasing tendency toward oversaving.[1] As we now know, the subsequent development of the U.S. economy made short shrift of the ideas of technical maturity, of the dearth of great industries, and of the danger of oversaving.

The theorists of the late 1970s and early 1980s – notably Ira C. Magaziner and Robert B. Reich – asserted that the "competitive declines" in textiles, apparel, footwear, steel, automobiles, and several other major U.S. industries were due to both slower economic growth and greater exposure to international competition. According to Reich, for instance, the slower growth was due to the gradual depletion of resources, the end of labor migration from the farm, the entry of young people and of women into the labor force, and the inconsistencies of government policies in regard to health, safety, and the environment. Because of slower growth, young industries, said Reich, were not "springing up of their own accord to replace the old," while concomitantly key industries were experiencing increasing unemployment and underutilized capacity. This might have changed if the government had eased the flow of capital and labor to the most competitive businesses within an industry or outside the industry on the basis of systematic programs "helping industries to restructure themselves and salvage their most competitive parts."[2] Meanwhile, manufacturing workers unable to find full-time jobs utilizing their skills and providing enough income to support their families were drifting toward low-paid jobs in the service sector. In a 1982 book entitled *The Deindustrialization of America* – a work which Alfred Kahn described as "an ideological tract . . . intensely irritating but important" – Barry Bluestone and Bennett Harrison asserted that the country's decline was marked by "plant closings, community abandonment, the dismantling of basic industry," and the displacement of workers, who were forced to look for jobs in low-paid, low-skill service industries. All this was attributable to a large extent to the "desperate attempt" of the managers of basic industries – particularly of the old smokestack plants of the frostbelt states – to restore or preserve in the 1970s the rates of profit to which they had become accustomed in the halcyon days of the 1950s and 1960s. Many managers allegedly abandoned competition, reduced investment, cut the workforce, curtailed labor costs, circumvented taxes and regulations, and shifted capital as rapidly as possible from one activity in one region or nation to another, and in the process "the industrial base of the American economy began to come apart at the seams."[3] Others asserted that the moves offshore were also accompanied by a "wave of mergers and acquisitions . . . financed by running down older production capacity."[4] When producers moved their plants abroad, their suppliers also moved offshore, thus speeding up the emergence of their own competitors. Such moves blinded the firms' managers to the possibilities and needs of automating at home, and, moreover, helped build expertise in offshore management rather than in the management of most advanced technologies at home. In short, America must reverse course and "automate, not emigrate."[5]

Contrary to the 1930s maturity and stagnation theses, this time the source of the U.S. decline was attributed to *under*saving rather than to *over*saving. According to such commentators as Jerry J. Jasinowski (then assistant secretary for policy in the U.S. Department of Commerce), less job creation, modest production increases, and lower productivity were due to the rising cost of capital, particularly in relation to other factors of production, resulting in insufficient investment relative to the growth in the labor supply and to the increasing technological obsolescence of existing capital.[6] Richard W. Rahn (chief economist of the Chamber of Commerce) summarized the same basic idea in a short formula: "The decline of real capital formation – i.e., savings and productive investment – is at the root of the decline."[7] Others attributed underinvestment to the bad habits of middle-class consumers, who had "taken up spending in advance of income through the use of consumer credit,"[8] and still others added later that the chief counterpart of our overconsumption in the 1980s had been underinvestment, following which "the historical trend toward more capital-intensive production – that is, more capital on average for each worker – has all but stopped."[9] Lester C. Thurow proclaimed forcefully that America did not have "an economy marked by world-class inputs." Its investments in plant and equipment were below those of Japan and Western Europe. In theory, added Thurow, one does not need to have "a world-class level of savings to have a world-class level of investment," since the necessary investment can be borrowed, but the interest payments become a drag on the U.S. economy. This means, concluded Thurow, that "higher investment rates will in fact require higher saving rates," but whether such changes can be sold as necessary for economic growth remains to be seen.[10]

To the assumed characteristics of decline – industrial aging, shift of labor away from manufacturing and toward services, unfavorable savings-investment relationship – one must also add the allegedly overall *poor performance* of American manufacture. According to Charles P. Kindleberger, for instance, there seemed to be in the U.S. of the mid 1970s "a dearth of new products, or old products produced cheaply by new processes, to take their place." Moreover, American R&D did not seem to produce "the commercial winners of the past."[11] In the same vein, a group of MIT writers charged at the end of the 1980s that American industry was not producing as well as it used to, as well as it ought to, or as well as other nations were now succeeding in producing. Our factories were said to be inefficient, our workers poorly trained, and our designers and engineers mired in lagging technologies. Fears of economic decline, added these writers, "are surely linked to larger doubts about the nation's ability to retain its influence and standing in the world at large"; and they then concluded that though there were various encouraging indications, their verdict was that "American industry indeed shows worrisome signs of weakness," signs symptomatic of "systematic and pervasive ills."[12]

A whole group of authors – notably Lester C. Thurow and Robert B. Reich (subsequently President Clinton's secretary of labor), Laura d'Andrea Tyson (President Clinton's first chairperson of the Council of Economic Advisers), and some of her co-authors, such as John Zysman and Stephen Cohen, to mention only the most representative – have consistently subscribed to the contention that America's economy has been slowly unraveling since the late 1960s, and that its weakening position and its waning preeminence in international industrial competition revealed the picture of a troubled national adjustment to a changing world economy. Relative to its competitors, the U.S. supposedly displayed a "radical inability to apply high-tech to the production of traditional goods and to maintain our competitive position by diffusing technology and know-how widely throughout the manufacturing economy."[13] This inability to transform the economy and to compete was allegedly due to the conjunction of business executives' myopia about the value of immediate profits in lieu of investment in long-term projects and our nation's and our government's *ideology,* which forbade us "to accept the need for a *national strategy*" to respond quickly to international market changes and particularly to Japan's willingness "to invest years of effort and to lose hundreds of millions of dollars to maximize global market share."[14]

This alleged slowing down of America's vitality, along with its inability to change technologically and to compete, were attributed by Kindleberger to the passing of the U.S. "through some critical stage of the economic aging process – a climacteric, change of life, or economic menopause." Kindleberger added that the series of stages which any living organism exhibits – following a Gomperz S curve with its slow start, rapid progress, and ultimate return to slowdown – were simply "a fact of economic (as it is of all) life." He went on to say that the U.S. climacteric was analogous to the "climacteric of the British economy at the end of the last century" – a kind of natural follow-up, a century later, to the rise and fall of another great power.[15]

Incidentally, the opinions of the historians are divided as to the alleged climacteric phase of Britain. Economic historians do agree that the British economy went through a particularly stressful period in the early 1870s, a time of deep economic crisis when the rising competitive challenges of Germany and of the United States started to loom increasingly large. Alfred Marshall himself noted that Britain had moved from overconfidence at the beginning of 1870 to a "feeling of disquiet" as the commercial depression started in 1873. This feeling grew with the perception of increasing competition, particularly from Germany, whose leadership was rapidly growing "in industries in which academic training and laboratory work can be turned to good account."[16] But the notion of the alleged British climacteric phase – aside from its crude determinism – does not fit the facts. No uniform pattern of economic slowdown is discernible in Britain at the end of the last century. Indeed, while Britain's "black country" declined in the decade 1876–86 as a center of coal and iron production, new industries and new processes expanded in that country from the 1890s onward. Certainly, late in the Victorian era, international competition increased sharply as the Western world reached a high level of economic development characterized by growing industrialization – notably of the United States as well as of Germany and France. But the decade of 1913 was in fact marked by important transformations and adaptations in the British economy. The expansion of industrialization abroad did not turn Britain into a loser: considerable advantages accrued to it from this process. While there has been a decline in Britain's *world status,* its "economic descent" has been marked by periods of recovery, advances, and successes, with material wealth rising, not falling, over the long term.[17] (I shall return in detail to some of these issues in Section 8-1.)

It is on the basis of the decline diagnosis, of the alleged dangerous parallelism of the United States' economic fate with that of Britain and other great powers of the past, juxtaposed with the increasing successes of its competitors, that the proponents of strategies to "restructure" America's investment in manufacturing formulate their proposals. In Section 4-2, I shall present these strategies in detail, complete with the suggested measures for their implementation, the institutions to be created, and the conceptual changes concerning the operation of the market which such policies would entail. Then, in Section 4-3, I shall critically evaluate the decline diagnosis, and in Section 4-4 the industrial policy proposals. The concluding comments of Part II are set out in Section 4-5.

4-2   Holistic industrial policy proposals

An industrial policy is a program of supply-oriented recommendations focusing the government's attention on the country's *technological advances,* on the mobilization of its *financial means for industrial investment,* and on the development of its *human resources.* The implementation of such a policy should lead to the restructuring of the country's manufacture, to the accelerated growth of its "industries of the future," to the increase of its productivity rates, and to the recasting of the patterns of skills and employment of its workforce. The proper combination of these results should yield increased competitiveness in the global market, a competitiveness ensured by adequately *managed trade.*

Some of the measures needed to carry out such recommendations may seem similar to the ad hoc forms of government intervention discussed in Chapter 2. Actually, a holistic industrial policy supposes an *integrated, fully coherent set* of measures with regard to technology, investment, human resources, and trade. Predicated on the contentions of U.S. decline – its sliding productivity rates, its deindustrialization, its technological retardation, and its failure to compete, not to mention its competitors' unfair trade practices – industrial policies call into question many standard economic conceptions concerning the functioning of the market and the role of the government, as we shall see immediately below.

The debate on industrial policy peaked in the congressional elections of 1982 and in the presidential race of 1984, subsequently being revived in the presidential race of the early 1990s. In September 1982, just in time for congressional elections, the House Democratic Caucus Committee on Party Effectiveness issued a crucial report entitled *Rebuilding the Road to Opportunity: A Democratic Direction for the 1980s.* The report, with its yellow cover (promptly dubbed "The Yellow Brick Road") recommended in particular "investment to retool our basic industries and to expand growing industries in the high technology and information sectors"; investment "not only in bricks and machinery, but in our work force as well"; investments in infrastructure; and a "national economic strategy" to monitor "the vitality and changing nature of our domestic economy and the economic strategies of our major competitors." In the summer of 1983 the main Democratic candidates again stressed the urgency of formulating and adopting such a policy. Gary Hart, for instance, affirmed that a coherent industrial strategy including more investment in job training and education was indispensable, as was a "modernization and growth agreement" between employers and trade unions guaranteeing jobs for specified periods in exchange of deferred wage demands. Walter F. Mondale, the Democratic candidate-designate, made industrial policy – a policy largely based on Robert B. Reich's study *The Next American Frontier* (1983) – the heart of his campaign, asserting that as far as competition was concerned he would match "other countries' subsidies product for product and dollar for dollar." An expanded sequel to *Rebuilding the Road of Opportunity,* crafted by the top leaders of the Democratic Party in 1983, was launched in January 1984 by the House Democratic Caucus under the title *Renewing America's Promise: A Democratic Blueprint for Our Nation's Future.* The document dismissed the views of those who "cannot see beyond the myth of the free market to the long-standing reality of interaction between government and private enterprise," and stressed again the urgency of increased government involvement in education, support for R&D, innovation, infrastructure, and "industrial policies, rather than just [in] the energies of individual firms, to influence competitive success." While the defeat of the Democrats seemed to seal the fate of such programs, and while the Republicans dismissed the latter as revivals of the ideas of "statism" and "planning," President Reagan did establish a Commission on Industrial Competitiveness which bore at least a nominal euphemistic kinship with the Democrats' terminology.

Throughout the 1980s, discussions on industrial policy and competitiveness continued both inside and outside the government and produced an enormous assortment of publications. As an observer noted, if one were to attempt to compile a list of even the Congressional hearings bearing on these subjects, the project would soon get out of hand just in deciding which debates on which bills should be included.[18] What I shall try herein is to extract from this mass what I believe to be significant with regard to industrial *targeting;* the *instruments* to be used; the ways of *institutionalizing* industrial policies; and finally, the *conceptual* changes that such policies called forth.

To start with, let me indicate that a "holistic" industrial policy implies both a rejection of the prevailing ways in which government-business relationships are carried out and many basic economic views concerning the operations of the market in general and of foreign trade in particular. The proponents of holistic programs view prevailing U.S. government-business relations as being based on what they disdainfully call "ad hoc-ism" or "ad hockery," allegedly in sharp contrast with the policies of our main trading partners. As Robert F. Wescott rightly put it, our government industrial policies have indeed *not* been industry-specific, have *not* chosen national champions and *not* aimed at nationalizing the "core" industries, have *not* encouraged cartelization or promoted mergers, have *not* enforced coordinated industry programs, and have *not* provided comparatively strong government support for exports.[19] Rather (as I indicated in Chapter 2), the U.S. has relied upon a *series* of measures of widely diverse scope and effects on industry. It is precisely this approach which Ira Magaziner and Robert Reich, for instance, rejected as "the product of fragmented, uncoordinated decisions" of executive agencies, the Congress, and regulatory agencies without "an integrated strategy to use these programs." Reich complained in another work that the policies designed by the government have resulted in a hodgepodge of public policies "bearing no direct relation to overall industrial growth." Moreover, added Reich, in the absence of an integrated policy, industries and firms can impose costs on those unrepresented in the government-business bargains, namely consumers, emerging industries, employees, and communities.[20]

A rather specious critique of the classical views of technological change and of free trade – i.e., the conception of comparative advantage – has been put forth by Laura d'Andrea Tyson and her co-writers. According to them, the classical theory reveals only "the benign face of trade," namely that material gains arise through expanded exchange. But the theory masks "a malign face of trade," namely that there can be losers as well as winners from trade, depending on each national level of development, which can be actively shaped by *government policies.*[21] The classical theory fails to capture the modern "technological essence" of production and hence constitutes only an imperfect guide to both industrial policy and trade policy. A proper approach to these policies must take full account of the characteristics of the industrial structure, as well as of its changes, the patterns of trade which it conditions, and the circumstances in which this trade takes place. Within such a framework, *static* considerations are not helpful; what matters are *dynamic* comparative advantages. Tyson and her associates thus resuscitated arguments used not long ago by policy advisers to less developed countries in favor of import-substituting industries. "Static" advantage accruing to each of two trading partners concentrating efforts and trading on the products of their most efficient lines of production, given their prevailing resources, scale, and technological endowments *at any point in time,* were dismissed as being of secondary importance. What mattered in trading, they said, is not the ability of traders to take advantage of *prevailing* differences, but rather the ability of the government to *modify* these differences via appropriate, "strategic" trade choices. In this light, the traditional "policy prescription implied by international trade theory is no longer obvious."[22] Indeed, "the competitive advantage of a nation's producers in world markets *is created by policy* rather than given by immutable resource and technological endowments."[23] In essence, a nation forges its own comparative advantage by the efforts of its government and industries to focus on and to capture certain specific undisputable trade advantages (defined in the context as *absolute advantages*) in the market.[24] This advocacy of strategic trade policies found immediate favor with the Executive Council of the AFL-CIO. The Resolution on International Trade and Investment adopted in 1989 by the Eighteenth Convention of that organization stated in its special style: "It is increasingly clear that the academic abstractions of the free trade theory and comparative advantage, upon which current U.S. government policy is based, are not guides to the management of economic issues between nations but a rationale for policies that support the interests of international business."[25]

While Laura Tyson and her co-authors tried to build some kind of theoretical basis for their contention that government policies shape a nation's trade advantage, most of the other partisans of industrial policies took this idea for granted. What they stressed was that the United States should aim specifically to achieve absolute advantage in *high-value-added exports*, and that this kind of advantage could be brought about by appropriate, coherent microeconomic policies concerning investment. Magaziner and Reich reproached the U.S. government with having "failed to help our companies gain competitive productivity in world markets," and deplored the fact that no government program affecting resource-allocation decisions directly or indirectly had been viewed as a part of "a coherent industrial policy."[26] Subsequently, Robert Reich further extended this idea of high-value-added targets to jobs. Americans have become part of the international labor market, he stated, and what matters ultimately is the *quality* of one's labor force.[27] Thus, competitiveness finally boiled down for him to the urgent need for investment in *human capital,* an investment in which the government would be called upon to play the decisive role.

Which, then, are the critical components of holistic national strategies in regard to (a) manufacturing, (b) trade and competitiveness, (c) employment and training?

Concerning manufacture, one may distinguish three industrial-policy strategy options: *defensive, offensive,* and *adaptive.* The first entails direct government support, particularly to basic industries, combined with variously selected forms of protection. The second posits the targeting of certain industries for special subsidies and support, and the raising of investment rates up to the levels of the competitors. To the first approach (freezing existing production patterns) and the second (promoting targeted industries) the third adds the idea of helping industries to adapt to change via adjustment assistance and, at times, efforts to delay the pace of change.[28] While the Republicans have consistently inclined toward the traditional mix of the defensive and adjustment approaches, from the early 1980s on the Democratic center has been moving toward a mix of defensive and offensive strategies, with the latter increasingly dominating. Already during the last years of the Carter administration, a number of top officials urged the president to "create [industrial] winners," encourage high-tech industries, restructure the less efficient ones, and facilitate "positive adjustment." But at the time most high economic advisers, including the chairman of the Council of Economic Advisers, Charles L. Schultze, remained strongly skeptical about such policies.[29] Subsequently, however, the promotion of the idea of coherent industrial policies was taken over by various congressional committees, by Democratic congressional leaders, and by their best-known advisers, Robert Reich and Lester Thurow.[30]

With regard to trade and competitiveness, the fundamental policy options involve a *passive* or a *positive* strategy. The passive strategy is predicated on the assumption that problems involving U.S. international competitiveness are not issues of direct concern for the U.S. balance of payments. Any given trend in the trade balance can reverse itself, income from U.S. investments abroad can offset declines in the trade balance, and substantial current-account deficits can be continually financed by capital inflows. The positive strategy, on the other hand, is predicated on the assumption that government policy creates comparative advantages and, moreover, that foreign interference with competition negates the need for a domestic policy of competition enforced by law. The government must attempt to ease international barriers while revamping domestic industry, expanding the infrastructure, unshackling exports by removing any restrictive legislation, and making imports less attractive. The last can be achieved either through protectionist measures or through an exchange rate devaluation. These measures coalesce two overlapping sets of interests: those of industries struggling against manufactured imports, and those of industries competing in the global market to expand exports.[31]

Clearly, a holistic industrial policy joins a positive strategy toward competitiveness with an offensive strategy vis-à-vis manufacture. Such a combination further requires the continual training and retraining of the workforce – moving it increasingly away from routine production and, in Reich's vision, increasingly toward "high-value symbolic-analytic activities" (including in particular "problem-solving, problem identifying and strategic brokerage activities").[32]

Which specific measures would all the aspects of such a holistic national strategy involve, and how would they interact in its implementation? To answer this question let me first recall briefly the connections between government goals, policies, and instruments. Government economic *goals* usually refer to employment and growth, stabilization, distributional equity, and allocative efficiency. The goals are implemented through various *policies* – fiscal, monetary, foreign-trade, industrial, welfare, environmental, educational, and so on. The policies are executed via the use of various *instruments.* The latter may be grouped into instruments of direct control (of enterprises, branches, and sectors and of foreign trade); of public finance (related or not to direct controls); of money and credit (again, related or not to direct controls); and of institutional change (affecting the other instruments or the production framework). Besides reliance on instruments of pubic finance and of money and credit, a holistic national strategy with the indicated characteristics would also have to resort eventually to instruments of direct control (such as control of investment, control of prices and wages, exchange control, control of import and export prices and mixes) and possibly to institutional changes concerning the system of direct controls, the system of subsidies, the tax system, regulations and antitrust statutes, and the extent of public ownership as well.[33]

Various proposals have been put forth as to the institutions which would select the industries to be supported, coordinate the policies involved, and provide for their financing. Felix G. Rohatyn, for instance, suggested that a single institution, a revived Reconstruction and Finance Corporation (RFC) of the 1930s type, could receive proposals from the industries which wanted to be "rejuvenated" and decide case by case which ones should be supported. The proposal was criticized as implying that the RFC would *determine* rather than *discover* the successful enterprises or industries. More commonly, proposals have asserted the need for two institutions. A bill proposed by Senator William V. Roth would have established a new Department of Trade and Industry on the model of the Japanese MITI, combining the Office of the U.S. Trade Representative and elements of the Department of Commerce; an amendment to the bill would have created, in addition, an Office of Competitive Analysis to assemble and analyze data more strategically. Other proposals have stressed the need for an industrial or an industrial competitiveness board, and for a supporting financial institution. Congressman Stan Lundine sponsored a National Industrial Development Bank which would raise and lend its own funds, and Congressman John J. LaFalci introduced other bills which would have created a Council on Industrial Competitiveness and a Bank for Industrial Competitiveness to invest in and lend to firms in mature or emerging industries.[34] These and other proposals of the same nature would require, as Robert W. Russell points out, a massive delegation of congressional authority to entities located within the executive branch or wholly outside the government. But this would involve fundamental changes in the character of Congress and in the existing legislative process.[35]

The formulation and implementation of a coherent, holistic national strategy concerning manufacturing and trade raises, as I noted at the outset, problems connected with the nation's traditional beliefs and with the functioning of a primarily market-directed economy and policy. As Magaziner and Reich have regretfully noted, the U.S. is not a nation of "planners" and lacks the experience of an "expert and independent civil service," and "the hurly-burly of its democratic system mirrors the untidy competitive marketplace." Britain and

America, noted Reich in another place, are trapped in an "ideology" that does not recognize the need of a national strategy to respond quickly to change. This ideology allegedly sidetracks the country into endless debates about free markets and planning instead of letting it become aware that the real choice now is between "evading the new global context or engaging in it." Another staunch defender of industrial policies, Chalmers Johnson, affirmed that the idea of such policies challenges many American beliefs, notably "the commitment to the market mechanism as the supreme arbiter of economic decisions." And Lester Thurow assures us that if one is looking for the key to Japan's successes, one need not look in "the economics of Anglo-Saxon profit maximization" but rather in the analysis of empire builders, in "the universal desire to build, to belong to an empire, to conquer neighboring empires, and to become the world's leading economic power." Those remembered by history, added Thurow, "are not the great consumers. They are the conquerors, the builders, the producers – Caesar, Genghis Khan, Rockefeller, Ford."[36]

Thus, in the opinion of the most representative exponents of holistic industrial policies, changes in industrial structure, in the way "winning" industries are selected, in the level of government investment, in the education of human resources, and in the country's approaches to international trade are indispensable not only to properly restructure the economy's framework and assure economic growth, but also in order to change traditional beliefs and misconceptions about the market, and thus guarantee the nation's future and its leadership in the concert of nations.

4-3   Critique of the decline thesis

At the core of the thesis of U.S. decline is, as we saw, the crucial contention that the country's course is set toward *deindustrialization* – a process involving all kinds of detrimental shifts in the structure of the country's employment, its manufacturing branches, and its position in the world market.

As can be seen from Table 4-1, from 1960 to 1990 there was indeed a sharp and steady decrease in the *relative* share of manufacturing employment in total private-sector employment. While this latter total increased by over 99 percent between 1960 and 1990, manufacturing employment increased by only slightly over 13 percent. Further, during the 1980s, while total employment in the private sector expanded by a hefty 17.3 million jobs, manufacturing employment lost 1.2 million jobs (and an equal number of production workers).

However, these different trends in employment reflect to a large degree not an economy careering toward deindustrialization, but a leap in rates of productivity. Manufacturing output increased remarkably between 1960 and 1989; on the basis 1982 = 100, it rose from 55 to over 150. During the 1980s alone, it went from 106 to 151. Again, between 1960 and the end of the 1980s the share

Table 4-1. *U.S.: quinquennial changes in manufacturing employment, 1960–1990: absolute figures (thousands) and percentages*

	1960	1965	1970	1975	1980	1985	1990
Total Employees*	54,234	60,185	70,880	76,945	90,406	97,519	109,782
Private Sector	45,881	50,741	58,325	62,259	74,166	81,125	91,478
Manufacturing Employees	16,796	18,062	19,367	18,323	20,285	19,260	19,062
Of Whom Production Workers	12,586	13,434	14,050	13,043	14,214	13,092	12,979
Percent of Manuf. Employees in Total in Private Sector	36.6	35.6	33.2	29.4	27.4	23.7	20.8

*All full- or part-time employees who received pay.
Sources: Statistical Abstract of the United States 1961, p. 221; 1971, p. 219; 1981, p. 396; 1990, p. 395; 1992, p. 406; U.S. Department of Labor, Bureau of Labor Statistics, Monthly Labor Review, September 1992, p. 67.

of manufacturing in the real gross national product, at 1982 prices, rose from 21 percent in 1960 to 23 percent in 1988.[37] It is often asserted that the U.S. economy has been driving newly unemployed manufacturing workers to "hamburger flipping." It is true that employment in drinking and eating places increased in the 1980s by 1.8 million workers, but larger increases were registered during the same period in health services (2.2 million) and in business services, including computer and data processing (2.3 million), along with smaller increases in legal, educational, and social services; mechanical and transportation services; utility services; general merchandise stores; finance and insurance; and other specialized services.

The general contentions about the aging and decay of U.S. manufacture reflect a rather simplistic, static view of this sector, its branches, their production facilities, their technologies, and their interrelations. To begin with, dramatic shifts took place from 1947 to 1987 in total employment and in the value added by manufacture, both as a whole and between the constituent manufacturing industries, reflecting complex changes in the patterns of demand, of growth, of productivity, of technological change, and of products, along with changes involving the closing down of obsolete units, the transfer abroad of various facilities, and the establishment of extensive new international connections. Food and kindred products, which held 2nd place in manufacturing employment in 1947, had fallen to the 6th rank 40 years later; textile mill products dropped from 3rd rank to 13th; primary metal products, from 5th to 11th. On the other hand, transport equipment rose from the 4th to the 1st rank; electrical machinery, from the 8th to the 3rd; instruments, from the 18th to the 8th. Out of the 20 two-digit groups of manufacturing, only 4 secondary groups maintained their relative ranks (17th to 20th). The value-added rankings exhibit the same shifts, with the moves to 1st, 2nd, and 3rd rank of transport equipment, electrical machinery, and nonelectric industrial machinery, respectively.[38]

In regard to vast transformations *within* industries, of particular interest are the cases of iron and steel, of machinery (machine tools in particular), and of microelectronics. Employment in U.S. blast furnaces and in iron and steel products has shrunk spectacularly – from 653,000 in 1960 (compared to 674,000 in 1950) to 627,000 in 1970, 512,000 in 1980, and, most precipitously, to 278,000 by the end of the 1980s. Faced by a declining demand for their products, more uses for lighter materials, expanding competition from both the new domestic minimills and imports, the managers of the old large integrated steel mills were confronted by a number of crucial choices. In the early 1980s there were 14 such integrated mills: of these, 3 suffered bankruptcy, 1 closed, and 1 became owned by its employees. In the meantime 50 minimills were in operation; they were aggressively innovative, achieving high product specialization, lower capital costs (they use scrap metal as inputs), and high productiv-

ity. The minimills have drastically reduced the minimum economic scale necessary to produce steel efficiently, and have often proven to be in a better
position in terms of costs to meet certain kinds of foreign competition. The
minimills are bent on increasingly shifting production from low-quality items
to a typical Big Steel product, the flat-rolled steel used in automobiles and
appliance parts. By the end of the 1980s, they had succeeded in accounting for
as much as 21 percent of U.S. consumption, against 18 percent for imports. Big
Steel at first responded slowly to the pressures of the minimills and foreign
competition. The indispensable shift of the industry to continuous casting –
which forms molten steel directly from semifinished shapes – got under way
slower here than it did among America's Japanese and European competitors.
But ultimately, the Gary Works, the largest steel plant in North America (USX
Corporation), having reduced its workforce from some 28,000 employees to
8,000, introduced a new cast at the beginning of 1990, enabling it finally to
achieve a critical turnaround in the man-hours needed per ton of steel (5.3,
compared to the international standard of 5.4 to 5.6). While not a single major
American steel company has been bought outright by foreign makers, there are
by now a number of joint ventures with Japanese steelmakers, and more will
occur as the industry tries again to become fully competitive worldwide. The
ideas that this "basic" industry is decaying technologically, or that it can
maintain the same level of employment as before, or that it can change only
behind protectionist walls, are clearly all far off the mark. Incidentally, according to the Federal Reserve Board, the amount of steel needed to sustain one
point of domestic production fell from 1950 to 1965 by 38 percent, and during
the following 15 years (1965–80) by over 41 percent.[39]

Crucial technological changes are also in process within the basic traditional
group of industrial machinery and equipment (excluding electrical) and in
three of its subgroups, namely, metalworking machinery, special industrial
machinery, and general industrial machinery. Within the special industrial
machinery subgroup, the crucial link between intermediate products processed
from raw materials and finished products has been provided by the small but
critical *machine tools industry,* comprised of a metal-cutting sector (SIC 3541)
and a metal-forging sector (SIC 3542). This industry, which reached its postwar peak in 1979–81, suffered a deep drop in production and exports in the
early 1980s, relieved only by a relatively shallow recovery at the end of that
decade. Yet meanwhile, foreign competitors – Japanese and German – had
been making deep inroads in its markets and in addition had come to cover a
large share of America's needs. Many analysts now view our industry as
parochial, fragmented, lagging technologically, and handicapped by the significant shifts in the demand patterns of manufacturing – particularly of its traditional clients, the automakers and the rapidly evolving aerospace industry. The
trend toward expanded automated manufacturing, in which machine tools are

but *one* of a number of linkage components including robotics, automatic handling equipment, sensors, and computer controls, is in the process of radically changing the operations of machine tools. Computer-related developments, combined with changes in the traditional mechanical industries, are pushing events toward the creation of a *new manufacturing base* involving both mechanical and electronic elements. As an MIT study of the U.S. machine tools industry put it, the old mechanical-engineering base of machine tools is no longer adequate by itself. Electronic skills are needed to build controls, programming skills are needed to develop software; users, too, now need programming skills to program their parts. But these needed changes also create new opportunities outside the traditional structural and technological base of the machine tools industry. In the prospective development of an *integrated* machine tool base, the U.S. holds leading positions.[40]

Rapid critical advances are occurring also in microelectronic hardware and software which have engendered both new successful products and vast reorganizations of the industry's dominant firms. The giant IBM, the dominant force in the world computer industry since its beginnings, has been deeply shaken by a shift away from IBM mainframe computers – the huge box-like machines serving as the computing nerve center of large businesses – toward its competition's workstations or personal computers (PCs), performing, much more cheaply, some of the tasks formerly done by mainframes. IBM has hastily undertaken deep workforce cuts, far-reaching structural decentralization, the incorporation of new technologies, and changes in its commodity-style competition in software and services. But IBM is hardly alone – the big Japanese computer makers have also been battered by these new trends. While in the early 1980s "Japan Inc." was perceived as the pacesetter in the field, by the beginning of the 1990s American companies had abruptly retaken the lead. The United States' Intel, the world's largest maker of microprocessors, the brains of PCs, has become the dominant factor in the PC surge, while the United States' Microsoft is the new leader in software. New families of mainframes built on microprocessors have been launched by Hewlett-Packard and by Digital Equipment Corporation (which in its turn has problems with adapting to the development of PCs). Such turmoil and continuous upheaval have effectively put to rest not only contentions about the alleged "incapacity" of U.S. high-tech manufacturing to compete in the global market and to develop new products, but also misconceptions about the ease of making valid predictions in fast-changing technological fields – a fact which raises serious doubts about governments' ability to appropriately guide industries' future developments.[41]

The claims that gross fixed capital formation has tended to falter in manufacture are likewise not supported by the data. The fact is that real capital formation has increased in this sector during each decade from 1950 onwards. At 1982 prices, expenditures on new plant and equipment rose from $344 billion in the 1950s, to $550 billion in the 1960s, to $870 billion in the 1970s, and to $1.377 trillion in the 1980s (i.e., at a rate of over $137 billion per year in the 1980s). However, the rate of growth of expenditures on new plant and equipment in nonmanufacturing exceeded the rates of the corresponding expenditures in manufacturing: the ratios of these latter to the former expenditures fell from a level of over 70 percent in 1960 to 67 percent in 1970, to about 65 percent in 1980, and then to some 57 percent in the late 1980s. In addition, the incremental capital to output ratio in manufacture increased, in real terms, from a low of less than 3 in 1960 to close to 5 in 1970 and over 5 at the end of the 1980s. This means that increasingly more units of capital were needed per unit of increment in output from the 1970s on. In part, the rate of increase of equipment in certain service sectors may be accounted for by expansion of the contracting out ("outsourcing") to service firms of a number of functions previously carried out within manufacturing firms, including notably data processing, accounting, laboratory research and testing of various kinds, mail services, and other types of jobs.[42]

The dark side of manufacturing's rise in output and technological transformations has been the permanent layoff of workers, the shutting down of inefficient plants, and an erosion of wages. The share of wage and salary disbursements in manufacture (excluding employer contributions for social insurance), given the expanded shares of services and other income, decreased in terms of total personal income. The share of manufacture itself contracted from 21.9 percent in the early 1960s to 14.7 percent at the end of the 1970s and then to about 12.4 percent at the end of the 1980s. In relation to GNP, this share dropped from 17.1 percent at the beginning of the 1960s to 13.3 percent at the end of the 1970s and to 10.4 percent at the end of the 1980s. At constant (1977) dollars, average hourly earnings in manufacture fluctuated throughout the 1970s and 1980s very close to the $5.30 level.

How do all these U.S. changes compare with the developments which took place in Japanese and German manufacture? But, to start with, are these manufactures structurally comparable? If they are – leaving aside differences in size for the moment – how did the pace of growth of output, employment, gross capital formation, and productivity differ among the countries with which we are concerned?

As can be seen from Table 4-2, the structures of manufacturing output were very similar in the three highly industrialized countries considered: the dominant industries were *chemicals* and *fabricated metal products,* with the latter including production of transport equipment, nonelectric machinery, and, last, electrical machinery. Output of fabricated metal products as a group increased during the 1980s by 51 percent for the United States, 62 percent for Japan, and 93 percent for Germany, a pace which exceeded by far the growth of the rest of manufacturing. Out of the total investment in manufacture in 1989, investment

Table 4-2. *United States, Japan, and Germany (West): comparative structures of manufacturing output,* 1989 (percentages)*

	U.S.		Japan		Germany (West)	
Food, Beverage & Tobacco	14.0		10.6		11.5	
Textile, Apparel & Leather	5.1		4.4		4.4	
Wood Products & Furniture	3.1		2.5		2.7	
Paper, Paper Products & Printing	9.9		6.7		4.4	
Chemical Products	19.0		14.1		20.6	
Non-Metallic Mineral Products	2.4		3.4		2.8	
Basic Metal Industries	5.0		7.5		6.2	
of which Iron & Steel		2.8		5.7		4.1
Fabricated Metal Products	40.2		49.3		46.9	
of which Metal Products		5.2		6.0		6.7
Nonelectric Machinery		10.0		12.8		14.0
Electrical Machinery		7.2		15.2		11.2
Transport Equipment		13.8		14.0		14.6
Professional Goods		4.0		1.3		0.4
Other Manufacturing	1.3		1.5		0.5	
Total	100.0		100.0		100.0	

*Underlying data at current prices in national currencies.
Source: Computed from OECD, Industrial Structure Statistics 1989/90, pp. 42, 70, 140.

in this group alone was on the order of 37 percent in the U.S., 49 percent in Japan, and 48 percent in Germany (West).

At the end of the 1980s, U.S. manufacturing output was estimated to have reached $1.815 trillion, that of Japan $1.279 trillion, and that of Germany (West) $684 billion – i.e., Japan's output was equivalent to 70 percent of U.S. output, and Germany's to 37 percent. For the entire period 1960–89, Japan's total manufacturing output increased at a faster pace than that of the United States or of Germany: the average annual rate of growth in manufacturing output was 8.8 percent for Japan, 3.6 percent for the United States, and only 2.9 for Germany. Japan, as we noted in Section 3-1, also excelled in the pace of *average output per hour* – i.e., the pace of change of productivity – in this sector: during the same period the average annual rate of change was 7.6 for Japan, 4.1 for Germany, and only 3.0 for the United States. What may seem paradoxical is that unit labor costs rose much faster in Germany and Japan than in the United States. The annual average rates of change in this sector during the same years were 6.9 percent for Germany, 6.5 for Japan, and only 3.1 percent for the United States. In short, the United States kept a tighter rein than its challengers on wages (and on employment) changes during this long period. On the other hand, the pace of its *productivity* change failed to meet that of Japan or Germany. This may suggest that the mix of wage incentives, technological change, organization of production, capacity utilization, and inputs may not have been as effective as it should have been in at least some of the branches of this sector.[43]

However, let us note for now that the United States' decrease in employment in manufacturing, particularly in the 1980s, and the slower annual pace of growth in output and, above all, in productivity do not signify either that U.S. manufacturing is tending toward disappearance or that it is bound to lag technologically in relation to its challengers. The examples of steel and of machine tools show the potential opportunities that exist for reviving and transforming traditional industries, while the example of the upheavals in electronics demonstrates the great potential for change through domestic competition and innovation within the new high-tech industries. New combinations are arising even between such old and fiercely competing industries as railroads and trucking, involving centralized loading and the moving and unloading of heavy freight (or trailers) over long distances by high-speed trains. One cannot know what is obsolete and what is potentially in ascendancy. Clearly, possibilities for innovations in industries old and new, for new and unexpected alliances and combinations inland and offshore, and for dynamic change in new products, new-product quality, and factor prices are not being missed by creative leaders in United States manufacturing. Moreover, ups and downs can affect not only the United States, but also its challengers.

In the section below, I turn to an extensive discussion of holistic industrial policies, of their underlying assumptions, specific strategies, and combinations with, or substitutions for, a range of policies in other associated areas.

4-4   From the New Deal to a holistic industrial policy

Speaking for himself and for "many Democrats," Lester Thurow affirmed in the mid 1980s that the New Deal was dead, and that what the Democrats needed henceforth was "a new vision to replace the old New Deal goals." He defined these old goals as aggregate demand management, a social safety net, equal access to education, and economic opportunity. The new vision which he offered to the Democrats as a guide over the next 20 to 30 years was "the problem of competitiveness in the world economy," a long-term problem equivalent for him to "the problems that the Roosevelt Administration set out to conquer in the 1930s."[44]

The interest in recalling these quotations is that they accurately summarize the positions of at least a part of the leadership of the Democratic party – let us call it its center – that was defeated in the presidential race of 1984 but victorious in 1992. What the shift from the old vision implies is a departure from Roosevelt's emphasis on consumption and income redistribution, away from the *increase in demand* – in the language of the 1930s, the increase of the "purchasing power" of farmers, workers, the needy, the old – toward a significant *increase in investment*. This shift would at first blush seem a Democratic conversion to the main principle of the Republican credo, as reaffirmed in the early 1980s by President Reagan. Indeed, Reagan was the first to initiate and to implement a shift away from the *welfare tenets* of the New Deal. But the similarity stops there. The Republicans had always stressed that the government should step aside in virtually all respects, leaving the key task of investment to the private sector, via the higher savings of the higher income receivers. Contrariwise, the Democratic shift to investment posited from the beginning first of all a *more activist government* than ever, a government active with respect to the allocation of this investment, a government expanding its relationship with business, a government directly concerned with the level of savings, the volume of R&D, and the quality and skills of the labor force. The new "competitive problem" which commanded all these adjustments required that we learn from the Japanese *where* to go and from the French what dirigiste *instruments* to use. It required a government capable of "practic[ing] triage and kill[ing] off weak companies unable to develop the new products needed to fight off [Japan's] Komatsu."[45] The centrist Democrats have thus abandoned demand policies aiming to control the business cycle in favor of investment policies aiming to control economic growth. Both policies proceed from the dubious assumption that "fine-tuning" is possible: on the demand side by the use of macro measures; on the investment side, by micro measures.

The rise of Japan to the joint position of bête noire and model in a curious fashion replaced the position held by the Soviet Union until the early 1980s. While the Soviet Union took until 1991 to crash and dismember itself, by the turn of 1980 informed observers and a number of U.S. policymakers had already radically changed their views about the strengths and weaknesses of that economy. From 1955 to 1980 one can distinguish *grosso modo* three basic shifts in American policymakers' perceptions of Soviet economic power and performance. During the first period, from 1955 to 1965, the feeling was one of surprise, then one almost of awe about its rapid achievements in mathematics and science, particularly after the launch of Sputnik in 1957. Soon, however, a period of mounting skepticism and then of placidity followed, lasting from 1965 to 1975, as the Soviet economy's difficulties increased and its leaders attempted and failed to quasi-rationalize its pricing system. Finally, from 1975 on, one finds increasingly condescending appraisals of the Soviet Union's economic performance, still accompanied by deep uneasiness about Soviet military might and its uses in the international arena.[46] While the Soviet Union was demoted from the position of economic and scientific challenger, Japan was hoisted onto the empty pedestal. We are slowly but surely coming out of the first phase of our fascination with the new bête noire model, with more and more people taking into account the fact that Japan, which packs roughly one half of our population in a country the size of California, has few minerals, no oil, and no gas, and is still highly dependent both on the U.S. market and on U.S. technological developments.

The advocacy of competitiveness as a problem allegedly equivalent to the problems that the Roosevelt Administration had to conquer in the 1930s raises the following questions. Can the U.S. rapidly strengthen its manufacturing base, erase its deficits, increase its savings rate, and expand its investments into the industries of the future? Can the U.S. improve its productivity rates, cope with Japan's pace of growth, match its competitiveness, and maintain or reassert a decisive lead in world markets?

Consider again the question of competitiveness. Those who claim that our competitiveness has been eroding focus on the decreasing share of the U.S. in world exports and its increasing share in world imports. I presented some of the relevant data in Section 1-4, but I wish to concentrate now on the particular role of *manufacturing*. The U.S. share in manufacturing production for the advanced industrial world – including the United States, Japan, and Europe, but excluding the former Soviet Union – was estimated at about 32 percent of the total in 1990, compared to 23 percent for Japan and the balance for Europe (of which close to 13 percent of the world total was accounted for by West Germany). In exports, as I noted, the U.S. remained dominant in aircraft, industrial chemicals, engines and turbines, drugs and medicines, and scientific instruments; Japan has reached important positions in office and computing machinery and in communication equipment; Germany remains a decisive force in industrial chemicals and machinery. By the end of the 1980s, the ratio of U.S. exports to imports was favorable (above 1) in "industrial supplies" and "capital goods"; it was in balance for "other manufacturing products" and unfavorable (0.4) for automotives. Even a cursory look at U.S. capital-goods exports and imports from 1960 to 1990 shows a rapidly falling ratio (from 3 to 1), as reconstruction had long since been achieved and development had long since been in full swing in the former enemy countries. Yet one should also note that Japan has continued to be not only the largest single market for U.S. agricultural products, but also a larger market for our manufactured products than Germany and France combined. Further, in considering the scope and extent of U.S. competitiveness, one cannot overlook the position of American multinational enterprises (MNEs) in foreign trade. Intrafirm trade, i.e., goods and services exchanged within U.S. parent companies and their affiliates, may account for more than 35 percent of U.S. exports and 40 percent of our imports. They alone account for a very substantial share of world trade: clearly, shifts in multinational corporations' sourcing decisions can have a relatively large impact on what is considered the United States' foreign trade performance. (I shall return to the role of MNEs in Chapter 7.) Judging from the success of the American MNEs in the world market, certain diminished U.S. trade positions may clearly result less from deficiencies in American managerial and technological leadership than from a host of other factors, such as productivity differentials, wage rates, taxation, cost of capital, and exchange rates.[47]

The movement of foreign investments into markets to be served is a global phenomenon which also deserves careful attention. Foreign companies are now catching up with U.S. firms, which have been at the forefront for much of the post-World War II period. In the 1980s, higher rates of foreign direct investments (FDI) by other countries lowered the U.S. share of world FDIs from 42.5 percent in 1980 to 28.3 percent in 1989. However, measured on a book value basis, that 28.3 percent by far exceeded the shares of the other main investors, namely the United Kingdom (with 16.7 percent), Japan (11.5 percent), and Germany (9.1 percent). The earning power of U.S. manufacturing FDIs is significantly larger than that of foreign manufacturing investments in the U.S.[48]

For advocates of a shift from consumption to investment – and, subsidiarily, of a decrease of the national debt – the crux of the matter is the persistence of the low level of U.S. savings in relation to that of the other industrialized countries, above all Japan. According to the IMF, between 1980 and 1990, for instance, U.S. national savings were 13.6 percent of GNP, compared to 31.9 percent for Japan, 22.7 percent for West Germany, 20.2 percent for France, 21.7 percent for Italy, 17.3 percent for the United Kingdom, 20.2 percent for Canada, and 20.6 percent for all industrial countries.[49] Are such rates as those of the United States, it is asked, adequate to promote growth rates for future outputs in line with those of other industrial countries and particularly of Japan – even assuming that the latter's rates will decline in the future? The promotion of higher levels of output in the future would of course require reductions in current consumption. There are no generally acceptable ways of resolving this intertemporal, intergenerational trade-off. It has been suggested that the most appropriate normative rule would be to treat the interests of all generations as equal. On the basis of this "golden rule," a steady balanced growth path of the economy would ensure that the per capita consumption of all generations would be maximized, subject to the resources available and the state of technology. Under various computations, this would involve an enormous increase in the savings rate in the case of the United States, from 13.6 percent of GNP to anywhere from 15.5 to 30 percent of GNP.[50] The desirability of pursuing such a course, however, is still a matter of dispute. To those who have been urging that the U.S. government should raise the rate of national saving, Herbert Stein (chairman of the Council of Economic Advisers under President Nixon) cogently answered: "Let us assume that we have discovered that we are saving too little.. . . Why should individuals require the help of government to carry out impartial saving decisions if that is what individuals want to do?" And Stein added: "There is no *critical mass* that the savings must reach."[51] Moreover, one should not forget that the same rates of savings in different countries do not necessarily generate the same rates of investment, the same rates of growth of the same industries, and the same path of development. The latter depend *inter alia* on the allocations they support, on the evolving interrelations between government and business, and on the socioeconomic framework within which they occur – a framework vastly different in the United States, Japan, and Germany.

In regard to rates of capital formation, the United States has fallen significantly below Japan. The annual average rates of growth of U.S. business' fixed investment during the sub-periods 1970–79, 1980–83, and 1984–88 closely paralleled those of the OECD, namely U.S. 4.0 (OECD, 3.9), then −1.8 (−0.3) and 6.7 (6.8). But these rates were below those registered by Japan in the same time intervals, namely 4.3, 3.5, and 8.9. According to the UN system of accounts, gross fixed capital formation as a percentage of GNP for the U.S. between the 1960s and the 1980s fluctuated between 17.0 and 18.0, compared to 31–35 for Japan.[52] Besides the underlying savings rates, a variety of causes played a role in this divergence: e.g., the level of inflation, the cost of capital, tax laws, regulatory processes, and uncertainty about future conditions. May one assume that in noninflationary circumstances, increased savings following significant reductions in consumption (via changes in taxes) and in the structure of government spending (with regard to welfare "entitlements" and the military) will support higher levels of capital formation, thanks to "appropriately" channeled investments into manufacturing? Certainly not. To start with, the assumption is predicated on wrong premises: insuperable obstacles are in the way of the implementation of some of these proposals.

The advocates of an industrial policy have asserted that broad changes are necessary with regard to *technology* and to *human resources,* not to mention a broad combination of activities involving *infrastructure, environmental technologies,* and the *downsizing of defense.* The changes, they assert, would radically and efficiently reshape the American economy. According to a series of recommendations made from the early 1980s on by the proponents of a holistic industrial orientation, as summarized in a policy study by Daniel F. Burton, Jr., Victor Gotbaum, and Felix G. Rohatyn entitled *Vision for the 1990s,* the United States should, first of all, *view technology as a national priority* and should treat it with the attention and care it received "during World War II and in the wake of the Sputnik crisis." A continuous "dialogue" should be engaged with industry, allowing the latter to discuss its technology needs and facilitating "more rapid, coordinated policy responses." A significant increase should be made in U.S. federal investment, on a matching basis, for industrially relevant R&D to promote long-term investment in R&D in both product and process technology. Encouragement should be given to cooperative research, with improved incentives provided for private sector investment.[53] With respect to *human resources, Vision* suggested a number of changes concerning labor-management relations, health care, education, and labor training and retraining. Finally, in regard to the *infrastructure,* the document enjoined the government to provide investments for such physical assets as office buildings and their equipment, as well as for environmental technologies, water-resource projects, and grants-in-aid to state and local governments for investment in highways, airports, and urban rehabilitation projects.

In order to carry out such complex and costly measures, *Vision for the 1990s* posited the need for tax increases to *cut consumption,* along with spending cuts and a reduction of the federal debt (as a necessary adjunct to increasing private savings). The measures for cutting consumption were to include a value added tax, a national sales tax, and a business transfer tax, along with separate tax increases on upper-income Americans, on Social Security payments to upper-income individuals, on gasoline, and on oil imports (in the form of fees).[54] As we shall see in Part IV, the Clinton-Gore administration eventually adopted many of the proposals included in *Vision for the 1990s* and raised them to the level of new national goals.

Consider now the implications of such choices with regard to each of the indicated "basic blocks." Active federal participation in the development of new technology has traditionally focused on four types of R&D expenditures: (i) *fundamental research programs* – destined to broaden our understanding of science and its applications, from which will emerge future technologies; (ii) *industry-oriented R&D* – targeting a specific set of technological problems affecting commercial technologies; (iii) *use of specific technologies* – aiming to encourage the private sector to adopt specific new technologies; and (iv) critical *national concerns* – involving defense and the environment. As far as methods of R&D support are concerned, the federal government has tended to oscillate between two extremes. At one extreme, it has permitted all important decisions regarding means and ends to be taken by decisionmakers in private companies and in the higher educational institutions; at the other extreme, it has insisted that the federal government alone should target the directions of research to be managed by government agencies and to be financed by project-specific federal appropriations.[55] The advocates of holistic industrial policies propose that the bulk of federal R&D investments should consist of industry-oriented R&D, and suggest that some expenditures for defense-oriented and fundamental research be curtailed. Besides their main focus, which was on the last two types of expenditures, the Republican administrations also offered small technology-oriented grants through the Commerce Department and encouraged federal laboratories to strike deals for cooperative research with private firms. Advocates of industrial policies incline instead toward Japanese and European dirigiste models of hands-on support for so-called cutting-edge industrial technologies. As we already know, these policies imply extensive cooperation between business and government of the Sematech type, stressing commercial research based on large federal subsidies, expanded cooperative research among private companies with government support, and permanent tax credits to help channel private R&D investment toward specified sectors, industries, companies, products, and technologies.

The objections of critics to such centralized government choices stress five ideas. (1) That in undertaking their crucial investment decisions, private firms have profits and jobs at stake, as well as better information concerning the market than the government can obtain. (2) That efficiency requires not one-shot decisions but continuous evaluation and reevaluation of appropriate timing, amounts, and directions of resource allocation. (3) That the government's efforts to change the patterns of investment within and between industries involve creating not only "winners" but also "losers" – i.e., taking resources from certain industries and from the economy in general (more often from consumption in particular) to support technological projects whose outcome is uncertain. (4) That just as the stagnationist theoreticians of the 1930s assumed, erroneously, that the economy had exhausted its growth possibilities because of the lack of a new great industry, so the 1980s advocates of industrial policy have mistakenly assumed that only their selections of cutting-edge industries can increase productivity and secure an appropriate growth rate for the GNP. And (5) that, in the last analysis, competition among companies for government aid will ultimately require these companies to devote a considerable amount of time and energy to maneuvering to obtain this aid – resources which could be put to better use.

The notion of strategic choice concerning human resources – defended by the advocates of industrial policies as well as by some of their adversaries – was largely based on the theory of *human capital* developed in the 1960s by Theodore Schultz and Gary Becker of the University of Chicago. The heart of the theory is that expenditures on health, education, job security, information about job opportunities, migration to take advantage of these opportunities, and on-the-job training *are investments rather than consumption,* whether such expenditures are undertaken by individuals on their own behalf or by society on behalf of its members. The key issue is not who spends what, but rather the fact that the decisionmaker, whoever he or she is, spends not for present but for *future* return.[56] Proponents of industrial policy have continually affirmed that government assistance to business must explicitly aim at upgrading both capital and labor. As the Senate Democratic Caucus *Jobs for the Future* report had already put it in the early 1980s, "nothing is more important than investment in people."[57] Two critical problems arise in this respect: health care and labor training.

The U.S. health-care system has for decades been based on a mixed public-private arrangement. The federal and state governments have run two large public programs: *Medicare* (purely federal) for the aged, established in 1965 under the Social Security System, and *Medicaid* (joint state-federal) for some of the poor. Business has provided the bulk of health-care insurance for the "non-aged." The big concerns since the 1980s have been the *rising costs of the system* and the fact that a substantial number of people have remained *without health-care insurance*. The shares of federal and state budgets devoted to health-care outlays in 1990 were over 15 percent of total federal expenditures and over 11 percent of state outlays. Further, about one person in seven had no insurance at all – many of them in small firms that did not offer group insurance. And many who were employed by businesses that did provide insurance were worried that their coverage would be reduced when they retired, or would be eliminated altogether beforehand if they lost or changed jobs. A federally operated insurance program covering the entire nation was considered by the Roosevelt administration in 1935 but was never proposed to Congress. A federally operated insurance program – modifying or replacing the mixed public-private setup – must necessarily involve an *intergenerational shift* of care resources from the aged to "investment" in the "non-aged" labor force.[58]

Lester Thurow and others argued in the mid 1980s that we must "invest in people as well as in machines" if we want to "increase productivity and restore growth." However, such programs are controversial, costly, and not easily implementable. Indeed, there is no consensus on what to do about overhauling the school system, be it elementary or high school. The same is true of workers' vocational training, for which the U.S. has always lacked a coherent national policy. Many employers look upon apprenticeship, for instance, as an expensive proposition which does not pay off; it has been typical only for the building trades and for certain manufacturing industries with low rates of employee turnover. While in most industrialized countries apprenticeship is a work-study arrangement for teenagers who have left full-time school – a system which smooths the transition from school to work – in the United States typically apprenticeship is not for teenage youth: in certain manufacturing industries where apprenticeships are available, starting apprentices are usually aged 20 or over. Apprenticeship training in the United States exists as a voluntary partnership between labor and management, private business and public agencies, and the federal and state governments, which varies across trades and localities and tends to produce irregularly distributed young skilled workers. The overhauling of this system may turn out to be very costly.[59] Concerning the requirement that every employer should provide continuing education and training for *all* workers, one wonders which specific goals such training would have to achieve. There is no solid evidence that there is a "mismatch" between the skills needed in the economy as a whole and the skills possessed by the labor force.[60] Further, there is no clear-cut evidence of specific mismatches in specific industries. Robert Reich suggested in the early 1980s that the government should explicitly assist business to upgrade capital and labor. According to him, businesses that receive such restructuring assistance should in exchange agree "to maintain their labor force intact.. . . If the firms diversify, they will have to retrain their workers to take on jobs in the new lines of business. The virtue of this scheme is that it will connect capital adjustment to labor adjustment." But this kind of scheme, allegedly patterned on the Japanese model, where "when workers must be laid off, they do not go on welfare, they go to work," is devoid of realism.[61]

Are declining investments in plant and equipment, or in education, really the causes of the productivity slump? Paul Krugman points out that "in fact the American economy placed about as high a share of its resources into investment, and a higher share in education, in the 1970s and 1980s as it did in the 1950s and 1960s. It just didn't work as well."[62] One may surmise that both the demand-supply shifts in the international market and the deep transformations taking place in a number of U.S. industries (communications technologies, automotive industry, machine tools, steel, and materials in general) have simply rendered the "orthodox prescriptions" of accelerating productivity growth less effective than they might have been in different circumstances.

The claims that investment in the physical infrastructure would boost employment, productivity, and output may also turn out to be overstated. Without altering existing methods of planning highways, for instance, and without doing something to discourage congestion, more investment in highways, bridges, and airports will merely constitute an incentive to clog up these facilities anew and lead to their rapid deterioration. What some economists have proposed instead is that the government change the ways it *charges* for the use of highways and airports. In a properly devised system, drivers, for instance, would have to pay charges scaled to the degree of congestion on the highways on which they travel. Over the long run, such charges would provide incentives to modify both traffic patterns and firms' locations.[63] The imposition of congestion-related charges to pay for airports and highways would generate billions of dollars while reducing the waste in traffic jams and delays. Scheduled developments of information and environmental technologies (concerning, for instance, water and toxic wastes) could be better carried out by extensive *privatization.* Such problems cannot be properly treated as they still are – as a matter of *engineering* efficiency using an administrative, supply-oriented approach. It is, rather, necessary to focus on the economic efficiency of both the demand and the supply of such goods as information and water.[64] The implementation of these as well as of all the other programs raises two germane questions: their *financing* and their *coordination.*

There is a kind of mystique about what "guided" investment and broadened R&D might produce with regard to technological change, output, jobs, productivity, and competitiveness. The dominant idea enshrined in industrial policy is the shifting of resources from consumption toward centrally conducted investment. Note that this departure from the New Deal's emphases on consumption and increase in demand does not involve a break with *latter-day* Keynesianism. In the broader framework of the so-called neoclassical synthesis, it is held that measures to create jobs need not be wasteful per se and need not focus exclusively on augmenting the national propensity to consume. Further, as James Tobin has pointed out, there is nothing specifically Keynesian about the welfare state. Welfare structures have grown to different extents in all the industrialized countries. The Keynesians could take any side in the controversies about Social Security, socialized medicine, and urban renewal. But what the Keynesian economists do suggest is that modern capitalism is sufficiently robust to progress while striving to remain humane and equitable.[65]

In the central guidance of investable resources, industrial policy involves *selection:* this may mean not only picking "winners" – or actually *making* "winners" out of the industries and companies picked for subsidies – but also protecting at least some of the "losers." The latter would back subsidies for the former in exchange for their support for trade protection. No cogent economic standards are available either for picking a future winning industrial combination or for selecting a rational assemblage of industries to be protected and restructured. There are many important things that only a government can do – and I shall discuss them in detail in examining the debates on the "agenda" in Chapter 6. But the one thing which a democratic government, and especially the American one, cannot do well at all is to make deliberate final choices among industries, municipalities, and regions, and determine their ultimate progress or failure.[66]

The assertion that guided investment, and possibly also augmented protectionism, should be undertaken in order to create jobs is combined with the assertion that the budget deficit must be cut, since it is alleged that the budget competes with private business for funds. No matter what one may think of budget deficits, their reduction for whatever reason also affects aggregate demand. Certain cuts – for instance, those imposed by the obvious need to convert defense industries and downsize the military, whose expansion in the 1980s pumped up the national debt – will affect aggregate demand for years to come. In addition, when one adds to this the cuts in welfare "entitlements," along with those in Medicare (part of the Social Security insurance system), and then also figures in higher taxes on many Social Security beneficiaries – in order to contribute both to cutting the national debt and to shifting resources from consumption to guided investment – these multiple cuts in the purchasing power of the (mostly) aged might harm the economy as a whole more than they would help the "winners" picked among manufacturing firms in order to expand the country's jobs and ensure its technological leadership.

Neither increased guided investment and expanded R&D spending, nor lower industrial prices and costs and higher productivity rates, will necessarily improve America's trade balance. Investment unaccompanied by higher savings could lead to large current-account deficits. More R&D spending may lead to the increased output of certain goods produced more cheaply abroad. Lower prices may actually yield a *decline* in the trade balance if the demand for the goods in question is not responsive to price. And finally, an increase in productivity might, paradoxically, lead to higher wages and profits, to the detriment of our competitiveness. No single indicator – investment, R&D, technological change, price level, productivity rates – will serve as a reliable predictor of performance.[67]

Recall that coordinated approaches to industrial policy are supposed to end the existing erratic "ad hocism," even though the very concept of *selection* which industrial policy implies entails the use of a variety of criteria, the correct weighting of which is not obvious, and thus leads to ad hocism again. Be that as it may, a powerful central council (capping the existing U.S. government agencies, or independent of them) would have to make the critical decisions involving selections. The choice of these critical real decisionmakers may prove elusive. The creation of a *professional elite* rivaling the movers and shakers of the private sector, focused on the task of picking "winners" – of the kind suggested by Lester Thurow – may require radical changes in the U.S. civil service. The federal government rarely provides incentives for those presumed to be the most qualified in this area to pursue careers at such high levels of government. The U.S. could hardly draw from U.S. society, supposedly on Japan's or other countries' model, the top-flight, well-trained talent needed who would be entrusted with the virtual guidance of the key decisions affecting our complex economy.[68] Congress, on the other hand, has always guarded control, as far as possible, over executive branch offices and has enforced its supervision with the power of the purse. The idea that economic issues of national importance could be resolved, so to speak, outside or above Congress and the results brought to Congress for automatic approval and implementation would require, as Robert W. Russell put it, the "reinvention" of Congress.[69] But even if one supposed that the temptation for Congress to micromanage the cutting of this "national investment" pie could be overcome, why would one believe that such an apparatus would yield sounder judgments than those coming from industries and firms immersed in the market? Eventually political pressures could extract "remedies" that would favor particular companies, municipalities, and regions over others, or call forth protectionist measures at enormous costs to the economy as a whole. Yet both during the 1992 electoral campaign and soon after – as we shall see in Part IV – the successful Democratic candidates, later President Clinton and Vice-President Gore, forcefully advocated some of the proposals put forward by the "holistic" industrialists. I shall examine in Chapter 7 the ways in which some of these proposals have been reformulated, and up to what point their implementation may shape the future development of the American economy.

Japan's development under MITI's guidance, which many advocates of industrial policy are ready to emulate, may have helped that country to move along certain technological paths already opened by the United States. But it did not necessarily help it to open new paths, as the unsuccessful experiences of the "Fifth Generation" computer project and of HDTV based on a dated technology readily suggest. As another example, the currently grim prospects of large computer giants like Fujitsu and Hitachi, modeled on IBM and based like it on the utilization of mainframes, may ultimately push these companies to restructure drastically or face the terrible risk of following IBM over the cliff. The big problems of the future require not the *imitation* of established techniques – even temporarily successful ones – but the opening of new technological paths. The tradition of setting up new companies, pursuing new ideas, and charting new paths is still more typical of the U.S. than of its current challengers.

4-5   Concluding comments

The destruction wrought by time and the ubiquity of decline have been associated since the remote past with such notions as twilight, autumn, senescence, exhaustion, and decay – along with their antonyms dawn, spring, youth, energy, and vitality – involving thought in terms of *natural cycles* and *biological metaphors*. As Matei Calinescu noted in a study on the "Idea of Decadence," the myth of decadence was known to nearly all ancient peoples and has constituted the core of numerous religious traditions. The actual or alleged inferiority and misery of the present have often been contrasted with an earlier, more felicitous time, that of a so-called Golden Age from which decline was inevitable. Ancient Greece speculated extensively about models of ideal states and of social forms, from which a declining path was ineluctable.[70] Many historical analysts have since then used the same kind of schemata. Adam Smith noted ironically how common such practice had become in his beloved England from the time of the restoration of the monarchy in 1660 to the publication of *The Wealth of Nations* in 1776. As he put it, the country's "annual produce" was certainly much greater in 1776 than at the earlier date. "Yet, during this period, five years have seldom passed away in which some book or pamphlet has not been published, written too with such abilities as to gain some authority with the public, and pretending to demonstrate that the wealth of the nation was fast declining, that the country was depopulated, agriculture neglected, manufactures decaying, and trade undone."[71]

Now five years have seldom passed since the early 1970s without someone's pretending to demonstrate that America is aging and declining. Recall Kindleberger's diagnosis of the crippling middle-age "climacteric" allegedly weakening Britain at the end of the last century and then the U.S. at the end of this one. Robert Reich, for instance – to pick another of those who try hastily to arrive at broad conclusions – has discovered another disease which has afflicted the great powers, from the Italian city-states of the 17th century to Holland in the 18th century and Britain in the 19th. The disease – whose manifestations are absence of public spirit, conservatism, and possession of privileges which undermine the capacity to adapt to change – leads remorselessly to decay unless it is overcome by the "civic spirit." The U.S. is at a crossroads: either it discards "outmoded forms of organization" and learns to respond to economic change (viz. the "global market"), or else it will continue to transit toward "a slowly shrinking economic pie divided into ever smaller slices."[72]

In contrast to analysis in terms of natural or sociopolitical cycles and biological metaphors, progress may be viewed as having to do more with *technological change* and *mechanics*. Interestingly enough, the dysfunctional aspects of technological progress are at times also identified with the notion of decline or with that of decadence. The underlying logic of such identification relies on the assumption that the present is always worse than the past, i.e., it is always at the low end of a declining trajectory. But, for most other people, progress has consistently been identified with the machine age and with its advances under the impact of science. Given this specific connection with the surge of industrial, technological and commercial development in the West, progress has also been associated either with the growth of individual freedom (on the British and French models) or with its opposite, the notion of the crucial role of the government in society (notably on the model of Bismarck's Germany).

The very existence of the Soviet Union often tended to bolster the perception that progress involved some kind of "rational," centralized drive toward the organization of the economy and of society on an "ideal" model. The same impression was given by various postwar experiments with state interventions in the economy, including those which took place in various West European countries (particularly France). Yet, curiously, the collapse of the Soviet Union and of its satellites, and the abandonment by the West European countries of the attempts toward centralized controls over the direction of the economy, have not led to the complete discrediting of the idea of "planned," comprehensive state intervention in the broader form of "managed competition" or "organized capitalism" (in its German or Japanese shape). The size, diversity, and technological levels of certain so-called strategic manufacturing branches continue to be viewed as constituting the *core* of advancing economies – though exactly which manufacturing areas *are* the strategic transforming industries on which everything else is supposed to depend is not always clearly discernible. Certainly, at the beginning of the 20th century, iron, steel, and machine tools could easily be perceived as the strategic transforming industries – *if* one overlooked the crucial concomitant transformations in transportation and communication. But by the end of this century the overlooked branches of yesteryear had surged to the fore: this is certainly the case with aircraft and satellites, new materials, biotechnology, and of course computer technologies. As toward the end of the 19th century the very spread of industrialization was alleged to have plunged England into decline and disaster at the very moment when British industry was in fact opening up new markets for its products, so at the end of the 20th century the spread of high technology outside the United States is allegedly portending this country's downfall. Actually, as I noted, the future development of high tech is infinitely more difficult to chart than was that of the civilization based on heavy industry. Not that this discourages would-be prophets. Indeed, some analysts assume that the U.S. has already lost the battle for "the economic honors of owning the twenty-first century," to use a strange expression coined by Lester Thurow to define the stakes in the battle for industrial supremacy in the coming century. This battle, according to Thurow, is winnable by the "House of Europe" "no matter how well either the United States or the Japanese play the economic game." This is so, adds Thurow, because "the House of Europe holds the strongest starting position on the world's economic chessboard."[73] Such readings of the future are based on many erroneous assumptions, including the one that what America needs in order to "win" is to catch up with its competitors – Japan and the "House of Europe" (centered on Germany) – by discarding its "individualistic" approach to market capitalism in favor of the postulates of organized capitalism and of all-pervading industrial policies, whose patent failures seem to have completely escaped their committed defenders. As we have seen, the United States continues to be by far in the forefront of the world's economic powers. This is true whether one looks at the size of its investable mass, at the size of its scientific establishment, at the diversity of its contributions, or at the vast size of its market.

Part III

The long-run development of the U.S. economy

Introductory note

After outlining America's growth and change from the early post-World War II years on up to the critical turning point marked by the debacle of East European and Soviet communism, and after examining the nature and scope of the new economic challenges now facing the United States, a number of questions are in order. How does America's postwar development fit into the historical development of its industrial economy, starting from its strong post-Civil War expansion begun around 1869? How do transformations in the patterns of production and employment as well as in underlying technological structures in agriculture, industries, and services relate to one another during the various "phases" of the economy's growth since then? How do capital flows, the rise and the fall of tariff rates, and the dismantlement and the erection of nontariff barriers relate to debt, balances of trade, and competition? Last but not least, how do the proposals for industrial policy and managed trade emerging from the United States' post-World War II experiences resemble or diverge from previously suggested policies concerning the nature and scope of the state's interventions in the economy?

In trying to answer these questions and in attempting, for the purpose, to sketch in broad outline the ways in which the U.S. evolved from an agricultural to an industrial setting, I do not aim to present a kind of short economic history, but only to establish certain *points of reference* with regard to a limited number of characteristics of this development. Of the two chapters of this section, the first (Chapter 5) focuses on certain structural transformations of the economy in the broad processes of growth and change from 1869 to 1989; the second centers on the nature and main features of the expansion of the role of the state during this period.

In Chapter 5 I pay particular attention to changes in *manufacturing* and in private *services.* The transformations in the agricultural sector seem relatively simple: the decrease in its share of total employment and income, with which I am concerned here, is easy to document and illustrate. Quite different are the changes in manufacturing and in related industries. The intricate transmutations they underwent in response to shifts in demand and the imperatives of technological inventions, along with the complex modifications and adjustments in the patterns of investments, in interindustry flows, and in outputs and employment, represent clear warnings against the illusion that such multiple interrelations can be easily and appropriately manipulated on the basis of certain industrial policies.

I view *services* as being comprised of *productive services,* which are tied in multiple ways to the other sectors of the economy, and *personal services,* which focus specifically on individual needs. Within the productive group I distinguish distributive, financial, technical, and professional services, increasingly expanding their connections with the rest of the economy in a rapidly changing fashion. Centralized computing and accounting services, to take a recent example, may serve an ever augmenting number of manufacturing firms and commercial enterprises, as well as government departments, with a view to reducing costs and personnel. Finally, I believe that the state complex does not belong to the heterogeneous bloc called "services." In the allocation of resources, we do distinguish clearly between private consumption and private investment and the government. We should just as clearly distinguish, in the economy's employment, between the private economy and the state.

The latter constitutes a special, *sui generis* complex, whose growth and development (detailed in Chapter 6) involve accretions of diverse tasks as the economy itself evolves and changes. With regard to economics, the state pursues multiple objectives besides the allocation of resources, income distribution, and stability. These involve special problems concerning public welfare, natural resources and the environment, science, space, new technology, safety, health, and the development of human capital – as well as protection of the consumer on the one hand and of the producer on the other.

In its conclusion this section also considers the U.S. performance in manufacturing over the entire period under review, in relation to that of the other industrialized countries now joined in the so-called Group of Seven. It also examines the arguments advanced in favor of the theory that the U.S. has become a "post-industrial society" and points out the weaknesses of this paradigm.

In Part IV I shall reexamine, in the perspective of the findings set out in Parts I–III, the ideas that survival of the U.S. as an advanced economy requires it to plan and implement industrial policies patterned on various foreign models, and to systematically pursue "strategically" oriented policies for gains in the world market.

5   The structural transformations

5-1   Phases of growth and change, 1869–1989

This section presents in broad outline the deep transformation of the American economy as it evolved out of a predominantly agricultural matrix into a predominantly industrial and service-oriented economy. First, I shall try to disengage the main trends concerning the rates of growth of GNP during various sub-periods; the major impacts of business fluctuations; the relations between the growth of capital stock, the workforce, and the growth of the GNP; and increases in the level of productivity. Second, I shall try to illustrate the changes which took place in the structure of the economy, that is, in the interrelations between its basic sectors – agriculture, industries, and services – and their components. I shall indicate the effect of these changes on patterns of occupations and income, as well as on the volume and composition of foreign trade from 1869 up to the threshold of the 1990s. Finally, I shall try to show how the entire post-World War II period analyzed in Chapter 1 fits into long-term U.S. development trends.

From 1869 onward, the United States evolved from a preponderantly agricultural setting, in which it depended on and was oriented toward foreign commerce, into a growing industrial and service-oriented economy with a vast and expanding domestic market at its disposal. Its rapid and powerful economic growth, increasingly evident by World War I, continued further unabated while Europe, then being torn apart by Germany, destroyed and impoverished itself. Europe's self-destruction, on the one hand, opened the door to the rise of Soviet communism and, on the other hand, left the United States the world's chief industrial nation – and its main creditor. After the depression and unrest of the 1930s and the upsurge of Nazism in Germany, Europe was again plunged by the "new" Germany into the carnage of total war, while Japan, the Nazis' ally, pushed China and a vast part of Asia into the furnace. Though this time the United States was drawn deeply into the war, once again it emerged at its end as the major military and economic power of the world. Its dominance, as I have already recalled, remained uncontested until the early 1970s, when, besides the menacing military and diplomatic challenge of the

Soviet Union, the forward surging of the reconstituted economies of Japan and Germany presented it with a new and powerful economic challenge as well.

Let us first take a careful look at some figures. From 1870 to 1913 the American economy grew at an average annual rate of 4.1 percent. In the 20th century, the highest average rates of growth of the U.S. gross national product occurred between 1900 and 1913 (3.9 percent), between 1920 and 1929 (4.3 percent), and between 1948 and 1973 (3.7 percent). The lowest average annual rates of U.S. growth were registered during the periods 1930–38 (0.4 percent) and 1973–81 (2.1 percent). Over the entire 20th-century period 1900–88, the average annual rate of growth of the GNP came to 3.1 percent. Put differently, from the turn of the century to the end of the 1980s, the real national product (at 1982 prices) rose to 15.7 times the 1900 level.

During the same period, the highest average annual rates of growth in real per capita income were attained in 1900–13 (2.0 percent), 1920–29 (2.7 percent), and 1948–73 (2.2 percent). The lowest rates were exhibited in 1930–38 (−0.3) and 1973–81 (1.1 percent). Between 1900 and the end of the 1980s – a period in which the U.S. population nearly tripled, growing from 84 million to close to 250 million – real per capita income increased at an average annual rate of 1.7 percent.[1]

Nothing inbuilt in the economy can ensure that total demand will grow in step with total production, that real nonresidential fixed capital per worker will grow at an accelerating pace and in perfect combination with new technology, that the workforce available will be fully employed, that productivity will not slacken, and that the actual growth of the economy will match its potential growth. In the 120 years between 1869 and 1989, the American economy experienced 27 business cycles – 10 during the first 40 years (1869–1909), 10 again during the next 40 years (1909–49), and 7 during the last 40 years considered (1949–89). In terms of their duration and the rates of unemployment for which reliable data are available, the deepest contractions occurred in the 1890s and in the 1930s. During the first contraction, the level of unemployment rose from 3.0 percent of the civilian labor force in 1892 to 18.4 percent by 1894; this rate then started to decline slowly, year by year, until it reached 12.4 percent in 1898, and finally fell back to 6.5 percent in 1899. The 1930s depression was also deep and long-lasting. The rate of unemployment of the civilian labor force rose from 3.2 percent in 1929 to 8.9 in 1930 and then kept climbing up to the unprecedented rate of 25.2 percent in 1933. It then started to crawl down, reaching 9.9 percent by 1941. Other very sharp 20th-century declines were recorded in 1921 (11.7 percent unemployment) and 1982–83 (9.6 to 9.7 percent). The 20th century's longest contraction (trough from previous peak) occurred from March 1933 to May 1937 (43 months). The two longest expansions in American history (trough to peak), took place between February 1961 and December 1969 (106 months) and between November 1982 and January 1991 (97 months).[2]

Table 5-1. *U.S. structure of investment in fixed nonresidential private capital: selected years, 1900–1989 (millions of 1987 dollars)*

	1900	1929	1959	1989
Information Processing and Related Equipment	0	1,103	7,815	128,634
Industrial Equipment	7,225	14,967	32,970	85,795
Transportation and Related Equipment	4,432	12,093	19,297	53,071
Other Equipment	1,511	12,043	29,575	79,068

Source: <u>Fixed Reproducible Tangible Wealth in the United States, 1925-89</u>, pp. 375, 377.

Throughout most of the 1900s, the United States had higher rates of investment in its capital stock than most other nations. The data available on real fixed nonresidential private capital (at 1987 prices) in all industries for the 65 years from 1925 to 1989 indicate that the real net capital stock of equipment and structures increased 4.4 times (from $1.05 trillion to $4.67 trillion). During the same years the labor force increased 2.6 times, and the real net stock of equipment per worker increased more than threefold.[3] As can be seen from Table 5-1, the *structure* of real investment (at 1987 prices) changed in dramatic fashion over the period 1900–89.

Most notably, information processing and related equipment (office computing and accounting machinery, communication equipment, instruments, and photocopying) increased at a frantic pace in the 1980s. It substantially exceeded investment in all other types of equipment, including industrial equipment (i.e., fabricated metal products, engines and turbines, metalworking machinery, materials handling equipment, and electrical distribution apparatus).

Over the long haul, labor productivity increased at an average rate of 2.0 to 2.6 percent per year. Thus, real GNP per worker-hour increased at an average annual rate of 2.0 between 1870 and 1913, of 2.6 percent between 1913 and 1950, and again of 2.0 percent from 1950 to 1987. The highest average yearly growth rates of labor productivity were scored between 1960 and 1973 (2.8 percent); the lowest, between 1973 and 1982 (0.5 percent).[4]

The far-reaching structural transformations of the American economy from 1869 to 1989 are presented in Table 5-2 and illustrated (on a decennial basis) in the graphs of Fig. 5-1. As can be seen from the upper part of the table, the share of agriculture, forestry, and fishing in national income fell in rapid steps through each of the time intervals considered, declining from over 22 percent in 1869 to a little over 2 percent by 1989. A different trajectory appears in the

Table 5-2. *U.S. national income and employment by sectors: selected years, 1869–1989: totals and percentages (underlying data for income in current dollars)*

Years	Totals*	Agric. Forestry Fishing	Industries					Services				Government	Discrepancies
			Total	Mining	Construction	Manufacturing	Transp. Commun. Utilities	Total	Trade	Finance Insurance Real Estate	Other Services		
1869	6.827	22.2	32.7	1.5	5.7	14.6	10.9	40.9	15.2	11.5	14.2	4.2	0.0
1899-1903	17.313	18.2	36.1	2.9	4.3	18.6	10.3	39.6	16.6	12.7	10.3	6.0	0.1
1929	87.194	9.9	42.7	2.4	4.4	25.2	10.7	40.6	15.5	15.1	10.0	5.8	1.0
1959	414.300	4.0	44.9	1.3	5.2	30.1	8.3	38.2	15.8	11.8	10.6	12.0	0.9
1989	4,270.800	2.3	33.0	0.8	5.5	19.2	7.5	49.8	14.2	14.8	20.8	14.2	0.7
1869	11,910	48.3	28.9	1.3	4.9	17.2	5.1	19.3	7.8	0.4	11.1	3.5	0.0
1899	26,861	36.9	35.1	2.5	4.9	20.0	7.7	23.9	10.8	1.2	11.9	4.1	0.0
1929	46,461	27.5	36.3	2.1	3.2	22.4	8.6	29.4	13.9	3.3	12.2	6.8	0.0
1959	62,870	11.7	38.7	1.1	4.7	26.5	6.4	36.7	17.6	4.1	15.0	12.9	0.0
1989	117,342	2.7	32.4	0.6	6.5	18.4	6.9	49.8	20.6	6.8	22.4	15.1	0.0

*Upper table grand totals are in billions of dollars; lower table grand totals represent thousands of workers. Figures in all other columns are percentages.
Sources: Upper table (national income by industry) compiled from: (for 1869) Long-Term Economic Growth 1860-1965, Washington, D.C., U.S. Department of Commerce, October 1966, p. 79; (for 1929) The National Income and Product Accounts of the United States, 1929-1976, Washington, D.C., U.S. Department of Commerce, September 1981, pp. 229-233; (for 1959) The National Income and Product Accounts of the United States, 1959-1988, Washington, D.C., U.S. Department of Commerce, September 1992, p. 207; (for 1989) Survey of Current Business, Vol. 70, No. 1, January 1990, p. 19. (The 1929-89 data are without capital consumption adjustment for industry.) Lower table (persons employed) compiled from (for 1869 and 1899) Historical Statistics of the United States: Colonial Times to 1970, Washington, D.C., U.S. Department of Commerce, 1975, Part I, p. 240; (all other data) The National Income and Product Accounts 1929-1976, pp. 248-252, and 1959-1988, p. 220; Statistical Abstract of the United States 1992, pp. 400 (data for 1989 "Employment in Industry"), 410.

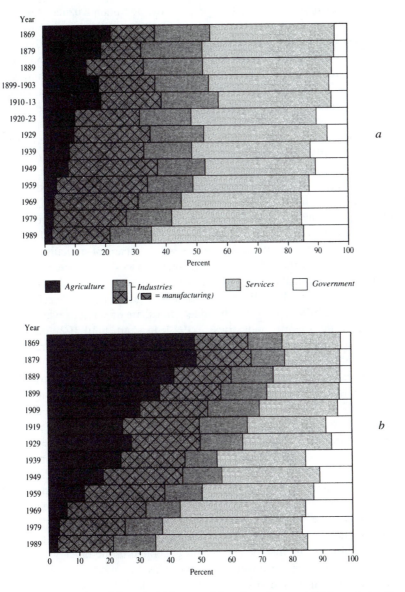

Figure 5-1. U.S. national income (*a*) and employment (*b*) by sectors: selected years, 1869-1989. "Government" excludes minor statistical discrepancies and residuals from "Rest of the World." *Sources:* As in Table 5-2.

share of all industries – in which category, following Simon Kuznets, I include mining, construction, manufacture, power and light utilities, transport, and communications. While industry's share grew significantly up to 1959, namely from close to 33 percent in 1869 to close to 45 percent in 1959, it had fallen back to 33 percent by 1989. The decline was due to contractions in manufacturing as well as in mining, utilities, transport, and communications. In contrast, nongovernmental services – in the broadest sense of this term – grew from some 41 percent of the total in 1869 to close to 50 percent by 1989.

The dimensions and the directions of change are better grasped when we compare the shifts in income shares with the sectoral shifts in the distribution of the persons engaged in production. As can be seen from the lower part of the table, the amplitude of certain changes in employment was far wider than that for changes in income shares. In 1869 the agricultural sector was the *dominant* employer, providing almost half of all the jobs available. Agriculture remained the largest employer until the end of the 19th century. By 1909 (see Fig. 5-1) the share of industry (39.0 percent) *exceeded* the share of agriculture (30.4 percent), as well as that of nongovernmental services (25.9 percent). Sixty years later, by 1969, the share of services (excluding government) finally exceeded the industry share. If we were to include government in services – as is usually, and I believe erroneously done – the share of services would stand ex equo with the share of industries in 1929. In short, until 1929, industry, services, and government jointly absorbed the excess of the labor force freed from agriculture. From 1969 on, nongovernment services alone started to absorb the excess labor freed both by agriculture and by industry, whose share in total employment had finally decreased to slightly over 32 percent by 1989. Only after 1949 does manufacturing's share in total employment exceed that of agriculture – but it *never* exceeds that of services, even when one excludes government from this sector, as I do. The United States has thus never been a predominantly "industrial society," a fact to which I shall return further on.

A comparison of the share of income per person employed during the period considered (namely the *ratio* of the percentage of income generated in a given sector to the corresponding percentage of persons employed in that sector and in any of its subdivisions) shows some trends worth noting. In 1869, the income per person in agriculture tended to be less than one fourth, and then about one third, of the income per person generated in the other sectors. By 1959, the income per person in agriculture was just over one third of the income per person in nongovernmental services and was equal to some 30 percent of that in industry. Finally, however, by 1989, the drop of the income per person in both industry and in nongovernmental services, coupled with the increase of the income per person in agriculture, raised the level of the latter to about 80 percent of the income per person generated in the other two sectors. These altered relations have been due to many factors, including changes in

Table 5-3. *U.S. major occupation groups of the experienced civilian labor force, 1900–1989 (percentages)*

	1900	1930	1960	1989
	100	100	100	100
White-collar Workers	17.6	29.4	42.2	56.8
Managers, Officials & Proprietors	5.8	7.5	10.1	12.7
Professional & Technical	4.3	6.8	11.0	16.4
Sales Workers	4.5	6.2	6.2	12.0
Clerical Workers	3.0	8.9	14.9	15.7
Blue-collar Workers	35.8	39.5	39.6	27.1
Craft & Kindred Workers	10.5	12.8	12.7	11.8
Operatives, Kindred Workers & Laborers	25.3	26.7	26.9	15.3
Service Workers*	9.1	9.8	11.8	13.2
Farm Workers	37.5	21.3	6.4	2.9

*Private household workers and other.
Sources: Computed from (for 1900, 1930, 1960) Historical Statistics of the United States: Colonial Times . . ., Part I, p. 139; (for 1989) Statistical Abstract of the United States 1992, p. 395.

demand patterns, in employment structure, and in productivity differentials in any given sector and in their respective components. As can be seen from Table 5-3, profound changes took place in the structure of the employed workforce during this period. The share of white-collar workers rose by 1989 to over 56 percent of the total "experienced civilian labor force," compared to around 18 percent at the beginning of the century. In this group, continual increases were recorded in the shares of managers, professionals, and technical workers, as well as in those of sales workers and clerical workers, who account for the bulk of the growth in services. The share of blue-collar workers significantly decreased, to less than 30 percent of the total, in particular because of the decrease in operatives, kindred workers, and laborers. Finally, as one might have expected, the share of experienced farm workers shrank dramatically.

The fast overall growth of the American economy led during certain periods to rapid increases in the flow of trade with other countries. From 1870 to 1913, and again from 1950 to 1987, our exports grew quickly, while they ran at a much slower pace from the onset of World War I up to 1950. In the next chapter I shall examine the commercial policies which, along with other factors, sharply molded the flows of trade. Let me note for now that from 1870 to 1913 and from 1950 to 1987, the average annual percentage change in real exports came to 4.9 and 5.2 respectively; from 1913 to 1950 this rate was 2.2 percent. These accelerations and slowdowns in trade flows can also be perceived when we relate the growth of exports to the growth of GNP. Thus, from 1869 to 1878, exports were on the order of 6 percent of GNP; by the turn of the century the rate had risen to 8 percent. From 1929 to 1949 the rate fell from 7 to around 5 percent, and then it climbed toward the end of the 1980s to 12 percent. Imports, however, grew faster than exports from 1983 on. The highest level of imports in relation to exports was reached in 1987, when imports were 12.5 percent of GNP.[5]

The structural changes which the entire economy underwent from 1869 to 1989, as well as the changes in U.S. trade policies, are well reflected in the changing structure of merchandise exports and imports. As could be expected, our merchandise exports shifted increasingly away from raw materials – mainly mineral fuels, logs and lumber, and metal ores and scrap – and also, eventually, away from manufactured foods and semimanufactured goods. These were to be displaced by finished manufactured products, now primarily including machinery of all kinds; transport equipment – both automotive and aircraft, plus parts – and scientific instruments. In 1869 raw materials accounted for some 53 percent of our exports, while finished manufactures amounted to 17 percent. By 1929, raw materials accounted for 22 percent, while finished manufactures had risen to 49 percent. By 1989 the percentages were less than 11 and over 54 respectively. Interesting changes also took place on the import side. In 1869, imports of raw materials accounted for some 12 percent and those of machinery for 37 percent of total imports. By 1929 the share of raw materials (including oil) rose to 35 percent, while that of machinery fell to less than 23 percent. Eventually, the share of raw materials was brought down again, while that of finished manufactures increased rapidly: by 1989 raw materials once more accounted for some 12 percent, while finished manufactures (including automotives) rose to close to two thirds of all imports.[6]

How did the post-World War II period – from the mid 1940s to the turn of 1990 – fit into the long-run development trends of the American economy? The average annual rates of GNP growth achieved from, say, 1948 to 1988 – namely, 3.3 percent – exceeded the rate of 2.8 percent scored in the preceding period (1913 to 1950). With regard to the per capita product, the average yearly rates of change were very close in the two periods considered, specifically 1.9 and 2.0 percent. The depth of the contractions during business fluctuations was less profound, and the usual length of recovery periods registered in the 1960s and the 1980s had no historical counterparts in the preceding years. On the other hand, the general level of unemployment in the 1980s tended to hover, year in and year out, above the level of 4–5 percent common in the preceding years. As for the sources of growth, real net capital stock increased appreciably in the 25 years from 1960 to 1985, at a yearly compound rate of change of 3.3 percent, compared to the 1.3 percent annual rate registered during the preceding 35 years. The real net *equipment* stock per worker increased at a faster pace from 1960 to 1985 than during the preceding 35 years. Yet in regard to labor productivity, the annual rate of change of less than 2.0 percent for 1950–87, while not far out of line with the average annual percentage change of the preceding years, was disappointing considering the levels attained by Japan and Germany during that period – 6.2 and 4.7 percent, respectively. However, in long-run perspective, the average annual gain in labor productivity of 2.6 percent scored by the U.S. in the period 1870–1950 was far superior to the yearly rates achieved by Japan and Germany, specifically 1.3 and 1.1 percent.[7]

It has often been asserted that the 1980s were characterized by a deliberate tax-engineered shift toward more income inequality. While the data available show that income inequality indeed tended to grow in the 1970s and 1980s, at least part of the change is attributable to deep modifications in the composition of families and households, the growing number of persons living in nonfamily situations, and the growth of the elderly stratum. Further, notwithstanding the postwar period's structural economic transformation and its large shifts in the patterns of employment and unemployment, poverty rates have broadly tended to fall. From a high of over 30 percent of the population in 1950, the poverty rate fell to 19.5 percent in the early 1960s – when the official "war on poverty" started – and to 11.1 percent in 1973, though it then rose again slightly, to less than 13 percent by the end of the 1980s. During the entire period, in absolute terms the official number of the poor decreased from 45.8 million in 1950 (out of a population of 151.6 million) to 31.5 million in 1989 (out of a population of 248.7 million).[8]

To better grasp the complex transformations of the American economy during the long period under review, I propose now to take a close look at the specific changes in U.S. manufacturing (Section 5-2), to classify in new ways the ensemble called services (Section 5-3), to detail the changes in the United States' balance of payments, debt, and investment positions (Section 5-4), and to conclude with a comparison of the economic development of the most industrialized countries of the world – the so-called Group of Seven – from 1900 to the end of the 1980s (Section 5-5).

5-2   *The making and remaking of manufacturing*

Perhaps nothing is more erroneous with regard to manufacturing than the notions that interindustry relations are unchangeable, that some particular industries must mandatorily achieve and maintain certain arbitrarily selected levels of output and employment, and that final demand must be constituted *predominantly* of certain types of goods, e.g., producer goods or high-tech goods. Yet these notions underpin theories about the alleged deindustrialization of the United States. (I shall return to some of these issues in Section 7-5.)

The fact is that manufacturing is continually reshaped by a variety of factors which remold it in innumerable fashions. First, transformations take place within the processes of production and in the interrelations between inputs and outputs. These mutations are due to a vast number of adjustments, large and small, within the nation's operating plants under the impact of skill development, of training and retraining, and of science and engineering advances, inventions, and innovations. Second, manufacturing alters under the multifarious impact of changes in *other* sectors – changes which at times may dramatically reshape the entire economic and social landscape. Deep changes may take place in the composition of final demand not only under the impact of transmutations in other sectors, but also under the influence of the expansion and deepening of the market due to changes in the incomes, tastes, and spending patterns of consumers. Indeed, technological changes in manufacturing have been complexly intertwined with factors as diverse as movements toward increased specialization, toward the generation and increased availability of applied power, and toward the economical use of raw materials, along with improvements in the scale of factory operation, in engineering design, in transportation, in information, in market scope, and in opportunities for mass production.

The growth of the railway net, for instance, from 1850 to 1890 – when it reached the limits of the continental United States – spurred the boom in the manufacture of iron and steel, copper, power machinery, explosives, and heavy equipment. Our iron and steel industry reached world-class status in 1890 and remained a top American industry until 1928. The automotive revolution started in the late 19th century, generating a colossus within the span of less than 30 years. By 1916, the country had passed the one million mark for cars and trucks "made in the U.S.A." By 1927, this industry, now in full expansion, was transforming the rubber, glass, and petroleum industries along with the entire social and economic fabric of the country. That same year a tremendous leap forward further increased the scope of the transformation of transportation. The rapid growth of commercial aircraft fleets and of airports in operation opened new horizons. From 268 airplanes in use in 1927, commercial aircraft increased to 1,209 flying machines in 1950 and to 4,665 powerful transport engines by 1990. But perhaps no other industrial change of the past, no matter how deep and spectacular, equals the immense change brought about – and still in progress – by the *combination* of the enormous advances in the speed and capacity of air transport to move people, materials, and work in progress with the equally astounding advances in and growth of information technology and electronics. The past achievements in information technology – the telegraph, begun in 1844, and the telephone, developed in 1876 and expanded on a colossal scale ever since – are by far overshadowed by the transformations brought about by this new combination and by its capacity to link industrial, financial, and other enterprises worldwide, to rapidly modify and readjust processes and production methods, to achieve savings in the use of materials, to increase specialization, and to integrate markets, thanks to satellite and fiber optic communications, along with the spread of computer networks.

Concomitant expansions in the size and the depth of the domestic market during the entire period under review have reflected both the structural transformation of the nation's economy and the diversification of its manufacturing outputs, as well as the growth of population via natural increase and immigration, and the rise in total and per capita product. From 1869 to 1929, the U.S. population increased from fewer than 40 million people to 120 million, while real income per capita almost tripled. And again from 1929 to 1989 population more than doubled, while income per capita once more increased about three-fold. Household demand expanded continually, not only for food, clothing, and housing, but also for cars, vacuum cleaners, washing machines, refrigerators, radios, stereos, televisions, and personal computers. At the same time, the U.S. share in world manufacturing production increased, according to various estimates, from 23 percent in 1870 to 42 percent in 1929. It eventually decreased to about 31 percent of a greatly expanded world production capacity in the 1980s. The volume of American exports grew in pace with the vast expansion of the domestic capacity to produce. According to the calculations of Angus Maddison, from 1870 to 1913 the volume of our exports grew at an average annual compound rate of 4.9 percent; between 1929 and 1950, this yearly rate fell to 2.2 percent, but then it rose dramatically between 1950 and 1973, when it reached the very high level of 6.3 percent. It then maintained itself, between 1973 and 1989, at the still high level of 4.7 percent, yielding for the entire period 1870–1989 the impressive annual average compound growth rate of 4.3 percent.[9]

Manufacturing responded to the expansion of demand and to demand's changing structure by appropriately increasing its size and shifting the allocation of its investments. Indeed, during the period under review, manufacturing grew and changed enormously in the number and size of its establishments, total employment, structural makeup, and value added. In 1869, U.S. manufacture counted some 250,000 factories and hand and neighborhood industries, employing 2 million workers and accounting for a total value added of $1.3 billion. By 1929 manufacturing numbered 206,000 factories – excluding handicraft and neighborhood industries – with a total of 9.6 million gainfully employed (of whom 8.3 million were production workers), yielding a value added of $30.5 billion. By 1989 the industry counted some 370,000 establishments with personnel of 19.4 million (of whom 12.3 million were production workers) with a value added of $1.3 trillion. The analysis of the structure of the value added, based on the shares of 20 SIC two-digit groups of industry, shows that during the period under review sharp drops took place in the value-added shares of tobacco products, textile mill products, apparel and related products, and leather and leather products, while powerful increases were registered in the shares of chemicals and allied products, petroleum and coal products, rubber and plastic products, electrical machinery, transport equipment, and instruments and related products. The shifts in manufacturing may be further illustrated by comparing the sharply changing lists of the top 10 three-digit industries at various points in time (see Table 5-4).

These changes in manufacturing, as well as changes in market concentration resulting in ever larger firms, are further reflected – though in a curious fashion – in the changes in the Dow Jones average of American stocks. In 1896, the Dow Jones average was based, for the first time, on 12 so-called industrial stocks (at its beginnings, in 1895, the Dow Jones included 12 railroads and 2 industrial stocks). These 12 industrials were companies dealing notably in cottonseed oil, sugar, tobacco, gas, cattle feed, lead, iron, leather, rubber, and electricity. A new list of 20 industrials replaced the old list of 12 in 1916. The new list involved companies dealing in canning, cars, locomotives, smelting, copper, leather, rubber tires, iron and steel, electricity, and communications. Twelve years later, in 1928, the list was expanded to 30 industrials, this time covering in particular canning, chemicals, smelting, sugar, tobacco, oil, steel, cars and trucks, tires, electricity, breakfast cereals, agricultural machinery, and aircraft. The 1990 list in use, also of 30 industrials, covers in particular companies engaged in the production of aluminum, steel, cars, aircraft, agricultural machinery, communications, advanced technologies, electricity, oil, beverages, and soaps and detergents.

The growth and changes we have been examining were accompanied by a vast expansion of capital stock and by deep structural modifications. The net stock of equipment and structures in manufacture increased between 1925 and 1989 at the average annual compound rate of 2.8 percent (of equipment only, at the average annual rate of 3.1 percent). Put differently, the real net stock of manufacturing equipment septupled between 1925 and 1989 (from $80 billion to $567 billion). The fastest growth in investments was registered in chemicals and related products, electronics and other electric products, and industrial machinery and equipment. During the most recent decades the biggest volumes of investments were again concentrated in these same industries, along with motor vehicle equipment.[10]

According to various computations, between 1869 and 1913 manufacturing output increased no less than eightfold, between 1919 and 1950 threefold, and between 1950 and 1989 about fourfold.[11] Excluding the food and textile industries, the highest average annual percentage change in multifactor productivity was registered in the post-World War II years in chemicals and electrical

Table 5-4. *U.S.: the ten leading manufacturing industries: selected years,*
1860–1987

Rank	1860	1900	1947	1987
1	Cotton textiles	Foundry & machine shop products	Motor vehicles & equipment	Motor vehicles & equipment
2	Lumber	Lumber	Blast furnaces & steel mills	Aircraft parts
3	Boots & shoes	Printing & publishing	Cotton & rayon	Computer & office equipment
4	Iron	Iron & steel	Beverages	Fabricated rubber products
5	Flour milling	Malt liquors	Electrical industrial apparatus	Communication equipment
6	Men's clothing	Tobacco	Industrial organic chemicals	Drugs
7	Gold mining	Cotton goods	Lumber & lumber products	Commercial printing
8	Steam engines	Men's clothing	Pulp & paperboard	Navigation equipment
9	Woolen goods	Bakery products	Petroleum refining	Newspapers
10	Leather	Cars & railroad	Women's & misses' clothing	Soap & cleaners

1860 range: from $60 million (1st) to $20 million (10th).
1900 range: from $435 million (1st) to $108 million (10th).
1947 range: from $3.8 billion (1st) to $1.4 billion (10th).
1987 range: from $65.7 billion (1st) to $1.5 billion (10th).
Sources: 1860 and 1900: Herman E. Krooss, American Economic Development, Englewood
Cliffs, N.J., Prentice-Hall, 1974, p. 437; 1947: U.S. Department of Commerce, Bureau of
the Census, Census of Manufactures: 1947, Washington, D.C., GPO, 1950, pp. 24-31; 1987:
Statistical Abstract of the United States 1990, pp. 735-739.

machinery, followed by the instruments industries and nonelectrical machinery.[12] As I have already noted, in contrast to the growth of chemicals, our steel
industry, once the world's largest and the most modern, was forced to engage
in a deep and intricate restructuring in order to adjust to declining demand for
its products both at home and abroad.

The vast and complex shifts in manufacturing's structure, equipment, technology, outputs, and employment sketched above in broad strokes for the period 1869–1989 have taken place, as I indicated, at various speeds at different points in time. The importance of these developments has not always been perceived immediately but rather only after all kinds of delays, and their implications have not always been assessed properly. Perhaps similar misinterpretations and misunderstandings are to be expected in regard to the current and impending changes in manufacturing. Large-scale interpenetrations are now developing between manufacturing industry and various service industries. The emergence and growth of service industries capable of producing competent, commercially available technical, engineering, legal, accounting, data processing, and other professional services, readily replacing in-house functions traditionally confined to individual manufacturing firms, has opened up *new avenues* for manufacturing *outsourcing.* This outsourcing is different in kind and in implications from the farming out of parts or processes from a manufacturing center to manufacturing satellites. The capacity to link with an abundance of specialized, centralized services – i.e., the transformation of the latter into virtual manufacturers – will lead both to the simplification of manufacturing's hierarchical managerial structure and to decreases in its total employment. In this light, growth and change in services and in their capacity to provide new intermediate (and final) outputs for other industries are of crucial importance in the process of structural change and development, not only of manufacturing, but of the economy as a whole.

5-3   *The changes in services*

Services are usually defined as outputs other than those commonly categorized as goods. In addition, it is noted that goods can be stored, while services are unstorable and are produced and consumed simultaneously. But, given the extreme heterogeneity of the conglomerate called "services," such definitions immediately call forth all kinds of qualifications. Thus, while it can be said that, in general, services make available to business and consumers the products of the goods-producing industries, one must also add that in so doing, certain services actually channel *inputs* into the production of various goods and should therefore be viewed as *producer services.* Furthermore, it may, with good reason, be argued that the transport of goods and persons, as well as the transmission of electric power and of information are part and parcel of the production of goods as well as of services. The production and channeling of clean water are often treated as services simply because these activities have been traditionally placed outside the market framework, though they actually belong to the market. In this work, as I have already noted, I include transportation, communications, and utilities in the broad group of *industries.*[13]

What exactly, then, should be included in "services"? The *Standard Indus-*

trial Classification Manual (1987) and the *Statistical Abstracts of the United States* list under services hotels and other lodging places; personal services; business services; auto repair and miscellaneous repair services; amusement and recreation services; health, legal, educational, and social services; and engineering and management services. The *Manual* also lists wholesale and retail trade independently as services, as well as finance, insurance and real estate. I believe that the *Manual* listing points to the need to *disentangle* the heterogeneous conglomerate called services. It seems to me that what is now included under the term "services" could be conveniently divided into *three different groups*. The first would include services directly tied to the activities of the other sectors of the economy; the second, personal services. The third, the public sector, which is only partially related to services, should in fact be listed *separately* from them.

In the first group I include the following subgroups: distributive services; financial intermediation and real estate; and business, professional, and technical services. I do not separate personal services into related subgroups. The suggested classification of services into these two groups, with their subgroups and subsections, is presented in Table 5-5 together with a set of benchmark employment figures for each category. Both of the main service groups have evolved in terms of structures, technologies, variety of product offerings, and effectiveness. But clearly the most significant changes have taken place in the first group, whose ties with the other sectors of the economy have expanded on a grand scale and will continue to do so in the future.

Let us now consider the main patterns of change and evolution in employment within each group and subgroup, starting with Group I. In the *distributive services,* during the period 1869 to 1989 the personnel engaged in wholesale trade has increased 38-fold (from 169,000 to 6.441 million gainfully employed) and in retail trade 27-fold (from 716,000 to 19.580 million gainfully employed), while the country's total population has increased a little over sixfold (from 39.0 million to 246.3 million). In the 19th century, most wholesale establishments started as retail firms. The concerns expanded, diverged from retail, and diversified in pace with the great changes which started to take place in farming and in manufacturing. Toward the end of the 19th century, a number of manufacturers started to bypass some of the wholesale firms in order to service retailers directly. The *dominant* role of both wholesalers and manufacturing in guiding production and marketing declined somewhat from the 1920s on as large-scale retail chains started to develop. However, wholesale trade activities continued to grow and diversify in the incessantly expanding economy.[14] The present gamut of wholesaling fields is indicative of the vast economic reach of this area. As of 1989, in descending order according to sales volume, the largest wholesale trade categories involved groceries and related products; farm products and raw materials; motor vehicles and auto-

Table 5-5. *U.S.: classification and evolution of employment in services: selected years, 1929–1989 (thousands)*

Group I	1929	1959	1989
i. Distribution Services	6,441	12,262	25,851
a. Wholesale Trade	1,757	3,351	6,271
b. Retail Trade	4,684	8,911	19,580
ii. Financial Intermediation & Real Estate Services	1,520	2,668	6,724
a. Depository Institutions	540	849	2,287
b. Nondepository Institutions		N.A.	364
c. Security & Commodity Brokers	156	124	431
d. Insurance Carriers	367	795	1,449
e. Insurance Agents, Brokers, Service	145	265	654
f. Real Estate	312	615	1,314
g. Holding & Other Investment Offices	N.A.	20	225
iii. Business, Professional & Technical Services	2,160	5,977	17,430
a. Business Services	189	755	4,931
b. Legal Services	98	292	892
c. Engineering & Managerial Services	N.A.	N.A.	2,383
d. Health Services	429	1,730	7,551
e. Educational Services	1,368	2,942	1,673
f. Miscellaneous Repair Services	76	258	N.A.

Group II	1929	1959	1989
Personal Services	1,983	3,778	8,521
a. Individual Services	661	1,185	1,083
b. Hotels & Other Lodging Places	398	666	1,601
c. Automotive Repair, Services, & Parking	N.A.	361	887
d. Motion Pictures	158	165	376
e. Amusement & Recreation Services	313	294	1,047
f. Social Services & Membership Organizations	453	1,107	3,527

Sources: The National Income and Product Accounts of the United States, 1929-1976, p. 248; The National Income and Product Accounts of the United States, 1959-1988, p. 219; Statistical Abstract of the United States 1992, p. 410.

motive equipment; metals and minerals except petroleum; and electrical goods – followed at a lower rate of sales by apparel and related products, paper and paper products, and hardware and miscellaneous products.[15]

The transition from small-scale shopkeeping to large-scale retailing commenced in earnest after World War I and has grown incessantly since then. The physical size of such stores in the 19th century is exemplified by Filene's of Boston, which in 1881 had 2,400 square feet and was described as "one of the most modern." Today a retail store covering 100,000 to 150,000 square feet is by no means unusual, and a 25,000- to 50,000-square-foot establishment is commonplace.[16] The pyramid that personifies the growth of retailing is the modern shopping center mall (there were some 35,000 such centers in the U.S. in 1989). What the retail experts worry now about is not the limitations of "smallness," but the dangers of "bigness." The retailer performs many functions similar to that of the wholesaler, but in addition, in order to be successful, he or she must efficiently serve a large and diverse block of customers and supervise an enormous variety of activities including complex choices of commodities, their purchase, and their appropriate display. Retail sales, which in 1989 amounted to 1.7 trillion dollars, were carried out through the following types of outlets, in descending order by sales volume: automotive dealers, food stores, general merchandise group stores, eating and drinking places, and gasoline and service stations – followed on a much lower level of sales by building materials and hardware stores, furniture and home furnishing stores, apparel and accessory stores, drug retailers, liquor stores, and mail order houses (department store merchandise). Out of the $1.7 trillion in sales, about one third was accounted for by multiunit organizations, which represented roughly one fourth of total retail establishments.[17]

The *financial intermediation channels* between savers (lenders) and borrowers (users of funds) have also increased and diversified impressively along with the expansion of the economy, in particular from the early 1900s on. Since that date, to the usual channels through which loanable funds flow (commercial banks), there have been added savings and loan associations, mutual funds and insurance companies, the Federal Reserve banks, public and private pension funds, government insurance and lending agencies, credit unions, private investment companies, and others. With increasing speed and effectiveness, the existing highly specialized financial institutions gather information about the sources and uses of funds and the creditworthiness of potential borrowers, issue liabilities to the public against themselves (indirect securities), and also achieve lower transaction costs in buying, holding, and selling direct securities (stocks and bonds). They play a key role in stimulating the flow of savings and investment and in achieving an efficient allocation of resources in the economy as a whole. The powerful development of the post-World War II credit market is illustrated in Table 5-6. As can be noted, the private sector's debt grew at a far faster clip than the government's debt. In 1949, the share of private sector

Table 5-6. *U.S. credit market debt outstanding: end of year, 1949–1989 (billions of dollars)*

Year End Outstanding	1949	1959	1969	1979	1989
I. Private Sector Debt	156.1	429.0	1032.0	3037.7	8053.9
a. Mortgages	62.4	190.6	440.8	1328.2	3540.1
b. Corporate bonds	37.3	84.8	177.4	464.9	1502.6
c. Consumer credit	17.4	60.7	129.4	383.4	790.6
d. Open market paper	0.4	4.4	38.1	256.2	579.2
e. Bank loans*	19.9	53.5	145.2	410.9	820.3
f. Other loans	18.7	35.2	101.1	294.1	821.1
II. Government Debt	239.6	310.3	454.3	1214.8	4333.6
a. U.S. government securities	217.7	244.8	321.2	893.2	3512.4
b. State and local obligations	21.9	65.5	138.3	321.6	821.2
Total Credit Market Debt	395.7	739.3	1486.3	4252.5	12387.5

*Not elsewhere classified.
Sources: Federal Reserve System, Flow of Funds Accounts: Financial Assets and Liabilities, Washington, D.C., June 1972, August 1983, and September 1990.

debt in total credit market debt was 39.4 percent, compared to 60.6 for government debt; in 1989, the share of private sector debt was the dominant one, namely, 65 percent, as against 35 percent for government debt. In fact, the share of government debt fell continually from decade to decade until it reached the level of 28.5 percent in 1979, starting to rise again only in the 1980s. Those who focus only on government debt fail to notice the size and the structure of private sector debt and the role which both play in capital formation.

The third subgroup of crucial services critically tied to the other sectors of the economy – *business, professional, and technical services* – has been growing at a meteoric pace; this was particularly so during the 1970s and 1980s. This growth has been tied, first of all, to developments in computer and data-processing services (involving in the 1980s alone growth in the gainfully employed from 304,000 to 745,000), followed by growth in engineering, architectural and surveying services, in management and public relations services, in accounting, auditing, and bookkeeping services, in legal services, in research and testing services, and in advertising and miscellaneous other business services. I have included in this subgroup also the industries that create *human capital* – namely, much of the education and health industries, which add to productive capacity. The advertising industry, which is at least as old as the bazaar, has experienced massive absolute increases in media expenditures, particularly since World War II. Traditional economic models have cast doubt – up to a point, legitimate – upon the value of advertising. Advertising has been treated as wasteful, anticompetitive, deceptive (which in some cases it certainly is), and inimical to welfare. But newer analyses of the so-called neo-Austrian school have also now drawn attention to the existence of imperfect knowledge within the context of a dynamic disequilibrium system of market functioning, and stress the importance of certain advertising as a means of increasing the information available to consumers, decreasing monopoly power in certain markets, and improving overall business performance.[18]

In the second group of services, personal services – to which I believe the term "services" applies most directly – I include individual services (which according to the SIC manual comprise laundry, cleaning, and garment services; photographic services; beauty and barber shops; and funeral services); hotels and other lodging places; automotive repair services and parking; and amusement and recreation, including motion pictures. As I have already pointed out, much attention is paid to the growth in employment in eating and drinking places (which are included in retail trade) and in such consumer services as laundromats, as if they were the most representative of what has been happening in services in terms not only of employment, but also of output, sales, wages, and relation to the rest of the economy. Actually, there are a number of special factors which determine sales and wages in regard to eating and drinking places, along with laundromats and similar services. Let me point out first that between 1960 and 1989 employment in retail trade increased roughly two times over, while employment in eating and drinking places increased close to fourfold. On the other hand, the share of eating and drinking places in the total volume of retail sales increased only from some 7.5 percent in 1960 to close to 10 percent in 1989, with clear implications as to what must have happened to the level of wages in these professions (i.e., slow growth translates into depressed wage levels). Further, the increase in employment in eating and drinking places reflected to a large extent the increased participation of women in the labor force and the corresponding shift of various in-house services to the market. Note that in 1960 there were 21.8 million women gainfully employed out of a total employed labor force of 65.7 million (i.e., 33 percent was accounted for by female labor). In 1989 there were 53.0 million women gainfully employed, out of a total of 117.3 million (i.e., 45 percent of the total was accounted for by women).[19] Moreover, severe pressure is exercised on the wage levels in certain service activities by the methodical shift toward *self-service,* most notable now in fast food restaurants but potentially increasingly important in banking, with the increasing use of teller machines, along with more important changes in shopping in general and in entertainment, in health testing, and in the new technologies for learning.

As noted earlier, the last group usually included in services – federal, state, and local government – does not in fact fit into this category. Plainly, the government performs many key functions other than services, above all capital investment. Moreover, services provided by the government are very hard to disentangle from *transfer payments* (so-called entitlements), as well as from expenditures on economic development. As government expenditures devoted to services one could count outlays on hospitals and health, education and libraries, some veterans' services, the postal service, public safety, parks and recreation, and sewerage and sanitation (though I include this last category in "industry"). But expenditures on health and education may legitimately be viewed as investments in *human capital.* These kinds of investments are also important in state and local budgets. Such expenditures vary from state to state, with the heavier expenditures, besides those on education, on public welfare, insurance benefits, and health. At the local level, outlays also involve such local services as police protection and fire and sanitation, besides health and public welfare. Employment per dollar of expenditures is high in certain services (e.g., in the postal service), while it is very low in others – for instance, in the case of retirement benefits from Social Security.

The data available on private employment in services (i.e., excluding government) over the 60-year period 1929–89 indicate an increase from 12.1 million to 58.5 million persons employed, at an average annual rate of growth of 2.6 percent. The highest annual rate of growth in employment – namely 3.5 percent per annum – was registered by the subgroup of business, professional, and technical services, followed by the financial intermediaries and real estate subgroup (2.5 percent per year). The lowest was displayed by distributive services (2.3 percent per year). On the other hand, in terms of share in total employment in private services, the highest shares were those of the distributive services (44.2 percent), followed by business, professional, and technical services (29.8 percent). Finally, it is interesting to compare these shares to the changes in the volume and structure of real investments in service equipment and structures. The total yearly real investment (in 1987 dollars) in *nonresidential private capital in services* increased massively during the postwar period (1947–89), from $3.7 billion in 1947 to $248.0 billion in 1989. Out of the latter sum the largest share, 59 percent, went to the group of financial intermediaries and real estate (each accounting for about one half of this total). Put differently, the highest investments took place in the group accounting for the smallest share in total employment in services: the total real investment in this group in 1989, namely, $146.5 billion, even significantly exceeded total real investment in manufacturing as a whole, which stood at $121.0 billion.[20]

Notwithstanding many conceptual drawbacks and statistical difficulties, it is roughly estimated that between 1948 and 1981, total factor productivity in the service sector increased at an average annual rate of 1.3 percent, compared with 2.2 percent in goods production. Although productivity grew less in services than in goods production, both labor and total input are estimated to have grown proportionately more in services, so that real gross product in this sector grew during the period considered at an average annual rate of 2.2 percent, compared to 0.6 percent in goods production. With restructuring, new forms of organization, standardization, and expanding technology, notable advances in productivity are bound to be registered in this sector.[21]

The trade in services across frontiers involves an entirely different composite from the one responding to domestic demand. Trade across frontiers is estimated to generate significant surpluses, though the estimates available vary widely. As I have already pointed out, in the broadest sense foreign trade in services involves all transactions across frontiers concerning the movement of producers, consumers, knowledge, information, or legal instruments. Note that the export of services may involve consumption or use in the exporting country, the importing country, or even a third country. Moreover, sales of services abroad, either directly or through foreign affiliates of U.S. companies, as well as sales of services in the U.S. through U.S. affiliates of foreign companies, must also be taken into account.[22] On these bases, as trade in services we may count the following (excluding direct defense expenditures and U.S. miscellaneous services included in calculations for balance of payment purposes): (i) spending by foreigners on goods and services in the U.S. – both by visitors on hotels, restaurants, airfares, etc. and by students (i.e., foreign enrolled in U.S. universities); (ii) business and technical services that earn royalties and license fees abroad; and (iii) sales of U.S.-generated goods and services abroad, either directly by U.S. companies or indirectly by their affiliates, including management and engineering services, legal services, travel offices, credit card offices, waste management companies, and entertainment industry sales (which count as the nation's second largest exporter, after aerospace). As a trade analyst writing in *The New York Times* once put it, "If goods and service trade data are lumped together – they aren't, because of an outdated Commerce Department convention – it becomes clear that the U.S. has an ace-in-the-hole in world trade."[23]

Evidently, the growth in domestic as well as in trade services has responded to a number of different factors: the growth in population, various changes in its age structure, shifts in the composition of the labor force, increases in per capita income, the transfer of in-house services to the market, and, increasingly, the transfer, both at home and abroad, of in-firm services (in manufacturing, commercial establishments, or even government) to outside, specially organized service enterprises. As we saw, the service sector is composed of *different groups* of service providers, with important differences within each group and subgroup. It is wrong to assume that the kinds of jobs that all the service groups offer are either low-paying or menial; this is certainly not the case in many lines of services – e.g., in the case of financial intermediaries or of business, technical, and professional services. It is wrong to assume that service production is primarily labor-intensive, low in productivity, and devoid of high technology. Again, this is a misconception which assumes that what is happening in certain lines of retail trade is characteristic of all the service groups and subgroups. Another misconception is that the growth of government causes a nation to become a service economy. Actually, as I pointed out earlier, government employment – besides the fact that it does not necessarily belong to "services" – has increased at a slower pace over the last 60 years than employment in certain private services (viz. the average annual rate of growth for government employment has been on the order of 2.8 percent, compared to 3.5 percent for business, professional, and technical services). It is erroneous to visualize the U.S. economy as turning away from the production of goods; rather, the *nature of production* is undergoing deep changes, with increasing dependence of the goods-producing industries on financial intermediation and on business, professional, and technological services.[24] As Earle C. Williams rightly put it, "National policies relating to the service sector are so outdated and imperfect that we are failing to fully benefit as a nation from the unique strengths we have created or that are within our ability to create."[25]

5-4   Debt, investment, and competitiveness

From the point of view of *capital flow*, the period 1869 to 1986 can be conveniently divided into four subperiods. During the first, from 1869 to 1914, the United States – which had always been characterized by negative capital outflows – acquired the status of the world's main *debtor* country. During the second subperiod, from the end of World War I to the threshold of World War II (1939), the United States' status changed for the first time in its history: it turned from main debtor to *main creditor*. During the third subperiod, from 1940 to 1970, the U.S. completely dominated the capital market; it also extended a vast amount of grant money and other aid to numerous countries, including, after World War II, its former enemies. During the fourth subperiod, from the early 1970s to 1986, the U.S. domination of the capital market started to be challenged in various respects by the reconstituted economies of Japan, Germany, and the Common Market, while foreign assets in the United States of all forms – official foreign assets, foreign direct investments, private portfolio investments (stocks and bonds) – started to grow until, in 1986, the United States again turned from main creditor into the world's *main debtor*.

Up to 1914, high tariffs by and large provided sufficient revenue to the federal government, so that only once, in 1895, did the U.S. government directly call on foreign capital markets. But in general federal government bonds attracted few foreign investors. The situation was different in the private sector, where foreign investment became increasingly significant. Foreign investors – particularly British and French – focused first on the financing of the national railroad system, but subsequently expanded their lending activities to public utilities, farming, mining, manufacturing firms, banking, and retail trade. The sums they invested played a particularly important role in a number of manufacturing industries, notably in the first synthetic fabric industry; in the new electrochemical industry; in automotives; and in rubber tire plants.[26] In relation to the 1914 GNP of $38.6 billion, the $7.2 billion worth of foreign assets in the United States was equivalent to 18.7 percent. U.S. assets abroad amounted to $5.0 billion – a total which, though respectable, left the net U.S. international position at –$2.2 billion (see Table 5-7).[27]

The United States emerged from World War I as a strong net creditor, whose foreign obligations had shrunk by 1919 to $3.3 billion and whose investments abroad had jumped to $9.7 billion. Put differently, U.S. foreign liabilities had fallen to the equivalent of 3.9 percent of GNP, which then stood at $84.2 billion. By the end of the 1920s, U.S. assets abroad exceeded foreign assets in the U.S. by $8.1 billion. (In addition, foreign governments owed the U.S. government some $11.7 billion on a war debt account, but these sums soon proved uncollectible and therefore do not figure in Table 5-7.) Until 1929, the 1920s were to be a very prosperous decade for the American economy. By 1928 the U.S. GNP had reached $97.1 billion. But the economic slowdown of 1929 and the onset of the great depression in 1930 affected both our foreign trade and the relation between our assets abroad and foreign assets in the United States. With the depression, our foreign trade declined sharply. In addition, various defaults on interest and payments due from foreign bor-rowers, both government and private, discouraged any further support of de-mand for American goods with large extensions of long-term credit. On the other hand, fear of the future and the desire to protect accumulated savings pushed other foreigners to shift "hot money" toward the United States. Even though the United States had no need for borrowed funds, by the end of the decade (as can be seen from Table 5-7) foreign investments in the U.S. matched declining U.S. assets abroad.[28]

This situation changed appreciably with the beginning of World War II. By 1940, although foreign portfolio investment continued to grow, U.S. assets abroad in the form of both direct and portfolio investment increased at a far quicker pace. In that year our assets abroad exceeded foreign assets in the U.S. by $20.8 billion. During the war, lend-lease assistance was used in lieu of war loans on a grand scale: by the end of the war, the U.S. grants and credit net amounted to over $40 billion. And by 1949, thanks to continued U.S. as-sistance through a variety of programs, the grants and credit net climbed to $65

Table 5-7. *U.S. international investment position: selected years, 1869–1989 (billions of dollars)*

Investments	1869	1914	1919	1929	1939	1945	1959	1969	1986	1989
Net international position of U.S.	-1.4	-2.2	6.4	8.1	0	19.9	43.1	67.2	-74.1	-439.6
U.S. assets abroad	0.1	5.0	9.7	17.0	12.5	36.9	82.2	158.1	1319.1	1672.5
Direct investments abroad	N.A.	2.7	3.9	7.6	7.3	8.9	29.8	71.0	414.1	1536.0
Foreign assets in the U.S.	1.5	7.2	3.3	8.9	12.5	17.0	39.1	90.8	1393.2	2112.2
Direct investments in U.S.	N.A.	1.3	0.9	1.4	2.9	2.5	6.6	11.8	266.5	433.7

Sources: For 1929, 1939: Cleona Lewis, The United States and Foreign Investment Problems, Washington, D.C., Brookings Institution, 1948, p. 26; for 1986 and 1990:Statistical Abstract of the United States 1992, p. 785; all other years: Historical Statistics of the United States: Colonial Times _____, Part II, pp. 868-869.

billion.[29] The lend-lease policy, the Bretton Woods conference on the International Monetary Fund and the International Bank for Reconstruction and Development, and the crucial 1947 General Agreement on Tariffs and Trade (GATT) all played a decisive role in achieving successive reductions in tariffs throughout the postwar years. The level of trade protection fell substantially, especially from the 1960s on, resulting in both drastic tariff reductions for most industrial goods among the developed countries and in a powerful expansion of world trade.

Within the new framework created by GATT and by a reciprocal U.S. agreement with the European Community (the Trade Expansion Act of 1962), our merchandise exports continued to exceed our imports. However, American investments abroad drained the balance of payments, first by small amounts, later by increasingly significant ones. In the decade of the 1950s, our balance of payments was unfavorable by about $18 billion. By the end of that decade our *net* international position amounted to $43 billion, while total foreign assets in the United States reached only some $39 billion, i.e., the equivalent of less than 10 percent of our GNP (then $406.7 billion). In the next decade, the balance of payments deficit rose to $25 billion, even though the balance of trade remained in our favor. By the end of the 1960s the net international position of the U.S. had increased to $67.2 billion, while foreign assets in the U.S. had also climbed – to over $90.8 – yet they still constituted only around 11.5 percent of the growing GNP (by then $780.7 billion).

Even more radical changes started to shape up in the decade of the 1970s. As I noted in Chapter 1, revitalized foreign competition turned our balance of trade and our current-account balance unfavorable throughout both the 1970s and the 1980s – with a few exceptions in certain years. During the 1970s U.S. assets abroad continued to grow, as did foreign assets in the U.S. – but at a quickened pace. By the end of that decade, the U.S. net international position had risen to $332.9 billion. But foreign assets in the U.S. had also increased massively, from $90.8 billion in 1969 to $449 billion in 1979, i.e., to close to 18 percent of a GNP then reaching the very high level of $2.5 trillion.

The speed of increase of foreign investments in the U.S. accelerated in the 1980s, for a large number of reasons already examined in Sections 1-4 and 1-5. Here I would like to draw particular attention to certain changes in the postwar framework of multilateral trade – changes which tend to be overlooked when, in discussing capital flow, one focuses only on the relation between national savings and national investments. With GATT deterring tariff increases, mounting *barriers to trade* started to be erected by the United States against the increasing economic challenge of the reconstituted economies of Japan, Germany, and the EEC, and of the "Little Tigers" of Asia as well. To stave off the competition, the United States went beyond such familiar methods as government subsidies to national producers and special standards and regulations, resorting to a number of extraordinary measures such as voluntary export restraints (VER), trigger price mechanisms (TPM), and targeted trade practices. The use of VERs on Japanese automakers amounted to an effective quota on U.S. imports of Japanese cars. VER agreements were also directed against Taiwan and other countries, e.g., in regard to machine tools. TPMs – the establishing of minimum prices for sale in the U.S. – were set in motion in regard to steel and semiconductors in order to "eliminate dumping." Finally, under the Omnibus Trade and Competitiveness Act of 1988, the U.S. was allowed (temporarily) to designate specific countries as unfair traders which it could then try to compel to change their trading practices.

The reaction to these measures, above all in Japan, was the upgrading of the mix of cars sold in the U.S., along with expanded investment in U.S. production, mainly in manufacturing capacity, in order to acquire a market share unconstrained by VER limitations. The Japanese also pursued the same policy in Europe, for automotives as well as for semiconductors and consumer electronics. U.S. companies also established new manufacturing facilities in Europe – again, most notably for the production of semiconductors. In short, the increased thrust toward building global market shares, the acceleration in the 1980s of penetration into foreign markets with unprecedented levels of investment, and the internationalization of manufacturing are not only the consequences of sharpened competition, but also, paradoxically – up to a point, at least – the result of devious protectionist barriers to trade.[30] (See also Section 7-3.)

From the end of the 1970s to the end of the 1980s, the United States' largest single source of investment in new plants and new plant expansion was Japan. Assets of foreign manufacturing affiliates as a percentage of the total assets of U.S. manufacturing corporations rose from 5.2 percent in 1977 to 12.2 percent in 1987. During the same years, the number of employees working for foreign manufacturing affiliates rose, as a percentage of total U.S. employment, from 3.5 to 7.9 percent.[31] Thanks to the inflow of British, Canadian, and Japanese investments, total foreign assets in the U.S. rose to $1,393 billion in 1986, and the U.S. again became, for the first time since 1914, the world's major debtor country (see Table 5-7). The indicated liabilities amounted at this point to close to 30 percent of our GNP of $4.2 trillion dollars.

The enormous increases in foreign assets in the U.S. through the 1980s, and the change in U.S. status from world's main creditor to world's main debtor – with a deficit of close to $440 billion by the end of the 1980s – has sharpened the debates about the consequences of foreign investment and about possible responses via our trade policies. The partisans of such investments have asserted that it increases U.S. productive capacity, provides employment, reduces interest rates, and constitutes a crucial instrument for the international transfer of resources, techniques, and skills – just as our own investments and our own companies and their affiliates abroad do – obviously, in exchange for income-earning assets in the form of equities or debt obligations. The opponents of this view have stressed (as we noted in Section 1-5) not only that the dividends and interest on these investments go abroad, but also that "undue penetrations" of foreign capital may endanger our national security. They insist that the nationality of a company's ownership (as Laura d'Andrea Tyson has regularly suggested) is of paramount importance, and that competition among states and local authorities to attract foreign investment (via reduced taxes and other subsidies) distorts market mechanisms and penalizes American producers.[32] (Actually, given the expansion of joint companies and of other forms of international investment combinations, it is often difficult if not impossible to distinguish neatly between an American and a foreign company.)

Temporarily at least, an informal understanding seems to have developed about giving higher priority to helping foreign companies to expand production in the United States rather than to assisting domestic companies to expand production in their factories overseas. This policy represents quite a departure from the more traditional view of foreign investment and from the policy of according priority to American companies *regardless* of whether their factories are at home or abroad. The shift is clearly dominated by the preoccupation with where and for whom the *jobs* are provided.[33] Yet it may be premature to believe that such decisions will necessarily apply to *all* foreign companies.

5-5   *The Group of Seven and U.S. performance*

U.S. economic development throughout the period under review can be best assessed by comparing it to that of the other most industrialized countries of our time, namely, the countries which, along with the United States, form the so-called *Group of Seven*. As can be seen from Table 5-8, the U.S. share in world manufacturing production in 1870 was already exceeded only by that of the United Kingdom; it was, in fact, exactly equal to that of Germany and France combined. By the end of the century, in 1896/1900, the U.S. share in world manufacturing output by far exceeded all the shares of the big industrial countries, including the U.K., and now equaled the total of the remaining five shares. On the eve of World War I, in 1913, the U.S. share in total manufacturing equaled the shares of the United Kingdom, Germany, and France combined. Again, on the eve of World War II, in 1936/38, the United States by far exceeded the combined shares of all the other principal combatants of the war, excluding Russia, namely Germany, Japan, Italy, France, and the United Kingdom.

The great changes undergone since the 1970s are illustrated in the last two rows of Table 5-8. In the total manufacturing output of the OECD in 1987, representing most of the world's industrial production in that year, the share of

Table 5-8. *Group of Seven: percentage distribution of manufacturing production: selected years, 1870–1936/38, of world output; 1980 and 1987, of OECD output*

Period	U.S.	Japan	Germany	France	Italy	U.K.	Canada
1870	23.3	N.A.	13.2	10.3	2.4	31.8	1.0
1896/1900	30.1	0.6	16.6	7.1	2.7	19.5	1.4
1913	35.8	1.2	14.3	7.0	2.7	14.1	2.3
1936/38	32.2	3.5	10.7	4.5	2.7	9.2	2.0
1980	33.5	18.7	12.1	7.6	4.7	7.3	N.A.
1987[a]	32.0	20.2	11.9	7.2	4.8	7.1	N.A.
1987[b]	37.4	25.1	10.5	4.9	3.1	8.2	N.A.

[a] Total manufactures.
[b] High-tech manufactures.
Sources: 1870-1936/38: League of Nations, Economic, Financial, and Transit Department, Industrialization and Foreign Trade, New York, League of Nations, 1945, p. 13; National Science Board, Science and Engineering Indicators 1991, p. 401.

the United States still exceeds the combined shares of its European partners in the Group of Seven – namely Germany, France, Italy, and the United Kingdom – but the share of Japan, negligible in the past, has increased to a very high level, equivalent to two thirds of that of the United States (20.2 percent vs. 32.0 percent of the total). In high-tech manufactures the shares of both the United States and Japan are very high, with the U.S. share still by far exceeding all others.

The extraordinary performance of the United States in relation to that of all the principal industrial countries over the entire period under review is further illustrated by the data on income per capita and growth of the total gross domestic product. As can be seen from Table 5-9, in *all* the years considered – 1900, 1913, 1950, 1973, 1987 – U.S. income per capita (in constant 1980 prices) exceeded by far that of each of the other members of the Group of Seven. Among the other six members, the most remarkable changes occurred in the GDP per capita of Japan: the lowest in 1900, by 1987 it exceeded the GNP per capita of such highly developed countries as France, the United Kingdom, and Italy.

GNP per capita is usually taken as the main – and at times as the only – criterion of economic development. I believe that what has to be taken into consideration *simultaneously* with it is the amount of investment at the disposition of each country at various points in time. Indeed, to reach higher and higher levels of development, critical masses of investment – i.e., threshold

Table 5-9. *Group of Seven: GDP per capita and total GDP (millions of international dollars at 1980 prices): selected years, 1900–1987*

Period	U.S.	Japan	Germany	France	Italy	U.K.	Canada
1900	2911	677	1558	1600	1343	2798	1808
1913	3772	795	1907	1934	1773	3065	2773
1950	6697	1116	2508	2941	2323	4171	4822
1973	10977	6622	7595	7462	6824	7413	9350
1987	13550	9756	9964	9475	9023	4178	12702

1900	222352	29840	53259	65154	44718	107502	9864
1913	368132	41102	77864	80636	64066	130623	21775
1950	1019725	93342	125361	123051	108657	210041	66240
1973	2326225	719530	470687	388908	371649	416686	206386
1987	3308401	1198943	606404	527602	515158	520270	329525

Upper part of table: GDP per capita.
Lower part of table: Total GDP (millions).
Source: Excerpted from Angus Maddison, The World Economy in the 20th Century, OECD Development Center, Paris, OECD, 1989, pp. 19, 113.

sizes of funds – must necessarily be available in order to propel an economy beyond its prevailing technological level. Such critical investable resources are needed for achieving significant structural changes, viz. the passing from, say, the production only of iron and steel to that of airplanes, then again to that of satellites and of such high-tech products as have been developed at the end of the 20th century. Using the GDP data presented in Table 5-9, we can, under various assumptions, visualize the possible shifts in the positions of these countries in the process of their economic development, i.e., of their *structural changes*.

Notice first the great differences in total GDP between the members of the Group of Seven, differences due both to the *size* of the countries considered, in terms of human and natural resources, and to the *speed* of their economic growth as fueled by the amount of their investments due to higher saving rates and/or possibly also of increasing direct foreign investments. In 1987, for instance, the population of the United States totaled 246 million persons, compared to 122 million in Japan and 55, 57, and 57 million in France, Italy, and the United Kingdom respectively. The population of Canada amounted to only 25 million people. The speed of growth of total GDP also varied greatly over the period 1900–87. According to Angus Maddison's data, the annual

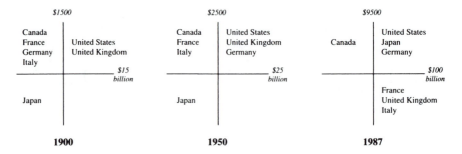

Figure 5-2. Development changes, 1900, 1950, and 1987.

compound growth rate of the GDP over the entire period was on the order of 3.2 percent for the United States, exceeding the yearly rate of 2.4 for France and 2.8 for Germany and Italy, but bettered by the rates of growth for Canada (4.1 percent) and Japan (4.3 percent). Size and speed of growth combined were bound to affect changes in investments available, technological changes, and position of these countries relative to one another. Schematically, one can illustrate such shifts on the basis of some reasonable assumptions concerning level of income per capita and the potential amount of investment at different points in time. Assume that in 1900, 1950, and 1987, for instance, the per capita GDP of a developed country was above $1,500, $2,500, and $9,500 respectively (these figures are closely related to the data presented in Table 5-9). And assume, on the other hand, that each country, in each of the years considered, allocated or could have allocated around 20 percent of its total GDP to investment. (On the basis of the data for 1980–87, the figure of 20 percent was actually exceeded in 1987, for instance, by Japan [29.9 percent] and not met by the U.S. [15.5 percent] and the U.K. [17.5 percent]; the percentage allocated to investment by the other four countries ranged between 20 and 22.) With this approximation, assume that the critical level of investment required for achieving the appropriate structural changes commanded by advancing industrial technology was on the order of $15 billion in 1900, $25 billion in 1950, and $100 billion in 1987 – a total corresponding on the average to GDPs of $75 billion, $125 billion, and $500 billion respectively (roughly corresponding to the midpoint levels of the G7).

As can be seen from Fig. 5-2, in 1900 only the United States and the United Kingdom had both higher GDP per capita and a higher amount of potential investment than the $15 billion level set. Canada, France, Germany, and Italy all had higher GDP per capita than the norm, but a lower investable mass. Finally, Japan was below the mark set for both GNP per capita and the investment norm. By 1950 the United States and the United Kingdom, now joined by

Germany, were above the $2,500 per capita GNP level and above the theoretical investment norm of $25 billion. Canada, France, and Italy were above the level set for per capita GDP, but below the suggested investment level. Japan was still below the two benchmarks. Finally, in 1987, by a highly sustained effort, Japan moved dramatically close to the United States and Germany, rising above the high mark of $9,500 per capita GDP and above the investable level of $100 billion. France, the United Kingdom, and Italy each also commanded an investable amount above the $100 billion benchmark, but their income per capita fell below the set level of $9,500. Finally, Canada reached an income per capita high above the mark, but its investable amount remained well below the criterion set. Continual shifts and reorderings thus occur in the process of growth and change. With its large population and enormous productive machine, the United States remains the "fixed point" around which all the reorderings take place.

Communist countries (past and present) have constantly claimed that, year in, year out, their investable means, as well as the rates of growth of their GNP, far exceeded those of the industrialized capitalist countries. These claims – particularly those of the former Soviet Union, as well as those of Communist China – always involved questionable calculations of GNP and of both the size and structure of the national investment. While this is not the place for a detailed analysis of these issues, let me recall in passing that already before the collapse of the Soviet Union it had become evident to its principal leaders that the performance of the economy, guided according to the traditional "Soviet strategy for economic growth," was yielding increasingly poor results. As is known, this strategy posited the allocation of a large share of GNP to investment: first of all to industry, and then, within industry, to producer goods. Until the collapse of their economies, the East European communist leaders, and then the Russians, hoped that they could avoid disaster by experimenting with various forms of "market socialism." The collapse of the system showed that a reduction in the detail and scope of central plan instructions, the introduction of leasing and of other forms of "commercialization" of state enterprises, and the authorization of more or less extensive markets at the borders of the state's "commanding heights" – with the party continuing to hold large-scale industry, banking, transportation, and most wholesale trade in its hands – were not sufficient to avoid catastrophe.[34] Notwithstanding these examples, China's experiments with "market socialism" seem to convey to some people the conviction that China's own way of traveling over a germane road could transform it into one of the industrialized giants of the 21st century. The Chinese have indeed engaged in a *sui generis* kind of market socialism since 1978, without following a particularly well-defined path. Essentially, in order to cope with agricultural stagnation, they liberalized (between 1978 and 1984) direct state control over the rural economy; then, in order to cope with the inefficiency of state enterprises, they created (between 1984 and 1988) the so-called director responsibility system, involving the transfer of management power over enterprises from party secretaries to directors. Further, while liberalizing market transactions, thanks to the growth and development of urban and rural small industries, they maintained a mandatory planning component of the economy, a two-tier price system, and a loosely defined public, collective, and private property regime. China's "socialist market economy," with a per capita income of some $400 and a total GNP of some $500 billion by the mid 1990s, is supposed to be lifted "into the ranks of industrialized countries by 2050." The experience of the former communist countries, and first of all the Soviet Union itself, makes the realization of such predictions quite doubtful.[35]

6   The state machine and the evolving economy

6-1   The state and its agenda

How large has the state machine in the United States become? How much have its functions expanded with regard to the allocation of resources, the distribution of income, the regulation of the market, the content and direction of foreign trade? How significant have become the federal government's receipts, outlays, and deficits in relation to GNP? In which ways, and why, has the state agenda been broadened?

Paradoxically, while the state's *functions* have grown only in step with the growth of the economy, growth in the state's *machinery* has far outpaced that of the economy, first during the great depression and then, at an even faster rate, through World War II. This growth continued through the following decades, but at a somewhat lower rate. Thus in the 15 years from 1914 to 1929, the federal workforce increased by 77,000; employees in the following 10 years increased by 360,000. In the decade 1929–39, total government employment – federal, state, and local – increased from 1.0 million to 1.7 million. In the following decade it rose to well over three and a half times the previous total, namely to 6.2 million. It then doubled through the next two decades, rising by 1969 to 12.6 million. Finally, in 1989, it reached 17.7 million – that is, exactly 10 times the 1939 level. As can be seen from Table 6-1, employment in government rose from 2.2 percent of the labor force in 1929 to 15.1 percent 60 years later. Incidentally, the increase in the "state machinery" has also been appreciable in relation to the total U.S. population. The machine rose from 1.3 percent of total population in 1929 to 7.1 percent in 1989. While the media clamor continually against the increase in federal employment, it is interesting to note that over the period 1939–89 employment in the federal government grew a little over threefold, while during the same period employment in state and local government increased over 18-fold. This divergence between the pace of growth of the federal government and that of state and local government would increase even more dramatically if a *federalist orientation* were to be adopted, as suggested, for instance, by Alice M. Rivlin. According to the federalists, the states should take charge of the pri-

Table 6-1. *U.S. government employment (thousands), 1914 and decennial changes, 1929–1989*

	1914	1929	1939	1949	1959	1969	1979	1989
1. Federal Government	483	560	920	2,047	2,399	2,969	2,898	2,988
2. State & Local Government	N.A.	496	797	4,156	6,088	9,716	13,315	14,781
3. Total	N.A.	1,056	1,717	6,203	8,487	12,685	16,213	17,769
4. Employed Labor Force	36,281	47,630	45,750	57,651	64,630	77,902	98,824	117,342
Ratios: 1/4	1.3	1.2	2.0	3.6	3.7	3.8	2.9	2.5
Ratios: 3/4	N.A.	2.2	3.7	10.8	13.1	16.3	16.4	15.1

Sources: Statistical Abstracts of the United States; Economic Report of the President . . . 1991, p. 322.

Table 6-2. *U.S. gross national product by end use, at current and at constant prices: decennial changes, 1929–1989*

	1929	1939	1949	1959	1969	1979	1989
Personal Consumption	74.4	73.4	68.5	63.8	62.0	62.4	66.3
Gross Private Investment	16.0	10.4	14.0	16.2	15.9	18.1	14.8
Gov. Purchases of Goods & Services	8.6	14.9	15.0	19.7	21.5	18.7	19.7
Net Exports	1.0	1.3	2.5	0.3	0.6	0.8	-0.8
Total GNP	100.0	100.0	100.0	100.0	100.0	100.0	100.0

Personal Consumption	66.4	67.0	62.7	60.1	60.1	62.8	64.5
Gross Private Investment	19.6	12.0	15.2	16.6	16.9	18.0	17.4
Gov. Purchases of Goods and Services	13.3	20.1	20.4	24.4	24.4	19.1	19.4
Net Exports	0.7	0.9	1.7	-1.1	-1.4	0.1	-1.3
Total GNP	100.0	100.0	100.0	100.0	100.0	100.0	100.0

Upper part of the table at current prices; lower part, 1982 prices.
Source: Computed from Economic Report of the President . . . 1991, pp. 286-287, 288-289.

mary public investments, especially in regard to education and infrastructure, with their revenue systems to be strengthened accordingly with the assistance of the federal government. In turn, the latter should eliminate most of its programs in education, housing, highways, social services, economic development, and job training, while focusing on health-care financing and on balancing the budget.[1] Though such a program of decentralization may have merits, its adoption and eventual implementation are unlikely. As Charles L. Schultze has noted, careful control of the civilian budget expenditures by Congress "reflects the fact that even minor decisions about *the means of achieving social ends* intimately affect income distribution, political power relationships, and group attitudes toward social questions."[2]

The allocation of resources among the competing needs of private consumption, private investment, and government purchases of goods and services is, as James Tobin once put it, "the central and classical theoretical problem of economics." As the data presented (at current prices) in Table 6-2 show, in relative terms personal consumption has generally tended to decline (except in the 1980s), falling from close to 75 percent of GNP in 1929 to 66 percent in

Table 6-3. *U.S. federal government and total government receipts,*
expenditures, surpluses, deficits, and gross federal debt as percentages of
GNP: decennial changes, 1929–1989, with 1995 estimates

	1929	1939	1949	1959	1969	1979	1989	1995
Fed. Gov. Receipts as Percent of GNP	3.7	7.1	14.9	16.5	20.1	18.9	19.3	20.0*
Fed. Gov. Outlays as Percent of GNP	3.0	9.1	14.7	19.1	19.8	20.6	22.3	20.0*
Surplus or Deficit as Percent of GNP	0.7	-2.0	0.2	-2.6	-1.7	-1.7	-3.0	N.A.
Gross Federal Debt as Percent of GNP	16.2	44.2	95.7	59.7	39.4	33.9	55.9	65.1
Total Gov. Receipts as Percent of GNP	10.9	16.7	20.7	23.8	29.3	28.5	29.6	N.A.
Total Gov. Outlays as Percent of GNP	9.9	19.2	20.8	26.8	29.1	29.1	31.6	N.A.
Surplus or Deficit as Percent of GNP	1.0	-2.5	0.1	-3.0	0.2	-0.6	-2.0	N.A.

Sources: For 1929 and 1939: Economic Report of the President . . . 1991, pp. 286, 375, 379;
all other: Historical Tables, Budget of the United States Government, Fiscal Year 1992, pp. 15,
17, 23, 71, 178, 180.

1989. Over that entire period, gross private investment has oscillated between
14 and 16 percent (except in the great depression years, when it fell to 10
percent, and in the stagflation years of the 1970s, when it rose to 18 percent).
Government purchases have increased significantly, rising from around 9 percent in 1929 to between 19 and 21 percent in the decades from 1959 to 1989.
While in real terms the changes have been less dramatic, the same basic
underlying tendencies are apparent. Personal consumption has tended to
decline (except in the 1980s), while gross private investment has oscillated
between 12 and 17 percent of GNP over the years, remaining below its 1929
level (even in the 1970s). Government purchases of goods and services have
risen well above the level of gross private investment, being 19–20 percent
overall, and in certain years 24 percent.

The budget of the federal government packs enormous power to affect
growth and stagnation, employment and unemployment, inflation and defla-
tion, and the extent and forms of income transfers. The growth of federal power
lies in the growth of the federal budget, not of federal employment. As can be
seen from Table 6-3, a comparison between 1929 and 1989 shows that the

share of federal outlays in the GNP increased from 3.0 percent to 22.3 percent, compared to 3.7 and 19.3 percent for receipts, leading during the years considered to a surplus equivalent to 0.7 percent of GNP in 1929 and to a deficit equivalent to 3.0 percent of GNP in 1989. During the 60 years considered, deficits have pushed the gross federal debt from 16.2 percent of GNP in 1929 to as high as 95.7 in the years immediately following World War II; the debt decreased to close to 34 percent of GNP in 1979 but then shot up dramatically again, reaching close to 56 percent of GNP by the end of the 1980s.

In terms of receipts, the total government share (including state and local governments) increased from around 11 percent of GNP in 1929 to close to 30 percent in 1989. In terms of outlays, the share increased from about 10 percent to about 32 percent. Put differently, close to one third of the country's GNP is now cleared through the government, which is why the United States is said to have a *mixed economy* whose beginnings may be traced to the 1930s. As far as the deficit and the gross federal debt are concerned, raising taxes and cutting spending are obvious ways of balancing the budget. However, given the influence the government exerts on private spending, lending, and borrowing, one may wonder to what extent the government is actually free to use either or both of these methods at significant levels in periods of sluggish or of no economic growth.

In 1869, the public debt of the federal government amounted to $2.5 billion. By the beginning of World War I, the total had fallen to less than half that amount, namely to $1.2 billion. By 1929 this public debt had risen to $15.1 billion, by 1939 to $34.9 billion, and by the end of World War II to $260 billion (then equal to 122.5 percent of GNP). Under Truman's presidency, from 1945 to 1952, the federal debt total fluctuated slightly, settling at $259 billion in 1952. From then on, it climbed under each presidency as follows: under Eisenhower (1953–60), by $22 billion; under Kennedy and Johnson (1961–68), by $79 billion; under Nixon and Ford (1969–76), by $259 billion; under Carter (1977–80), by $180 billion. Finally, and paradoxically, it rose in a period of peace, under the Republican administrations of Reagan and of Bush (considered herein only from 1981 through 1990), by the extraordinary amount of $2.298 trillion.[3] Clearly, the functions and the obligations of the government have moved far away from the modest "state agenda" of Adam Smith.

According to Smith, the agenda of the state was to be limited to defending the society; supporting the dignity of the chief magistrate; administering justice; maintaining good roads and communications (supported by tolls); and providing for institutions of education and religious instruction (though Smith adds that these latter two expenses "might perhaps with equal propriety, and even with some advantage, be defrayed altogether by those who receive immediate benefit of such education and instruction").[4]

If the federal agenda were to correspond to that of Adam Smith, the federal

Table 6-4. *U.S.: shares of Smith's governmental "core" in total federal budget outlays: percentages for 1940 and decennial changes, 1949–1989, with 1995 estimates*

Functions	1940	1949	1959	1969	1979	1989	1995
National Defense	17.5	34.2	59.0	52.1	28.8	32.6	24.3
Administration of Justice	0.8	0.4	0.4	0.5	1.0	3.9	1.3
Education and Training	20.1	0.4	0.9	4.7	7.5	1.0	3.8
General Government	2.9	2.1	1.1	1.2	3.0	0.9	1.1
"Core" as Percent of Total Fed. Outlays	41.3	37.1	61.4	58.5	40.3	38.4	30.5

Source: Computed from **Budget of the United States Government, Fiscal Year 1992**, Part Seven, pp. 30-36.

government would collect taxes to the extent needed for covering expenses for defense, justice, education, and the general government (with or without Smithian connotations of "the dignity" of the chief magistrate). In the modern federal budget understanding of these terms, a vast gamut of activities are involved. *Defense* concerns military personnel, operation and maintenance, procurement, R&D testing and evaluation, military construction, family housing, and more. *Administration of justice* covers federal law-enforcement activities, federal litigative and police activities, federal correctional activities, and criminal justice assistance. *Education* (including training and employment) involves disbursements for elementary, secondary, and vocational training, for higher education, for research and general education aids, and for certain labor services. Finally, the term *general government* covers legislative functions, executive direction and management, central judicial operations, general property and records management, general-purpose fiscal assistance, and other miscellaneous functions. Leaving aside "the maintenance of good roads and communications," which represent a small part of federal allocations for transportation, Smith's agenda would have involved around 42 percent of total federal budget outlays on the eve of World War II. At their highest point, in 1959, they would have come to 61 percent. In 1989 they would have accounted for some 38 percent, and in 1995 they should barely exceed 30 percent (Table 6-4).

Clearly, the modern agenda has extended well beyond Smith's concepts. Besides the indicated "core," it now covers outlays for public welfare, as well as a vast spectrum of expenditures on economic development (as we shall see in the next section). Even within the indicated "core," the array and scope of outlays has, of course, been appreciably broadened. Note that regulatory policies which may be considered part of the allocation function are not primarily a part of budget policy. (I shall return to some special aspects of regulation in Section 6-3.)

6-2   The federal budget and the agenda

From the beginnings of the 19th century up to 1921, as Charles L. Schultze reminded us, federal agencies submitted their budget requests directly to Congress. The president had no central staff to exert control over the size and composition of these requests, and no authority to amend them. The Congress was highly concerned to limit the power of the executive by specifying the appropriations in detail. The first major change in this system took place through the Budget and Accounting Act of 1921, which established, for the first time since the beginning of the republic, an *executive* budget. On the basis of this act, the president, rather than the individual departments, submitted budget requests to Congress. This consolidated request thus became the *president's budget.* The subsequent expanded activities of the federal government, both during the New Deal and then more strongly during the 1960s and the 1970s, led to a substantial broadening of the budgetary role of the president. Since the New Deal, the scheduled allocation of resources among the different federal programs has always involved "implicit evaluations of program benefits in light of presidential objectives."[5] In principle, it is within this basic framework – which Congress may and often does reject, but not completely – that budget decisions are finalized in Congress. Any budget involves not only *objectives* but also suggested *means* to carry them out: the choice of means is just as critical as that of the ends, and involves no fewer political decisions than the latter do. In the preceding section, we looked at the allocation of resources among consumption, investment, and government. I shall now turn to the federal budget's *distribution* functions, which are carried out by a combination of income taxes on high-income households and subsidies to low-income households.

Income taxes are now the mainstay of budgetary receipts. They have been increasing rapidly since 1940, when they accounted for less than 14 percent of total government receipts, to between 40 and 47 percent in the following years. The social insurance taxes which supply the Social Security system have also increased appreciably, but most of them are accounted off budget. Other federal taxes, notably corporate and excise taxes, have decreased since the 1950s. In relation to GNP, individual income taxes rose between 1940 and 1989 close to 10-fold (from 0.9 to 8.7 percent). Social insurance taxes and

Table 6-5. *U.S.: synoptic composition of federal receipts and outlays as percentages of GNP, 1940, 1959, and 1989*

RECEIPTS

	1940	1959	1989
Individual Income Taxes	0.9	7.6	8.7
Corporate Income Taxes	1.2	3.6	2.0
Social Insurance Taxes and Contrib.	1.9	2.4	7.0
(On Budget)	(1.3)	(0.7)	(1.9)
(Off Budget)	(0.6)	(1.7)	(5.1)
Excise Taxes	2.1	2.2	0.7
Other	0.7	0.6	0.9
Total	6.8	16.5	19.3
(On Budget)	(6.3)	(14.7)	(14.2)
(Off Budget)	(0.6)	(1.7)	(5.1)

OUTLAYS

Defense	1.7	10.2	5.9
Nondefense, including:	8.2	8.9	16.4
Payments for Individuals	1.7	4.7	10.4
Direct Payments	(1.4)	(4.2)	(9.1)
Grants to State and Local Gov.	(0.3)	(0.5)	(1.3)
All Other Grants	0.6	0.8	1.1
Net Interest	0.9	1.2	3.3
All Other	5.2	3.1	2.3
Undistributed Offsetting Receipts	-0.3	-1.0	-0.7
Total Outlays	9.9	19.1	22.3

Source: Budget of the United States, Fiscal Year 1992, Part Seven: Receipts, p. 23; Outlays, pp. 30-36.

contributions have almost quadrupled in relation to GNP during the same span of time (from 1.9 to 7.0 percent). (See Table 6-5.)

Outlays for defense rose between 1940 and 1989 from 1.7 percent of GNP to 5.9 percent – but the increases in certain war years were of course massive. Thus, in 1944 and 1945 the share of defense amounted to close to 40 percent of GNP. In the early 1950s, during the Korean War, the share in question stayed around 9 to 10 percent of GNP. One should not forget, however, that through-out all these years the U.S. defense provided the shield of the Western world against the Soviet military buildup. Nondefense expenditures have varied in-versely with expenditures on defense.

The budget of the United States separates federal outlays by superfunctions and functions, i.e., defense, human resources, physical resources, net interest, and other functions. I prefer to group the outlays in a different way, namely as expenditures on public welfare, on economic development, on net interest, and other. As can be seen from Table 6-6, public welfare has accounted for around or over a quarter of federal outlays, except in the 1950s and 1960s. The main item in this group is *income security* – including general as well as federal retirement and disability insurance (excluding Social Security), unemployment compensation, housing assistance, food and nutrition assistance, and other income security. Excluding retirement disbursements, expenditures in this category to a large extent reflect care for the disadvantaged as well as correc-tive responses to economic fluctuations. The *economic development* expendi-tures, while broadly decreasing as a share of total outlays, encompass a vast range of supports for critical economic activities. I have also included in this group the expenditures concerning *human capital* – education and health – which will certainly be radically modified in the years to come. Clearly the Clinton administration would prefer to expand expenditures on economic development, including not only those earmarked for health, but also those devoted to support for investment incentives, R&D, business tax rebates, and subsidies for industrial policies, but prospects in this regard are still uncertain (see also Chapter 7).

The question of *net interest* generates considerable confusion among the public. When considering just the size of its share in total expenditures – which, as we see in Table 6-6, had reached 18 percent of federal outlays by the end of the 1980s – people not unnaturally become deeply worried about its economic impact. However, when one considers the *structure* of the federal debt, one notices first of all that on the threshold of the 1990s almost a quarter of this debt was held in government accounts (federal agencies and the Social Security Trust) and that an additional 7 percent was held by the Federal Re-serve banks, the rest being held by "private investors." Less than 15 percent of the total federal debt was held by *foreign* investors. Thus, most of the interest on the debt was disbursed in the U.S. either to government accounts or to private institutions such as foundations, pension funds, credit unions, and, finally, personal investors. As Robert Eisner once put it, the debt of the govern-ment is a debt to its own people. The greater the government debt, the greater the people's net worth.

The existence of a continually rising deficit does absorb a significant part of private savings which *might or might not* have gone to investment in housing

Table 6-6. *U.S.: percentage composition of federal outlays by function groups, 1940, and decennial changes, 1949–1989*

OUTLAYS BY FUNCTION GROUPS

	1940	1949	1959	1969	1979	1989
1. Public Welfare						
Income Security	16.0	8.3	9.9	8.2	16.4	14.6
Social Security (on budget)	N.A.	N.A.	N.A.	0.3	0.2	0.5
Veterans' Benefits & Services	6.0	17.2	6.5	4.8	4.9	3.2
Medicare	N.A.	N.A.	N.A.	3.6	6.6	9.1
Subtotal	22.0	25.5	16.4	16.9	28.1	27.4
2. Economic Development						
Natural Resources & Environment	10.5	2.8	1.9	1.8	3.0	1.7
Commerce & Housing	5.8	2.1	2.3	N.A.	1.2	3.2
Transportation	4.1	2.4	4.4	4.1	4.3	3.0
Community & Regional Development	3.0	N.A.	0.3	0.9	2.6	0.6
General Science, Space & Technology	0	0.1	0.4	3.2	1.3	1.4
Agriculture	3.9	5.0	5.4	3.8	2.8	1.8
Energy Supply	0.9	0.9	0.5	0.6	2.3	0.3
Education & Training	20.8	0.4	0.9	4.8	7.5	3.9
Health	0.6	0.5	0.8	3.2	5.0	5.2
Subtotal	49.6	14.2	16.9	22.4	30.0	21.1
3. Net Interest	9.5	11.8	6.9	8.0	10.6	18.1
All other nondefense	1.4	14.3	0.8	0.6	2.5	0.8
Subtotal	10.9	26.1	7.1	8.6	13.1	18.9
4. National Defense	17.5	34.2	59.0	52.1	28.8	32.6
Total Federal Outlays on Budget	100	100	100	100	100	100

Source: Computed from **Budget of the United States Government, Fiscal Year 1992**, Part Seven, pp. 30-41.

or in business plant and equipment. That is, a decrease in the deficit and a corresponding increase in the resources available for private investment might or might not actually generate additional productive investment. On the other hand, reduction of the deficit without, say, the offsetting effect of a marked easing in monetary policy would certainly reduce demand, employment, and output, slowing down the economy's growth.

The agenda is thus continually shaped by policy *choices* which reflect political philosophies; the complex and conflicting changes in the society's approaches to economic, social, and ethical problems; and the deep shifts in military as well as economic patterns in the world at large. The range of choices of both ends and means is, of course, limited both by the overall resources available and by certain fixed obligations or commitments reflecting decisions taken in the past.

6-3   *The state and the consumer's interests*

As I stated, regulation is not primarily a budget problem. But the regulatory agencies, which engage in an enormous range of controlling activities, do account for large administrative expenditures absorbing billions of dollars per year. In the analysis of government-business relations presented in Chapter 2, I focused on the ways in which certain regulatory activities, supervisory actions, allocative processes, and promotional supports have modeled the framework of business operations and have limited or expanded the scope of business activities. In the present section I wish to center the reader's attention on a variety of measures enacted by the government in order to stop and/or modify a number of business methods and practices and thereby to *protect the consumer.* Such measures complete certain budgetary provisions concerning welfare and extend the scope of the latter to the population as a whole.

Everyone is familiar with the oft repeated adage reigning in the competitive arena: "Let the consumer beware" (*caveat emptor*). In the market framework, consumers are indeed masters of their choices and pay for their own mistakes. Yet a broad network of government measures is also continually setting various limitations in the market processes, with the object of protecting the consumer and of "letting the seller beware" (*caveat venditor*). I shall focus here on three groups of regulatory activities, attempting to show in historical perspective how they have developed and how they are interconnected. I shall refer first to regulatory measures concerning monopolistic price fixing; second, to measures against certain abusive procedures in the securities markets and in banking; and third, to the complex set of measures concerning control of the true characteristics of goods to be sold, the processes used in their production, and their impact on the population. These three sets of measures coalesced during three nodal historical periods: the rise of industrialism at the end of the 19th century, the great depression of the 1930s, and the great stagflation of the 1970s. I shall sketch for each of these sets the broad historical background, the main debates which took place at the time about what should be done, and finally the measures actually taken and their subsequent development.

The post-Civil War years, on which I intend to focus now, witnessed a powerful transformation in the country's economic structure, involving dramatic shifts from a predominantly agricultural to a preponderantly industrial setup. Technologically, farming also advanced rapidly, but in the process many farmers suffered from the adverse effects of output expanding beyond market demand (particularly falling prices); high rates of rail transport; high prices of manufactured goods protected by tariff walls; tight credit; increased indebtedness; and shrinking income. In the almost permanent farm depression marking the post-Civil War decades, the farmers began to agitate first against the high rates of rail transport for farm products (higher than for industrial ones), then against tight credit and scarce money (in favor of bimetallism), and finally and increasingly, against the wave of trust and monopoly formation. Manufacturing and related industries were indeed expanding rapidly, and large-scale concentrations of business into fewer and fewer hands were becoming the rule, particularly from the 1880s on. Firms' combinations on the model of the railroads' organization were generating trusts, holding companies, mergers, and cartels aiming aggressively at eliminating "excessive competition," restricting output, and fixing prices. The opinions of the professional economists of the time were divided as to how to assess the nature and the impact of these changes. Arthur T. Hadley of Yale, a former president of the American Economic Association, asserted in 1899 that competition in the old sense of the term was "a thing of the past" and that we could not continue to have such competition without "disastrous fluctuations in price and the danger of commercial crises due to irregular investments of capital."[6] In the same year, John R. Commons of Columbia University, while recognizing that the "competitive system had broken down," affirmed that the new system led to the "misuse of power" by "trustees" without any legal or commercial penalties, and that the task of the economists was to aim to break down these monopolies and to abolish the laws they had enacted in their favor.[7] An intermediate position was formulated by John Bates Clark, also toward the end of the 1890s. Contending that it was impossible either to restore "internecine" competitive war or to force the monopolies into "illegal forms," he suggested that "to regulate combinations is possible and, in some directions, desirable; to permanently suppress them is impossible."[8]

Public sentiment, meantime, had come to incline – though not necessary consistently – against industrial concentration, particularly in the railroads, and in favor of some legislation with regard to business combinations. Under the farmers' so-called Granger movement, and subsequently under the auspices of the Populist movement (a combination of farmers, workers, inflationists, and other reformers, especially those of the Knights of Labor and the American Federation of Labor), more or less effective pressures were generated on policymakers in the states and in Congress to write into law prohibitions against monopolies, restraint of trade, and price fixing. In 1887 Congress passed the Interstate Commerce Act, prohibiting formation of pools among the railways and also creating the Interstate Commerce Commission, the first major federal regulatory agency. Some 32 states and 2 territories passed antitrust laws, and in 17 states antitrust provisions were inserted in the state constitution. Finally, in 1890 Congress adopted the Sherman Anti-Trust Act, the foundation of our antitrust legislation. Yet during the six or seven years following its adoption, neither Congress nor the general public exercised active pressure in favor of its enforcement. Paradoxically, the entire period 1898–1903 was a time "of more frenzied trust formation, at least relatively speaking, than at any other time in American history."[9] But from 1903 on, antitrust law was increasingly a force to be reckoned with, as the administration of the law, its scope, its judicial interpretation, and its enforcement were recast and strengthened. A series of laws and measures adopted through the years – notably against price discrimination and unfair competition – supplemented the Sherman Act (e.g., the Clayton Act of 1914, the Robinson-Patman Act of 1936, the Antimerger Act of 1950). These acts plugged some loopholes and introduced various procedural changes. Did all these measures markedly help the consumer? The evidence is not always compelling, nor is public opinion unanimous on the issues involved. Critics of antitrust policies contend that the antitrust laws have been ambiguous, their theoretical foundations faulty, and many antitrust rules and court decisions inappropriate. Yet the defenders of the policy continue to enjoy public support, and the further expansion of antitrust enforcement continues to be viewed by many as useful.[10]

The second climactic event which dramatically widened the scope of government regulation of business and of its attention to consumer protection was the New Deal, the complex set of policies aimed at overcoming the great depression of the 1930s. The debacle of the stock market on Thursday, October 24, 1929, saw the convulsive collapse of share prices and the wiping out of billions of dollars of investments. Further stock market plunges on October 28 and 29 increased the scale of the disaster. The prices of commodities and commodities groups fell at varying speeds; money supply and credit operations tightened spasmodically; currency and demand deposits shrank abruptly; and loans and discounts of all banks dropped dramatically. The number of the unemployed rose rapidly. In the presence of the general mood of despair and discouragement, the economists, like the decisionmakers and the public at large, were deeply divided on the question of what the government should do: should it intervene or not in the economy? And if it should, in which ways should it recast the relation between business, labor, and itself? While some economists viewed the depression as a purely monetary phenomenon, others saw in it an expression of a chronic demand deficiency, while still others asserted that the institutional setup concerning money and credit, the operation of business, and the distribution of income were at fault.

The New Deal covered a period of seven years: from March 1933 to June 1940, when the beginning of war preparations lifted the economy out of its still prevailing difficulties. Under the complex pressures building up in the economy from 1930 on, under the pull and push of the division of public opinion impacting the media and the policymakers, President Roosevelt developed his own strategy of *relief, recovery,* and *reform* – a strategy not always consistent, yet coherent at least in some fundamental respects. Through a series of measures he attempted to increase demand via expansion of the "purchasing power" of farmers, workers, the old, the needy, the debtors. But through a set of other measures he aimed to facilitate concerted reductions in output and increases in price by the suppression of antitrust legislation – measures which canceled, up to a point, the raising of "purchasing power." In regard to the defense of the consumer, on which I intend to focus here, the New Deal affected the stock market and banking as follows. Much attention was being paid at the time to such abuses in stock market transactions as the "watering down" of stocks (i.e., the issuing of stocks whose initial value exceeded the book value), misrepresentation of facts and other distorted information hampering rational buying decisions, unlicensed and unregulated brokerage activities, and illicit stock price manipulations. A series of laws, beginning with the Security Act of 1933 (the so-called Truth in Securities Act), followed in 1934 by the Securities and Exchange Act (which created the Securities and Exchange Commission) and in 1935 by the Public Utility Holding Act (protecting the public against the collapse of such companies), established a *structure of controls* over the issue and negotiation of *securities.* Most notably, it prohibited the interstate sale of securities without adequate information, extended federal regulation to the securities markets, and devised appropriate measures for protecting the public against the collapse of utility holding companies. With regard to banking, the big problem of the time was the multiplication of bank failures and the apparently imminent collapse of the entire banking system. The so-called Glass-Steagall Act of 1933, designed in particular to weaken the connection between speculation and banking and to give added powers to the Federal Reserve, along with the Banking Act of 1935, further broadened the powers of the Federal Reserve and extended the government's control over banking. An additional layer of protection was added by Congress in the form of federal deposit insurance. These guarantees of bank safety, stabilizing banking operations and protecting the depositor, though slightly modified by subsequent legislation, are still in effect.

The third cycle of complex regulations of business was likewise aimed at preventing certain abusive forms of marketing and product promotion as well as protecting the consumer in a number of directions. Already under way before the 1970s, but coalescing during the great stagflation and in its aftermath, it involved legislation to ensure not only pure food, drugs, and cosmetics, but above all *product safety* and *product liability*, as well as *environmental policies* with crucial implications for the population as a whole.

Let us briefly recall the course of the great stagflation. The slowing down of the economy after the Vietnam War, the rise of Japanese competition in international markets and in our domestic market as well, and finally the Arab oil price hikes ushered in a difficult period, marked in the nine years between November 1973 and November 1982 by three recessions, two of which were severe. The largest of these dragged on for not less than 16 months. Its trough was reached by the first quarter of 1975. High inflation rates, high unemployment rates, faltering productivity, losses of leadership in certain technological fields, and a deterioration in the country's balance of trade were accompanied by appreciable decreases in the average growth of the GNP, personal consumption, public consumption, and private investment. The quandary facing the policymakers of the time, and particularly the Carter administration, which took office in 1977, is vividly summarized by Alice M. Rivlin, who noted that the 1970s were "a tough time for policy makers" because none knew how to deal with stagflation: *restrictive* policies would take the pressure off inflation but would probably raise unemployment; *stimulative* policies would reduce unemployment but very likely would aggravate inflation. Even with hindsight, as she concludes, it is not clear what set of policies could both have offset the inflationary pressures and curbed unemployment.[11] Carter applied first stimulative policies (as I pointed out in Section 2-1) and then restrictive ones without succeeding in pulling the economy out of its predicament.

In the area of business regulation, the Carter administration's concern for stimulation led it to focus first on dismantling various obsolete regulations hampering development (e.g., deregulation of the airlines), on exploring alternatives, potentially less costly, and on setting priorities among regulatory objectives. However, the administration and Congress soon did advance the legislative processes started in the immediately preceding administrations in favor of consumer protection with respect to consumer product quality, warranties, and safety; workplace health and safety; and environmental protection covering virtually every kind of manufacture and every kind of production process. Carter promised to create a consumer protection agency within the executive branch of government, but the legislation introduced to create it failed to clear Congress.[12]

The "consumer policy" which came to fruition in the 1970s, along with the "social regulation" with regard to health, safety, and the environment, are in fact and in law complementary to certain antitrust objectives and other measures aiming to prevent various really or potentially abusive business practices. Ultimately, these measures probably "strengthen open markets, encourage pluralist and voluntarist solutions, stimulate decentralization and experimentation, and establish a balance between *caveat emptor* and *caveat venditor*."[13]

6-4   The state and the producer's interests

In Chapter 2 I examined the interaction of the policies, instruments, and measures concerning property rights, contracts, and the rules and scope of regulations which establish the legal matrix within which the market operates and businesses function. In this section, I shall concentrate on the evolution of U.S. policies in *foreign trade,* from the early application of mercantilist-protectionist principles, to a free trade approach, and then on to a diffuse combination of the two courses aiming to protect the interests of domestic producers – though not always of all of them – against a variety of real or potential inroads by foreign competitors. The basic changes in U.S. foreign trade policies are illustrated by the changes in *tariff rates,* though the latter reflect the coalescing at given junctures of diverse and extremely complex underlying factors.

As can be seen from Fig. 6-1, the average tariff rate on dutiable imports reached a high plateau (with some variations) between the threshold point of the 1870s and the beginning of the 1900s, during the rise of American industrialism and its first period of feverish combinations, vast consolidations, and mergers. During these years, average tariff rates on dutiable imports reached between 43 and 48 percent. Between 1904 and 1920 – a period of vigorous economic growth – the average tariff rate on dutiable imports fell from the 48 percent peak to around 16 percent. Then again, during the early post-World War I years – enormously difficult ones for American agriculture – the rate on dutiable imports for agricultural and other products was pushed upwards, notwithstanding the otherwise booming economy, to 36 percent by 1924 and then on up to 40 percent by 1929. The beginnings of the Great Depression pushed this rate even higher, from 44 percent in 1930 to over 59 percent – the highest rate ever – in 1932. From the New Deal years onward, the rate declined to 35 percent in 1940 and to 13 percent by 1950. The rates of 12 to 13 percent held steady until the process of decline reasserted itself at the end of the 1960s, pulling the rate down to between 5 and 5.5 percent in the 1980s.[14]

Thus, after the Civil War and for the next 35 years, the average tariff rate on dutiable imports remained very high, in part because it was high duties that brought in most of the state's revenues until the adoption of the income tax amendment in 1913, and in part because of powerful pressures from various industries, particularly the heavy industries, which in the post-Civil War years

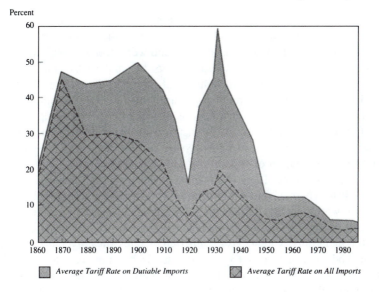

Figure 6-1. U.S. tariff rates, 1860-1987. *Source:* Department of Commerce; *Economic Report of the President . . .* 1989.

felt more secure in their drive for expanded production behind high tariff walls. But these high tariff duties kept the prices of certain industrial products high, and, as I have already pointed out, also nourished deep dissatisfaction among the farmers and in the lower urban strata. The significance of these high tariff rates for the development of American industry during the period in question is still under debate. Thomas K. McCraw, for instance, recalls that Frank Taussig in his classic early study *The Tariff History of the United States* argued that neither the iron and steel nor the woolen and cotton industries actually benefitted from this protection. However, though the evidence remained unclear, Taussig felt that later on the tariff "may" have stimulated the growth of these basic industries. McCraw himself does not doubt that the tariff did have very useful consequences, concluding that "in a significant measure the modern American industrial plant sprouted and grew to maturity behind high tariff walls." He also adds that a lobbyist of the time for the American Iron and Steel Association anticipated, in his 1876 book *The Industrial Policies of Great Britain and the United States,* with "uncanny accuracy" the terms of today's debate on industrial policy, namely "promotion of selected domestic industries, subsidies to exports, discouragement of imports, overall coordination of policy."[15] Incidentally, McCraw's interpretation of Taussig is not authoritative. In his introduction to the latest revised edition of Taussig's *Tariff History,* David M. Chalmers recalls first that the most important "protected" industries on which he focuses, iron, wool, and cotton textiles, owed their growth to factors other than the tariff. Woolen and cotton textiles gained major tariff protection only after they were established and were strong enough to sustain themselves, and the iron industry had developed from the 1830s on, thanks to the discovery of anthracite. On the other hand, he asserts that combinations and concentrated power were the products of large-scale production rather than of protection.[16] The latter led to other consequences than the "growing to maturity" of the iron and steel industry, for instance. As Frank W. Tuttle and Joseph M. Perry cogently point out in *An Economic History of the United States,* the tariff on the importation of certain iron and steel products permitted the perpetuation of certain obsolete technological processes in the U.S., e.g., refining iron ore via the charcoal method "long after it had become a relatively high cost process in world markets." Since the prices of steel products were kept high, the railroads, then the main customers for these products, incurred high fixed costs for their rails, which pushed up freight rates (heavily burdening the farmers) and passenger fares. By the end of the 1890s, however, steel started to be increasingly used in the construction of buildings, bridges, and tunnels. Even though the tariff rates kept the cost of imported steel high relative to domestic prices, steel imports increased, since the expanding American mills were still not large enough to meet the exploding demand. Also the rates of return on capital tended to be higher here than in Europe, a fact which attracted here large amounts of foreign portfolio investment as well as direct foreign investment.[17]

As American manufacturing grew and surpassed European manufacturing outputs, Congress oriented itself, first cautiously and then more resolutely, toward the decrease of tariff rates. But no sooner had the average tariff rate on dutiable imports reached its above-mentioned low of 16 percent in 1920 than pressures built for a return to high rates. The "Emergency" Tariff Act of 1921, and then the Fordney-McCumber Act of 1922, took the average tariff rate on dutiable imports back up to 29 percent in 1921 and to 38 percent in 1922. With the end of the 1920s, under the Hoover administration, Congress finally enacted the last of the old-style tariffs, the Hawley-Smoot Act. The worst-conceived and most disastrous tariff in our history, Hawley-Smoot raised the indicated average tariff rate to 44 percent in 1930, to 53 percent in 1931, and to 59 percent in 1932. America's actions sparked a series of reactions which led to convulsive contractions in world trade and to the deepening of the great depression. As I recalled above, from 1933 on the new Democratic administration started to shift steadily away from the economic policies of narrow nationalism, increasingly aware that tariffs had to be set with the world market as well as domestic industry in mind. Notwithstanding heavy pressure from the protectionists, an amendment was added in 1934 to the Hawley-Smoot Act, known henceforth as the Reciprocal Trade Act, adopted at the time as an "emergency" antidepression measure. The path chosen was selective reductions of tariffs to up to 50 percent of the Hawley-Smoot levels via bilateral agreements and the use of other means of import control. Between 1934 and 1940, 23 trade agreements were negotiated, effecting over 1,000 reductions in the Hawley-Smoot tariff rates, out of the 3,000 rates in its schedule. The outbreak of World War II pushed the government to take over control of foreign trade. As in all the countries engaged or engaging in the conflict, ukases about purchases and sales, prices and means of distribution, all reinforced by quotas, licenses, and the rationing of exchange, displaced consumers and entrepreneurs from their normal decisionmaking roles in regard to trade. In 1940, the United States adopted the lend-lease policy, which ended U.S. neutrality and set out to transform America into the "arsenal of democracy."

As the war drew to a close, an array of organizations were created under American leadership with a view to placing international cooperation on new foundations. Yet, while the General Agreement on Tariffs and Trade (GATT) was created in 1947 on the basis of principles derived from America's trade agreements, the "liberal" U.S. tariff policy remained anchored in the Reciprocal Trade Act of 1934 until the radical Extension Act of 1962. The latter act directed new negotiations with the European Community and empowered the president to negotiate wide cuts in 1962 tariff levels and to eliminate duties altogether on various products supplied by the Europeans. A major step in international tariff cutting was completed in 1967 at the close of the so-called Kennedy Round (the sixth in the series of bargaining rounds promoted by GATT), leading to cuts in the tariffs of close to two thirds of our dutiable imports. The very success of the Kennedy Round eventually created other difficulties, as both domestic and international conditions changed and several of our industries started to scramble for protection. And, as I earlier recalled, with the rise of Japanese competition, the beginning of the great stagflation, and our increased balance of trade and current-account deficits, the resort to nontariff barriers increased in importance, and, along with them, nontariff overt or covert distortions of trade.[18]

Thus, paradoxically, while the average tariff rates on dutiable imports (and on all imports) remain low, the nontariff barriers to trade are flourishing. The focus in this development (as is usually also the case with tariffs) is allegedly a preoccupation with *jobs*, rather than with the *consumer*. The nontariff drive also affects the antitrust laws in an interesting way. Thus, the National Cooperative Production Amendment Act of 1993 states that firms notifying the federal government of investment in joint production ventures should be liable only for actual damages in antitrust laws. In addition, the legislation allows manufacturers to pool resources, share technology, and spread risk to help offset the costs of research, technology development, and capital equipment.

In the conditions of rising international competition – due, incidentally, not only to Japan, but also to the EU and certain industrializing former less developed countries – economists such as Laura d'Andrea Tyson suggest, as I recalled, that the U.S. must adopt an industry-targeting "strategic trade policy" against Japanese "planned" inroads into world trade. Other influential economists like Paul R. Krugman have developed an apparently intermediate position between the "conventional wisdom" of free trade and the orientation toward "strategic" trade policies. On the one hand he states that "free trade is not *passé*," but that it is an idea "that has irretrievably lost its innocence." On the other hand he asserts that he has looked "pretty thoroughly" into the "dynamic aspects" of aggressive trade policies and has found their policy implications to be limited.[19] In short, "the old time free trade position seems naive," while the "basher program" (to wit, bashing the Japanese) "seems equally unappealing." But after this distribution of merits and demerits right and left, Krugman himself concludes that "protection may, in some cases, actually be beneficial," and "an explicit, but limited, U.S. industrial policy" may be appropriate. And he even recommends that the U.S. should make a decision to "frankly subsidize a few sectors, especially in the high-technology area, that may plausibly be described as 'strategic.'"[20]

I do not believe that the cautious balancing of the idea that "free trade is not *passé*" and the discovery that the "bashing" of competitors is not appealing renders the recommendation of a "limited industrial policy" any more acceptable than the proposal of a "full" industrial policy. Who will trace these limits? Who will choose the industries that "plausibly" may be called strategic? Who will define the "high technology area"? Again, as I have already stated, I do not believe that selected state bureaucrats can make these decisions better than business and the private market can make them. However, Krugman may be right in one respect: a new, more confrontational tone in American foreign trade policy, expressing renewed confidence in the ability of the government to step in effectively where "unregulated markets appear to produce unsatisfactory results," is already increasingly audible, and may become even more so in the not too distant future.[21]

6-5   Concluding comments

According to a popular socioeconomic paradigm proposed most notably by Daniel Bell in his work *The Coming of Post-Industrial Society* (1973), the U.S. evolved during the period 1870–1970 from a *pre-industrial* to an *industrial* and then to a *post-industrial* society. This symbolic transformation, readily accepted and popularized not only by the media but also by some pseudoscientific publications, is based on a number of simplistic interpretations of the data concerning the changes over time in U.S. sectoral incomes and employment.

Following Daniel Bell, a pre-industrial society is one where the labor force is overwhelmingly engaged in the "extractive" industries, which he defines as consisting of mining, fishing, forestry, and agriculture. An industrial society is a "goods-producing" society centered on worker-machine relationships and using energy to transform the environment. Finally, a post-industrial society is based on services. Its dominant figure is the *professional* equipped by education and training to provide the skills which such a society requires. Focusing on the United States, Bell cannot, however, use the familiar identifications of pre-industrial society with agriculture *and* the *farmer*, and of the industrial society with manufacture *and* the *worker*. It is true that in 1869, for instance, agriculture was the predominant sector in terms of employment, but at no moment in U.S. history has manufacturing been the predominant sector in terms of its share in the labor force. Furthermore, the entire industries sector (defined, as it traditionally is, to include only mining, construction, and manufacturing) has *never* exceeded services (also defined in the usual fashion, that is, including services per se plus transportation, communications, utilities, and government).

Confronted with these dilemmas, Bell identified, as indicated above, the pre-industrial society with the "extractive" industries, and the industrial society with "goods producing." But this peculiar choice turns out also to be an unfortunate one. In 1869, for instance, on the strength of the "extractive" industry criterion, the U.S. was a pre-industrial society; that is, close to 50 percent of its labor force was still engaged in these industries. But the extractive industries were also *goods-producing* industries, and if to the "extractive" workers we add those in manufacturing (then employing 17.7 percent of the labor force), then they already jointly accounted for the largest shares of both employment and output, to an extent which, according to Bell, would indisputably make the American society of 1869 an "industrial society." Following Bell's criteria, the United States remained an industrial society from 1869 to 1939, when services – defined in the usual fashion – finally reached 50.8 percent of total employment, compared to 49.2 percent for the goods-producing sector. Thus, in Bell's schemata the United States ceased to be an industrial society at precisely the moment when manufacturing started to powerfully expand its relative share of both total income and employment, a situation which continued roughly until 1969 (refer back to Fig. 5-1). Bell's implicit axial idea of the transition from the centrality of the farmer to that of the industrial worker, and finally to that of the professional, also does not comfortably fit the data. As we saw in Table 5-3, all blue-collar workers accounted, from 1900 to 1960, for roughly the same percentage (36 to 39 percent) of the experienced civilian labor force. The advanced craft and kindred workers also kept their relative share fairly steady during the entire period considered (this share fluctuated between 10.5 and 12.5 percent). Finally, from 1900 to 1989, professional and technical employment grew rapidly, namely from some 4 percent to over 16 percent of the experienced workforce. But only together with the managers, officials, and proprietors did they finally account, by 1989, for a larger relative share of the indicated workforce than blue-collar workers did.

In discarding the post-industrial paradigm, I do not intend to hitch onto some other kind of archetype (e.g., the one contending that the U.S. has become "a mature industrial society" – as Alvin Hansen proposed it in the 1930s and as John Kenneth Galbraith reasserted it in the 1960s – or the one alleging that the U.S. is a "declining industrial society," as notably Robert Reich and Lester Thurow indicated in the 1980s). What it seems to me that a careful reading of the data suggests is this: the incessant transformations both *within* the technology of each economic sector and *between* sectors since the 1970s have certainly led to a shift increasing the relative share of nongovernmental services in total income and in employment. But this shift has involved first of all an expanding *interlocking* between industry and commerce (and eventually government) with a certain group of services, in particular business, professional, and technical services, due to the rapid growth and change of these services founded on the revolution in information technology. The relative decrease in the share of manufacturing in total income and employment reflects the consequences both of this expanding *outsourcing at home* and of continued *outsourcing abroad,* due in the latter case to other kinds of changes in competition and cooperation in production and trade.

The data presented in the preceding chapters also indicate clearly that the United States remains the leading manufacturing economy among the most industrialized countries of the world, a position which it gained and has kept since the end of the last century. In looking to the next century, we should not forget that the collapse of the Soviet Union will allow the United States to redirect many of its vast human and material resources toward the growth and transformation of a large number of nondefense-related activities. There are no valid reasons to believe in the pessimistic forecasts spun by Paul Krugman and Lester Thurow, who predict that "by the year 2000 the United States will have sunk to the number three economic power in the world," the number one position being held by "an increasingly unified Europe" and the number two position by Japan, whose national income will be "80 percent or more of the U.S. level."[22] Such forecasts rest on arbitrary projections and many shaky assumptions about the U.S. economy, about Europe's "increasing" unification, and about Japan's crisis-free growth.

Part IV

The road ahead

Introductory note

The collapse of the Soviet Union; the end of the cold war; and rising competition from Japan, certain newly industrialized Asian countries, Germany, and the European Union, have, as we have noted, changed many elements shaping the U.S. national economic scene and international economic relations. Now the overwhelming questions are: if the United States is to maintain its industrial and economic leadership and keep its high standard of living in the 21st century, how should it mold its economic policies, allocate its national product, and "manage" its foreign trade? Is the United States capable of keeping the lead in an ever changing technological environment? Who is actually overtaking whom in the perspective of the new century?

The two chapters of Part IV focus on various issues concerning *technological change*. In the first of the two I shall sketch the directions in which the Clinton-Gore administration has been trying to orient the U.S. economy, an orientation which is bound to have long-lasting effects no matter the administration. In the second I shall focus on the meanings of "catching up" and "surpassing" in the process of development; on the nature of changes in a technological matrix; and on the leading role of the United States in the unfolding revolutionary changes of the Age of Information.

To a large extent, America's pessimistic diagnosticians of the 1980s have succeeded in drawing the public's attention to two critical questions: Can America increase its rate of economic growth and preserve its standard of living without engaging in a complex, all-encompassing industrial policy? Can America keep its competitors from overtaking it in the battle for technological supremacy in the 21st century? While the diagnosis of America's economic "maturity" and "decline" is increasingly viewed as doubtful, the alarmist analysts of the late 1970s and early 1980s have nevertheless succeeded in convincing a significant part of the body politic that the time has come for the U.S. to "catch up" with its competitors and their achievements, via the implementation of a comprehensive *industrial policy* and the expansion of its trade within a subset of countries dominated by it.

Paradoxically, as we shall see in Chapter 7, the prescriptions of the literature on growth, development, and planning, which are intended for the less

207

developed countries, have found an increasingly receptive audience in the United States and in other developed countries. In order both to increase the speed of growth and to "catch up" with some real (or imaginary) successes by America's competitors, the Clinton administration of new Democrats has stressed the need for a fundamental shift in spending patterns, along with the implementation of a comprehensive industrial policy. As we shall see, this shift would allow sharp increases in business, public, and human-capital investment. Buttressed by various protectionist measures, joint government-business investments in support of the development of new technologies are to be carried out via a number of key close state-industry relationships. Alas, numerous examples of such alliances and measures show that many – though not necessarily all of them – prove costly and wasteful, and risk not infrequently yielding poor results. Certain investments in human capital with regard to national health, education, and job training and retraining, while essential in many respects, may also exhibit wide and often unfavorable discrepancies between costs and benefits. On the other hand, public investments in various forms of infrastructure, while also costly, in many cases turn out to be useful, even indispensable – as I believe to be the case with the gigabit information system, for example. After a discussion of the differences between "free trade" and "fair trade" and the formation of NAFTA, and after an analysis of the possible impact of technological change on employment and unemployment, I shall conclude the chapter with an examination of the assumptions underlying two different perceptions of the way structural change affects the process of development.

Chapter 8 takes the analysis of technological permutations further. I shall focus first on a classic example – the competition of the United States and Germany with the United Kingdom in the last quarter of the 19th century – in order to clarify the meanings of "catching up" and "surpassing" and to apply them to the current technological contest between the United States, Japan, and Germany. I shall then discuss the fact that any kind of technological system necessarily involves *specific coherences* between inputs and outputs, along with certain organizational, behavioral, and institutional relationships which jointly define it. These technical coherences are in a continuous state of alteration and realignment in a developed economy. But they can be and are radically transformed at various points in time through imitations and innovations, as well as through wars, massive migrations, and borrowings and adaptations of other (more advanced) technical relationships. The processes of catching up are *at the core* of development. Growth and change are in effect uneven within and between countries, given their inevitable differences in resources, size, ownership relations, patterns of response to stimuli, forms of income distribution, access to markets, and extent and forms of government intervention. Then, in order to show how deeply impending changes may affect both the technological matrices and the competitive postures of advanced countries, I shall examine ongoing efforts to develop advanced *telecommunications infrastructures*. The United States is deeply engaged in this process in order to help business operate and compete more efficiently and to aid the country as a whole to acquire better, cheaper, and more extensive services in a variety of fields, including research, education, jobs training, and health care. I shall note in conclusion the similarity between the United States' current efforts to strengthen "industrial competitiveness" and overtake its challengers and the efforts of Japan and the EEC four decades earlier (in the 1960s) to close the technological gap with the United States.

7   New priorities

7-1   *Paradigmatic reversals*

A marked change in conceptions and in emphases took place in the 1970s in the theoretical and practical approaches to the problems of economic development (ED). The ED literature of the 1950s and the 1960s promoted a grand vision of rapid and successful growth and change relying on central planning and heavy investment combined with a "multidimensional process involving the reorganization and the reorientation of entire economic and social systems."[1] This vision has been shattered. The devastating failures of many governments that had implemented forceful, wide-ranging centralized administrative interventions in the economy have become increasingly visible. The disregard of markets and prices, the incessant drive for higher and higher investment, the forced-draft methods of industrialization, and the insistence on autarky turned out to be unbearable burdens in some developed and in most less developed countries, even before the collapse of the antimarket standard bearers of centralized planning, Eastern Europe and the USSR.

These doctrinaire approaches to growth and change have given way, both in the development literature and in the practice of the less developed countries (LDCs), to empirically based observations in regard to all sectoral performances, to more sober perceptions of the role and functioning of markets and prices, to a better evaluation of rules in lieu of administrative diktats, and to a more prudent approach to import substitution, export promotion, and protectionism. Paradoxically, while these changes have been taking place in most LDCs, opposite trends have emerged in the United States, at first timidly and then strongly, in regard to some key functions of the market. Recommendations for holistic industrial policies, for jacking up savings and investments, and for massive intervention in foreign trade and in regard to foreign investment became increasingly insistent from the early 1980s on, in the name of furthering "competitiveness," ensuring leadership in the global market, and overtaking our competitors in this or that critical field. Yet there is clear evidence from both developing and industrial countries that it is better not to ask governments to intervene in the details of growth and change. As a World

Bank report sums up the situation, in "defining and protecting property rights, providing effective legal, judicial, and regulatory systems, improving the efficiency of the civil service, *the state forms the very core of development*"[2] – a core which allows *markets and prices* to play their complex roles in the processes of growth and change.

Notwithstanding the above-mentioned thrust of the literature on development of the past decades, this literature did bring to the fore a number of issues which continue to be relevant not only for the LDCs, but for the developed countries as well. Contributions concerning the *determinants* of economic growth, the *structural changes* arising in the process of growth, and the *optimal* linkages of policy goals and the instruments used have had significant impacts in a number of directions, including better assessment of drives to "catch up" with the "leaders" in this or that economic field. Certainly, many of these ideas influenced some of the "holistic" industrial proposals concerning the directions in which the United States should be guided in this and the next century. Let me recall briefly some of the highlights of this literature.

With regard to growth and its determinants, a highly simplified model inserted in the Keynesian framework had a particularly eventful life. In the 1930s Keynes focused on utilization of the labor and the stock of capital *already available,* disregarding the consequences of capacity-creating investment. First Roy Harrod and then Evsey Domar incorporated these consequences in the Keynesian framework. The ensuing Harrod-Domar model related per capita income growth (g) to the rate of realized savings-investment (s) divided by the capital-output ratio (k) minus the rate of growth of population (ΔL) (i.e., $g = s/k - \Delta L$). Many LDC central planners – unaware of the critical issues overlooked by the model concerning technological change and the rates of unemployment and of capacity utilization – seized upon this simple device as the perfect answer not only to the question of how much to save and invest in order to increase the per capita income to some arbitrarily set level, but also *how much to solicit* from the "international community" in order to make such an investment actually feasible. Many planners did in fact assert that their countries could not generate the savings rates needed for the scheduled development and that foreign aid had to fill this specious "savings gap." The "capital constraint" argument became a tool for justifying the need for massive transfers of capital and technological assistance from developed countries to the LDCs.[3]

One of the outstanding theoreticians of development, Arthur Lewis, suggested how the raising of *s* could be carried out through the growth of the sectors which generate profits. He indicated, with the help of a dualistic model comprising a subsistence sector and a modern, profit-maximizing industrial sector, that the "surplus labor" of the former could be absorbed by the latter at a wage level determined by the subsistence wage in agriculture (with some augmentation), thus helping the expansion of the capitalist sector while increasing the productivity of the subsistence sector (now freed from the burden of its excess population). Critics of the Lewis model argued that such models overestimated the capacity of the modern sector to absorb the underemployed in agriculture and to generate a special effect enabling the population at large to share in the benefits of growth. Other critics asserted that, on the contrary, it was first agriculture that had to increase its productivity (its surplus output) in order to fuel the expansion of industry. Much of the discussion on modernization and planning finally centered on the issues of raising the savings function by whatever means (on the back of agriculture), controlling capital-output ratios, and optimizing the pace and directions of the growth of manufacturing, the "profits-generating sector."

Meanwhile, concern with the sources of growth was also becoming acute in the developed countries. As James Tobin put it in the mid 1960s, "In recent years, growth has come to occupy an exalted position in the hierarchy of goals" both in the United States and abroad. Earlier, in the 1950s, Robert M. Solow's celebrated paper "A Contribution to the Theory of Economic Growth" solved some of the problems raised by the Harrod-Domar model, but in its turn left outside its scope the main factor in economic growth, namely technological change. Various subsequent studies emphasized the importance of what came to be known as *disembodied technology* – viz. changes due to innovation, R&D, infrastructural investment, management organization – over changes in the inputs of capital and labor. Eventually, critics asserted that, on the contrary, capital deepening was the main source of gains in productivity; capital stock was "indeed constituted of different vintages," with current technological progress incorporated in each new, more productive modernizing addition. And, they affirmed, the higher the rate of net investment *plus* that of replacement of the old capital (depreciation), the more efficient the resulting capital stock. Various other studies tried to pinpoint the relative contributions made by factor productivity and factor inputs.[4]

The exploration of the structural problems allegedly "imposed" by long-term economic growth led also to a wide variety of what might be called "structuralist" approaches to development. Among these one may first recall the revival of old *stage theories,* which flourished particularly in 19th-century Germany (including the Marxian model), as well as some modern additions made in the 1950s, notably by W. W. Rostow in his *The Stages of Economic Growth* (a so-called Non-Communist Manifesto). Further, one may point to the gestation of all sorts of models propounding dualistic relationships, not only between the subsistence and the modern capitalist sectors, but also between "dominant" and "dependent" countries, the world's capitalist industrial "center" and the underdeveloped "periphery," and so on. Other approaches to structural change were predicated on the historical patterns of transformation

which had taken place in the process of growth of the *developed* countries –
sketched in the 1950s and the 1960s, most notably by Simon Kuznets, in terms
of the shifts in *production* from agriculture to manufacturing and to other
activities. This work led various other economists to search for the variations in
development patterns caused by differences in *resource endowments, institutions,* and *policies.* Many researchers worked to distinguish and analyze what
they called the "stylized facts" of development. These "facts" bearing on a
nation's levels of surplus labor, education, industrialization, and differential
productivity growth, along with the nature of its export commodities and its
terms of trade – spillovers, so to speak, from the export sector to the rest of the
economy – were tested for different countries, periods, and typologies in order
to formalize sets of complex interrelations.[5] Other development economists
asserted that the LDCs are so different in structure and organization from the
most developed countries that the behavioral assumptions and policy precepts
of neoclassical economics simply did not apply to the LDCs: competitive
markets do not exist there; innumerable discontinuities and indivisibilities are
present in production and technology; markets are fragmented and monopo-
lized; consumers are not sovereign; producers have great power to determine
prices and quantities sold. In short, while recognizing that many arguments of
the neoclassical economists concerning the inefficiency and the wastefulness
of state enterprises and the powerful effects of government intervention are
well taken, this kind of "structuralist" economist still asserts that massive
government interventions are necessary and inevitable.[6] Such views, as Ian M.
D. Little rightly noted, provided a reason for distrusting the price mechanism
and for trying to bring about change by other means.[7]

At the heart of these proposals were the ideas of vast nationalizations of the
"means of production and distribution" and of a nearly exclusive reliance on
central planning. With regard to both expropriations of private property and
planning, many LDC leaders emulated both the Soviet model of *industrialization* and the Soviet planning *method,* based on the so-called balance system.
The method consisted in a crude equalization of planned material outputs with
planned distributions, all at arbitrarily set planned prices – a method which had
made barely any progress during the entire Soviet regime. But more sophisticated planning theories and techniques were eventually developed in a number
of directions in the West and eagerly applied to various LDCs by Western
researchers.[8] The principal advances in this regard emerged from studies of
control processes in military operations and from systems engineering. Optimal control – that is, optimum modes of processing the information data
available – aimed at defining optimal organizations of processes and control-
lers, along with optimal patterns of centralization and decentralization in organizations. It has found wide applications in policymaking, in capital theory
and growth, and in systems control. The general-control problem in "idealized"

frameworks was predicated, with regard to economic policy, on four types of data: the system's structure and its initial state; the targets set (reflecting the controller's preferences); the control variable (the policy instruments); and the performance index (comparing the effectiveness of various controls). With regard to optimal economic growth – i.e., the best way for an economy to expand, given the society's preferences – the controller's problem was shown to involve the allocation of resources so that the intertemporal combination of the values of the state variables (e.g., the values of the capital stock) and of the control variables (the chosen values of the policy instruments) will maximize the welfare function (the index of society's ranking of alternatives, as defined by the controller). In optimum system design, the study of the restructuring of idealized systems focused on the issues centralization-decentralization, control of aggregate production processes, and optimally linked decisionmaking hierarchies based on performance characteristics. Critics of the application of control theory to policymaking eventually pointed out that policy preferences were defined only over ultimate outcomes (e.g., employment, price stability), that policy instruments exhibited high degrees of variability, and that forecasts based on complex economic models (in vogue in the 1960s) yielded inaccurate and misleading results.[9]

In all optimal-control models, the planner was the ideal allocator, maximizer, optimizer. But in a system of perfect markets, of course, a central planner would be entirely superfluous. What the analyses in ideal frameworks attempted to determine was what the ideal controller might do given a set of problems (or goals), compared to what the market was likely to do *under various constraints*. The Soviet economists, for their part, tried to identify the ideal planner with his inefficient Soviet counterpart, and to assert that Soviet planning was perfect while the market's imperfections actually constituted its essential characteristics. In fact, the Soviet economists should have *contrasted* the Soviet planner with the ideal planner – but this would have discredited their own cause along with their clumsy planned economy. In the United States, as Herbert Stein has reminded us, there has always been an "undercurrent of support" for "something called 'economic planning.'" But the drive for planning has surfaced in the United States only from time to time. It had only a truncated existence during the great depression under the National Recovery Act. It developed in partial ways under various agencies and departments during the war. It reemerged during the period of concern about the shape of the postwar economy. It resurfaced again in the mid 1970s during the great stagflation, in the form of the Balanced Growth and Economic Planning Act of Senators Jacob Javitz and Hubert Humphrey.[10] This act was to lead the way to a "Balanced Economic Growth Plan." Eventually the so-called Full Employment and Balanced Growth Act of 1976 was adopted, but it played an insignificant role in the subsequent development of the economy. The idea of "industrial planning," combined with emphasis on investment for achieving rapid growth, reemerged in the 1980s and, as we shall see in the next section, may be gaining increasing influence in the unfolding struggle for industrial supremacy in the 21st century.

In summary, as I pointed out above, pragmatic shifts concerning the role of planning and of the market are taking place – but are moving in opposite directions – in the two extremes of less developed and more developed countries. In the specific case of the United States, many of the ideas typical of the old literature on development of the 1950s and 1960s concerning growth models, the determinants of growth, the interrelations between investment, factor inputs, technological changes, manufacturing, planning and controls, and foreign trade structure and balance made their way here in the 1980s and early 1990s in various mixes and in more or less obtrusive fashion. I shall discuss the question of technological priorities and industrial policy immediately below. I shall examine afterward the related concepts and procedures concerning "fair trade," "reciprocity of access," and other measures meant to guarantee "competitiveness" (Section 7-3). I shall then consider the possible impact of such changes on employment, unemployment, and the standard of living (Section 7-4). I shall conclude with an analysis of two perceptions of technological change as they apply to economic policy (Section 7-5).

7-2   *Technological strategy and industrial policy*

Both during the presidential campaign of 1992 and soon after their victory, President Clinton and Vice-President Gore released a number of documents emphasizing the importance of *technology* to America's economic development. However, their hazily defined policy in regard to economic growth and change clearly involves much more than a narrow technological approach to the country's problems. Actually, their key 1993 document, *Technology for America's Economic Growth: A New Direction to Build Economic Strength,* proposes a *decisive shift* in regard to technological objectives, along the lines propounded in the famous *Vision for the 1990s* (which I examined in Chapter 4) and in accord with the main thrust of a formal report on technology policy made in 1990 by Dr. Allan Bromley (President Bush's science adviser). The center of attention is moved from defense to innovation in the private sector. Specifically, *Technology for America's Economic Growth* projects (a) a strategic shift in technological priorities from defense to the private sector; (b) the creation of various forms of government-industry partnerships and of interindustry arrangements; (c) the expansion of public services to manufacture via the spread of appropriate extension centers; (d) increases in tax allowances and in research credits to industry; (e) extensive infrastructural developments, including changes in the information infrastructure; (f) far-reaching transformations with regard to human capital concerning education, training, and health programs. Let us consider these critical issues in turn.

Technology for America's Economic Growth asserts that the "traditional federal role in technology development," limited as it was to the support of basic science and of mission-oriented research in the Defense Department, NASA, and similar entities, was "a strategy appropriate for a previous generation." This strategy should be replaced with a decisive orientation toward "technologies crucial to today's businesses and a growing economy"[11] – technologies centered on *new techniques.* The old method of "serendipitous" applications of defense technology to the private sector has to give way to the recognition that the government can play "a key role helping private firms develop and profit from innovations." Such a shift will allow things to be done "beyond the reach of the private R&D dollar." This shift has become necessary in order to strengthen the country's *competitiveness,* to create *jobs,* and to stimulate and sustain long-term *economic growth.*

The reaching of the indicated goals further posits, according to the Clinton-Gore documents, the forging of "closer working partnerships" (CWPs) among the federal government, the state governments, and industry. Examples of such CWPs are *Sematech,* created, as we have noted, to develop semiconductor manufacturing technology (see Chapter 2); the *Concurrent Supercomputer Consortium,* focused on photovoltaic technology; the *United States Display Consortium* (USDC), involving an ARPA-funded group of industries in the building of new factories and the development of new technologies for flat-panel displays, now a Japan-dominated industry producing the thin screens used in laptop computers, video games, and jetliners' control panel displays; and the *United States Council for Automotive Research* (USCAR), an umbrella organization that since 1992 has overseen 10 formal consortia guiding cooperative R&D activities between GM, Ford, and Chrysler, aiming to develop technologies for a *new generation of vehicles* with a view to "reestablishing technological leadership and competitiveness in the U.S. automobile industry." There are, of course, numerous potential candidates for CWPs along these lines. At the head of the queue are industries and activities affected by the process of defense downsizing, particularly aerospace, and industries in expanding high-tech fields, such as those in biotechnology, robotics, and new materials. This enumeration is, of course, far from exhaustive. Any and all high-tech industrial firms may line up for such partnerships or participate in *other kinds of arrangements* meant to "accelerate technologies where market mechanisms do not adequately reflect the nation's return on the investment." Among such arrangements the Clinton-Gore document propounds the creation of (1) *cost-sharing partnerships* between all federal R&D agencies, including the nation's 726 federal laboratories, so that "federal investments can be managed to benefit both government's needs and the needs of U.S. businesses;[12]

(2) *regional technology alliances* designed to promote the commercialization and the application of critical technologies, by helping firms and research institutions clustered in a particular region to exchange information, share and develop technology, and develop new products and markets; and (3) so-called agile manufacturing programs, i.e., the forging of allegedly temporary *networks of complementary firms* aiming to "exploit fast-changing market opportunities." It is worth recalling that already, under the tolerant enforcement of antitrust legislation prevalent during the Bush-Quayle administration, intraindustry consortia developed among the Big Three automakers concerning electric car technology, and tie-ups were established by IBM with Apple and Siemens. *Technology for America's Economic Growth* states specifically that reviews of laws and regulations will be conducted in order both to increase government-industry communication and cooperation and to reform antitrust laws to permit joint production ventures (e.g., by extension of the National Cooperative Act of 1984).

The Clinton-Gore administration proposes to provide manufacture with a number of public services like the extension services designed to spur the advance of U.S. agriculture. Critical for this purpose is the creation of a national network of *manufacturing extension centers* engaging in the active dissemination of research results. The existing but limited state and federal centers managed through the Department of Commerce allegedly provide assistance to only a small number of businesses. According to the proposed plan, such services should henceforth be vastly expanded, so that *all* businesses would have access to the technologies, testing facilities, and training programs they need. The lack of active dissemination of research is said to particularly affect the United States' 360,000 small and medium-sized manufacturers, some of which are still using 1950s technology. The reorientation of federal R&D through CWPs with industry, along with the activities of other types of partnerships, combined with a vastly expanded diffusion of techniques through the manufacturing extension centers and through eventual changes in the federal information infrastructure (of which more below), should massively increase the speed with which technology and knowhow get into the hands of businesses and should augment their capacity to commercialize the results and bring new products to market.

To stimulate investment in manufacturing, which "remains the foundation of the American economy," the Clinton-Gore document suggests that industry consortia (including universities and possibly government laboratories) should receive continuous *matching funds* for advanced manufacturing R&D. To accelerate investment in advanced manufacturing and create an environment conducive to innovation and to private investment, *permanent tax credits* along with other fiscal means should be used to encourage research and experimentation (R&E). R&E by nature is *long-term,* and business should be able to plan knowing that the credits will be available when needed. Also, incentives should be provided for those willing to make high-risk, long-term venture capital investments in startups and other small enterprises. Moreover, incremental investment tax credits should be given for investment in equipment, taking into account that our competitors invest "twice what we do" in plant and equipment as a percentage of GDP.

In the Clinton-Gore framework, the rebuilding of America, the creation of "millions of higher-wage jobs," and the smooth transition from defense to a peacetime economy involve also the development of the world's best communication, transportation, and environmental systems.[13] Putting people to work will require the renovation of transportation – of roads and bridges, along with the creation of high-speed railroads, the expansion of highway capacity, and the encouragement of high-tech short-haul aircraft – and also advanced *environmental* technologies, without mistaken concern for "a false choice between protecting our environment and spurring economic growth." The building of a high-speed national telecommunications network is also viewed as necessary to compete successfully in the 21st century. I shall return to some of these issues in more detail in the next chapter. Let me note for now that the building of a gigabit national information infrastructure requires a continuous effort to achieve a working *consensus* with the private sector.

Finally, with regard to the improvement of the country's human capital, the Clinton-Gore team proposes various costly, and in some respects, highly controversial changes. It forecasts a "revolution in lifetime learning," involving, to start with, an overhaul of the public school system and support for students' jobs training or college studies. It also calls for the joint development with business of a *national apprenticeship system* and a requirement for every employer to spend a fixed percentage of payroll for continuing education and training "for all workers, not just executives." As noted earlier, the United States is now devoid of a system of national industry training boards, has no national program of testing or of training certification, and has not adopted a set of standards with regard to the relationship of apprenticeship to other training. Creating all these *ex nihilo* will pose a formidable challenge. As for workers' training which does not rely on an *employer-centered* system of direct, on-the-job training, the results are disappointing. For instance, a generous government program of retraining and redeployment of laid-off manufacturing workers hurt by foreign trade has turned out to be largely ineffective: only one in five retrained workers (in computer operation, nursing, accounting, and various other trades) could be steered into jobs paying at least 80 percent as much as their old jobs.[14] (I shall return to this case again further below.) Likewise, in health care, as I have already indicated (cf. Chapter 4), the nation will surely remain preoccupied for years to come with attempting to resolve seriously divergent approaches, in conception and, eventually, in practice, to the role of government, employers, health-care providers, the pharmaceutical industry, and insurers.

The redirection of America's programs in science and technology is to be led by a reinvigorated Office of Science and Technology Policy (OSTP), working with the vice-president and using the Federal Council on Science, Engineering, and Technology, along with other means, "to coordinate the R&D programs of the federal agencies." The National Economic Council will monitor the implementation of new policies.[15] This rather ambiguous coordination does not seem satisfactory to certain partisans of holistic industrial policies, who request the creation of an *integrated industrial-technology base* "that will serve both commercial and defense interests." They argue that a technical-industrial policy must be organized around private industry rather than government agencies, that the goals of public-private partnerships must respond to private opportunities, and that effective links must be achieved between the national laboratories, the training institutions, the information service providers, and the universities.[16]

Clearly, many of these Clinton-Gore approaches to "technological" policy involve potentially wide-ranging changes in the traditional patterns of government-business relations. As Herbert Stein rightly pointed out in the mid 1970s in connection with a somewhat similar government effort concerning planning, such policies necessarily lead to an increase in the *supervisory powers of the Executive Office,* and to a devaluation of departments and agencies, whose originally limited practical objectives would be replaced by central goals largely defined by politicized experts. Furthermore, central goals usually (and almost inevitably) focus on large firms, necessarily neglecting the political needs of medium-sized and small ones. They also conduce strongly to more government spending and controls, while the uncertainties which all this engenders may easily depress rather than encourage private investment.[17] It may also be added that certain studies across countries indicate that among *managers* in private industry, government actions to stimulate innovation are perceived as comparatively irrelevant and that in fact only in some cases do government incentives have direct effects on R&D decisions. According to these studies, such incentives are in practice too slow and tortuous in their response to industry's needs. Other studies assert, however, that technology development programs do not depend only on managers' views: technological progress and dissemination is determined by continuous cooperative involvements among the developer, the vendor, and the consumer. Many actions and objectives are involved, and any single evaluative standard for such programs may thus turn out to be insufficient.[18]

Be that as it may, the sweeping changes required for the full implementation of the Clinton-Gore technological-industrial policy will certainly cause, as they unfold, a series of drawn-out debates in Congress, the media, and the public at large. A lot of give and take is unavoidable with regard to *each part* of this complex program. In time, certain features of the background will also change: there will be new developments in technological innovation, in the international markets, and in domestic productivity and employment. Yet, given the unavoidable and unsettling decreases in defense-related spending, and given the increasing focus on civilian manufacture – both in the traditional "key" industries in process of readjustment and change, and in the newer and expanding high-tech fields – certain directions traced by the Clinton-Gore program are bound to persist for years to come. This may turn out to be true in particular with regard to government-industrial partnerships, manufacturing extension services, tax allowances and credits, and certain technological priorities, along with related measures in foreign trade, to which I turn in the following section.

7-3   Fair trade, reciprocity, and regionalism

In a *free trade* system, restrictions on imports are avoided, *no matter what other countries may do.* The beneficiary is the home *consumer,* who is thus able to buy as cheaply as possible. As Adam Smith, the great exponent of free trade, put it, in this system the interest of the producer "ought to be attended to, only so far as it may be necessary for promoting that of the consumer." Assuming perfect or nearly perfect competitive conditions, the system rejects government interventions in the economy in favor of some specific industry as leading to distortions and misallocations. In regard to exports and imports, a free trade system relies on comparative advantage, i.e., on nations' technological differences and specialization in the production of what they make best (which yields the best outcome for the exporter and the importer alike). Contrariwise, *mercantilist* orientations focus on the *producer.* Mercantilism advocates government protection and subsidies for some selected sector or industries, along with "restraints upon the importation of all foreign commodities which can come into competition with those of our own growth, or manufacture." The interest of the home consumer is sacrificed to that of the producer[19] – or rather of certain producers selected by the government on the basis of various criteria. Whenever possible (or deemed indispensable), mercantilist orientations may lead to aggressive unilateral trade measures taken against a weaker country deemed to be "unreasonable or discriminatory" or planning or scheming "export targeting" to undercut a more powerful country's commerce.[20] When various forces or interests prevent resorting to such measures, the more powerful country will call for bilateral or multilateral negotiations emphasizing *reciprocal* elimination of asymmetries in market access, the flow of capital, trade restrictions, or volume of trade.

Without espousing a mercantilist protectionist measure, one may envisage situations in which government intervention with regard to trade would be justifiable. In the 1950s and 1960s, certain trade theorists showed that this would be the case when the *terms of trade* had been distorted through the intervention of other governments aiming to tilt the global economic playing field and redistribute international welfare in their favor. Certain models emphasizing terms-of-trade effects also showed that industrial countries like the United States could gain by unilaterally raising tariffs or restricting exports. But in practice, decisions to resort to import duties or export taxes were avoided, either for fear of retaliation or because of the understanding that such measures would yield *lesser benefits* than previously prevailing ones. (Incidentally, in certain cases, the developed countries did accept the export restrictions applied by certain LDCs, for foreign policy reasons or on income distribution grounds.) In the 1980s, new trade theorists gave technological innovation a special role in "strategic" trade policy outcomes under imperfectly competitive conditions (contrasted to the assumption of perfect or near-perfect competition under free trade). In addition to emphasizing that strategic trade policies under oligopolistic market conditions created opportunities for shifting welfare from foreign countries to the home market, the new trade theorists also pointed to the existence of external economies (e.g., knowledge spillovers from high-technology industries) as a reason for government intervention. Eventually it was shown that "corrective" international trade policies would be appropriate only when an *international* distortion existed, as in the case of terms-of-trade or international oligopoly situations. But again, any retaliatory action would yield only questionable advantages. These analyses have thus pointed to both the difficulty of framing useful interventions with regard to trade and to the possibility that such interventions may turn out to be counterproductive. These conclusions combined themselves, as Paul R. Krugman asserted, "into a new case for free trade."[21]

The powerful United States that emerged from World War II enthusiastically espoused the doctrine of free trade. It attempted to promote it through GATT, and to a lesser extent through bilateral negotiations, throughout the Western world. As I have already mentioned, the GATT system did reduce quotas and tariffs and greatly facilitated the sizable postwar expansion of world trade. The United States would have continued these policies in a "free and undistorted market," as a publication of the U.S. Congress put it – but with the 1970s, the world profoundly changed. Analyses of these changes, and the ways in which the United States is supposed to answer them, were developed in a number of books published in the early 1990s, notably by the U.S. Congress' Office of Technology Assessment (OTA), whose conclusions and recommendations, as we shall see immediately below, concur with the arguments developed by Laura d'Andrea Tyson and correspond in many ways to the directions charted by President Clinton in regard to foreign trade, foreign investment, and competition in world markets for the balance of the century and beyond.[22] Like

Tyson, OTA focuses on the so-called high technology trade challenge and on the alleged "decline" of our competitiveness. It asserts that the intensification of international competition, along with the severe payment imbalances experienced by the United States, heightened U.S. awareness about the complex obstacles to access in certain foreign markets; the asymmetries prevailing in international capital flows; the detrimental impact of various foreign investments in the United States in regard to certain critical technologies; and the dangers involved in the growing globalization of various businesses. Let us consider in turn the bill of particulars drawn up by OTA.

According to OTA, while the United States' policy has traditionally been that "manufacturing firms should make it on their own," many of the United States' trading partners, including the EU, Japan, South Korea, and Taiwan, have regularly employed a variety of tools aiming to enhance their manufacturing outputs and exports while protecting their markets and limiting imports. The nations of the European Community have provided support for their national industrial "champions" – including direct cash infusions, preferential access to government procurement, and tolerance of national cartels – while sheltering their own markets. Targeted industries in Japan, South Korea, and Taiwan have benefitted from financial and regulatory assistance, infant-industry policies, and outright protection from imports while being encouraged to seek economies of scale via high exports.[23]

While the United States and Great Britain applied "free market principles" to the inward and outward flow of investment capital, the other trading nations, and in particular Japan, imposed a variety of restrictions and conditions on foreign direct investments (FDIs). These obstacles have *inter alia* compelled U.S.-based multinational enterprises (MNEs) to reconfigure their operations by engaging in "minority joint ventures or licensing technologies and market rights to indigenous firms" in order to gain access to this exclusive national market. Many U.S.-based MNEs are painfully aware that at the same time as they face barriers in Japan, they must battle Japanese and European competition for market share in the United States. This kind of imbalance in market access is partially reflected in the U.S. trade deficit.[24]

To fully appreciate the impact of foreign-based firms on certain U.S. critical technologies, the OTA suggests that one must take into account *all* foreign-owned production, i.e., both FDIs and imports. Foreign firms accounted in 1988 for only 4.1 percent of the total domestic product but for 14.7 percent of the assets and 10.5 percent of the gross product of our manufacturing. Europe remains the leading investor, but Japan's share has been rising rapidly. Furthermore, Japan is the most diversified of all foreign investors, and often it is its major producers who invest here, "giving critics a sense that Japanese investment is enveloping the U.S. economy." This investment differs from traditional investment patterns: it is "more coherent, comprehensive, and strategic than European patterns of FDIs."[25]

Concerning globalization and the formation of international strategic alliances (ISAs) among MNEs, OTA notes that while such alliances are now concentrated in a few manufacturing industries, their numbers are rising. ISAs involving U.S. firms have been formed in such well-established industries as automotives, as well as in high-tech industries such as aerospace, information technology, new materials, and biotechnology. The OTA writings point to a number of dangers in the participation of U.S.-based MNEs in ISAs: some foreign markets restrict access unless the U.S.-based MNEs supply critical technologies, manufacturing capabilities, and distribution rights to their foreign partners; the above-mentioned asymmetries between different foreign government investment, industrial, technological, and trade policies may impede the ability of U.S.-based MNEs to use the strategic alliances competitively; and combining manufacturing, technology, marketing network, and other assets of competing firms into ISAs may concentrate too much power in coalitions of U.S. and foreign firms for which it is difficult to devise appropriate *national* treatment policies.[26]

Implicitly, the OTA publications raise the following questions. Why should the United States continue to tolerate asymmetries in both market access and investment capital flows? Why should the United States, as some critics put it, accept the continuation of competition among our states for FDIs, when the costs of incentives may outweigh the benefits and when unregulated FDIs potentially endanger our manufacturing firms and technological base? And how should the United States tackle the problems of the twin forces of global financial integration and of MNE expansion, which diminish U.S. capacity to control the pace and direction of adjustment to economic change?[27]

With regard to some of these key issues, the Clinton-Gore document *Technology for America's Economic Growth* stresses that the U.S. must turn toward "a trade policy that encourages *open but fair trade*." This implies a trade policy that "strengthens high-technology industries"; that guarantees "full access to overseas markets and effective protection of intellectual property rights"; that is consistent with a domestic program of "vigorous public research and development" concerning manufacturing; and that fosters cooperative projects which "enhance U.S. access to foreign sources of science and technology, contribute to the management of global problems, and provide the basis for marketing U.S. goods and services." *Fair trade* – often considered a code word for protectionism – thus implies the administration's will to end *asymmetries* with regard to access to markets *and* with regard to the development of "vigorous" R&D domestic policies (which, as we have seen, involve expanding government support to research by industry and by government-corporate consortia). It implies further that cooperation between U.S.-based firms and foreign associates will entail not one-way transmission of U.S. science and technology, but rather U.S. access to foreign sources of science and technology and an open path for U.S. products and services. All this involves a much broader interpretation of the idea of reciprocity and equivalence than the simple matching of mutual restrictions. It posits not only the search for full access to overseas markets for U.S. goods and services, but also a simultaneous commitment to the strengthening of high-tech industries and to the maintenance of complex domestic supports for manufacturing.

Critics, notes an OTA publication, "have equated reciprocity with mercantilism and protectionism." But, adds that publication, the emphasis on reciprocity has a special "strategic advantage": it can be applied in the context of bilateral or multilateral negotiations while it allows the assertion of policies tailored to particular sectors and the carrying out of sanctions that are unilateral in application. Since the threat of protectionism could easily "escalate," the accent on reciprocity (tailored only to special sectors and carrying unilateral sanctions) may, it is asserted, evade "the simplistic choice between free trade and protectionism."[28] This peculiar reasoning assumes that only protectionism involves potentially undesirable outcomes such as retaliation or trade wars. In any case, present U.S. trade policy is oriented not only toward the selective assertion of reciprocity but also toward the formation of a *preferential set of agreements* among a *subset of nations*.

As I recalled previously (in Section 3-3) the trade pact known as the North American Free Trade Agreement (NAFTA) binding together the economies of the United States, Canada, and Mexico was signed by President Bush in December 1992. President Clinton saw in this accord a potentially important instrument for the assertion of America's competitiveness both within NAFTA and outside it. He added a wide range of agreements, along with special deals, to the trade pact signed by the previous administration. This won Congress' approval in November 1993. The pact, unlike the one that governs the European Union, does not prescribe common tariffs and other barriers against the rest of the world and does not involve efforts to combine currencies, welfare programs, and immigration policies. NAFTA, as permitted under GATT's Article XXIV, is motivated by other immediate goals and long-run priorities than those of the EU. At the time of the formation of the European Community, in 1958 – an action sponsored by the United States – political and military goals were at least as important as economic ones, given that the Soviet threat against the Western world was then at its height. The turn toward NAFTA, by contrast, addresses the position of the United States in the world economy after the collapse of Soviet communism and after the strong competitive surge of Japan, the EU itself, and some new industrial powers in the world market. It concerns not only broader relations within an area from the Arctic to Acapulco – phasing out tariffs in the 15 years from 1994 to 2008 – but also, as President Clinton put it, the capacity of the United States "to win trade concessions from Japan and Europe." While much of the focus of the public debate has been on whether NAFTA will create or destroy U.S. jobs, whether American workers' wages will fall, and whether the federal budget deficit will grow, many analysts have overlooked the importance of the pact as one of several instruments that can be used "to pressure the Europeans and the Japanese to make trade concessions unpopular in their own countries."[29] Such an agreement is bound eventually to involve protectionist measures against nonsignatory countries. Within GATT's world framework, NAFTA is bound to be in constant use to further broaden U.S. objectives concerning investments, intellectual property, settlement mechanisms, and coverage of certain products.[30] As students of international trade well know, the case for preferential trade agreements is different from the case for free trade for all; while the latter is a first-best case, the former, by contrast, reflects second-best considerations – and may not necessarily be welfare-improving, either for its members or for the world at large.[31]

7-4   Spending shifts and living standards

As mentioned above, President Clinton has predicated his *Vision of Change for America* on a fundamental shift of spending from consumption to investment. He has repeatedly asserted that America has been *underinvesting* and that this situation must be radically changed. If, like the new Democrat writers, we overlook any and all intermediate phases of recession and recovery and focus upon 1973 as the *turning point* of the entire postwar era, we can easily bring forth some stark contrasts between the pre- and post-1973 periods, contrasts which are taken as compelling indicators of the need for rapid change.

Thus, from 1950 to 1973 GNP grew at an average rate of 3.6 percent per year, while during the following (rather unrepresentative) period, from 1974 to 1990, it grew at an average rate of 2.4 percent per year. Physical capital per worker grew, up to 1973, at the average rate of 2 percent per year; from 1974 to 1990, at 0.6 percent per year. Productivity grew in the indicated first period at 2.8 percent per year; in the second, at 1 percent per year. With regard to the standard of living, refer to two important indicators. Up to 1973, GNP per capita grew at the yearly rate of 2.1 percent, while after 1973 it grew at 1.5 percent per year (i.e., at the former rate, per capita income would double in 34 years; at the latter rate, in 47 years). Real disposable income per capita closely followed the same trends: it rose during the first period at 2.4 percent per year; in the second period, at 1.4 percent per year. The number of persons below poverty level fell between 1959 and 1973 from 39.5 million to 25.5 million, then rose again to 33.6 million in 1990. The poverty data reflected more or less similar trends in unemployment, people on food stamps, and people on welfare – though in regard to employment the average rate of growth actually rose in the second period to 1.9 percent per year, compared to 1.6 percent per year in the first period. Finally, according to the data on the structure of the GNP, in 1950 consumption accounted for 60.9 percent of the GNP and investment for 19.5 percent. These levels remained quite stable until 1973, when the respective percentages were 61.5 and 18.9. But by the 1990s these percentages stood at 64.5 and 16.6 of that year's GNP. At a minimum, the "reversal of the drift" concerning consumption and investment may be interpreted to imply a shift back to the pre-1973 levels.[32] As we know by now, President Clinton has been favoring increased taxes (on middle and upper incomes), decreased government-financed consumption, and expanded government investment. To achieve much the same ends, the Republicans have advocated less government spending, lower transfer payments, and faster reduction of the national debt.

Looking toward the future, one may safely assume that the growth of investment and implementation of the basic levels of industrial policy will result in the creation of new jobs and in high productivity in industries and services (related, for instance, to the continued transformation of information transmission and use). On the other hand, such changes also lead to the elimination of occupations in superseded industries and often leave behind them pockets of displaced workers and of eroded, low-income communities. Recall the rapid transformation of agriculture after World War II. In 1947 there were still over 8 million people engaged in this sector, with an output per person of some $6,500 (at 1982 prices). By 1957 employment in this sector had fallen below 6 million, with an output per person (in constant prices) of over $10,000. By 1987 the population engaged in agriculture had fallen to 3.2 million, with an output per person in real terms of over $26,000. Notwithstanding this astounding per capita productivity growth and the capacity of manufacturing and of other sectors to absorb most of the agricultural surplus population, significant numbers of underemployed persons were left in poor, neglected rural areas. Mining and the extractive industries have also experienced rising per capita productivity, declining employment, and concomitant erosion of the basis of many mining communities. This has also been evident in specific manufacturing industries – e.g., automotives – and, in some respects, in manufacturing as a whole. Thus, the output per person employed in manufacturing rose in real terms (again, at 1982 prices) from $14,500 in 1947 to $19,300 in 1957. If we focus only on the strictly comparable sets of data for 1977, 1985, and 1987, the output per capita in real terms increased to $33,700, then to $40,200, and finally to $44,500. What is interesting to note with respect to these data is that the labor force in manufacturing decreased in these years from 19.6 million workers to 19.3 million and then to 19.0 million.[33] Technological change and rising per capita productivity may thus leave a trail of displaced workers and declining communities (e.g., in the "rust belt").

It may be appropriate to recall that the term "technological unemployment" dates from the 1920s, when many workers were left without jobs by the postwar economic shakedown. Certainly, questions of employment, under-employment, and unemployment depend not only on technological change "in general," but also on differences in the speed of change among branches and sectors, on changes in the demand for goods, on shifts in markets and prices, on imports and exports, and on many other factors affecting the country's eco-nomic life. In no small measure, the post-cold-war need to downsize the armed forces and military production has impacted not only industries directly related to armaments but also others supplying these industries and their workers, thus increasing the tendencies toward downsizing and reengineering throughout the economy. All this has strengthened awareness that more could be obtained with fewer people employed. Moreover, the pressure to downsize, coupled with expanding competition, has led to complex changes in industrial organization and in hiring and firing, affecting not only the numbers of skilled and unskilled workers employed, but also the *conditions* of their employment. Typical of lean organizations is the employment of "contingent workers," i.e., of workers not entitled to the usual benefits and to job-security provisions. Related, though separate, problems for the future are needed improvements in education and in the training of noncollege workers, and the necessary effort to erase the in-grained distinction between technical-vocational and college work. The Clin-ton program of apprenticeship and the national service program cannot suc-ceed unless the administration can narrow this deep divide in the labor force by making noncollege training and careers as valuable *in status and income* as the careers of college graduates.[34] Of course all these changes nurture deep anx-ieties among those who feel their livelihoods threatened by them. Looking in the mid 1960s at the balance of employment and unemployment, the labor economist Eli Ginzberg remarked that both before the war (in the 1920s) and after World War II, *employment opportunities* did not expand at a sufficiently rapid rate to provide *jobs for all,* i.e., both for those who were dislocated by technological and other changes and for the new entrants in the labor force. Rising productivity had enabled the entire goods-producing sector to turn out a greatly enlarged output without significant increases in employment. Ginzberg then added that the American economy had come to be characterized by "underemployment prosperity."[35] One should not forget, however, that this underemployment was at least partly mitigated by transfer payments and other efforts. Professor Sumner H. Slichter perceptively pointed out in the early 1930s that insofar as the costs of change fall upon the community at large, e.g., upon those whose property and occupations are rendered obsolete, rather than upon those who make the innovations, "change is being subsidized just as much as if Congress appropriated millions to accelerate it." Change is thus subsidized in practice – with or without the direct subsidies involved in industrial policies – through the inevitable costs generated by economic transformations.[36]

There is no method by which the benefits of innovation and technical change can be balanced against their costs. Exactly how these changes affect the standard of living is not immediately ascertainable. One can only note that in historical perspective, accelerated technological changes calling forth new industries, new processes and products, and new interbranch and intersector relations, along with rising per capita productivity, did bring in their wake complex displacements and adjustments throughout the economy, but did also finally bring a higher standard of living for the majority and then for the population as a whole. As the annual report of the President's Council of Economic Advisers pointed out in January 1993, "each generation of Americans has started life with the prospect of achieving a higher standard of living than the preceding generation." Indeed, "real national income today is 15 times greater than it was in 1900."[37]

7-5   *Contrasting perceptions of growth and structural change*

Certain indicators of structural economic change, involving in particular the growth of industry and of certain types of manufacturing, have traditionally been viewed as the main gauges of technological change. The latter has been specifically identified with (a) sustained growth in the ratio of the manufacturing workforce to total manpower; (b) a higher proportion of the workforce in industry (say, in manufacturing plus power generation and transportation) than in agriculture; (c) a higher ratio of industrial output to total production compared with either agriculture or services; (d) higher percentages of total industrial output in iron and steel, machine tools, and power generation; (e) the growth of a mobile, adaptable labor force subservient to the needs of the expanding use of machinery in manufacturing.

Actually, the economic changes which have unfolded in the United States, Germany, and Western Europe since the last decades of the 19th century, have shown that both the underlying assumptions and the indicators on which such a perception of change is based are highly questionable. In practice, (a) a continuously expanding share of the industrial workforce (artisanal, mining, and manufacturing) in total employment may be a sign of chronically low industrial productivity rather than of modernity and advancing technology. In the United States and other developed countries, the manufacturing labor force has tended to *decrease* in the second part of the 20th century, from some 30 to 40-plus percent to 20-plus percent of the labor force – a percentage which has varied only slightly even in periods of great industrial expansion. (b) The identification of modern economic change with a crossover to a society with more manufacturing than agricultural workers is misleading. Such a crossover indeed took place in England around 1810, but in the United States it happened only in 1959, and in the United States, employment in services – even in the narrowest sense of this term – had long before exceeded that in agriculture. As I have already noted, the United States simply crossed over directly from an agricultural to a so-called service society in 1929 without ever passing through a predominantly manufacturing phase. Also, as I pointed out in Chapter 5 (Table 5-2), agriculture, forestry, and fishing accounted for 36.9 percent of the persons engaged in production in 1899; manufacturing, for 20 percent; and the rest of the economy, for 43.1 percent. Twenty years later, the agricultural group stood at 27.5 percent and industry at 22.4 percent, but services, even in the indicated narrow sense of the term, were at 29.4 percent. (c) There is no compelling reason whatever why agriculture's output share should not equal or exceed that of manufacturing. This depends on factor endowments, not on preconceived symbols of development. As for services, they form a composite in *a state of accelerating process* of differentiation. The *growth of certain services* is in fact an excellent indicator of a high level of development (i.e., of a high per capita income and of a high process of outsourcing from production to services). (d) Any particular industry cannot hold more than a temporary lead in total output. Crucial technical advances are discontinuous. They involve sequences of numerous small inventions and, at unexpected moments, of major inventions which cause permutations in the economy's technological matrix and in its industries' rankings, ultimately leading to new integrated *technological concordances*. Machine tools are no more a permanent "fitting base of modern industry" than, say, chemistry is. Incidentally, a sustained increase in the output of a group of industries, e.g., of "producer goods" (i.e., of raw materials, intermediate products, and machinery) – an often-used indicator of economic growth and development – may be an indicator of underdevelopment if the increase is exclusively due to expansion of the production of raw materials. (e) While the 18th-century industrial revolution found ad hoc ways of replacing certain scarce skills with machines devised by skillful, intelligent, self-taught practitioners, modern economic change has increasingly depended on scientific investigation and scientific design and, because of this, necessarily on *highly trained personnel*. Among the latter, the key figures have been the scientist, the engineer, and the laboratory researcher who have at their disposal a complex theoretical apparatus rather than simply "mechanical ingenuity of the old sort."[38] Certainly, no matter how one looks upon the nature of development, one must recognize the crucial role of the innovator, the adaptor, the entrepreneur without whom no practical changes would ultimately occur. Yet one must not forget that innovators operate in a continually advancing scientific matrix which influences and expands their choices. (I shall return to some of these issues in the next chapter.)

The emergence from the late 19th century on of key industries, and the creation, thanks to them, of new technological interrelations suggest that an appropriate way of grasping the nature and rationale of technological change is to examine how new concordances arise between various *clusters* of interindustry flows as a new major technological breakthrough takes hold, rather than to focus on the growth of manufacturing's share of total employment and output. A critical role in technological change, perceived already in the latter part of the 19th century, was played by two complexes: one formed by the chemical industries and the other subsequently formed around the automobile. Now a similar critical role in economic transformation is played by the "information industry" and its underlying electronic communication and computing industries. Such clusters, no matter in which sector or branch they arise or what their specific succession in time, ultimately impact *the entire* technological matrix. Also interesting for assessing various aspects of technological development is the analysis of the changing interrelations occurring between broader complexes, for instance those arising between agriculture and the industries dependent on it (including the textile and food-processing industries) on the one hand, and the rest of manufacturing and services on the other.

Economic growth entails not only a long-term rise in the overall capacity to supply goods and services, along with some of the previously mentioned structural shifts, but also various changes which cannot be fully anticipated. Bold leaps in science, along with discrete, cumulative, and wide spread changes in design and in plant configurations, will render certain types of processes and products obsolete, willy-nilly flinging the fortunes of particular industries and branches to the top or the bottom of the heap. Technological mutations may abridge the economic life of invested capital and cause investment patterns to change in an environment of continuous uncertainty. When a profound technological breakthrough occurs in one sector, changes are bound to reverberate through the other sectors as well, necessitating numerous readjustments over time with regard to inputs and outputs. As far as capital stock is concerned, technological change may at any point in time increase its value, decrease it, or leave it constant (in real terms). The traditional view of the process of change as tending to increase the "organic composition" of capital (i.e., the ratio of capital outlays to wages and value added), especially in manufacture, is devoid of substance. An "industrial policy" focused on some specific and well-protected interindustry relations may retard rather than help along the processes of growth and change.

As I pointed out, changes in techniques and in markets may generate technological unemployment even on a large scale, and of a permanent character. The faster and more encompassing the technological change, the more difficult the adjustments in the labor market. Technological change may or may not require more technical personnel; in any case, it requires more intensive training for at least some new entrants in the workforce. The incentive system governing the production of fundamental and applied knowledge varies, of course, from country to country and period to period, depending also to a large extent on a nation's overall cultural level. Along with the other changes indicated above, the pace of growth of scientific-technical personnel will obviously remain a significant indicator of actual and/or potential capacity to *produce* new products, to *absorb* new and spreading technologies, and to *adapt* such technologies further.

The contrasting perceptions of technological change enumerated above focus on entirely different indicators of development. The first is predicated on the erroneous idea that what matters are a fixed set of crude statistical ratios concerning capital deepening, the relative size of the manufacturing workforce, and the structure of its output. The second perceives change as a discontinuous process in which wide and often unpredictable shifts take place in the economy's production technologies. A technological breakthrough ultimately generates a new *technological system* in which are forged new interbranch, intersector technological compatibilities, along with new patterns of employment. Change depends on many factors, some of which may be subtle and not readily apparent. Yet, obviously, inventions and innovations depend *decisively* on a highly qualified and well-trained workforce. I shall return to some of these issues, in historical perspective, in the next chapter.

8 Contests at technological frontiers

8-1   On "catching up" and "surpassing"

In comparative analyses of growth and change, often no clear-cut distinction is made between a competing country's *industry or industries* catching up with and/or surpassing those of a foreign country, and the catching up with and the surpassing by the competing country of the leading foreign country's *level of development*. Yet the phenomena are different and are signaled by different indicators. The catching up with and surpassing of a particular industry or industries can be verified with the help of such measurements as volume and value of output and so on. The catching up with and surpassing of a country's level of development, however, is indicated by two other very specific measures: respective per capita income and total income. The latter variable, as I suggested before, determines the capacity of a country to generate a given investable mass supporting a given manufacturing complex and economic structure.

Clearly, a less developed country can see its industries catch up with and surpass a given industry or group of industries in a more developed country without necessarily catching up with *that country's level of development*. Indeed, in the process of growth and change, a developed country often abandons certain kinds of productive activities – even entire industries – and shifts the allocation of its investments. But while a developing country may follow up on such moves and achieve higher outputs in these industries, or register a breakthrough in certain other industries by innovative imitation or by a more rapid application of immediately available advanced technological methods, this by no means implies that it can catch up with or surpass the *level of development* of the more advanced country for years to come. Such changes often underlie misconceptions about the "aging," the "decline," or the "inefficiency" of the advanced country, along with magnified assessments of the achievements of the developing country. Yet certainly *all* processes of catching up involve interesting searches and solutions which may influence the more developed country in its efforts to maintain its leadership.

In order to illustrate these processes, I shall attempt first to sketch in broad outline the efforts of Germany and the United States to catch up with and surpass the United Kingdom in the last quarter of the 19th century. I shall then try to compare, cursorily, these processes with the drives of Germany and of Japan to catch up with and overtake the United States in the last quarter of the 20th century. I have already pointed out that those who contend that the United States is in economic "decline" are assuming that this phenomenon is a close replica of the process of "decline" of the United Kingdom in the last century. I shall attempt to show their essential differences, along with the implications of these distinct events.

Consider first the situation of the United Kingdom on the threshold of the last quarter of the 19th century. From the late 1840s until 1873, the U.K. experienced both a great expansion and a far-ranging transformation of its industrial structure. By the beginning of the 1870s it was leading the world not only in textiles, but also in heavy industry – in iron and steel, machinery construction, and shipbuilding. By then, its industrial workforce was three times as large as its agricultural workforce. At the time, its main competitors were just emerging from difficult but finally successfully concluded conflicts. Germany had been at war with Denmark (1864), then with Austria and, up to a point, the German confederates (1866), and then with France (1870). The United States had ended the Civil War (1861–65) and was integrating its three economic areas, the North, the South, and the Midwest.

While the United Kingdom and the newly industrializing countries suffered along with the rest of the world from a severe depression and a long downswing in prices during the years 1873–96, from the end of the 19th century and up to World War I all three experienced a period of "golden prosperity." Through all the years from the early 1870s to 1913 industrialization spread at an accelerated pace both in Germany and in the United States, and these newly industrialized countries sharply increased their challenge to British supremacy. The perseverance and enterprise of the Germans started to make themselves keenly felt in both the British and the overseas markets. Moreover, both Germany and the United States were surpassing Britain's industrial techniques in a number of key industries, including machinery and machine tools. All these changes, along with higher rates of GDP and productivity growth in both countries, were supposed to certify Britain's "loss of industrial spirit," its exaggerated interest in services (viz., investment in fixed-interest securities rather than in technological change), its reluctance to modernize, its incapacity to modify its "old style capitalism" rooted in small-scale, family-owned firms, and its inability to create "a system of scientific and technical education" that would facilitate the introduction of new scientific developments into industry. Actually, none of these contentions were necessarily proven by the German and U.S. successes, which in many respects differed in nature, as we shall see further below.

Let me note for now that as far as technological change is concerned, the unsystematic use of science mentioned earlier seems to have been characteristic of British development until the end of the 19th century. Neither the industrial revolution, i.e., the transition from crafts to machines and factories, nor the vast mechanization and transformation of Britain in the mid 19th century required systematic recourses to science. However, some authors stress the existence of a significant body of knowledge at the beginnings of the industrial revolution and note that by then mathematics had been used not only in astronomy, but also in such practical arts as navigation, cartography, ballistics, shipbuilding, mining, and surveying, as well as in the manufacture of telescopes, microscopes, barometers, and chronometers.[1] Other historians add that renowned innovators like James Watt had exchanged ideas with Dr. Black, the great chemist of Glasgow, while Watt's partner, the machine builder Matthew Boulton, had entertained relations with other distinguished scientists of the age.[2] But all this does not prove either that science was sufficiently advanced at the time, or that it had been put to use in a methodical fashion by British entrepreneurs. As for the great transformations of the mid nineteenth century, some sectors of Britain's engineering were undoubtedly advanced, yet most engineers up to 1900 still came up through an apprenticeship. Many first-class engineers were still trained in a traditional environment, and found it hard to break with the past.[3] A system of formal technical education developed slowly in England. As late as the end of the 19th century, the educational system was viewed as a "hopeless muddle." The education of the upper and middle classes was based on a value system that elevated the status of service to the state and the liberal professions, to the detriment of involvement in trade and, more particularly, in manufacturing industry. Eventually newer colleges, following the examples of Germany and the United States, started to serve as centers of research for industry and for manpower training.[4]

Just the opposite situation developed in Germany, where science and scientific education and training eventually supplied Germany's key leverage in the processes of catching up with and surpassing the United Kingdom in a number of industries and technical fields. However, at its beginnings, Germany's approach to industrialization did not differ from that of England. The early German industrialists had neither scientific training nor special technical qualifications. Some of them had been landlords, traders, or handcraftsmen, or had exercised other, most unusual occupations. Thus, for instance, the initiator of the German optical industry, Duncker (1801), was originally a parson; F. A. Winzer, the founder of the gas industry (1804), a balloon aerialist; F. Harkort, one of the first German machine builders (1815) and later on one of the country's great railroad and canal constructors, a tanner; I. E. H. Alban, the initiator of the machine industry of Mecklenberg, an eye doctor. Other industrialists who were to play leading roles in equipment production or rail construction – e.g., J. A. Maffei, J. Meyer, N. A. Otto – had initially been wholesale or retail dealers. F. Dinnendhal, who had been successively a farm-hand, a miner, a mechanic, and finally a machine builder (1808), later associated himself with both Harkort and Friedrich Krupp, the founder of the Krupp dynasty.[5]

But even before the second half of the 19th century, the industrialists' response to the increasingly complex technical demands of the state and the private market were beginning to be facilitated by both rapidly expanding cooperation – or even partnerships – between the industrialists, the "technologists," and scientifically trained researcher-entrepreneurs like Karl Achard.[6] The technologists were often themselves grouped into such societies as the Association for the Advancement of Trade Skills – Beuth Foundation (1821) and the Polytechnic Association (1839). Various modifications started to occur from around the mid century in the process of importation, imitation, and adaptation of the British pattern of development, modifications which were to completely alter the nature and directions of German industrialization.

The first impetus to change came from the clearing away of local particularisms and various other trade obstacles encumbering the domestic market, and from the simultaneous expansion of international markets, which proved increasingly receptive to the new and diversified products of German industry. At the same time, deep changes started to take place via a methodical interaction of science and techniques. This was a specifically German brand of development – a professionalized approach to technological change combined with a methodical concentration, diversification, and expansion of manufacturing and of transports and communications. In the 30 years between 1830 to 1860, the Germans established a powerful network of "polytechnicums" (technical universities), supported by a vast number of high schools emphasizing mathematical training, the sciences, and technology.[7] Under various French and British influences, the Germans succeeded, in their own novel way, in integrating scientific theory and practical instruction in the classroom, the laboratory, and industry. As Alfred North Whitehead put it, the Germans created the appropriate methods of reaching "the deeper veins in the mine of science" – methods involving the discarding of haphazard scholarship, the professionalization of scientific research, the creation of disciplined science – in essence, the routinization of "the method of invention" itself.[8]

On the other hand, also in contrast to Britain, Germany's powerful industrial expansion occurred within a framework of "organized capitalism." As I noted before, in such a scheme much is due to vigorous state intervention and to its provision of various kinds of services – electric power, communications, land improvement, education, health facilities – along with high, protectionist tariffs. Also important were the rapid increase of the rate of investment and the coalescing of manufacturing and mining industries in "cartels" and "trusts," often under the guidance and supervision of large banks.[9] Within this framework, by 1913 Germany had become Europe's leading industrial power, challenging Britain's supremacy in the overseas markets in many fields. It had overtaken Britain in the production of iron and steel; had developed new and important branches of manufacturing, such as the chemical, electrical, and shipbuilding industries; and had become a larger exporter of woolen cloth, synthetic dyes, electrical appliances, and machinery.[10] But *in terms of per capita income and total output* Germany did not catch up with and surpass the United Kingdom until the 1960s. Put differently, before the 1960s Germany, with a significant part of its population still relatively backward farmers, was an *underdeveloped* economy in relation to the U.K., even though it had surpassed it in the growth and output of certain industries. According to the computations of Angus Maddison (Table 8-1), Germany's GDP and its productivity did grow at higher rates than those of the U.K. between 1870 and 1913. But by the latter date its annual per capita income was (in constant prices) $1,907 vs. $3,065 for the U.K.; its GDP stood at $77.8 billion vs. $130.6 for the U.K.; and its overall productivity was well below that of the U.K.

The United States, the other great challenger of Britain's supremacy in the mid 19th century, also departed eventually from the British industrialization model, but it achieved this break thanks to a unique combination of other factors. In the mid 19th century U.S. per capita income was already probably the highest in the world. Southern cotton agriculture – unfortunately based on the inhuman slave system – was then an important source of growth. This brutal system was destroyed by the Civil War. The latter, however, did not prevent agriculture from continuing to be an important source of growth, thanks to the increase in family farms, the expansion of land under tillage for wheat and corn, the improvement in agricultural implements and machinery, and the rise in agricultural productivity. This growth underpinned industrial growth in both older and newer areas. Development received a further boost from massive immigration (particularly after 1880), rising urbanization, the growth of transport (subsidized by the government) and communications, the expansion of banking and finance, and the continuous growth and diversification of both the domestic market and exports. The increases in industrial output itself were made possible by large-scale imitation and adaptation, first of foreign and then of domestic inventions and innovations; increased standardization and mechanization; the rise of entirely new industries (e.g., the automobile); and the integration of industrial operations into big enterprises. As I indicated in a previous chapter, the end of the 19th century and the beginnings of the 20th century witnessed large-scale concentrations of American businesses into holding companies, trusts, and cartels managed by great entrepreneurs and by innovative and audacious "captains of industry."

Only in the 20th century did U.S. industry finally resort to the employment

Table 8-1. *Economic growth in three leading economies, 1870–1913, 1900, and 1913*

Countries	Average annual compound growth rates, 1870-1913		GDP per capita (1980 prices in $)		Total GDP (billions of $ at 1980 prices)		Productivity (GDP per man hour; U.S. = 100)		Value of exports f.o.b. (billions of $ at 1980 prices)	
	GDP	GDP per hour worked	1900	1913	1900	1913	1900	1913	1900	1913
United Kingdom	1.9	1.2	2798	3065	107.5	130.6	82	74	20.5	35.0
Germany	2.8	1.9	1558	1907	53.2	77.8	49	48	12.4	27.7
United States	4.2	2.0	2911	3772	222.3	368.1	100	100	12.3	16.4

Sources: First 2 columns: Angus Maddison, "Growth and Slowdown in Advanced Capitalist Economies: Techniques of Quantitative Assessment," Journal of Economic Literature, Vol. 25, June 1987, p. 650; 1900 and 1913 data: Maddison, The World Economy in the 20th Century, pp. 19, 113, 89, 141.

of scientists on a large scale. State-supported higher education on the German model started its development slowly and relatively late – only from around the 1870s on. By 1900 U.S. institutions of higher learning had awarded a total of 382 doctorates. Few corporations had set up laboratories prior to 1900: the advancement of knowledge and the tracing of new directions in industry and communications were due to such brilliant, ingenious independent inventors as Samuel F. B. Morse, Alexander Graham Bell, and Thomas A. Edison. It is this unique American combination of factors – advanced agriculture, massive immigration and urbanization, rapid industrialization, and large-scale innovation – which permitted the U.S. (with a population of over 75 million, compared to 56 million for Germany and 41 million for the United Kingdom) to catch up with the U.K. by 1900, not only in terms of the technology and output of certain industries, but also in terms of the average yearly rates of growth of GDP and of productivity – and, finally, in terms of the *levels* of both total and per capita GDP (see Table 8-1).

Compare now these measurements and achievements to the economic growth patterns of the U.S., Germany, and Japan after 1973, i.e., when U.S. competitors had allegedly caught up with it with regard to the technical level of certain industries. As can be seen from Table 8-2, Japan overtook the U.S. in terms of the average *rates* of annual growth of the GDP and of productivity, and Germany in terms of the *rates* of growth productivity, but neither one reached the *level* of the U.S. with regard to total and per capita income, productivity, *or* total exports. This underlines not only the arbitrariness of comparisons concerning the allegedly similar "aging" of Britain and the United States at the end of the 19th and 20th centuries respectively, but also the fact that "catching up" has involved different *indices* and different *domains* which must be clearly specified. It is arbitrary to speculate on the efficiency of industries, on their ability or inability to apply new technologies, and on the modernity or obsolescence of their processes and products, on the basis of the *levels* of development in which the various performances of the countries compared are actually taking place.

8-2   *Changing the technological system*

Technological change involves advances in knowledge concerning the industrial arts – advances which lead to changes in production techniques and in the organization of production. Advancing technologies are a key element in the competitive struggle among firms, industries, and nations. To better visualize such changes – which may affect either the nature and the *kind* of a country's industries and/or the volume of *inputs* needed to produce certain outputs – recall the *input-output schema* devised by Professor Wasily Leontief and presented in Chapter 1. As indicated there, the economy's *processor* is constituted

Table 8-2. *Economic growth in three leading economies, 1973–1984, 1973, and 1987*

Countries	Average annual compound growth rates, 1973-1984		GDP per capita (1980 prices in $)		Total GDP (billions of $ at 1980 prices)		Productivity (GDP per man hour; U.S. = 100)		Value of exports f.o.b. (billions of $ at 1980 prices)	
	GDP	GDP per hour worked	1973	1987	1973	1987	1973	1987	1973	1987
United States	2.3	1.0	10,977	13,550	2326.2	3308.4	100	100	13.4	20.6
Germany	1.7	3.0	7,595	9,964	470.6	606.4	64	79	15.1	15.8
Japan	3.8	3.2	6,622	9,756	719.3	1198.9	40	51	3.2	7.3

Sources: As Table 8-1.

by the web of interindustry transactions. The *production function,* i.e., the relation of inputs to outputs, is assumed to have fixed technological coefficients, that is, the output of industry *i* used as input in industry *j* is a *fixed proportion* of the total output of industry *j.* The assumption of fixed input-output relations is restrictive, but it is nevertheless useful, since it simplifies parameter estimation while not substantially distorting the true picture. This approach can be applied if we assume that proportions remain unchanged only over short periods of time. The web of interindustry flows can then be appropriately depicted with the help of three matrices: an *accounting* matrix showing interindustry sales (of industries *i*) and purchases (of industries *j*) (as shown in Fig. 1-2); a *transformation* or technological matrix presenting the technical coefficients, i.e., the *ratios* of the outputs (of industries *i*) used as inputs (for the outputs of industries *j*); and an *interdependence* matrix portraying how changes in the demand (of consumption and investment goods) affect interindustry relations.

Competition may stimulate, in innumerable ways, the acceleration of the pace of technological change, on which the rate of economic growth heavily depends. Changes are achieved via inventions, scientific discoveries, and innovations, as well as through imitation, borrowing, and adaptation of techniques and procedures applied in other firms, branches, industries, or countries. Inventions are due to intuition, insight, and the ingenuity of individual inventors or groups of researchers in small- or large-scale establishments. These inventions may involve syntheses of known inventions and discoveries or be due to original perceptions of ways of creating, using, or combining various resources. As Simon Kuznets has noted, innovations (i.e., applications of an invention) provide opportunities and pressures as they spread, not only for related innovations but also for new tools, new insights, and new puzzles for scientific study, which in turn stimulate new inventions and new technological changes. As in any process of development, industries, branches, and sectors are impacted in different ways and degrees, and this inequality of impact inevitably generates social and economic problems that require adjustment. Kuznets adds that regardless of the rate of adjustment to other opportunities of displaced capital and labor, displacement and readjustment costs may rightly be *debited* to the particular technological innovation that is their source.[11] In practice, as Sumner H. Slichter taught us, the society as a whole and not the innovator bears the costs of readjustment.

The imitation and adaptation of innovations often encounter innumerable snags when such transplantations occur in highly different social and economic frameworks with wide discrepancies between them in terms of scale of production, prevailing techniques, capital availability, workers' training, and general production relations. On the other hand, many developed countries inaugurating new types of production or military techniques have traditionally erected all kinds of barriers to their export. In the late 18th century and in the 19th, British machines were smuggled out in pieces, recreated from memory, or copied from blueprints; only eventually were they allowed to be exported under license. These procedures have remained in practice in the 20th century and will continue into the next one, as will smuggling and industrial espionage. Until the collapse of the Soviet Union and its satellites, the United States and Western Europe tried to keep tight control and/or embargo on the export of many materials and technologies directly or indirectly related to advances in the production of weapons. Certain technologies continue to be tightly protected and "inexportable," even among the industrialized countries.

The interplay of competition, imitation, and adaptation – and in particular innovative adoptions – may lead to all kinds of unexpected results. In his study on the evolution of technology, George Basalla tells us that in 1953, while on a trip to the United States, Masaru Ibuka, one of the founders of Tokyo Telecommunications, was told by Western Electric about the release for sale of patent rights to the transistor. The transistor had been invented at the Bell Laboratory in Murray Hill, New Jersey, on December 23, 1947. A device which used semiconductor material to amplify an electrical signal, it was not viewed at the time as one of the "major inventions of the century." When Tokyo Telecommunications bought the transistor license in 1954, other Japanese firms showed little interest. Ibuka sent technicians to the United States to visit laboratories, talk to engineers and technicians, and assimilate the oral and written information concerning semiconductor technology and transistor use. By 1955, the Japanese had started to manufacture their own transistors; they used them to make a pocket-sized radio receiver, and changed the name of the increasingly profitable Tokyo Telecommunications to Sony – a name now known around the world. It is interesting to note that American technology promptly developed new kinds of transistors and that the American semiconductor industry supplied the high-technology markets opened by the growth of the computer and the needs of space and military programs. Unfortunately, the American consumer product industry adopted the new technology only slowly.[12]

A mixture of misconceptions and misevaluations of Soviet strength and technological sophistication may, however, have had a useful impact on U.S. technological achievements. Toward the mid 1950s, as the then Soviet Union was getting increasingly embroiled in its problems both at home and in its satellites, prospects of an international detente seemed at hand. Then, in 1957, the launching of the Soviet Sputnik, the first artificial satellite, shook the world. Though the Sputnik in fact represented only a small step in the progress of technology, but a big step in Soviet propaganda, it certainly accelerated the development of a U.S. space program and opened extraordinary vistas to the progress of U.S. science in many directions.

How exactly does a *technological matrix* change under the impact of such diverse stimuli as inventions, innovations, imitations, and adaptations? Consider some specific examples. An invention or innovation usually affects first the persons or the firms or the industrial branch using it, and then these uses have certain primary effects which eventually engender derivative effects. The primary effects may flow in different directions, and they are not exerted all at once. Let us look, for instance, at the electronic revolution and at certain of its computer and noncomputer effects. With electronics one can control the disposition of small or large amounts of energy and power, much the way the brain directs the action of muscles. With its inner transformation from the transistor to the microprocessor, electronics has continued to expand the scope of its uses in defense, manufacturing, banking, trade, transportation, and communications, as well as in medicine and education. Other complex changes have been occurring with regard to control, extraction, and bioprocessing methods for the developing biotechnologies. The latter are in their turn affecting microbiology, enzymology, fermentation, separation, and purification technologies, and are serving an expanding spectrum of activities, notably in agriculture and animal husbandry, food production, textile manufacturing, waste treatment, and health care. These and other changes – as already noted, for instance, with regard to photonics, advanced composites, and metallic structures – clearly lead to changes not only in the production functions of an increasing number of industries, but also to the elimination of certain industries and to the creation of new ones. Thus, eventually a new technological matrix – i.e., a new technological system – takes shape. In time, these accumulated complex changes require for their efficient use a scale of production, a stock of fixed capital, and relations between labor and the factors of production entirely different from those of the earlier technologies. The difficulty of properly assessing the sources and the widespread and elusive impact of *technological change* continues to hamper the efforts of economists to fully integrate it in the models of economic growth (i.e., of making it endogenous).

Inventions and discoveries, imitations and adaptations, may or may not be supported by the state. Historically, the state's involvement in the economy has been complex, diverse, and often infelicitous. The main state emphasis has been on the development of weapons and of related industries. In modern times, from the end of the 15th century on, the state's interventions in the economy have been due to an incessant expansion of its functions involving efforts to bring cities and regional economic units under a central authority, along with incessant struggles with other (emerging) states. Up until the 18th century, the states which eventually gained the upper hand were those who knew "how to put the might of their fleet and admiralties, the apparatus of customs laws and navigation laws . . . at the service of the economic interests of the nation-state." In accordance with emerging mercantilist theories – in essence, theories of *state making* – the ideas of self-sufficiency of the nation and of its manufacturing and the pursuit of a favorable balance of trade (looked upon as the nation's "net profit" from its annual trading) became the guiding rules of governments in many countries.[13] While mercantilist ideas were discarded up to a point in 19th-century England, they have *never* ceased to assert themselves there and in *all* other countries, in a variety of forms, and with different intensities. State intervention has ranged from direct state ownership of certain natural resources, industries, and banks to promotion of selected industries, expanded state activities in public works, extensive regulation of production and sale, a gamut of covert and overt subsidies, price fixing, tariff protection, and a variety of discriminatory measures concerning the inflow and outflow of capital and technology.

8-3   *Advancing in the age of information*

Obviously, the areas in which international competition is at its fiercest are the areas of rapid technological change – microelectronics, new materials, and biotechnology, and their expanding applications. In regard to the expansion of microelectronics, one frenetic competition at the technological frontier concerns transmutations in information technologies. Let us look more closely at this particular issue in order to get a feeling for the complexities of the Information Age.

The creation of a *national information infrastructure* – accessible to all and as easy to use as our transportation and communications infrastructures – will undoubtedly have a deep impact on our prospects of growth and change in the 21st century. The information infrastructure will reshape the ways in which business performs, laboratories and libraries operate, and individuals and families work, travel, play, educate their young, and care for their old. It will be a giant high-speed, high-volume broadband network of interconnected public networks (i.e., open to use by anyone) and private networks (i.e., linked for use by specific groups of people, such as company networks) to deliver voice, images, and computer data simultaneously from coast to coast. The first computer network – that is, the first system of interconnected users – was ARPANet, which, as I have already recalled, began in the 1960s as a research project of the Department of Defense's Advanced Research Project Agency (ARPA, later called DARPA, and under the Clinton administration again ARPA). Much progress has been registered since then in many directions, including in computing, electronics, and the networking needed for such a giant endeavor.

In order to build the broadband network, the High Performance Computer (HPC) Act of 1991 called for the upgrading of federal computing networks (which connect federal laboratories and universities) to *gigabit* networks. This would represent a 20-fold increase over the most capable links in the networks now in use. (The latter transmit 45 million bits per second; a gigabit is 1 billion bits.) To achieve this objective, six prototype gigabit networks, or "testbeds," are being funded as part of the Federal High Performance Computing and Communications (HPCC) Program, a multiagency endeavor that supports research on advanced supercomputers, software and networks. The HPCC, whose annual budget is close to $1 billion, aims to upgrade first the National Research and Education Network (NREN) into an advanced network, operating at gigabit speeds by 1996 and serving, at least up to a point, as a testing ground for broadband technologies eventually to be applied to commercial networks. Yet, as it develops, the national information infrastructure will necessarily comprise for a time numerous networks operating with diverse and evolving transmission technologies servicing different communities of users at affordable costs. To ensure openness among the many components of these technologies, the government will set the rules (so-called protocol standards) in cooperation with the industries' standard writing bodies (which focus on strategic barriers to interoperability). Moreover, the complex national network will have vast outside connections. Already Internet, as previously mentioned, consists not only of the government-subsidized portions (such as NREN) but also of growing commercial and overseas networks. New players such as the coordinated European market and the former Eastern bloc countries are broadening the field, and more commercial information providers and networks, such as Dialog and CompuServe, are establishing connections to the continually expanding Internet.

The building of the broadband national information infrastructure will require complicated new systems (like high-capacity switches that will allow two-way high-bandwidth communications) and redesign of the components that link computers to the network. These links are usually made of copper (either "twisted pair" or "coaxial" cable) or fiber optics (which have several advantages over the other types), and may consist also of satellite and microwave links. Television and telephone service use analog technology, i.e., a modulated wave which takes a relatively large amount of bandwidth to transmit a small amount of information. The creation of the information superhighway offers the opportunity to eventually use the same technology we have in computers, namely *digital* technology, in transmitting the three forms of information – voice, images, and data – integrated through the same switches and transmission media. This, as the specialists point out, will mean the ability to use software to dramatically expand the capacities of telecommunications networks. Large investments are needed to access the technologies which will help achieve leading-edge price/performance improvements in such communications areas, including fabrication lines making state-of-the art chips, fiber communications including the "last mile" to homes, the growing demand for software, and so on. In many network products, the United States fortunately holds a technology lead and commands a strong market position.[14]

The building of the giant broadband information infrastructure will have a deep impact on almost all aspects of economic life. It will profoundly impact all the mass-media services – cable television, publishing in all forms, postal services, telephone, research data, and services. It will affect business performance with regard to productivity, costs, and quality of product and services, via changes in engineering design, tests, marketing methods, competitiveness, and job creation. It will open opportunities for useful employment for both able-bodied and disabled workers, who will find it easy to "telecommute" to their place of work for special tasks and/or for office work. It will transform education and training, making better schools, teachers, and courses available to students of all ages without regard to distance or disabilities. It will help improve America's health-care system and respond to other important needs when and where they arise.

The existing U.S. information structures have been in many respects the most efficient and the most affordable in the world. These structures exhibit a very high line density, high level of telephone and television cable usage, and a continual emphasis on modernization. However, competition in all these fields is sharply increasing in the integrated Age of Information. Other nations are also trying to develop the most advanced technologies and networks. Because countries have different characteristics, sizes, backgrounds, and overall development levels and capabilities, international comparisons of often incomplete and noncomparable data must be treated with caution, and proper adjustments must be made as far as possible. Consider, for instance, the issues involved in telecommunications investments, modernization, telephone penetration, new advanced technologies, and service quality. No comprehensive evaluations of *total* investment in public and private telecommunications facilities are available. With regard to *public* investment only, data for 1980–89 show the U.S. below other countries, including Germany and Japan. Concerning modernization, the U.S. trails Switzerland, but is far ahead of Germany and Japan. With regard to advanced out-of-bank signaling information in digital form, the U.S. trails France and Canada. With respect to service quality, the U.S., like the other industrialized countries, can boast a high level.[15]

Clearly, all this expresses itself in the form of a high-speed race in highly advanced technological processes. America's most important partners and competitors have embarked upon ambitious long-term development and modernization of their telecommunications networks. Thus Japan's principal service provider, NTT, has inaugurated a 25-year program to build a broadband network to begin offering videotext and interactive television in the year 2005 that will reach "every school, business and home by the year 2015." The nation which will emerge victorious in the contests at the technological frontier, and which will at the same time build the skilled workforce capable of taking advantage of these achievements, will reshape the entire world technological system, accelerate its growth rate, increase its productivity, and eventually secure a high and increasing standard of living for its population. None of those objectives are lost either on the U.S. administration or the U.S. Congress, nor, for that matter, on the big telephone and cable companies ready to consolidate their positions in cyberspace.

8-4   *Policy emphases, priorities, and goals*

In an economy based on private property, the market and the price system are the primary instruments of economic organization within the framework determined by law and custom. The market feeds the drive for economic growth and change via incentives to produce and to invest; the market encourages the accumulation of material capital and the growth of labor skills; the market directs the allocation of production between consumption and investment; the market allocates the factors of production among their various uses; the market distributes incomes among the production factors. As the economy develops, both the scope and the extent of the domestic market, and of its relations with other markets, grow and diversify.

In the 20th century, within a *mixed* economy, the state has been shaping its economic policies and determining its interventions in the economy in response to rapid and at times deep changes in the economic, social, ethical, and political conditions of increasingly complex societies. Thus, the state has become intensely concerned with such issues as the levels of output and employment, the nature and extent of structural economic changes, the evolution and the application of science and technology, the balances of income and expenditures and the distribution of income, relations with other economies, and the ensemble of factors which affect the society's patterns of development. This does not mean, however, that the policy *emphases* – or the "strategies" – to reach these goals, and the *set of priorities* which they determine, are either unchanged or unchangeable. From the early 1930s to the early 1990s and beyond, two basic policy emphases have been dominant in the United States: one emphasizing *demand* and its linkages to supply, the other emphasizing *supply* and its linkages to demand.

The great depression of the 1930s raised many thorny questions, among which the most pressing were whether the market, "left to itself," would provide necessary and sufficient incentives to invest when attractive opportunities for domestic investment seemed to have suddenly vanished, effective demand was contracting spasmodically, and unemployment was rising at an alarming rate; whether the allocation of factors of production among their uses had been the right one, when many branches and even sectors were falling behind technologically while rapid progress was registered abroad far and wide; whether the output mix had been appropriate to ensure the wherewithal for the subsequent expansion of production; whether the combined lags and "myopia" concerning future growth, and an undue emphasis on protection, were hampering foreign trade; and whether the results of the market distribution of income were not diminishing both consumption and growth.

Out of the depression's problems – as perceived at the time by the Democratic leadership – emerged, as we know, the strategy of emphasis on *demand* and the national goals of full employment, increased production, and increased "purchasing power." These objectives, embodied in Keynesian demand-side management, were reasserted after World War II in the Employment Act of 1946 and remained the guiding principles of economic policy – with variations and additions but without changes in substance – until the 1970s. At that time, the whole policy of fine-tuning the business cycle became discredited.

From the stagflation of the 1970s and its aftermath emerged a mix of old and new problems involving, as I have noted, the issues of "deindustrialization," technological "decline," rising deficits, and new competitive challenges in world markets. The strategy of emphasis on demand was abandoned, and the attention, first of the Republicans and then of centrist Democrats, shifted toward the supply side of the economy. Then in the 1990s, the Clinton-Gore administration brought forth a new set of priorities as set forth in *A Vision of Change for America*. As I have already recalled, these priorities stressed a fundamental shift toward investment, a new government-business "partnership" (to be "financed by a fair tax system"), and an integrated technological–industrial policy – all aiming at "raising the rate of productivity and boosting living standards." With the shift to the supply side, the set of priorities aiming at "full employment, increased production, and increased purchasing power" has changed to others emphasizing "increased investment, a broad technological policy, and increased productivity" along with a "fair trade strategy." In essence, in the demand approach everything hinged on *full employment;* in the supply approach, everything hinges on *technology.*

Paradoxically, advanced technology used to be viewed, at least by the technologically displaced workforce, as a major source of *un*employment. Times have changed. The apparent Japanese technological superiority – more apparent than real, and limited to certain fields – has become such a national obsession that the objective of leadership in technology in *all* fields has become a fully accepted *national* goal. An appearance taken for a reality can indeed be as influential as reality itself.

8-5   Concluding comments

The uneven and asynchronous growth of technologies and their applications has necessarily led to various *technological gaps* in the industrial history of even the most developed countries of the world. The search for the appropriate policies for bridging these real, or at times imaginary, gaps has been particularly frantic during the post-World War II years.

In the late 1950s, for instance, the shocks generated by the launching of the Soviet Sputnik were felt most intensely in the United States. The mistaken perception of Soviet achievements in science and in space exploration technology engendered in the U.S. an anguished examination of our presumed failures and shortcomings. Partly in response to the Soviet space probe, President Eisenhower appointed a *Commission on National Goals.* The report of the Commission, published in 1960, was significant because it recognized the importance of a critical examination of these goals. But no attempt was then made to evaluate the internal compatibility of such goals, the relative priorities to be followed in pursuing them, or the costs involved in terms of dollars or resources for carrying them out.[16] Eventually, the U.S. space program found its own path to success in space technology and exploration.

In the 1960s, few people continued to believe in the superiority of Soviet technology. By that time, Europe and the rest of the world were fascinated by U.S. developments and by what the French political writer Jean-Jacques Servan-Schreiber called, in a famous book, *The American Challenge.* In his foreword to the English translation of this book, the American historian Arthur Schlesinger, Jr., asserted that its author had "stated the European dilemma with brilliant clarity, precision and urgency," and had also indicated the "way to a solution." Simply put, Europe's choices consisted of facing economic *decline* or engaging in "discriminating Americanization." The United States was indeed seizing the opportunities created by the Common Market in order to achieve "the economic invasion of Europe." The gap – technological and managerial – between Europe and America was due to the latter's "dynamism," whose secret lay in its "art of organization" and in its marshaling of "intelligence and talent to conquer not only invention but development, production and marketing." America's industries were spilling out across the world "primarily because of the energy released by the *American system.*" Servan-Schreiber himself warned European leaders that the time had come to concentrate "on this strange phenomenon, dangerous and massive in its size and power." Europe, he added in his special kind of prose, was engaged in a peculiar war, "to be fought without arms or armor" – remembering that "General Motors, after all, isn't the Wehrmacht" – but a war nonetheless, whose solution lay in "the fabulous struggle for the conquest of Titan's metal, or the ferocious effort to master the mental world of integrated circuits."[17]

From that time until the early 1970s, Europe and Japan concentrated – on the model of Kennedy's America – on accelerating the rate of economic growth and on the rapid development of science and technology as a means of modernizing their economic structures and as a source of critical innovation. In order to bridge the gap with these United States, most countries drafted plans in the 1960s to promote large-scale extensions of their scientific and technological infrastructures. Some countries even institutionalized technological policy-making and implementation in separate ministries. In other countries, ministries of education were either given separate boards to promote science policy, or science policy received autonomous status. Many European countries increased R&D expenditures, pinning their hopes on the creation of large-scale establishments. Frenzied merger activity took place in all the industrialized countries – including the United States – to concentrate the means needed, particularly in the development of massive new technologies. During that period in most industrial countries "the government became the principal commissioner or risk bearer of complex research programmes, which were increasingly carried out by a limited number of companies active in a few selected fields."[18] In the early 1960s, West Germany instituted the Ministry of Scientific Research, the precursor of the early 1970s Ministry of Research and Technology. Germany's generous subsidies were directed toward companies' projects in the machinery industries, with indirect subsidies also being channeled toward a number of other industries. At the same time, France introduced a number of "Grand Programs" to boost its aerospace, aircraft, computer, and nuclear industries. The United Kingdom set up a Ministry of Technology in 1964 and focused its attention on machine building, electronics, computers, and telecommunications. Japan's by then well-anchored MITI also oriented its attention to machine building, electronics, computers, and the aircraft industry.[19]

A complete reversal started to occur all of a sudden from the 1970s on. At that time, most industrial countries, including the United States, were being confronted by stagflation, decreasing private investment, drops in the rate of productivity increases, rising unemployment, and the energy crisis, while the star of feverishly rebuilding Japan started to rise on the horizon. As I have noted in many places in this book, this time the *technological gap* was allegedly developing between the United States and the empire of the Rising Sun. Undoubtedly unconsciously following the kind of logical pattern embodied in Servan-Schreiber's book, many American economic and political analysts of the 1980s started to speak of America's *decline* and of Japan's superbly organized capitalist system, capable of formulating and carrying out strategies ensuring its dominance in all markets. Dynamic Japan was "invading" our domestic market – just as we had supposedly been "invading" Europe two decades previously – and our only hope of closing *the gap* with it was to copy the "Japanese system," with its method of organizing rapid growth and of strategically determining its position in the "global" market. In short, salvation lay for us in a kind of "discriminating Japanization" of America.

The end of the U.S. recession of the late 1980s to the beginnings of the 1990s and the ensuing U.S. growth, coinciding with continuing recessions in Germany and Japan, have awakened the awareness of various writers to the fact that the U.S. economic machine wasn't after all as "broken" as they had thought it was. A number of publications have hastily rediscovered the strength of both the U.S. economy and of U.S. manufacturing. As *The Economist* put it at the beginning of 1994, the "U.S. patient was never as sick as *he* thought he was." And *The New York Times,* following suit, noted under the headline "The American Economy, Back on Top" that the ideas that America was "a has-been? An also-run?" were disproved by the data and that "perceptions" were "beginning to change."[20] Concomitantly, other newsmakers started to note that "the pendulum of confidence" was swinging back, that the Japanese were developing an "inferiority complex" and were now "bashing themselves," that Japan's apparent invulnerability had "popped," and that the "allegations about its challenge" were "passé."[21]

Exaggerations of course cut both ways. On the threshold of the 21st century it is undoubtedly even less certain than during the last decades of the 20th where every critical technological gap lies. Clearly, the United States' managers, entrepreneurs, and scientists continue explorations in many new directions, as can be seen by daring initiatives in the advancing Age of Information, while Japan seems to fall behind in some areas, from PCs and cable TV to the expanding mail and computer networks. But one should not forget, as A. Roobeek reminds us, that the phrase *core technologies* or *key technologies* – which has come to embody the "renewed panache" with which governments try to tackle any and all crises at hand – is actually a *generic* name covering a host of intricate and diverse fields from microelectronics, computers, and control instruments to biotechnology, new materials, robotics, energy technology, environmental technology, and, of course, telecommunications. All these fields need the support of vast and complex interindustry flows, of powerful industrial-technological networks. It is possible – in fact, it is certain – that in some specific, limited fields, Japan and the EU countries may register innovative successes. Indeed, as we have seen, the fight for supremacy in the 21st century takes place simultaneously in many directions and at many technological frontiers.

On the other hand, there is certainly not one contest from which the United States can or does wish to be absent, no matter who the challenger or challengers might be. We should not forget that the United States is still the country with the highest total and per capita income, the most technologically advanced industry, the largest and most diverse scientific and engineering core of the workforce, the most extensive and receptive market for high-tech processes and products. In the struggle for industrial supremacy in the 21st century, it has already secured for itself technological and market leadership in many fields.

Its economy will continue to move forward energetically and enterprisingly if growth and change are left to emerge from within the private economy. Indeed, this economy can perform at its best in response to market-directed incentives, rather than in response to centrally devised and highly subsidized industrial policies and export "strategies."

Notes

Chapter 1. Postwar growth and change

1 For a detailed discussion of some of these phases, see my study *Managing the American Economy from Roosevelt to Reagan*, Bloomington, Indiana University Press, 1989.

2 *Economic Report of the President Transmitted to the Congress January 1989, Together with the Annual Report of the Council of Economic Advisers*, Washington, D.C., GPO, 1989, p. 31.

3 These and the immediately following data have been computed, in the indicated order, from *Economic Report of the President Transmitted to the Congress February 1991*, Washington, D.C., GPO, 1991, pp. 288, 317, 347, 322, 338.

4 Computed from ibid., pp. 288, 347; and Department of Commerce, Bureau of Economic Analysis, *Fixed Reproducible Tangible Wealth in the United States, 1925–1989*, Washington, D.C., GPO, 1993, pp. 216, 391.

5 *Economic Report of the President Transmitted to the Congress February 1990, Together with the Annual Report of the Council of Economic Advisers*, Washington, D.C., GPO, 1990, p. 122.

6 Ibid., pp. 123–124.

7 U.S. Department of Commerce, Bureau of the Census, *Statistical Abstract of the United States 1990*, Washington, D.C., GPO, 1990, p. 742.

8 Donald L. Losman and Shu-Jan Liang, *The Promise of American Industry: An Alternative Assessment of Problems and Prospects*, New York, Quorum Books, 1990, pp. 62–63; see also J. C. Derian, *America's Struggle for Leadership in Technology*, trans. Severen Schaeffer, Cambridge, Mass., MIT Press, 1990, p. 48.

9 *Economic Report of the President . . . 1991*, pp. 149–152.

10 Aerospace Industries Association *Newsletter*, Vol. 1, No. 7, 1990.

11 *Statistical Abstract of the United States 1990*, p. 747; U.S. Department of Commerce, *1990 U.S. Industrial Outlook: Prospects for over 350 Manufacturing and Service Industries*, Washington, D.C., U.S. Department of Commerce, January 1990, p. 17.

12 Ibid., p. 749 (for import penetration); for production, see *Statistical Abstract of the United States 1991*, p. 750.

13 "Output per Hour, Hourly Compensation, and Unit Labor Cost in Manufacturing: Fourteen Countries or Areas, 1950–1989 (Average Annual Rate of Change)," mimeo., U.S. Department of Labor, Bureau of Labor Statistics, Office of Productivity and Technology, April 1991.

14 For the underlying data see *Economic Report of the President . . . 1991*, pp. 288–289.

15 See Dennis J. Encarnation, *Rivals Beyond Trade: America vs. Japan in Global Competition*, Ithaca, Cornell University Press, 1992, pp. 89–95; see also OECD, *Economic Surveys 1990/1991: Japan*, Paris, OECD, 1991, pp. 69, 70, and *The New York Times*, June 23, 1992.

16 Aerospace Industries Association, *Key Speeches*, Vol. 4, No. 5, June 1991.

17 Computed from *Economic Report of the President . . . 1991*, p. 404.

18 Computed from ibid., pp. 308–309.

19 See the interesting discussion on service trade and international competition in *The United States in the World Economy: NBER Summary Report*, ed. Martin Feldstein (Andrew Berg, rapporteur), New York, NBER, 1987, pp. 39–43.

20 See for instance *Economic Report of the President Transmitted to the Congress February 1983, Together with the Annual Report of the Council of Economic Advisers*, Washington, D.C., GPO, 1983, p. 54, and *Economic Report of the President Transmitted to the Congress February 1988, Together with the Annual Report of the Council of Economic Advisers*, Washington, D.C., GPO, 1988, p. 90.

21 William G. Dewald and Michael Ulan, "The Twin-Deficit Illusion," *Cato Journal*, Vol. 9, No. 3, Winter 1990, p. 702. See also *Economic Report of the President . . . 1989*, p. 127.

22 Paul A. Samuelson, "America's True Decline Without Exaggeration or False Optimism," testimony for U.S. Senate Committee on Banking, Housing, and Urban Affairs, November 15, 1989, mimeo.

23 Peter K. Kilborn, "Is the Deficit Still Dangerous? Maybe Not, Some Start to Say," *The New York Times*, January 23, 1989.

24 *Economic Report of the President . . . 1989*, pp. 107, 133–134.

25 C. Fred Bergsten, *America in the World Economy: A Strategy for the 1990s*, Washington, D.C., Institute for International Economics, November 1988, p. 50.

26 Ibid., pp. 7, 51.

27 Paul Krugman, *The Age of Diminished Expectations: U.S. Economic Policy in the 1990s*, Cambridge, Mass., MIT Press, 1990, pp. 43, 47, 50.

28 Robert Eisner, "The Federal Budget Crisis," in *The Changing American Economy*, ed. David R. Obey and Paul Sarbanes, New York and London, Blackwell, 1986, pp. 85–107, and "The Real Federal Deficit: What It Is, How It Matters, and What It Should Be," *Quarterly Review of Economics and Business*, Vol. 26, No. 4, Winter 1986, pp. 6–21.

29 Alan Reynolds, "Praising Keynes," *The Wall Street Journal*, May 22, 1986 (review of Robert Eisner's book *How Real Is the Federal Deficit?* Free Press, 1986).

30 Krugman, *The Age of Diminished Expectations*, p. 71.

31 Herbert Stein, *Governing the $5 Trillion Economy*, New York, Oxford University Press, 1989.

Chapter 2. Government-business relationship

1 J. M. Clark, "Some Current Cleavages Among Economists," Papers and Proceedings of the American Economic Association, Fifty-Ninth Meeting, *American Economic Review*, Vol. 37, No. 2, May 1947, pp. 1–11.

2 David E. Rosenbaum, "Parties March to Different Drummers into Hearings on Reviving Economy," *The New York Times,* December 5, 1991.

3 *First Annual Report to the President by the Council of Economic Advisers,* December 1946, Washington, D.C., GPO, 1946, p. 4.

4 *The Economic Report of the President Transmitted to the Congress January 6, 1950, Together with a Report to the President by the Council of Economic Advisers,* Washington, D.C., GPO, 1950, p. 80.

5 *The Economic Report of the President to the Congress, January 7, 1949, Together with a Report "The Annual Economic Review, January 1949" by the Council of Economic Advisers,* Washington, D.C., GPO, 1949, pp. 2, 3, 10, 43; *The Midyear Economic Report of the President to the Congress, July 11, 1949, Together with a Report, "The Economic Situation at Midyear 1949," by the Council of Economic Advisers,* Washington, D.C., GPO, 1949, pp. 6–14.

6 *The Economic Report of the President Transmitted to the Congress January 16, 1952, Together with a Report to the President by the Council of Economic Advisers,* Washington, D.C., GPO, 1952, pp. 25, 137. See also "Annual Message to Congress, Fiscal Year 1953," January 21, 1952, in *Public Papers of the Presidents of the United States: Harry S. Truman, Containing the Public Messages, Speeches, and Statements of the President, 1952–53,* Washington, D.C., GPO, 1956, p. 77.

7 *The Economic Report of the President Transmitted to the Congress January 14, 1953, Together with a Report to the President, "The Annual Economic Review," by the Council of Economic Advisers,* Washington, D.C., GPO, 1953, pp. 17, 22.

8 "Annual Message to the Congress on the State of the Union, January 30, 1961," in *Public Papers of the Presidents of the United States: John F. Kennedy, Containing the Public Messages, Speeches, and Statements of the President, January 20 to December 31, 1961,* Washington, D.C., GPO, 1962, p. 19.

9 "Special Message to the Congress: Program for Economic Recovery and Growth, February 2, 1961," in ibid., p. 41.

10 *Economic Report of the President Transmitted to the Congress January 1962, Together with the Annual Report of the Council of Economic Advisers,* Washington, D.C., GPO, 1962, pp. 8–9, 68, 72, 74.

11 "Annual Message to Congress on the State of the Union, January 14, 1953," in *Public Papers of the Presidents of the United States: John F. Kennedy, Containing the Public Messages, Speeches, and Statements of the President, January 1 to November 22, 1963,* Washington, D.C., GPO, 1963, p. 12; *Economic Report of the President Transmitted to the Congress January 1963, Together with the Annual Report of the Council of Economic Advisers,* Washington, D.C., GPO, 1963, pp. 37, 46.

12 *Economic Report of the President . . . 1962,* p. 9.

13 "Annual Message to the Congress on the State of the Union, January 8, 1964," in *Public Papers of the Presidents of the United States: Lyndon B. Johnson, Containing the Public Messages, Speeches, and Statements of the President, 1963–64,* Book 1, *November 22, 1963 to June 30, 1964,* Washington, D.C., GPO, 1965, p. 112.

14 *Economic Report of the President Transmitted to the Congress January 1965, Together with the Annual Report of the Council of Economic Advisers,* Washington, D.C., GPO, 1965, pp. 8–9.

15 *Economic Report of the President Transmitted to the Congress January 1966, To-gether with the Annual Report of the Council of Economic Advisers,* Washington, D.C., GPO, 1966, pp. 4, 6, 10.

16 *Economic Report of the President Transmitted to the Congress January 1969, To-gether with the Annual Report of the Council of Economic Advisers,* Washington, D.C., GPO, 1969, pp. 62–63.

17 *Economic Report of the President Transmitted to the Congress January 1978, To-gether with the Annual Report of the Council of Economic Advisers,* Washington, D.C., GPO, 1978, pp. 50, 51, 83–85, 93.

18 *Economic Report of the President Transmitted to the Congress January 1979, To-gether with the Annual Report of the Council of Economic Advisers,* Washington, D.C., GPO, 1979, pp. 72–75, 80.

19 *Economic Report of the President Transmitted to the Congress January 1980, To-gether with the Annual Report of the Council of Economic Advisers,* Washington, D.C., GPO, 1980, pp. 95, 98.

20 *Economic Report of the President Transmitted to the Congress January 1981, To-gether with the Annual Report of the Council of Economic Advisers,* Washington, D.C., GPO, 1981, pp. 3, 8–9, 38–39, 46–47.

21 *Economic Report of the President Transmitted to the Congress January 28, 1954,* Washington, D.C., GPO, 1954, pp. 54–55, 113–114.

22 *Economic Report of the President Transmitted to the Congress January 20, 1959,* Washington, D.C., GPO, 1959, pp. IV, 2.

23 "Annual Budget Message to the Congress – Fiscal 1959," January 13, 1958, in *Public Papers of the Presidents of the United States: Dwight D. Eisenhower, 1958, Containing the Public Messages, Speeches, and Statements of the President, Jan. 1 to Dec. 31, 1958,* Washington, D.C., GPO, 1958, p. 29.

24 "Annual Message to the Congress on the State of the Union, January 9, 1959," in *Public Papers of the Presidents of the United States: Dwight D. Eisenhower, 1959, Containing the Public Messages, Speeches, and Statements of the President, Jan. 1 to Dec. 31, 1959,* Washington, D.C., GPO, 1959, p. 7.

25 *Economic Report of the President Transmitted to the Congress January 18, 1961,* Washington, D.C., GPO, 1961.

26 See notably "The President's News Conference of January 27, 1969," in *Public Papers of the Presidents of the United States: Richard Nixon, 1969, Containing the Public Messages, Speeches, and Statements of the President,* Washington, D.C., GPO, 1970, p. 22; "Special Message to the Congress on Fiscal Policy, March 26, 1969," in ibid., p. 253; "Statement on the Control of Inflation, May 15, 1969," in ibid., p. 376; "The President's News Conference, September 26, 1969," in ibid., p. 755; "Remarks at the 'Briefing for Businessmen' Meeting, November 21, 1969," in ibid., p. 958.

27 "Address to the Nation on Economic Policy and Productivity, June 17, 1970," in *Public Papers of the Presidents of the United States: Richard Nixon, 1970, Contain-ing the Public Messages, Speeches, and Statements of the President,* Washington, D.C., GPO, 1971, pp. 502, 506.

28 President Nixon's "Address to the Nation" of August 15, 1971, *The New York Times,* August 16, 1971; *Economic Report of the President Transmitted to the Congress*

January 1972, Together with the Annual Report of the Council of Economic Advisers, Washington, D.C., GPO, 1972, p. 101.

29 See *Economic Report of the President Transmitted to the Congress January 1973, Together with the Annual Report of the Council of Economic Advisers,* Washington, D.C., GPO, 1973, p. 51; *Economic Report of the President Transmitted to the Congress February 1974, Together with the Annual Report of the Council of Economic Advisers,* Washington, D.C., GPO, 1974, pp. 3–4, 99, 103.

30 "Annual Budget Message to the Congress, Fiscal Year 1976, February 3, 1975," in *Public Papers of the Presidents of the United States: Gerald R. Ford, 1975, Containing the Public Messages, Speeches, and Statements of the President,* Book One, Washington, D.C., GPO, 1977, p. 147; *Economic Report of the President Transmitted to the Congress February 1975, Together with the Annual Report of the Council of Economic Advisers,* Washington, D.C., GPO, 1975, pp. 3, 4, 7.

31 In regard to regulation, see notably *Economic Report of the President . . . 1975,* pp. 147, 159; and *Economic Report of the President Transmitted to the Congress January 1977, Together with the Annual Report of the Council of Economic Advisers,* Washington, D.C., GPO, 1977, p. 8. Also, for taxes and productivity, the 1977 report, pp. 4–5, 24, 55.

32 *Economic Report of the President Transmitted to the Congress February 1982, Together with the Annual Report of the Council of Economic Advisers,* Washington, D.C., GPO, 1982, pp. 3–7, 33–35, 42–43, 59–60, 109, 118–119. Emphasis supplied.

33 *Economic Report of the President Transmitted to the Congress February 1985, Together with the Annual Report of the Council of Economic Advisers,* Washington, D.C., GPO, 1985, pp. 21–24, 27–30, 65–69.

34 *Economic Report of the President Transmitted to the Congress January 1989, Together with the Annual Report of the Council of Economic Advisers,* Washington, D.C., GPO, 1989, pp. 40, 56–57, 255–256, 262–263.

35 *Economic Report of the President . . . 1990,* pp. 25–26; *Economic Report of the President . . . 1991,* pp. 38, 46, 59, 71, 77.

36 Daniel F. Spulber, *Regulation and Markets,* Cambridge, Mass., MIT Press, 1989, pp. 10–12, 464–465; also Martin C. Schnitzer, *Contemporary Government and Business Relations,* 3rd ed., Boston, Houghton Mifflin, 1987, pp. 121–134.

37 Schnitzer, *Contemporary Government,* pp. 329–341; Robert W. Crandall, *After the Breakup: U.S. Telecommunications in a More Competitive Era,* Washington, D.C., Brookings Institution, 1991; Agis Salpukas, "Electric Utilities Brace for End of Regulation and Monopolies," *The New York Times,* August 8, 1994.

38 Schnitzer, *Contemporary Government,* pp. 241–254; Murray L. Weidenbaum, *Business, Government and the Public,* Englewood Cliffs, N.J., Prentice-Hall, 1977, pp. 92–96.

39 See Spulber, *Regulation and Markets,* pp. 62–65, 78, 385–392, 493–494; Schnitzer, *Contemporary Gernment,* pp. 274–289; Stephen Breyer, *Regulation and Its Reform,* Cambridge, Mass., Harvard University Press, 1982, pp. 96–97; "U.S. Is Proposing New Restrictions for the Labeling of Foods," *The New York Times,* November 6, 1991.

40 See Harold Koontz and Richard W. Gable, *Public Control of Economic Enterprises*, New York, McGraw-Hill, 1956, p. 63.

41 Spulber, *Regulation and Markets*, pp. 79–80.

42 Ibid., p. 79; Schnitzer, *Contemporary Government*, p. 311; Koontz and Gable, *Public Control*, p. 63; Weidenbaum, *Business, Government*, p. 4.

43 Molly O'Neill, "New Rules on Labeling May Change Foods Too," *The New York Times*, November 13, 1991.

44 Weidenbaum, *Business, Government*, pp. 300–319.

45 See William A. Hosek and Frank Zahn, *Monetary Theory, Policy, and Financial Markets*, New York, McGraw-Hill, 1977, pp. 20, 30–33; also Weidenbaum, *Business, Government*, pp. 4, 15.

46 Spulber, *Regulation and Markets*, pp. 392–394.

47 Breyer, *Regulation and Its Reform*, pp. 73, 78–79; also Koontz and Gable, *Public Control*, pp. 224–233.

48 For federal credit and government-sponsored enterprises (GSEs), see Office of Management and Budget, *Budget of the United States Government, Fiscal Year 1992*, Part Two, Washington, D.C., GPO, 1991, pp. 220–267. See also Donald L. Losman and Shu-Jan Liang, *The Promise of American Industry: An Alternative Assessment of Problems and Prospects*, New York, Quorum Books, 1990, pp. 76–77. For agriculture, see notably Harold C. Halcrow, *Agricultural Policy Analysis*, New York, McGraw-Hill, 1984, pp. 38–39, 95; see also William Robbins, "Policy Shift Raises Hopes of Farmers," *The New York Times*, October 27, 1986, and by the same author, "As Prices Plunge, Farmers Discover a Bonus Linking Two Programs," *The New York Times*, October 31, 1986.

49 *Budget of the United States . . . Fiscal Year 1992*, Part Two, pp. 201–215.

50 Ibid., pp. 207–214; also Schnitzer, *Contemporary Government*, pp. 377–389.

51 Mervyn A. King and Don Fullerton, eds., *The Taxation of Income from Capital: A Comparative Study of the United States, the United Kingdom, Sweden, and West Germany*, Chicago, University of Chicago Press, 1984, pp. 255, 279, 300, 303.

52 Schnitzer, *Contemporary Government*, pp. 407–419.

53 Weidenbaum, *Business, Government*, p. 119.

54 See interesting precedents for this situation in Kent Weaver, *The Policy of Industrial Change: Railway Policy in North America*, Washington, D.C., Brookings Institution, 1985, pp. 69–70.

55 Le Roy J. Haugh, "Procurement – Lightning Rod for Reform," Aerospace Industries Association *Newsletter*, Vol. 4, No. 5, November 1991, pp. 1–2.

56 The entire issue of the *Newsletter* cited in n. 55.

57 See Weaver, *The Policy of Industrial Change*, pp. 72–73, and Paul W. MacAvoy et al., *Privatization and State-Owned Enterprises*, Boston, Kluwer Academic, 1989, pp. 77–89.

58 National Science Foundation, *National Patterns of R&D Resources: 1990, Final Report*, by J. E. Jankowski, NSF 90–316, Washington, D.C., 1990, pp. 47, 55.

59 See notably Annemieke J. M. Roobeek, *Beyond the Technology Race: An Analysis of Technology Policy in Seven Industrial Countries*, Amsterdam–New York, Elsevier, 1990, pp. 36–38.

60 For information on DARPA, see notably *High Performance Computing*, Hearing

Before the Subcommittee on Science, Research, and Technology of the Committee on Science, Space, and Technology, U.S. House of Representatives, One Hundred First Congress, 1st Session, Washington, D.C., GPO, 1989; *High Performance Computing Act of 1990,* Report of the Senate Committee on Commerce, Science, and Transportation, S. 1067, One Hundred First Congress, 2nd Session, Washington, D.C., GPO, 1990; *Department of Defense Appropriations for 1991,* Hearings Before a Subcommittee of the Committee on Appropriations, House of Representatives, One Hundred First Congress, Washington, D.C., GPO, 1990; "The Government's Guiding Hand," interview with Craig Fields, *Technology Review,* Vol. 94, No. 2, February/March 1991, pp. 35–40; "Pentagon Wizards of Technology Eye Wider Civilian Role," *The New York Times,* October 22, 1991. (Under the Clinton administration DARPA retook its original name ARPA – a change meant to emphasize its reorientation toward the general needs of the entire economy.) On Sematech, see *The Future of the U.S. Semiconductor Industry and the Impact on Defense,* Hearing Before the Subcommittee on Defense Industry and Technology of the Committee on Armed Services, United States Senate, One Hundred First Congress, 1st Session, Washington, D.C., GPO, 1990; *Infrastructure,* Hearing Before the Subcommittee on Commerce, Consumer Protection, and Competitiveness of the Committee on Energy and Commerce, House of Representatives, One Hundred First Congress, 2nd Session, Washington, D.C., GPO, 1990. See also *Economic Report of the President . . . 1989,* pp. 244.

61 See Departments of Veterans Affairs and Housing and Urban Development, and Independent Agencies Appropriations Bill, 1991, Senate Committee on Appropriations, *Report* (to accompany H.R. 5158), One Hundred First Congress, 2nd Session, Washington, D.C., GPO, 1990; Edmund L. Andrews, "The U.S. Rekindles a Dream for Space," *The New York Times,* March 10, 1991; Richard H. Truly, "Space Exploration 1991," Aerospace Industries Association, *Key Speeches,* Vol. 4, No. 9, November 1991, pp. 1–5. See also *Key Technologies for the 1990s,* a report of the Technical Council of the AIA, Washington, D.C., Aerospace Industries of America, November 1987.

62 See *Obstacles to Technology Transfer and Commercialization at Federal Laboratories,* Hearing Before the Subcommittee on Regulation, Business Opportunities, and Energy of the Committee on Small Business, House of Representatives, One Hundred First Congress, 1st Session, Washington, D.C., GPO, 1989; *Technology Programs,* Hearings Before the Subcommittee on Science, Research, and Technology of the Committee on Science, Space, and Technology, House of Representatives, One Hundred First Congress, 2nd Session, Washington, D.C., GPO, 1990; U.S. Congress, Office of Technology Assessment, *Making Things Better: Competing in Manufacturing,* Washington, D.C., GPO, February 1990, pp. 27, 190.

63 Cited by Ann R. Markusen, "Defense Spending as Industrial Policy," in *Industrial Policy: Business and Politics in the United States and France,* ed. Sharon Zukin, New York, Praeger, 1985, p. 75.

64 Andrew Pollack, "In U.S. Technology, a Gap Between Arms and VCR's," *The New York Times,* March 4, 1991.

65 *Statistical Abstract of the United States 1991,* pp. 740–744.

66 National Science Foundation, *National Patterns of R&D Resources: 1990*, pp. 65, 66.

67 Losman and Liang, *The Promise of American Industry*, p. 66.

68 "U.S. Industry Is Rated on Competitiveness in Technology," *The New York Times*, March 21, 1991.

69 National Science Foundation, *National Patterns of R&D Resources: 1990*, p. 3.

70 Ibid., p. 23; computed from *Statistical Abstract of the United States 1991*, p. 590.

71 Jurgen Schmandt and Robert Wilson, eds., *Promoting High-Technology Industry: Initiatives and Policies for State Governments*, Boulder, Colo., Westview, 1987, p. 3.

72 U.S. Congress, Office of Technology Assessment, *Making Things Better*, p. 175.

73 *Varied Uses*, Hearing Before the Subcommittee on Science, Research, and Technology of the Committee on Science, Space, and Technology, House of Representatives, One Hundred First Congress, 1st Session, Washington, D.C., GPO, 1989.

74 U.S. Congress, Office of Technology Assessment, *Making Things Better*, pp. 177–178.

75 *Competitiveness Challenge Facing the U.S. Industry*, Hearing Before the Committee on Commerce, Science, and Transportation, United States Senate, One Hundred First Congress, 2nd Session, Washington, D.C., GPO, 1990, p. 65.

76 David Osborne, *Economic Competitiveness: The States Take the Lead*, Washington, D.C., Economic Policy Institute, 1987, pp. 5, 62.

77 Alfred D. Chandler, Jr., *Scale and Scope: The Dynamics of U.S. Capitalism*, Cambridge, Mass., Belknap Press of Harvard University Press, 1990, pp. 608–609.

78 *Handbook of Industrial Statistics 1988*, Vienna, United Nations Industrial Development Organization, 1988, p. 74.

79 See the brilliant analyses of Alfred D. Chandler, Jr., in *Scale and Scope*, pp. 617–621.

80 See notably *The Future of the U.S. Semiconductor Industry and the Impact of Defense*, Hearings Before the Subcommittee on Defense and Industry of the Committee on Armed Services, United States Senate, One Hundred First Congress, 1st Session, November 29, 1989, Washington, D.C., GPO, 1990, pp. 76–79; *Infrastructure*, Hearing Before the Subcommittee on Commerce, Consumer Protection, and Competitiveness of the Committee on Energy and Commerce, House of Representatives, One Hundred First Congress, 2nd Session, May 9, 1990, Washington, D.C., GPO, 1990; William G. Howard, Jr., "Semiconductor Industry," in *National Interests in an Age of Global Technology*, ed. Thomas H. Lee and Proctor P. Reid, National Academy of Engineering, Washington, D.C., National Academy Press, 1991, pp. 134–137; "Electronic Components and Equipment," in *U.S. Industrial Outlook '92: Business Forecasts for 350 Industries*, U.S. Department of Commerce, Washington, D.C., GPO, January 1992, pp. 16–1 to 16–12; and John Markoff, "I.B.M. in Chip Deal with Toshiba and Siemens," *The New York Times*, July 13, 1992.

81 Janet H. Muroyama and H. Guyford Stever, eds., *Globalization and Technology: International Perspectives*, Proceedings of the Sixth Convocation of the Council of Academies of Engineering and Technological Sciences, Washington, D.C., National Academy Press, 1988, pp. 82–83.

82 "Motor Vehicles and Parts," in *U.S. Industrial Outlook '92*, pp. 36–1 to 36–20; see also Walter Adams and James W. Brock, "The Automobile Industry," in *The Structure of the American Economy*, ed. Walter Adams, New York, Macmillan, 1986, pp. 134–135.

83 Melvyn A. Fuss and Leonard Waverman, *Cost and Productivity in Automobile Production: The Challenge of Japanese Efficiency*, New York, Cambridge University Press, 1992, p. 229.

84 *Industry and Development*, Global Report 1989/90, Vienna, United Nations Industrial Development Organization, 1989, p. 34.

85 David Sanger, "A Defiant Detroit Still Depends on Japan," *The New York Times*, February 27, 1992.

86 See Brian H. Rowe, "Aircraft Engine Industry," in *National Interests in an Age of Global Technology*, ed. Lee and Reid, pp. 93–97; "Aerospace," in *U.S. Industrial Outlook '92*, pp. 21–1 to 21–7; Aerospace Industries Association, *Key Speeches*, Vol. 5, No. 1, February 1992; and John McDonnell, "Between the Devil and the Deep Blue Sea," *Key Speeches*, Vol. 5, No. 5, June 1992, pp. 1–4.

Chapter 3. The challenge

1 See Sheridan Tatsuno, *The Technopolis Strategy: Japan, High-Technology and the Control of the Twenty-First Century*, New York, Prentice-Hall, 1986, p. 43; also Motoshige Itoh et al., *Economic Analysis of Industrial Policy*, San Diego, Academic Press, 1991, pp. 21–23.

2 "MITI's Loosening Grip," *The New York Times*, July 9, 1989; *Business Week – Innovations 1990*, special issue, p. 79.

3 For a cursory view of the plans – which Charles J. McMillan calls "a judicious mixture of government intervention, jawboning and cajoling" – see his book *The Japanese Industrial System*, Berlin, Walter de Gruyter, 1984, pp. 65, 72–78. See Kozo Iamamura and Yasukichi Yasubai, eds., *The Political Economy of Japan*, Vol. I: *The Domestic Transformation*, Stanford, Calif., Stanford University Press, 1987, pp. 566–567, 569–570. Concerning the "visions," see "A New Nippon? MITI's 'Vision' for 1990s," *The Wall Street Journal*, July 3, 1990.

4 See Hugh Patrick, "Japanese High Technology Industrial Policy in Comparative Context," in *Japan's High Technology Industries: Lessons and Limitations of Industrial Policy*, ed. Hugh Patrick with the assistance of Larry Meissner, Seattle, University of Washington Press and University of Tokyo Press, 1986, p. 14.

5 Daniel Todd, *The World's Electronic Industry*, London, Routledge, 1990, pp. 209–211.

6 Patrick, "Japanese High Technology Industrial Policy," p. 15.

7 National Science Board, *Science and Engineering Indicators 1991*, Washington, D.C., GPO, 1991, p. 343.

8 Chalmers Johnson, *MITI and the Japanese Miracle: The Growth of Industrial Policy, 1925–1975*, Stanford, Calif., Stanford University Press, 1982, pp. 20–23, 315–319. See also Chalmers Johnson's essay "The Institutional Foundations of Japanese Industrial Policy," which stresses "the different priorities and political principles found in Japanese government as contrasted with those of the United States." At the heart is

the "skewed" relationship which business maintains with the other two centers of power (the strong bureaucracy and the weak Diet) and the "extremely intrusive" role of the state in the economy – a role based, however, on "cooperation rather than on confrontation" with the private sector. The essay is published in *The Politics of Industrial Policy*, ed. Claude E. Barfield and William A. Schambra, Washington, D.C., American Enterprise Institute for Public Policy Research, 1986; see esp. pp. 188–189, 198.

9 See Patrick, "Japanese High Technology Industrial Policy," pp. 19–21; he comments cogently on the views of Trezise and others.

10 Michael E. Porter, *The Competitive Advantage of Nations*, New York, Free Press, 1990, pp. 384, 401, 411–416.

11 Michael E. Porter, "Japan *Isn't* Playing by Different Rules," *The New York Times*, July 22, 1990.

12 For Japan and the U.S. the set of data used for the latter comparisons is for 1988; the latest data available for the U.S. are for 1991: see *Statistical Abstract of the United States 1991*, Washington, D.C., U.S. Department of Commerce, Bureau of the Census, 1991, p. 744.

13 Data from U.S. Department of Labor, Bureau of Labor Statistics, Office of Productivity and Technology, "Output per Hour, Hourly Compensation, and Unit Labor Cost in Manufacturing: Fourteen Countries or Areas, 1950–1989 (Average Annual Rate of Change)," mimeo., April 1991.

14 Robert H. Hayes and Steven C. Wheelwright, *Restoring Our Competitive Edge: Competing Through Manufactures*, New York, Wiley, 1984, p. 352.

15 Ibid., pp. 350–374; Michael H. Best, *The New Competition: Institutions of Industrial Restructuring*, Cambridge, Mass., Harvard University Press, 1990, pp. 149–150, 157–160.

16 T. Ozawa, "Japanese Multinationals and 1992," in *Multinationals in Europe: Strategies for the Future*, ed. B. Bürgenmeier and J. L. Mucchielli, London, Routledge, 1991, pp. 146–148.

17 Porter, *The Competitive Advantage*, p. 394.

18 National Science Board, *Science and Engineering Indicators 1991*, pp. 136–137, 139, 401–404.

19 Ibid., pp. 401–404; see also Porter, *The Competitive Advantage*, pp. 384–395 (including the Japanese cluster of competitive industries in the mid 1980s); for trade data, see *International Trade Statistics Yearbook 1989*, New York, UN, 1991, pp. 467, 932.

20 Gavin Peebles, *Hong Kong's Economy: An Introductory Macroeconomic Analysis*, Hong Kong, Oxford University Press, 1988, pp. 46–47; Lawrence J. Lau, ed., *Models of Development: A Comparative Study of Economic Growth in South Korea and Taiwan*, International Center for Economic Growth, San Francisco, ICS Press, 1990, pp. 1–15, 237–243.

21 Computed from OECD, *National Accounts 1960–1988*, pp. 31–36, and OECD, *National Accounts 1977–1989*, pp. 31–38.

22 "A New Nippon?" *The Wall Street Journal*, July 3, 1990.

23 See Tatsuno, *The Technopolis Strategy*, pp. 43, 228; see also Daniel I. Okimoto,

Between MITI and the Market: Japanese Industrial Policy for High Technology, Stanford, Calif., Stanford University Press, 1989, pp. 95–97.

24 See Susan Stern, ed., *Meet New Germany: Perspectives,* Frankfurt am Main, Frankfurter Allgemeine Zeitung, 1991, pp. 104–107.

25 Henry C. Wallich, *Mainsprings of the German Revival,* New Haven, Yale University Press, 1955, p. 141. For a detailed discussion, see Malcolm MacLennan, Murray Forsyth, and Geoffrey Denton, *Economic Planning and Policies in Britain, France and Germany,* New York, Praeger, 1968, pp. 34–54; see also *Meet New Germany,* ed. Stern, pp. 234–236; and Colin Campbell, Harvey Feigenbaum, Ronald Linden, and Helmut Norpoth, *Politics and Government in Europe Today,* New York, Harcourt Brace Jovanovich, 1990, pp. 325–327.

26 W. R. Smyser, *The Economy of United Germany: Colossus at the Crossroad,* New York, St. Martin's, 1992, pp. 144, 146.

27 See notably Victoria Curzon Price, *Industrial Policies in the European Community,* New York, St. Martin's, 1981, p. 53; Graham Hall, ed., *European Industrial Policy,* New York, St. Martin's, 1986, pp. 92–97; Smyser, *The Economy of United Germany,* pp. 113–117, 119.

28 *European Industrial Policy,* ed. Hall, pp. 102–103; Smyser, *The Economy of United Germany,* p. 168.

29 Price, *Industrial Policies,* p. 50; Porter, *The Competitive Advantage,* p. 377.

30 *Meet New Germany,* ed. Stern, pp. 111–118; Smyser, *The Economy of United Germany,* p. 92.

31 Gustav Stolper, Karl Häuser, and Knut Borchardt, *The German Economy 1870 to the Present,* New York, Harcourt Brace and World, 1967, pp. 27–29; MacLennan et al., *Economic Planning and Policies,* pp. 68–72; John Zysman, *Governments, Markets, and Growth,* Ithaca, Cornell University Press, 1983, pp. 261–265; A. Jacquemin, ed., *European Industry: Public Policy and Corporate Strategy,* Oxford, Clarendon, 1984, pp. 45–46; Smyser, *The Economy of United Germany,* pp. 83–92.

32 Hayes and Wheelwright, *Restoring Our Competitive Edge,* pp. 338–345; Campbell et al., *Politics and Government,* pp. 279–281; Porter, *The Competitive Advantage,* p. 369.

33 *OECD Economic Outlook,* 48, December 1990, p. 120; *OECD Economic Outlook,* 46, December 1989, p. 29.

34 Smyser, *The Economy of United Germany,* p. 196; Porter, *The Competitive Advantage,* pp. 357–358.

35 Michael W. Klein and Paul J. J. Welfens, eds., *Multinationals in the New Europe and Global Trade,* Berlin, Springer, 1992, p. 51.

36 Robert O. Keohane and Stanley Hoffman, eds., *The New European Community: Decision Making and Institutional Change,* Boulder, Colo., Westview, 1991, pp. 10–13, 30–31; also Smyser, *The Economy of United Germany,* pp. 215–217; *European Industrial Policy,* ed. Hall, pp. 4–12; *Multinationals in Europe,* ed. Bürgenmeier and Mucchielli, p. 127; Heinrich Siedentopf and Jacques Ziller, eds., *Making European Policies Work: The Implementation of Community Legislation in Member States,* London, Sage, 1988, pp. 72–77.

37 Jacques Lesourne, "The Changing Context of Industrial Policy: External and Internal Development," in *European Industry,* ed. Jacquemin, pp. 26–27.

38 See Economic Commission for Europe, *East-West Joint Ventures: Economic, Business, Financial and Legal Aspects,* New York, United Nations, 1988, pp. 23, 26, 71.

39 *The New European Community,* ed. Keohane and Hoffman, p. 31; *Multinationals in the New Europe,* ed. Klein and Welfens, p. 187; Smyser, *The Economy of United Germany,* p. 199; "Now Everyone Wants In, But Can a 24-Member Club Work?" *The New York Times,* May 10, 1992.

40 See notably J. H. Dunning and J. A. Cantwell, "Japanese Direct Investment in Europe," in *Multinationals in Europe,* ed. Bürgenmeier and Mucchielli, pp. 155–166; and *Multinationals in the New Europe,* ed. Klein and Welfens, p. 30.

41 *Statistical Abstract of the United States 1971,* Washington, D.C., U.S. Department of Commerce, Bureau of the Census, p. 222; *1981,* p. 401; *1986,* p. 401; *1992,* pp. 395–396.

42 *Statistical Abstract of the United States 1991,* Washington, D.C., U.S. Department of Commerce, Bureau of the Census, 1992, p. 385.

43 Marvin H. Kosters, "Wages and Demographics: The Payoff to Education in the Labor Market," in *Workers and Their Wages,* ed. Kosters, Washington, D.C., AEI Press, 1991, pp. 7–8.

44 *Poverty in the United States: 1990,* Current Population Reports, Consumer Income, Series P-60, 175, Washington, D.C., U.S. Department of Commerce, Bureau of the Census, 1991, p. 9.

45 *Economic Report of the President . . . 1991,* p. 336.

46 *Handbook of Labor Statistics,* Bulletin 2340, Washington, D.C., U.S. Department of Labor, August 1989, pp. 312–313; *Employment and Earnings,* Vol. 39, No. 5, May 1992, pp. 83–103.

47 See for instance Neal H. Rosenthal, "The Shrinking Middle Class: Myth or Reality?" *Monthly Labor Review,* Vol. 108, No. 3, March 1985, pp. 3, 8; and Patrick J. McMahon and John H. Tschetter, "The Declining Middle Class: A Further Analysis," *Monthly Labor Review,* Vol. 109, No. 9, September 1986, p. 22.

48 Arthur L. Robinson, "Impact of Electronics on Employment: Productivity and Displacement Effects," *Science,* Vol. 195, No. 4285, March 18, 1977, pp. 1179–1184; Henry Levin and Russell Rumberger, "The Low-Skill Future of High-Tech," *Technology Review,* Vol. 86, No. 6, August-September 1983, pp. 18–21.

49 Herb Brody in *Technology Review,* Vol. 94, No. 5, July 1991, p. 44.

50 These and the following data are from National Science Board, *Science and Engineering Indicators 1991,* Appendix, pp. 261–304.

51 See *OECD Economic Outlook,* 46, p. 6; and *OECD Economic Outlook,* 48, p. 120. See also OECD, *National Accounts 1960–1988* and *1991,* OECD, Department of Economics and Statistics, 1989 and 1991, and *Statistical Abstract of the United States 1991,* p. 842.

Chapter 4. The implications

1 See George W. Terborgh, *The Bogey of Economic Maturity,* Chicago, Machinery and Allied Products Institute, 1945, pp. 77–79, 94, 173. See also R. D. Norton, "Industrial Policy and American Renewal," *Journal of Economic Literature,* Vol. 24, March 1986, p. 1.

2 Ira C. Magaziner and Robert B. Reich, *Minding America's Business: The Decline and Rise of the American Economy*, New York, Harcourt Brace Jovanovich, 1982, p. 203; Robert B. Reich, "Making Industrial Policy," *Foreign Affairs*, Spring 1982, pp. 853–854.

3 Barry Bluestone and Bennett Harrison, *The Deindustrialization of America: Plant Closing, Community Abandonment and the Dismantling of Basic Industry*, New York, Basic, 1982, pp. 15–16.

4 Pearl M. Kamer, *The U.S. Economy: Adjusting to the New Realities*, New York, Praeger, 1988, p. 10.

5 John Zysman and Stephen S. Cohen, "The International Experience," in *The Changing American Economy*, ed. David R. Obey and Paul Sarbanes, New York and London, Blackwell, 1986, pp. 47–48; Stephen S. Cohen and John Zysman, *Manufacturing Matters: The Myth of the Post-Industrial Economy*, New York, Basic, 1987, p. 3.

6 Jerry J. Jasinowski, "Impressions from the Industrial Policy Debate," in U.S. Department of Commerce, *1981 U.S. Industrial Outlook for 200 Industries with Projections for 1985*, Washington, D.C., GPO, January 1981, p. xiii.

7 "At Issue: Productivity," *Fiscal Policy Forum*, Vol. 1, No. 2, April 1983, p. 1; see also Allen J. Lenz, *Beyond Blue Economic Horizons*, New York, Praeger, 1991, p. 21.

8 Charles P. Kindleberger, "An American Climacteric?" *Challenge*, Vol. 16, No. 6, January-February 1974, p. 44.

9 Benjamin Friedman, *Day of Reckoning: The Consequences of American Economic Policy Under Reagan and After*, New York, Random House, 1988, pp. 28–29.

10 Lester C. Thurow, "Creating a World-Class Team," in *The Changing American Economy*, ed. Obey and Sarbanes, p. 172.

11 Charles P. Kindleberger, "An American Climacteric?" p. 42.

12 Michael L. Dertuzos, Richard K. Lester, Robert M. Solow, and the MIT Commission on Industrial Productivity, *Made in America: Regaining the Productivity Edge*, Cambridge, Mass., MIT Press, 1989, pp. 1, 2, 8.

13 See notably Robert B. Reich, *The Next American Frontier*, New York, Times Books, 1983, pp. 3, 21, 131; John Zysman and Laura Tyson, eds., *American Industry in International Competition: Government Policies and Corporate Strategies*, Ithaca, Cornell University Press, 1983, esp. pp. 15, 17, 20–23; Zysman and Cohen, "The International Experience"; Cohen and Zysman, *Manufacturing Matters*, p. 61.

14 Stephen S. Cohen, "United States-Japan Trade Relations," in *International Trade: The Changing Role of the United States: Proceedings of the Academy of Political Science*, ed. Frank J. Macchiarola, Vol. 37, No. 4, New York, 1990, p. 129.

15 Charles P. Kindleberger, "An American Climacteric?" pp. 35, 44.

16 Alfred Marshall, *Industry and Trade*, London, Macmillan, 1920, pp. 92, 93, 132.

17 See W. H. B. Court, *A Concise Economic History of Britain: From 1750 to Recent Times*, Cambridge, Cambridge University Press, 1954, pp. 216–225, 319–321. See also Peter Mathias, *The First Industrial Nation: An Economic History of Britain, 1700–1914*, London, Methuen, 1969, pp. 408–409; Andrew Gamble, *Britain in Decline: Economic Policy, Political Strategy and the British State*, Boston, Beacon, p. 53; David Coutes and John Hilliard, *The Economic Decline of Modern Britain: The Debate Between Left and Right*, London, Harvester Press, 1986, p. 208; Sidney

Pollard, *Britain's Prime and Britain's Decline: The British Economy 1870–1914*, London, Arnold, 1989, pp. 266, 270.

18 Robert W. Russell, "Congress and the Proposed Industrial Policy Structures," in *The Politics of Industrial Policy*, ed. Claude E. Barfield, Jr., and William A. Schambra, Washington, D.C., American Enterprise Institute, 1986, pp. 318–319.

19 Robert F. Wescott, "U.S. Approaches to Industrial Policy," in *An Economic Perspective*, ed. F. Gerald Adams and Lawrence R. Klein, Lexington, Mass., Heath, 1983, pp. 87–89.

20 Magaziner and Reich, *Minding America's Business*, p. 370 (also 255–256); Reich, "Making Industrial Policy," p. 874.

21 Laura Tyson and John Zysman, "American Industry in International Competition," in *American Industry*, ed. Zysman and Tyson, pp. 24–27.

22 Ibid., p. 311.

23 Laura d'Andrea Tyson and John Zysman, "Preface: The Argument Outlined," in *Politics and Productivity: The Real Story of Why Japan Works*, ed. Chalmers Johnson, Laura d'Andrea Tyson, and John Zysman, New York, Ballinger, 1989, p. xvi. Emphasis supplied.

24 Cohen and Zysman (quoting Tyson), *Manufacturing Matters*, p. 217.

25 *The Pocketbook Issues: AFL-CIO Policy Recommendations for 1990*, pamphlet reprinted from the "National Economy" section of the report of the Executive Council of the AFL-CIO to the Eighteenth Convention, Washington, D.C., November 1989, p. 22.

26 Magaziner and Reich, *Minding America's Business*, pp. 5, 255, 367–368.

27 Robert B. Reich, *The Work of Nations: Preparing Ourselves for 21st Century Capitalism*, New York, Knopf, 1991, pp. 172, 196. Emphasis supplied. Some business executives, such as John McDonnell, CEO of the McDonnell Douglas Corporation, are already subscribing to the idea that the commercial aircraft business, for instance, must be transformed, with U.S. citizens performing "more and more of the higher value-added jobs, the kind of jobs that are involved in thinking, creating, and managing," while the production of parts and sub-assemblies of our future jetliners would take place in various countries outside the United States. See John McDonnell, "Between the Devil and the Deep Blue Sea," Aerospace Industries Association, *Key Speeches*, Vol. 5, No. 5, June 1992, p. 3.

28 *Economic Report of the President Transmitted to the Congress February 1984, Together with the Annual Report of the Council of Economic Advisers*, Washington, D.C., GPO, 1984, pp. 87–90; Thurow, "Creating a World-Class Team," p. 172.

29 Otis L. Graham, *Losing Time: The Industrial Policy Debate*, Cambridge, Mass., Harvard University Press, 1992, pp. 38–39.

30 For some interesting details, see Sidney Blumenthal, "Drafting a Democratic Industrial Plan," *New York Times Magazine*, August 28, 1983, pp. 31ff.

31 *Economic Report of the President . . . 1984*, pp. 85–86; *The Reindustrialization of America*, by the Business Week Team, ed. Seymour Zucker et al., New York, McGraw-Hill, 1982, pp. 136–137; James K. Galbraith, "The Debate About Industrial Policy," in *American Economic Policy: Problems and Prospects*, ed. Gar Alperovitz and Roger Skurski, South Bend, Ind., Notre Dame University Press, 1984, p. 97.

32 Reich, *The Work of Nations,* pp. 89–90, 108, 182–183.
33 Reich fails to recognize the variety of U.S. policies. He assumes that there are only three kinds of policy – fiscal, monetary, and industrial – which constitute "the three legs of the economic stool." And he adds that "we in this country have clung tenaciously until recently to the notions it is all fiscal and monetary policy, that we don't have to worry about the countless microeconomic interventions . . . which have a profound impact on the pace and direction of industrial change." Statement of Robert B. Reich in *Industrial Policy,* Hearings Before the Subcommittee on Economic Stabilization of the Committee on Banking, Finance, and Urban Affairs, House of Representatives, Ninety-Eighth Congress, 1st Session, Part 5, Washington, D.C., GPO, 1984, p. 212. Reich's "three legs of the economic stool" have been transformed by Chalmers Johnson into an economic triangle: "as a set of policies, industrial policy is the complement, the third side of the economic triangle to a government's monetary policies . . . and fiscal policies." Cf. *The Industrial Policy Debate,* ed. Chalmers Johnson, San Francisco, Institute for Contemporary Studies, 1984, p. 7.
34 See notably Felix G. Rohatyn, *The Twenty-Year Century: Essays on Economics and Public Finance,* New York, Random House, 1983; Bruce R. Scott and George C. Lodge, eds., *U.S. Competitiveness in the World Economy,* Boston, Harvard Business School Press, 1985, pp. 488–490. See also Russell, "Congress and the Proposed Industrial Policy Structures," pp. 320–321.
35 Russell, "Congress and the Proposed Industrial Policy Structures," pp. 327–331.
36 Magaziner and Reich, *Minding America's Business,* pp. 377–378; Reich, *The Next American Frontier,* pp. 231–232; *The Industrial Policy Debate,* ed. Johnson, p. 5; Lester C. Thurow, *Head to Head: The Coming Economic Battle Among Japan, Europe and America,* New York, Morrow, 1992, pp. 118–119.
37 U.S. Department of Labor, Bureau of Labor Statistics, Office of Productivity and Technology, "Output per Hour, Hourly Compensation, and Unit Labor Cost in Manufacturing: Fourteen Countries or Areas, 1950–1989 (Average Annual Rate of Change)," mimeo., Washington, D.C., April 1991; *Economic Report of the President . . . 1991,* pp. 288, 299.
38 Data computed from U.S. Department of Commerce, Bureau of the Census, *United States Census of Manufactures: 1947,* Vol. 1, *General Summary,* Washington, D.C., GPO, 1950, pp. 24–31; and *1987,* pp. 1–24 to 1–29.
39 See Donald F. Barnett and Robert W. Crandall, *Up from the Ashes: The Rise of the Steel Minimill in the United States,* Washington, D.C., Brookings Institution, 1986; Jonathan P. Hicks, "Foreign Owners Are Shaking Up the Competition" and "U.S. Steelmakers Staging Comeback in World Markets," *The New York Times,* May 28, 1989, and March 31, 1992.
40 MIT Commission on Industrial Productivity, *The U.S. Machine Tools Industry and Its Foreign Competitors,* Cambridge, Mass., MIT Press, 1989, p. 7; William J. Corcoran, "The Machine Tools Industry Under Fire," in Donald L. Losman and Shu-Jan Liang, *The Promise of American Industry: An Alternative Assessment of Problems and Prospects,* New York, Quorum Books, 1990, pp. 227–248. See also Donald A. Hicks, ed., *Is New Technology Enough? Making and Remaking U.S. Basic Industries,* Washington, D.C., American Enterprise Institute, 1988.

41 John Markoff, "A Remade IBM Reinvents the Mainframe"; Steve Lohr, "Lessons for a High-Tech President," "Mainframe Computers Aren't All That Dead," and "Job Cuts by IBM May Rise," *The New York Times,* January 29, 1993, January 24, 1993, February 9, 1993, and February 11, 1993.

42 Computations are based on data from *Economic Report of the President . . . 1991,* pp. 298–299 (for implicit deflators), 347, and Bureau of the Census, *Plant and Equipment Expenditures and Plans,* quarterly.

43 National Science Board, *Science and Engineering Indicators . . . 1991,* p. 401; U.S. Department of Labor, Bureau of Labor Statistics, Office of Productivity and Technology, "Output per Hour."

44 Lester C. Thurow, "Healing with a Thousand Bandages," *Challenge,* November–December 1985, p. 24.

45 N. Spulber, *Managing the American Economy from Roosevelt to Reagan,* Bloomington, Indiana University Press, 1989, p. 105; see also "The Political Realities of Industrial Policy," ed. Allan M. Kantorow, *Harvard Business Review,* September–October 1985; Lester C. Thurow, "The Zero-Sum Society," *The New York Times,* August 28, 1983, and *The Zero-Sum Society,* New York, Basic, 1980.

46 N. Spulber, "Perceptions américaines du pouvoir économique soviétique (1955–1980)," *Cadmos,* Spring 1981, p. 57.

47 See Robert Lawrence, "American Manufacturing in the 1990s: The Adjustment Challenge," in *American Manufacturing in a Global Market,* ed. Kenneth W. Chilton, Melinda E. Warren, and Murray L. Weidenbaum, Boston, Kluwer, 1990, p. 89. See also Allen J. Lenz, assisted by Hunter K. Monroe and Bruce Parsell, *Narrowing the U.S. Current Account Deficit: A Sectoral Assessment,* Washington, Institute for International Economics, June 1992, p. 558; and *Economic Report of the President . . . 1989,* p. 234; also "Japan's Mythical Trade Surplus," *The New York Times,* December 9, 1990.

48 Lenz, *Narrowing,* pp. 75–76.

49 *World Economic Outlook May 1991: A Survey by the Staff of the International Monetary Fund,* Washington, D.C., International Monetary Fund, 1991, pp. 46–47.

50 Ibid., p. 49.

51 Herbert Stein, "Economic Growth as an Objective of Government Policy," in Papers and Proceedings of the Seventy-Sixth Annual Meeting of the American Economic Association, *American Economic Review,* Vol. 54, May 1964, p. 25. Emphasis supplied.

52 OECD, *Economic Outlook,* 48, Paris, OECD, December 1990, p. 192.

53 Daniel F. Burton, Jr., Victor Gotbaum, and Felix G. Rohatyn, eds., *Vision for the 1990s: U.S. Strategy and the Global Economy,* Cambridge, Mass., Ballinger, 1989, pp. 11–13, 21–24.

54 Ibid., pp. 14–18.

55 See Linda R. Cohen and Roger G. Noll, *The Technology Pork Barrel,* Washington, D.C., Brookings Institution, 1990, pp. 43–45.

56 See Mark Blaug, "The Empirical Status of Human Capital Theory: A Slightly Jaundiced Survey," *Journal of Economic Literature,* Vol. 14, Nos. 3–4, September 1976, pp. 827, 829.

57 *Jobs for the Future: A Democratic Agenda,* Report of the Senate Democratic Caucus, Washington, D.C., November 16, 1983, p. 11.

58 *Congressional Quarterly Almanac,* Eighty-Ninth Congress, 1st Session, 1965, Vol. 21, Washington, D.C., Congressional Quarterly Service, pp. 236–245; *U.S. Health Care at the Crossroads,* OECD Health Policy Studies, No. 1, Paris, OECD, 1992, pp. 7–17, 48–55.

59 See the valuable study by Robert W. Glover, *Apprenticeship: A Review and Synthesis of Domestic and International Practices,* Columbus, Ohio, National Center for Research in Vocational Education, Ohio State University, 1985 (mimeo.).

60 Frank Levy and Richard J. Murnane, "U.S. Earning Levels and Earnings Inequality: A Review of Recent Trends and Proposed Explanations," *Journal of Economic Literature,* Vol. 30, No. 3, September 1992, pp. 1372–1373.

61 Reich, *The Next American Frontier,* pp. 246–247, 252.

62 Paul Krugman, *The Age of Diminished Expectations: U.S. Economic Policy in the 1990s,* Cambridge, Mass., MIT Press, 1990, p. 15.

63 Charles L. Schultze, "The Public Use of Private Interest," *Harper's,* May 1977, p. 49.

64 Water is discussed extensively in Nicolas Spulber and Asghar Sabbaghi, *Economics of Water Resources: From Regulation to Privatization,* Boston and Dordrecht, Kluwer Academic, 1994.

65 James Tobin, "Keynes' Policies in Theory and Practice," *Challenge,* November–December 1983, p. 11.

66 See Charles L. Schultze, "Industrial Policy: A Dissent," *Brookings Review,* Fall 1983, pp. 9–10.

67 Robert Z. Lawrence, "U.S. International Competitiveness," in *U.S. International Economic Policy in the 1980s,* Joint Economic Committee, Ninety-Seventh Congress, 2nd Session, Washington, D.C., GPO, February 1982, p. 68.

68 See Joseph L. Badaracco, Jr., and David B. Yoffie, "Industrial Policy: It Can't Happen Here," *Harvard Business Review,* No. 6, November–December 1983, p. 99.

69 Russell, "Congress and the Proposed Industrial Policy Structures," pp. 289–290.

70 Matei Calinescu, *Five Faces of Modernity,* Durham, N.C., Duke University Press, 1987, pp. 151–153.

71 Adam Smith, *An Inquiry into the Nature and Causes of the Wealth of Nations,* ed. Edwin Cannan, New York, Random House, 1937, p. 327.

72 Reich, *The Next American Frontier,* pp. 255, 280–282.

73 Thurow, *Head to Head,* p. 247.

Chapter 5. The structural transformations

1 *Economic Report of the President . . . 1989,* pp. 27, 150.

2 U.S. Department of Commerce, Bureau of Economic Analysis, *Survey of Current Business,* April 1990, p. C-25; U.S. Department of Commerce, Bureau of the Census, *Historical Statistics of the United States 1789–1945,* Washington, D.C., GPO, 1949, pp. 126, 135.

3 Computed from U.S. Department of Commerce, Bureau of Economic Analysis, *Fixed Reproducible Tangible Wealth in the United States, 1925–1989,* p. 213; U.S.

Department of Commerce, Bureau of the Census, *Historical Statistics of the United States: Colonial Times to 1970,* Washington, D.C., GPO, 1975, p. 65; and *Statistical Abstract of the United States 1992,* p. 386.

4 *Economic Report(s) of the President . . . 1989,* p. 150, and *1991,* p. 338; Angus Maddison, "Growth and Slowdown in Advanced Capitalist Economies: Techniques of Quantitative Assessment," *Journal of Economic Literature,* Vol. 25, June 1987, p. 650. Subsequent calculations by Angus Maddison, presented in his study *Dynamic Forces in Capitalist Development: A Long-Run Comparative View,* New York, Oxford University Press, 1991, enable him to assert that the annual average compound growth rate of U.S. GDP per man-hour was 1.9 percent for 1870–1913, 2.4 percent for 1913–50, 2.5 percent for 1950–73, and 1.0 percent for 1973–87 (p. 51).

5 Computations based on *Economic Report of the President . . . 1991,* pp. 286–287.

6 Computed from *Historical Statistics of the United States: Colonial Times,* pp. 889–890, and *Statistical Abstract of the United States 1990,* p. 805.

7 *Economic Report of the President . . . 1989,* p. 150.

8 U.S. Department of Commerce, Bureau of the Census, *Money Income and Poverty Status in the United States 1989,* Current Population Reports, Series P-60, No. 168, Washington, D.C., September 1990; U.S. Department of Commerce, Bureau of the Census, *Poverty in the United States 1991,* Current Population Reports, Series P-60, No. 181, Washington, D.C., August 1992; *Statistical Abstract of the United States 1992,* p. 456.

9 Maddison, *Dynamic Forces in Capitalist Development,* p. 75.

10 *Fixed Reproducible Tangible Wealth in the United States, 1925–1989,* pp. 216, 362.

11 Data for 1869–1913 are based on Edwin Fruckey's Index of Industrial Output; for 1919–50, on the Federal Reserve Board index; and for 1950–89, on the Federal Reserve Board again – cf. *Historical Statistics of the United States: Colonial Times,* p. 667, and *Economic Report of the President . . . 1991,* p. 341.

12 Calculations of Baily and Chakrabarti, quoted in Michael L. Dertouzos et al., *Made in America: Regaining the Productivity Edge,* Cambridge, Mass., MIT Press, 1989, p. 28.

13 For various interpretations of the term "services," see Victor R. Fuchs, *The Service Economy,* New York, National Bureau of Economic Research, 1968, pp. 14–17; Thomas M. Stanback, Jr., et al., *Services: The New Economy,* Totowa, N.J., Allanhela, Osmun, 1981, pp. 2–6; Robert Summers, "Services in the International Economy," in *Managing the Service Economy: Prospects and Problems,* ed. Robert P. Inman, Cambridge, Cambridge University Press, 1985, pp. 29–30.

14 See Theodore Marburg, "Domestic Trade and Marketing," and Richard C. Clemett, "Mass Marketing of Consumer Goods," in *The Growth of the American Economy,* 2nd ed., ed. Harold F. Williamson, New York, Prentice-Hall, 1951, pp. 516, 517, 766, 767.

15 *Statistical Abstract of the United States 1992,* p. 771.

16 C. Winston Borgen, *Learning Experience in Retailing,* Pacific Palisades, Calif., Goodyear Publishing, 1976, p. 7; see also Charles A. Bearchell, *Retailing: A Professional Approach,* New York, Harcourt Brace Jovanovitch, 1975, p. 16.

17 *Statistical Abstract of the United States 1991,* p. 763.

18 See Robert B. Eklund, Jr., and David S. Saurman, *Advertising and the Market*

Process: A Modern Economic View, San Francisco, Pacific Research Institute, 1988, esp. pp. 8–15, 17–24.

19 *Statistical Abstract of the United States 1992,* p. 383.

20 For the data on employment see *The National Income and Product Account of the United States, 1929–1976,* p. 248; *The National Income and Product Account of the United States, 1959–1988,* p. 219; and *Statistical Abstract of the United States 1992,* p. 410. For the data on investment, see *Fixed Reproducible Tangible Wealth in the United States, 1925–1989,* pp. 358, 361, 367–371.

21 John W. Kendrick, "Service Productivity, Trade, and Market Structure," and Irving Leveson, "Services in the U.S. Economy," in *Managing the Service Economy,* ed. Inman, pp. 100, 118–119.

22 See Bernard Ascher and Obie G. Whichard, "Developing a Data System for International Sales of Services" and "Comments," in *International Economic Transactions: Issues in Measurement and Empirical Research,* ed. Peter Hooper and J. David Richardson, Chicago, University of Chicago Press, 1991, pp. 206, 207, 210, 235. See also *1990 U.S. Industrial Outlook,* Washington, D.C., Department of Commerce, January 1990, pp. 12–15.

23 Ralph T. King, Jr., "U.S. Service Exports Are Growing Rapidly but Almost Unnoticed," *The New York Times,* April 21, 1993.

24 See notably Ronald Kent Shelp, "An Industrial Policy for a Service Economy," in *Industrial Policy: Business and Politics in the United States and France,* ed. Sharon Zukin, New York, Praeger, 1985, pp. 211–213; and "Statement of Ronald Kent Shelp," in *The Service Economy and Industrial Change,* Hearings Before the Joint Economic Committee of the Congress of the United States, Ninety-Eighth Congress, 2nd Session, April 4 and 11, 1984, Washington, D.C., GPO, 1984, pp. 39–42.

25 "Prepared Statement of Earle C. Williams," in *The Service Economy and Industrial Change,* p. 24.

26 Mira Wilkins, "Foreign Investment in the U.S. Economy Before 1914," in *Foreign Investment in the United States,* ed. Michael Ulan, special issue of *Annals of the American Academy of Political and Social Science,* July 1991, pp. 9–21.

27 For the GNP data, see *The National Income and Product Account of the United States, 1929–76,* p. 72.

28 See Cleona Lewis, *The United States and Foreign Investment Problems,* pp. 28–29.

29 *Statistical Abstract of the United States 1950,* p. 831.

30 Committee for the Study of Causes and Consequences of the Internationalization of U.S. Manufacturing, *The Internationalization of U.S. Manufacturing: Causes and Consequences,* Washington, D.C., National Academy Press, 1990, pp. 28–30; see also Dominick Salvatore, "Trade Protection and Foreign Direct Investment in the U.S.," in *Foreign Investment,* ed. Ulan, pp. 91–105.

31 *The Internationalization of U.S. Manufacturing,* p. 10; Edward John Ray, "A Profile of Recent Foreign Investments in the U.S.," in *Foreign Investment,* ed. Ulan, pp. 50–65.

32 Michael Ulan, "Should the U.S. Restrict Foreign Investment?" in *Foreign Investment,* ed. Ulan, pp. 117–125.

33 See Keith Bradsher, "In Shift, White House Will Stress Aiding Foreign Concerns in U.S.," *The New York Times,* June 2, 1993.

34 Nicolas Spulber, *Restructuring the Soviet Economy: In Search of the Market,* Ann Arbor, University of Michigan Press, 1991, pp. 280–281.

35 See notably "China's State Industry: A Paradox of Rising Productivity and Declining Profitability," *Transitions* (World Bank), Vol. 5, Nos. 2–3, February-March 1994, p. 7; "China's Surge Toward a Market Economy," *Transitions,* Vol. 4, No. 2, March 1993; Kung-Chia Yeh, "Economic Reform: An Overview," and Anthony Y. C. Koo et al., "State-Owned Enterprise in Transition," in *China's Economic Reform,* ed. Walter Galenson, San Francisco, The 1990 Institute, 1993, pp. 11–32, 33–80; Mark Knell and Wenyan Yang, "Lessons from China on a Strategy for the Socialist Economies in Transition," in *Socialist Economies in Transition: Appraisals of the Market Mechanism,* ed. Christine Rider and Mark Knell, Brookfield, Vt., Edgar Elgar, 1992, p. 216.

Chapter 6. The state machine and the evolving economy

1 Alice M. Rivlin, *Reviving the American Dream: The Economy, the States, and the Federal Government,* Washington, D.C., Brookings Institution, 1992, p. 17.

2 Charles L. Schultze, *The Politics and Economics of Public Spending,* Washington, D.C., Brookings Institution, 1968, p. 4. Emphasis supplied.

3 *Historical Statistics of the United States: Colonial Times,* pp. 1116–1117; *Statistical Abstract of the United States 1992,* p. 315.

4 Adam Smith, *An Inquiry into the Nature and Causes of the Wealth of Nations,* ed. Edwin Cannan, New York, Random House, 1937, pp. 651, 767, 768.

5 Schultze, *The Politics and Economics of Public Spending,* pp. 6–8, 12–14.

6 *Papers and Proceedings of the Twelfth Annual Meeting of the American Economic Association,* December 1899, New York, Macmillan for the AEA, February 1900, pp. 53, 58–59.

7 Ibid., pp. 73–79.

8 For an admirably detailed presentation and analysis of the division of opinion at the time, see Hans B. Thorelli, *The Federal Antitrust Policy: Origination of an American Tradition,* Stockholm, Nordsted and Soner, 1954, esp. chs. 3 (pp. 108–163), 5, and 6 (pp. 235–368).

9 Ibid., pp. 276, 560, 587–588.

10 For an extensive discussion, see Dominick T. Armentano, *Antitrust and Monopoly: Anatomy of a Policy Failure,* New York, Wiley, 1982, esp. pp. 273–278.

11 Rivlin, *Reviving the American Dream,* p. 57.

12 See Martin C. Schnitzer, *Contemporary Government and Business Relations,* 3rd ed., Boston: Houghton Mifflin, 1987, esp. chs. 12 (pp. 271–299) and 13 (pp. 300–325).

13 Hans B. Thorelli and James M. Patterson, "Longer Live the Sherman Act," *Antitrust Bulletin,* Vol. 35, No. 3, Fall 1990, p. 545. Emphasis supplied.

14 *Statistical Abstract(s) of the United States 1946,* p. 930; *1971,* p. 781; *1992,* p. 805.

15 Thomas K. McCraw, "Mercantilism and the Market: Antecedents of American Industrial Policy," in *The Politics of Industrial Policy,* ed. C. E. Barfield and William Schambra, Washington, D.C., American Enterprise Institute, 1986, pp. 33, 39, 53.

16 David M. Chalmers, Introduction to Frank Tassig, *The Tariff History of the United States,* revised ed., New York, Capricorn Books, 1964, pp. xiii–xv.

17 Frank W. Tuttle and Joseph M. Perry, *An Economic History of the United States,* Cincinnati, South-Western, 1970, pp. 390–391, 498–499.

18 See Robert A. Pastor, *Congress and the Politics of U.S. Foreign Economic Policy, 1929–1976,* Berkeley, University of California Press, 1980, esp. pp. 117–123, 134–135.

19 Paul R. Krugman, "The Narrow and Broad Arguments for Free Trade," *American Economic Review,* Papers and Proceedings of the One Hundred Fifth Annual Meeting, January 1993, Vol. 83, No. 2, May 1993, pp. 365–366. Also Krugman, "Is Free Trade Passe?" in *International Economics and International Economic Policy: A Reader,* ed. Philip King, New York, McGraw-Hill, 1990, p. 91.

20 Paul Krugman, *The Age of Diminished Expectations: U.S. Economic Policy in the 1990s,* Cambridge, Mass., MIT Press, 1990, pp. 108, 130–131.

21 See for instance Keith Bradsher, "For Clinton 'Managed Trade' is Emerging as Policy Option," *The New York Times,* March 30, 1993.

22 Krugman, *The Age of Diminished Expectations,* p. 193.

Chapter 7. New priorities

1 Michael P. Todaro, *Economic Development in the Third World: An Introduction to Problems and Policies in a Global Perspective,* London, Longman, 1977, p. 50.

2 *World Development Report 1991: The Challenge of Development,* New York, Oxford University Press for the World Bank, 1991, p. 4. Emphasis supplied.

3 Todaro, *Economic Development,* p. 54.

4 On the massive and complex development of growth models, from the early aggregative theory, without optimizing agents, to the later formulations of growth models with explicit microfoundations for consumption and investment decisions, see the three volumes *Growth Theory,* ed. R. Becker and E. Burmeister, Aldershot, Edward Elgar, 1991. See also Robert M. Solow, "Perspectives on Growth Theory," and Howard Pack, "Endogenous Growth Theory: Intellectual Appeal and Empirical Shortcomings," *Journal of Economic Perspectives,* Vol. 8, No. 1, Winter 1994, pp. 45–54, 55–72.

5 See notably Hollis B. Chenery, "Structural Transformation: A Program of Research," in *The State of Development Economics: Progress and Perspectives,* ed. Gustav Ranis and T. Paul Schultz, New York, Blackwell Publisher, 1988, pp. 49–64.

6 Todaro, *Economic Development,* 4th ed., 1989, pp. 84–88.

7 Ian M. Little, *Economic Development: Theory, Policy and International Relations,* New York, Basic, 1982, p. 21.

8 Nicolas Spulber and Robert A. Becker, "Theoretical Issues in Optimal Planning," *International Journal of Development Planning Literature,* Vol. 1, No. 3, July–September 1986, pp. 237–253.

9 Steven M. Sheffrin, *The Making of Economic Policy: History, Theory, Politics,* Cambridge, Mass., Blackwell Publisher, 1989, pp. 139–140.

10 Herbert Stein, "Economic Planning and the Improvement of Economic Policy," in *The Politics of Planning: A Review and Critique of Centralized Economic Planning,*

ed. Bruce Briggs et al., San Francisco, Institute of Contemporary Studies, 1976, pp. 13–16.

11 These and the following quotations are from *Technology for America's Economic Growth: A New Direction to Build Economic Strength,* document released by the White House on February 22, 1993.

12 Since 1994 the authority of the Advanced Research Projects Agency (ARPA) has been expanded to fund hardware-oriented R&D defense projects and to waive the requirement for cost sharing. Previously the government required at least 50 percent cost sharing in cooperative agreements (LeRoy Haugh, "ARPA Funds Available for Defense R&D Programs," *AIA Newsletter,* Vol. 6, No. 8).

13 *Technology for America's Economic Growth,* p. 14; Governor Bill Clinton and Senator Al Gore, *Putting People First: How We Can All Change America,* Washington, D.C., Times Books, 1992, p. 9.

14 Peter T. Kilborn, "U.S. Says Its Training Effort Fails Displaced Job Seekers," *The New York Times,* October 16, 1993.

15 *Technology for America's Economic Growth.*

16 Lewis M. Branscomb, "Empowering Technology Policy," in *Empowering Technology: Implementing a U.S. Strategy,* ed. Branscomb, Cambridge, Mass., MIT Press, 1993, pp. 269–271.

17 Herbert Stein, "On Economic Planning," in *National Economic Planning: Six Papers Presented at a Conference in Washington, D.C., November 1975,* ed. Crawfurd D. Goodwin et al., Washington, D.C., Chamber of Commerce of the United States, 1976, pp. 55–56.

18 Roy Rothwell and Walter Zegveld, *Reindustrialization and Technology,* Armonk, N.Y., M. E. Sharpe, 1985, pp. 90, 94.

19 Adam Smith, *An Inquiry into the Nature and Causes of the Wealth of Nations,* ed. Edwin Cannan, New York, Random House, 1937, p. 625.

20 See, for instance, Omnibus Trade and Competitive Act of 1988, Public Law 100–418, Section 301, enacting provisions of the Trade Act of 1974 as amended, 19 U.S.C. 2411(d)3(B)(11), 2411(d)3(E), concerning Section 301.

21 For an examination of the "new" trade theories, see Robert E. Baldwin, *Are Economists' Traditional Trade Policy Views Still Valid?* NBER Working Paper No. 3793, Cambridge, Mass., National Bureau of Economic Research, July 1991, pp. 12–14, 17, 36–37, 39, 45, 50.

22 Laura d'Andrea Tyson restates her 1980s positions (discussed in Section 4–2) in a 1993 book entitled *Who's Bashing Whom? Trade Conflict in High-Technology Industries,* Washington, D.C., Institute for International Economics. Concentrating on the "trade challenge" to the latter, President Clinton's chief economist proclaims herself in favor of government's selective subsidies to these industries, aggressive efforts to achieve "reciprocity" in foreign markets, and the setting of targets to expand exports. In a cogent review of this book, Jagdish Bhagwati points out that the policies advocated by Tyson "would undermine for a sizable and growing segment of world trade, the current international trading system" (Bhagwati, "Rough Trade," *The New Republic,* May 31, 1993, pp. 35–39; see also Paul Krugman, "Competitiveness, a Dangerous Obsession," *The Wall Street Journal,* February 28, 1994).

23 U.S. Congress, Office of Technology Assessment, *Competing Economies: America,*

Europe and the Pacific Rim, Washington, D.C., GPO, October 1991, pp. 9, 117; U.S. Congress, Office of Technology Assessment, *Multinationals and the National Interest,* Washington, D.C., GPO, September 1993, p. 32–33.

24 *Multinationals and the National Interest,* pp. 7–8.

25 Ibid., pp. 51–52.

26 Ibid., pp. 115–120.

27 Ibid., pp. 8, 64, 66, 158.

28 Ibid., pp. 18–19.

29 "Gore and Perot Are Set to Debate Trade Accord," *The New York Times,* November 5, 1993.

30 See "Trade Pact Sale Relies on a Twist," *The New York Times,* November 7, 1993; also U.S. Congress, Office of Technology Assessment, *Competing Economies,* pp. 128–129.

31 See the cogent study by Jagdish Bhagwati, "Regionalism Versus Multilateralism," *World Economy,* Vol. 15, No. 5, September 1952, pp. 535–554. Note that the Uruguay Round of GATT was concluded on December 15, 1993, shortly after NAFTA went into effect. In the course of years the GATT agreement will be bound to further adjust to the eventual growth of NAFTA.

32 All these rates are computed on the basis of data in *Economic Report of the President . . . 1991.*

33 Ibid., pp. 229, 334.

34 Dorothy S. Zinberg, "Putting People First: Education, Jobs and Economic Competitiveness," in *Empowering Technology,* ed. Branscomb, p. 254.

35 Eli Ginzberg, *Manpower Agenda for America,* New York, McGraw-Hill, 1968, pp. 43–44.

36 Sumner H. Slichter, "Lines of Action, Adaptation, and Control," Papers and Proceedings of the Forty-Fourth Annual Meeting of the American Economic Association, *American Economic Review,* Vol. 12, No. 1, supplement, March 1932, p. 41.

37 *Economic Report of the President Transmitted to the Congress January 1993,* Washington, D.C., GPO, 1993, p. 225.

38 Norbert Wiener, *The Human Use of Human Beings: Cybernetics and Society,* New York, Doubleday, 1954, p. 146.

Chapter 8. Contests at technological frontiers

1 A. E. Musson and E. Robinson, *Science and Technology in the Industrial Revolution,* Toronto, University of Toronto Press, 1969, p. 23; D. S. L. Cardwell, "The Development of Scientific Research in Modern Universities: A Comparative Study of Motives and Opportunities," in *Scientific Change: Symposium on the History of Science,* ed. A. C. Crombie, New York, Basic, 1963, p. 664.

2 P. Mantoux, *The Industrial Revolution in the Eighteenth Century: An Outline of the Modern Factory System in England,* trans. Marjorie Vernon, New York, Harper Torchbooks, 1962, pp. 319, 379.

3 S. B. Saul, "The Market and the Development of the Mechanical Engineering Industries in Britain, 1860–1914," in *Technological Change: The United States and Britain in the Nineteenth Century,* ed. S. B. Saul, London, Methuen, 1970, p. 169.

4 See R. N. Rundle, *Britain's Economic and Social Development from 1700 to the Present Day*, London, University of London Press, 1973, p. 141; P. Mathias, *The First Industrial Nation*, New York, Scribner, 1969, p. 423; Sir E. Ashby, "Education for an Age of Technology," in *A History of Technology*, ed. Charles Singer et al., Vol. 5, Oxford, Oxford University Press, 1958, pp. 776–798.

5 H. Bechtel, *Wirtschaftsgeschichte Deutschlands im 19. und 20. Jahrhundert*, Munich, Callwey, 1956, pp. 158ff.

6 W. Zorn, "Typen und Entwicklingskräfte deutschen Unternehmertums," in *Moderne deutsche Wirtschaftsgeschichte*, ed. K. E. Born, Berlin, Kiepenheur and Wirtsch, 1966, p. 29; C. Day, *Economic Development in Modern Europe*, New York, Macmillan, 1933, p. 261.

7 K. Karmarsch, *Geschichte der Technologie seit der Mitte der achtzehnten Jahrhundrets*, Vol. 11 of *Geschichte der Wissenschaften in Deutschland*, ed. R. Oldenburg, Munich, Oldenburg, 1872, p. 59; also F. Paulsen, *German Education Past and Present*, trans. T. Lorenz, New York, Scribner, 1908.

8 A. N. Whitehead, *Science in the Modern World*, New York, New American Library, 1953, p. 98.

9 C. Trebilcock, *The Industrialization of the Continental Powers 1780–1914*, London, Longman, 1981, pp. 44, 62.

10 W. O. Henderson, *The Rise of German Industrial Power 1834–1914*, Berkeley, University of California Press, 1975, pp. 173–177.

11 Simon Kuznets, "Technological Innovations and Economic Growth," *Growth, Population and Income Distribution: Selected Essays*, New York, Norton, 1979, pp. 71, 73, 83, 95.

12 George Basalla, *The Evolution of Technology*, New York, Cambridge University Press, 1988, pp. 86–87.

13 See Eli F. Heckscher, *Mercantilism*, trans. M. Shapiro, London, Allen and Unwin, 1955, esp. pp. 317–324; L. H. Haney, *History of Economic Thought*, New York, Macmillan, 1936, pp. 117, 123, 127, 143; Thomas K. McCraw, "Mercantilism and the Market: Antecedents of American Industrial Policy," in *The Politics of Industrial Policy*, ed. C. E. Barfield and William Schambra, Washington, D.C., American Enterprise Institute, 1986, pp. 33–62.

14 U.S. Department of Commerce, National Telecommunications and Information Administration, *The NTIA Infrastructure Report: Telecommunications in the Age of Information*, Springfield, Va., NTIA, October 1991; House of Representatives, One Hundred Third Congress, 1st Session, *National Information Infrastructure Act of 1993: Report* (to accompany H.R. 1757), No. 103–173, Washington, D.C., GPO, 1993; statement of John Sculley in *National Communications Infrastructure*, Hearings Before the Subcommittee on Telecommunications and Finance of the Committee on Energy and Commerce, House of Representatives, One Hundred Third Congress, 1st Session, January-March 1993, Serial No. 103–12, Washington, D.C., GPO, 1993.

15 *Telecommunications in the Age of Information*, pp. 150, 153, 156–157, 170–171, 180–189, 190–191, 193, 198–199.

16 Leonard A. Lecht, *Goals, Priorities, and Dollars*, New York, Free Press, 1966, p. 5.

17 J.-J. Servan-Schreiber, *The American Challenge,* trans. Ronald Steel, New York, Atheneum, 1968, pp. vii–xv. Emphasis supplied.

18 Annemieke J. M. Roobeek, *Beyond the Technology Race: An Analysis of Technology Policy in Seven Industrial Countries,* Amsterdam–New York, Elsevier, 1990, p. 18.

19 Ibid., pp. 17–19.

20 "Who Is Sharper Now?" *The Economist,* January 15, 1994; Robert Samuelson, "The Rediscovery of the U.S. Economy," *Newsweek,* February 28, 1994; Sylvia Nasar, "The American Economy, Back on Top," *The New York Times* (Business section), February 27, 1994.

21 Andrew Pollock, "Now It's Japan's Turn to Play Catch-Up," *The New York Times* (Business section), November 21, 1993; James Sterngold, "The $6 Trillion Hole in Japan's Pocket," *The New York Times* (Business section), January 21, 1994; David E. Sanger, "Cutting Itself Down to Size: Japan's Inferiority Complex," *The New York Times* (Business section), February 6, 1994; Robert Ristelhueber, "Setting Sun: The Slide of Japanese Semiconductors," *Electronic Business Buyer,* Vol. 20, No. 4, April 1994, pp. 52–60.

Index